TOGETHER,
SOMEHOW

TOGETHER, SOMEHOW

MUSIC, AFFECT, AND INTIMACY ON THE DANCEFLOOR

LUIS MANUEL GARCIA-MISPIRETA

DUKE UNIVERSITY PRESS / DURHAM AND LONDON / 2023

Designed by Matthew Tauch
Typeset in Alegreya and Trade Gothic LT Std
by Westchester Publishing Services

Library of Congress Cataloging-in-Publication Data
Names: García-Mispireta, Luis Manuel, [date] author.
Title: Together, somehow : music, affect, and intimacy on the
dancefloor / Luis Manuel Garcia-Mispireta.
Description: Durham : Duke University Press, 2023. |
Includes bibliographical references and index.
Identifiers: LCCN 2022053342 (print)
LCCN 2022053343 (ebook)
ISBN 9781478025047 (paperback)
ISBN 9781478020080 (hardcover)
ISBN 9781478027058 (ebook)
Subjects: LCSH: Queer studies. | Electronic dance music—Social
aspects. | Electronic dance music—Social aspects—Germany—
Berlin. | Electronic dance music—Social aspects—Illinois—
Chicago. | Electronic dance music—Social aspects—France—
Paris. | Music and dance—Social aspects. | Dance—Social aspects. |
Sound effects music. | Affect (Psychology) | Intimacy (Psychology) |
Nightlife. | House music—Social aspects. | Ethnomusicology. |
BISAC: MUSIC / Ethnomusicology | SOCIAL SCIENCE / LGBTQ
Studies / General
Classification: LCC ML3918.T43 G373 2023 (print) |
LCC ML3918.T43 (ebook)
DDC 306.4/846—dc23/eng/20230419
LC record available at https://lccn.loc.gov/2022053342
LC ebook record available at https://lccn.loc.gov/2022053343

Publication of this book has been aided by a grant from the
AMS 75 PAYS Fund of the American Musicological Society,
supported in part by the National Endowment for the
Humanities and the Andrew W. Mellon Foundation.

To my sister Carla, and to dining above our station.
And to friendly strangers: you know who you are.

CONTENTS

When did this book really start? I am not sure I can pinpoint an exact moment. Maybe it started when I began going to raves in the 1990s as a Latino, queer, postmigrant boy in a conservative, midsized university town in Ontario. As I went to local raves, took long-distance buses, and carpooled with local friends to attend larger ones in Toronto and Windsor/Detroit, I was constantly having surprisingly intimate encounters with friendly strangers at parties, all the while sharing in exhilarating experiences of the latest house music, minimal techno, hardcore, and jungle. Maybe this book really started in 2004, as I was completing my MA in musicology and transitioning from being a historical musicologist (of thirteenth-century French polyphony—with a weakness for the French-Cypriot repertoire of Torino J.II.9) to an ethnomusicologist of popular music. I took an introductory ethnomusicology class, submitted an ethnographic essay profiling some of Toronto's post-rave nightclubs, and received encouragement to pursue the study of popular electronic dance music—despite this discipline's tendency to focus primarily on traditional/folkloric musics of exotic and colonized places. Perhaps most decisively, this book started when I was a PhD student and took a seminar with Lauren Berlant titled "The Intimate Public Sphere." I had already spent more than a year embedding myself into Chicago's house and techno scenes, and I was especially attuned to the ambivalent play of intimacy and distance that comes with being the new stranger in an established subcultural scene. As a young, queer, and brown raver and budding scholar, I was constantly navigating spaces and institutions that were not meant for me but perhaps could be.

The journey to getting published was not a simple or easy one, and I wish I had heard more of these difficult stories before working on this book, instead of the smooth and frictionless narratives that were fed to me in graduate school. As a multiply marginalized scholar working on an unconventional and low-prestige research project, I am committed to telling the kind of ambivalent, messy story that could have helped me. I started my PhD program a few years before the 2008 financial crash that crushed the academic job market, and I went on that job market only three years afterward, when the impact of the crash was still reverberating. We were in a bewildering "new normal" for academia, and most of the advice our mentors could give was woefully obsolete. Drawing on their own experience from the 1980s and 1990s, our mentors expected us to land a tenure-track job at a "modest" university directly after completing our PhD, with the presumption that our first monograph would provide the necessary leverage to move up to a suitably elite institution. And so, most of the career advice we got was about how to quickly turn a dissertation into a monograph while working as a new tenure-track faculty member, with all of the institutional supports that (used to) come with such a position. At *worst*, we might instead take a postdoctoral position somewhere (ideally an Ivy League "society of fellows"), where we could focus more intently on book production and spin-off articles, with the hopes of moving directly into a tenure-track position at an elite R1 institution (that is, a doctorate-granting university with the highest rank of research activity). Already in the years immediately after the 2008 recession the straight-to-tenure-track pipeline was collapsing, and graduates from my doctoral program were struggling to find postdoctoral positions of any sort, let alone tenure-track ones. Our supervisors and administrators simply stopped talking about the ones who "didn't make it," and that form of *damnatio memoriae* told us everything we needed to know about the perceived stakes of the career path they expected of us.

It was into this morass of attrition and toxic "survival of the fittest" ideology that I was launched into the academic job market with a research focus ill suited to the expectations of my discipline. Most ethnomusicology job postings were looking for specialists in specific world areas (such as "an Africanist"—yes, anywhere on that vast continent will do—or "a specialist in classical South Asian musics"); candidates would be expected to teach a highly problematic "Introduction to World Music" course and run a number of "world music ensembles," usually based on whatever non-Western musical instruments the university had already bought. And so, I found myself unable to get any traction with my focus on the popular electronic musics of Chicago, Paris, and Berlin—even less so with my interests in affect theory, queer studies, and urban locales.

I managed, very much at the last minute, to land a short postdoctoral position at the Freie Universität's Berlin Program for German and European Studies, leveraging the fact that I already had an ethnographic network built in that city. However, this program only ran for one year and, more problematically for this book, the program explicitly forbade postdoctoral scholars from "writing up" their doctoral thesis into a book. Instead, I was required to launch an entirely new research project, which is how I came to publish articles on techno-tourism and musical migration in Berlin during my first few years after receiving my doctorate. I managed to secure a few months of an extension to my fellowship while I desperately applied to academic jobs. At the same time, I began applying for a freelancer visa to stay in Berlin, with the plan of transitioning to full-time translation work. I was preparing to leave the field entirely.

By pure coincidence, I heard about a research group at a local Max Planck Institute that was focusing on emotions and music in Europe. Although the framing was primarily that of historical musicology, I hoped that my expertise in affect theory as well as my focus on Berlin would garner some attention. Although my application was ultimately successful, the research group leader's skepticism of my research topic, theoretical framework, and ethnographic methods resulted in a two-year (extensible to three) postdoctoral position being reduced to six months, with the potential for small extensions if I pleased the people in power. As a result, I spent the next two and a half years in constant, simmering precarity, begging for six-month extensions to my funding. For those readers who are familiar with the German immigration system, you can imagine having to return to the Ausländerbehörde (immigration authority) every five to six months—and this was back when there were no booked appointments: you showed up at 5:00 A.M. to queue for offices that would open two or three hours later.

In 2014, I landed my first teaching-focused job at the Rijksuniversiteit Groningen (Netherlands), on a two-year contract. I struggled to find time to work on this book as I adjusted to a workplace with far fewer support structures compared to the North American university system for which I had been trained. In the winter of 2016, I started a permanent appointment at the University of Birmingham, although this came with a precarious three-year probation period. In the United Kingdom, I struggled to adjust to a higher education system with notoriously high workloads and a class-striated division of labor and reward, to which I was alternately illegible, abject, or a tokenistic "clever pet" to be tolerated with bemusement. Progress on the book was slow and agonizing, with repeated interruptions.

Along with this came a cascade of personal, regional, and global events that buffeted this book project. For example, the Brexit vote in 2016 made my ongoing research in Berlin more difficult as well as less likely to attract funding. That same year, events such as the Orlando Pulse massacre, the US elections, and the European xenophobic backlash to the "refugee crisis" provided troubling indicators of the return of fascist and nationalist ideology. In 2018, a major health diagnosis emerged in my family, which required me to devote the usual academic "research summer" to caregiving; at the same time, my three-year probation period was soon coming to an end, and this book was explicitly tied to whether I would be retained as a lecturer. In 2020, with my probation already precariously extended as I nervously awaited a decision on my book manuscript from Duke University Press, the pandemic hit, and we went into lockdown. The massive disruption to work and the isolation of lockdown combined with the helpless uncertainty regarding my book and my probation to snowball into a crushing burnout. After more than two years of anxious alarm bells going off continuously in my head, my body decided to shut everything down and slide into catatonia: medically mandated leave, debilitating anxiety and depression, and a slow recovery while global events continued to worsen. And here I am now, in the summer of 2022, with a book that will finally be published, a promotion to associate professor that is barely two weeks fresh, and a world that still continues to fall apart.

For those early career scholars looking for an alternate roadmap to book completion in an era of upheaval, here is my retrospective timeline: I first pitched this book verbally to Duke in 2012, on the sidelines of a popular music conference (IASPM/EMP) in New York City. I am forever grateful to Ken Wissoker for taking the time to meet with me and hear me out, in my ill-fitting suit and beaded sheen of nervous sweat. I submitted a book prospectus and roughly half of this manuscript in 2014 (the introduction and chapters 1–4), after much struggle to find time to write and edit while precariously employed in Berlin. I received the first round of reader reports later that same year, after which I was asked to submit a complete and revised manuscript before being considered for a contract. After changing jobs (and immigrating yet again to new countries) twice, I submitted the full manuscript in 2019. Updated reader reports came in the autumn of 2020—along with a publishing contract—while I was slowly recovering from my burnout and teaching remotely from Toronto in order to support my family there. That bit of good news was a godsend, but I was also too depressed to rejoice in the accomplishment. I wish I could have savored that moment; I wish I could even remember what I did to mark the occasion, if anything. I hope I was kind to myself. In the summer of 2021, I finally submitted a fully revised manuscript, with final approval coming from the Duke advisory board in April 2022. I made final revisions, proofreading, and formatting during the summer of 2022, as I recovered from the COVID-19 coronavirus. The fact that this book exists at all is a bruised, aching triumph for me.

While writing this book was often a solitary experience, it would not have been even remotely possible without the support of friends, families, networks, and institutions. As this preface transitions into acknowledgments, I begin by thanking my closest and less formal support networks and work toward the institutional ones—with a last-minute swerve.

First and foremost, my thanks go to the Garcia-Mispireta family, including my parents, my siblings, my in-laws, and my four irrepressible nieces. I am especially grateful to my sister, Carla, who provided more emotional support and reality checks than any sibling should have to. Despite being bereft of feline companionship due to my move-to-a-new-country-every-few-years postdoctoral life, I am immensely thankful for the fuzzy, purring support of Carla's two cats, Petrarch and Gabriela, during my visits to Toronto (may their memories be a blessing).

Equally important to me—especially as a queer person—is my chosen family, that is, the pulsing and ever-blossoming networks of friends that I cultivated in every place where I have lived. Most of these networks have grown out of my involvement in local rave and club scenes, and I am especially indebted to the Berlin-based queer, feminist, and intersectional rave collective Room 4 Resistance. We began organizing parties as my employment took me further and further from Berlin, and returning to the city for the next R4R party served as a critical lifeline. My warmest, sweatiest, neon-splattered, tie-dyed, unicorn-ballooned thanks go to the whole R4R crew, who supported me through the toughest years between my PhD and this book. As we pivot toward community-building, mutual care, and interdependence, I look forward to the worlds we can create in this new decade. We are (mostly) still here, somehow!

I struggle to imagine what this project would have been without the generous support and guidance of my doctoral supervision committee, including Kaley Mason and Steven Rings. Special and tearful thanks go to the memory of Lauren Berlant, who took my ideas seriously and saw me in ways nobody else could or would. In addition to intellectual engagement, Lauren provided empathetic support through several institutional struggles, carrying my outrage and frustration so that I could continue to be the polite, nonthreatening brown boy I needed to be in order to survive in a predominantly white, ruthlessly classist and ableist institution. Lauren, you will never get to see this book, and I will never not be sad about it.

In a similar vein, my thanks go out to the mentors who held me up through various phases of my career, such as Celia Cain, Kristin McGee, Kyra Gaunt, and Maureen Mahon, to name but a few. Nearly all of these mentors have been women and nonbinary folks, and I am very cognizant of the gendered distribution of labor, when it comes to the work of mentorship. I am grateful, in turn, to my own supervisees and mentees, as brilliant as they were patient while I worked to finish this book; helping them grow as researchers and writers has had an immeasurable impact on my own writing.

Nor can I truly measure the impact of my network of intellectual accomplices, the former classmates, coeditors, contributors, conference buddies, and extremely online Twitter nerds who gave me advice, feedback, readings, and the occasional very necessary warning as I navigated academia without a map. There are too many to name—and I offer my apologies now to those who go unmentioned—but a selection of accomplices would include Robin James, my publisher-sibling Rumya Putcha (we did it!), Kaleb Goldschmitt, Michael Meeuwis, Christopher Haworth, Byron Dueck, Mark J. Butler, Maria Witek, Imani Mosley, and so, so many more of you. Thanks for sticking with me.

Of course, an ethnographic project on urban subcultural music scenes would have been entirely impossible without the support and engagement of the scenes themselves. First of all, my thanks go to my interviewees as well as those partygoers who spoke with me in more informal ways on the dancefloors of raves and clubs wherever I went. Furthermore, I am grateful to all of those who work tirelessly to keep the dance music scenes of Berlin, Paris, and Chicago thriving. From my time in Chicago, I am glad to have been welcomed into the Naughty Bad Fun Collective and the Souvenir crew, as well as SmartBar's extended family. We had no name for our crew of *fêtards* in Paris, but my love and all the *bises* in the world go out to those who gathered and danced at On Cherche Encore, La Mona, and Maria Peligro (*que descanses, Carlito*). In addition to Room 4 Resistance and the extended network of queer rave collectives that make up Berlin Collective Action and Whole Festival, I give eternal thanks to the crew of friends and lovers who gathered in the "music nerd zone" in Pannebar, that is, the space between the column and the left side of the DJ booth. Our love language was YouTube links to whatever tracks we could identify at the rave. And, finally, my warmest, cheesiest thanks go to my local Brum techno-nerd crew, especially Doris, Tony, Franklynne, and Mrs. Tibbs—at least 50 percent of which are cats.

I am particularly grateful to the institutions that provided logistical, material, or financial support during the various phases of this project. For example, the University of Chicago's Paris Center and its Assistanceship in Learning Technologies program provided an academic home as well as employment while I undertook fieldwork there. In Berlin, I am grateful for the informal support and community I found on the BerlinScholars mailing list, which helped me find temporary housing and navigate Berliner bureaucracy during my first visits to the city. Back in Chicago, the University of Chicago's Center for Gender & Sexuality Studies truly saved me with its Hormel Fellowship, in that final year when my scholarship was running out and I was facing barriers in my home department. Finally, I extend my thanks to the Freie Universität's Berlin European Studies Program as well as the Max Planck Institute for Human Development, both of which provided funding during my postdoctoral years in Berlin.

As a first-generation, postmigrant, queer, and Latino scholar who has worked on disciplinarily unconventional and low-prestige topics, I am committed to improving the representation of marginalized experiences in academia—and this must also include acknowledging the negative impacts that people have had on myself and my career. These disacknowledgments begin with the disciplinary patriarch in my graduate school program (and his enablers), who blocked my access to internal and external research funding as part of a broader pattern of bullying—of which I was not the sole recipient. I also recall the unnamed dissertation supervisor who quietly "forgot" to write recommendation letters for a whole year's worth of job applications. Special disacknowledgments go to the research group leader who turned a two-to-three-year postdoctoral position into five months on the basis of his disrespect for my research topic, parceling out additional months of funding in exchange for unpaid labor and favors. I cannot forget all the conference-goers who, upon seeing my name and my appearance, asked me what part of Latin America I researched, even though I was presenting and publishing research on North American and European electronic music scenes. Nor can I forget those colleagues and peers who could not conceal their contempt for popular music studies, electronic

dance music, and queer/trans life-worlds. I write these disacknowledgments in solidarity with those who have experienced and will experience
similar obstacles to their flourishing. This book is for you, specifically.

And, to finish on a more uplifting note, I give my messiest, spiciest
thanks to the grassroots support networks that have sprung up in the back-
channels of music academia in recent years. I am not too humble to start by
thanking my own groups, including The Scare Quotes and The Society for
Exhausted Ethnomusicologists, all of whom carried me through some of
the toughest times in these past few years. I also have endless warmth and
solidarity for student-led initiatives such as Project Spectrum and the growing number of graduate student unions. Similarly, *solidarité* to the University
and College Union (United Kingdom) and the DUP (Duke) Workers Union.
Unionize *everything*, kittens.

INTRODUCTION

The tricky thing about dancefloors is that they are places where both inclusion and exclusion happen. Whether subtle or conspicuous, club cultures always find ways to signal who is welcome to join in the dance. Electronic dance music scenes tend to emphasize their inclusivity while downplaying their exclusions, and this tendency can be traced back to their subcultural origins: from the clandestine, queer-of-color dance parties of early disco to the mass gatherings of suburban youth in the 1990s rave era, these scenes share a history of utopian longing for radically open inclusivity—especially for those who experience exclusion everywhere else in society. As a result, these music scenes avoid focused talk about who belongs and how, instead relying on vague references to shared musical tastes, open-mindedness, and "good vibes." This strategic vagueness is both a help and a hindrance, enabling dancers to temporarily enjoy a moment of belonging unburdened by the difficult work of "identity politics," while at the same time enabling them to ignore the exclusions and injustices taking place on those same dancefloors. Such vagueness helps to sustain social worlds that can feel exhilaratingly expansive and yet also precarious, liable to disintegrate as soon as their underlying tensions are exposed. How do dancers get along in these fluid social contexts, where learning the details of other dancers' identities, values, and political affinities risks undermining their utopian fantasy of universal togetherness? This book takes dancefloor utopianism seriously and, in so doing, works to push electronic dance music scenes in the direction of those dreams.

Together, Somehow sets out to explain this getting-along in terms of stranger-intimacy—that is, the gestures of social warmth, sharing, and vulnerability between strangers that occur with surprising frequency and intensity at electronic dance music events ("parties" hereafter). It draws on ethnographic fieldwork that I conducted in the "minimal techno" and "house music" subscenes of three cities (Chicago, Paris, Berlin) as the first decade of the new millennium came to a close (2006–2010). Using stranger-intimacy as a point of departure, I consider the roles that tactility, gender, sexuality, music/sound, affect, intense experiences, and subcultural knowledge play in lubricating social interactions with fellow partygoers. In the process, I work to rethink intimacy through the diffuse, light-touch sociability of festive crowds.

What do I mean by "light-touch sociability"? Consider a common colloquial German phrase, drawn from my fieldwork in Berlin: "Alles klar?" When phrased as a question, this translates idiomatically to something like "You alright?" or "Everything fine?" You can use it to "check in" with someone, to briefly inquire after their condition without inviting the more detailed report prompted by "Wie geht's dir?" (How are you?). In this sense, the phrase is an instance of light-touch intimacy, a gesture of stranger-sociability that is both warm and impersonal. By casually expressing interest and care, it can imbue an encounter with a sense of closeness and connection. It is well suited to contexts of loose and informal socializing, where strangers mingle in familiar-feeling environments. It is, in fact, just the sort of thing you hear often on the dancefloors of Berlin's nightclubs.

BERGHAIN / PANORAMA BAR, BERLIN; SUNDAY, JULY 26, 2008; 4:00 A.M.

I was dancing in the middle of Panorama Bar, part of the Berghain nightclub complex. Located in a former power plant dating from the German Democratic Republic (East Germany), the club's raw industrial interiors would later become a principal site for my research as well as this book. I was there to "see"—that is, dance and listen to—Heartthrob (Jesse Siminski), a recording artist signed to the high-profile minimal-techno music label M_nus. He had been booked at Panorama Bar as part of a tour showcasing his most recent album-length release, *Dear Painter, Paint Me* (M_nus, 2008), and so his performance that night featured the sonic materials of his album while also reproducing its overall style: long, sustained, atmospheric washes across the high-frequency range, grounded by relatively slow, resonant, and yet punctuating bass kicks. Like many artists signed to this label, Heartthrob's interpretation of minimal techno emphasized sparse textures and gradual change, unfolding at a pace that was slow even by the conventions of a musical genre that primarily develops in cycles of thirty-two and sixty-four beats. The sonic atmosphere bore a semblance to other sensory aspects of the dancefloor, too: shimmering washes of sound hung in the air like the omnipresent haze emanating from the smoke machines, while the loud bass-drum kicks thudded against my flesh like the crush of bodies on the dancefloor.

Typical of a summer Saturday night (or Sunday morning) at Berghain / Panorama Bar in 2008, the crowd had yet to hit its peak—as packed as it was. I was about halfway back on the dancefloor, near the two-story windows that looked out over the Berlin skyline and the entry queue below, but I could barely see beyond my arm's reach. And so, when a young man approached me, it seemed as if he had stepped out of a wall of shoulders. He had shoulder-length blond hair, light skin, patches of glitter on his high cheekbones, a slim frame, and an outfit that combined an oversized white T-shirt with shiny Adidas athletic shorts and running shoes. He could not have been more than twenty-five years old.

He had been in the process of pushing past me toward the bar, but he stopped to look me in the eyes, a smile on his lips. After a brief pause, he asked, "Alles klar?" And I, not entirely sure what he meant in this context but reluctant to impede the smoothness of our interaction, smiled and nodded, "Ja, alles klar." His smile broadened, as if that was all he wanted to hear, and then he caressed my face along my jawline from ear to chin and continued pushing his way through the crowd. I never saw him again.

In that moment, "Alles klar?" functioned as an opening to an exchange of surprising warmth between strangers, providing the setting for a tactile gesture that would have been entirely out of place "out on the street," in everyday urban life. What transpired then was a moment of intimacy that was improvised on the basis of corporeal copresence, a shared sensorium, and apparent aesthetic affinities; in other words, we were there in the flesh, sharing space, atmosphere, and sensuous enjoyment. This improvised intimacy succeeded in bringing about a fleeting connection, despite the anonymity of the crowd—or, as I will argue later, *because of it*. But this encounter was also risky, starting from an utterance only half understood and followed by a series of unscripted transgressions of polite decorum;

things could have unfolded quite differently, for example, if I had recoiled at his touch. And yet, for all the potential for awkwardness and rejection, something brought us together, somehow.

This book is devoted to making sense of moments like this one, to searching for the "something" and the "somehow" of intimacy on the dancefloor.[1] Part of what is remarkable about this story is how unremarkable it is for this subcultural context; countless similar exchanges fill my fieldwork notes as well as my years of personal involvement in electronic dance music scenes since the mid-1990s.[2] On and around the dancefloors of nightclubs, loft parties, and raves, partygoers engage in forms of stranger-intimacy that short-circuit the conventional narratives of intimacy and make a mess of everyday decorum.[3] This stranger-intimacy taps into the sort of bonds between strangers that are often imagined as binding mass society, where anonymity and foreignness sometimes elicit moments of surprising closeness. And yet, the face-to-face and erotic aspects of the dancefloor encounter alter the strangeness of strangerhood, too, adding layers of meaning to the stranger's fluid position between distance and proximity, anonymity and candor. How does such intense stranger-intimacy arise and endure? In what registers is it felt and articulated?

In the pages that follow, I grapple with these questions by braiding threads of ethnography, analysis, and theory. Working from an archive of interviews with partygoers, fieldwork observations, and analyses of cultural artifacts (e.g., music recordings, film, print, and online media), I track the intensification of social warmth across the loose bonds of a dancing crowd, with special attention paid to the role of music in engendering this sense of intimacy. I explore a range of phenomena that have been studied elsewhere under the rubrics of stranger sociability, collective musicking, affect, intimacy, crowd psychology, and political solidarity. To these fields of study, *Together, Somehow* offers insights into a subcultural nexus of feeling, sound, and belonging. My approach is also informed by the "affective turn" in the humanities and social sciences while adding to a similar turn in ethnomusicology, suggesting some inroads into an affect theory that is grounded in music and ethnographic fieldwork.[4] To affect theory and the ethnomusicological study of feeling and emotion, I offer an account of *how* affect articulates between music and belonging, by way of sonic experience, touch, and collective dancing. Inspired by ethnomusicology's abiding concern for musical collectivity, I rethink intimacy and solidarity in the context of dancing crowds, engaging with the study of crowd dynamics as well as queer theory's exploration of affective relations beyond the romantic couple form.

I aim not only to describe dancefloor intimacy but also to question its easy fluidity, to ask at what cost and at *whose* cost such seemingly frictionless interactions are made possible. Most partygoers (and party organizers) seem to wish for fluid, unconstrained, and capacious forms of belonging, usually imagined to be dancing crowds that are loosely held together by shared musical affinities and sensory intensities. In other words, they hope that enjoying music together is enough to make their social worlds work. And yet, they must contend with the contradictions that arise from embedding such utopian worlds of inclusion within a "real" world that is already striated with exclusions. In a sense, partygoers want distinction without discrimination, to belong to an intimate world unburdened by the baggage of identity. Despite the underlying frictions, they strive to sustain this fragile sense of fluid belonging by maintaining a sort of lubricating vagueness about what binds them, invoking affinities that pass through aesthetics and affect—"the music" and "the vibe"—rather than identity. Beneath these utopian fantasies of easy belonging, however, the testimony of less privileged partygoers (as well as my own observations) reveal inequities and exclusions that often go unexamined. And so, my analysis of festive intimacy includes an exploration of how electronic dance music scenes support these ephemeral-but-real, utopian world-building projects by striking an ambivalent bargain with vagueness, one that both makes these worlds feel possible and provides cover for their failures.

In fact, "vague belonging" is a key concept for this project, an ostinato that runs throughout this book's analysis of dancefloor intimacy. A central argument in this book is that these surprisingly intimate encounters are enabled rather than hindered by anonymity, crowds, and a persistent vagueness about who belongs and how. Music plays an important role here, providing a shared point of reference that enables partygoers to anchor their sense of belonging: *we're here, feeling and enjoying this music together, and maybe that's enough*. This sense of togetherness emerges out of crowds that are mostly heterogeneous and anonymous, composed of partygoers who seem to share little more than a dancefloor, a passion for a particular style of music, and a distinctive way of having fun.

On these dancefloors, vague belonging is supported by face-to-face encounters with strangers. Such stranger-sociability lends a sense of openness to these parties, making nightlife scenes feel like something more expansive than a closed community: an intimate public or "counterpublic," perhaps.[5] But such fluidity and anonymity also make these scenes extremely fragile; all of this vagueness can lead just as easily to feelings of disappointment, betrayal, and exclusion. Being a stranger can be strangely liberating, engendering a feeling of freedom from the constraints of social norms, identities, and relationships, but it can also be risky, unpredictable, and alienating.[6] And yet, despite these risks, countless partygoers go out every weekend and find intimacy among strangers. Thriving and perishing in the urban interstices, these fleeting nocturnal worlds take on a glowing utopian halo for many of their participants, providing a "somewhere else" where different ways of being together can be rehearsed, enacted, demanded, and enjoyed.

Feeling Utopian on the Dancefloor

Together, Somehow focuses primarily on *how* stranger-intimacy occurs on the dancefloor, but we should also consider *why* it does. How are such encounters valuable to those who engage in them? Each chapter in this book adds to a patchwork of answers, but in this introductory chapter I provide a condensed overview of dancefloor utopianism as historical and cultural context for the rest of the book. To put it simply, stranger-intimacy is a utopian practice of post-disco dance music scenes; it serves as a meaningful way through which partygoers can enact and experience the world they want to live in—one characterized by openness and warmth. Along with subcultural practices that enact sexual freedom, self-transformation, sensory amplification, and the oceanic bliss of self-dissolution, stranger-intimacy enables partygoers to briefly live in a world better than this one.

Utopian themes pervaded my fieldwork, both in the interviews I conducted and in the way that parties were planned, performed, and remembered in the "minimal" electronic music subscenes of Chicago, Paris, and Berlin. These themes often featured prominently at the beginning of interviews with partygoers, in response to my opening question: "Why do you party?" Teresa, for example, a Chicago-based DJ, party organizer, and flight attendant, began by describing techno parties as a way of escaping everyday struggles; but, as she went on to tell the story of how she discovered and joined the local techno scene, she reframed it as a burgeoning alternative community.

TERESA: I always looked at it as more of an escapist kind of activity that is just part of dealing with . . . a lot of what we have to deal with in our daily lives, the reality of what things are in our society. . . . After spending enough time, you realize that it's not just a way of escaping, but it's a community that you look forward to. . . .

I really enjoyed being able to go to this sort of underground thing. Most of the people in my high school had no idea that [*sarcastically*] "a local rave scene" was going on—didn't know about it, didn't care about it, whichever it was. And, all of a sudden, I'd find myself amongst another forty, fifty people who felt the same way that I did about the music, and I just loved that sort of small community. (Chicago, 2010)

Teresa's account of an underground, subcultural world serving as a vibrant alternative to "the reality of what things are in our society" highlights the utopianism so central to her experience of electronic dance music culture, while also keeping sight of the everyday struggles that make such utopianism meaningful. In doing so, she invokes a subcultural heritage that extends back to disco's emergence in the 1970s.

The dancefloor has long served to symbolize a world better than this one. Thriving at both the physical and imaginative center of electronic dance music events, dancefloors are celebrated as places of self-invention, experimentation, escape, comfort, refuge, transformation, connection, and communion. For the marginalized, they can be a place where the injustices and indignities of everyday life are not only temporarily relieved but to some extent redressed. Inasmuch as dancefloors can serve as spaces for experimentation with ways of living together that are better, more just, more caring, more fulfilling, or simply less harmful, they also function as sites of utopianism. This is not to suggest that nightclubs are fully realized utopias—far from it—but rather that their dancefloors are utopian in spirit: they provide concrete sites for the collective envisioning of a different kind of "good life."

Starting from disco's twilight years, one can follow a thread of writers reflecting on the utopian aspects of dancefloors and the music that animates them. Appearing in print after the mainstream success of the disco-themed film *Saturday Night Fever* and at a time when disco had saturated national and international media, Richard Dyer's essay for the *Gay Left*, "In Defense of Disco," argued for the political relevance of this new genre—despite the misgivings of critics on the political left.[7] He did so by pointing to disco's nearly successful mainstreaming of nonheteronormative eroticism, its subversion of rock/folk ideologies of naturalness and authenticity, its valorization of worldly pleasure without shame, its vision of a utopian "flight from banality" through romantic extremes of emotion, and its role as a utopian refuge for sexual minorities. David Diebold, a singer and producer of "Hi-NRG" disco, gave a similar account of gay dance clubs as utopian safe havens in his memoirs of San Francisco's club scenes, *Tribal Rites*. Since then, a growing archive of memoirs, journalism, and scholarship continues to expand and nuance these utopian accounts of dancefloors as sites of refuge and self-fashioning, often noting that these spaces are still striated by harshly enforced hierarchies of beauty, coolness, fabulousness, masculinity, and wealth.[8] Notably, most of these analyses focused on the nightlife scenes of marginalized groups—especially where such marginalities intersect, such as the predominantly queer Black and Latinx crowds of the early New York disco scene.

The downtown Manhattan disco scene of the 1970s has often served as a utopian point of reference for subsequent generations of dance music.[9] Vince Aletti, who penned the first report on New York's budding disco clubs for *Rolling Stone*, was struck by the social mixing at early disco parties, describing them as "completely mixed, racially and sexually, where there wasn't any sense of someone being more important than someone else."[10] At the height of disco's popularity in 1978, New York mayor Ed Koch marked "Disco Week" by giving a speech in which he described disco as symbolizing "a more harmonious fellowship towards all creeds and races."[11] Diversity and integration were indeed important utopian themes for disco, surfacing in the lyrics of gospel-inflected hits like the O'Jays' "Love Train" and Sister Sledge's "We Are Family"—both of which invited dancers to join a community that was bound together by shared feeling and music rather than by existing social structures.[12] Despite these utopian visions of open and equal belonging, however, systems of exclusion were part of the disco scene from the very beginning. For example, members-only policies were initially justified as self-protective and legally necessary—especially for unlicensed venues such as The Loft, David Mancuso's residence on the Lower East Side—but this evolved into a system of elitist social curatorship at clubs like Studio 54, selecting and excluding people on the basis of beauty, celebrity, glamour, and social connections.

These utopian imaginaries continued into the era of house music, which emerged out of the disco and post-disco scene in Chicago.[13] Frankie Knuckles, Ron Hardy, and other local DJs played an eclectic mix of disco,

Italo-disco, funk, gospel, hip-hop, and European electro-pop; but it was the practice of looping the instrumental breaks of their favorite tracks on reel-to-reel tapes and bolstering the percussion with drum machines that solidified the "house music" aesthetic, eventually leading to the production of original tracks by local producers. As with disco, utopianism is easiest to find in the titles and lyrics of house tracks, such as Joe Smooth Inc.'s "Promised Land," featuring a vocal performance by Anthony Thomas: atop bright, high-tempo conga drums and lush, sustained synthesizer chords, Thomas sings lyrics with clear political and utopian themes, addressing the audience as "brothers" and "sisters" and invoking Christian tropes of "the promised land" as a collective goal and destination.[14] Perhaps the most well-known example of house music's utopianism is Larry Heard's 1988 anthem-cum-manifesto "Can You Feel It?," released under the moniker Fingers Inc.[15] The track features a spoken-word performance by Robert Owens, who uses a declamatory style reminiscent of a Black charismatic preacher to recount a musical creation-narrative that riffs on several biblical creation myths: "In the beginning, there was Jack / And Jack had a groove." Alluding to the book of Genesis in particular, this musician-creator brings house music into being by proclaiming, "Let there be house," and dubbing himself "the creator"; but this is soon followed by the declaration that this newly created house is a collective space, in which gaining membership is as easy as stepping onto the dancefloor:

> But I am not so selfish, because once you enter my house
> It then becomes our house and our house music
> And, you see, no one man owns house
> Because house music is a universal language
> Spoken and understood by all
> You see, house is a feeling that no one can understand, really
> Unless you're deep into the vibe of House
> House is an uncontrollable desire to jack your body
> And, as I told you before, this is our house and our house music.[16]

In these few lines, house music becomes a shared utopian world: a common point of understanding but also an ineffable affective experience; a festive public sphere with open membership but requiring deep immersion and bodily surrender. At several points in the track, this sermon is interpolated with sonic indexes of affective intensity, including the sound of cheering crowds responding to a shouted call: "Can you feel it?" In proximity to Owens's euphoric sermonizing, the "it" of this vocal sample remains unspecified but nonetheless resonant with potential meanings.[17]

Utopianism is not difficult to find in the United Kingdom's acid house scenes as well as the subsequent regional rave scenes, influenced as they were by post-hippie culture from the Balearic.[18] Indeed, the 1988–1989 boom in acid house was dubbed the "Second Summer of Love," a direct reference to the first Summer of Love in 1967, when the hippie movement became both a cultural revolution and a mass-cultural phenomenon.[19] Along with tie-dyed patterns, psychedelic graphic design, fluorescent color palettes, and smiley-face icons, the United Kingdom's early rave scenes adopted a great deal of hippie-era utopian rhetoric, including visions of universal inclusivity and a surging sense of revolutionary possibility through euphoric communion. Unlike the hippie movement, however, ravers did not seem to share an explicit political agenda—aside from getting along and having fun. Nonetheless, the euphoric sense of community cultivated at UK rave events seemed to remedy a certain sense of stuckness that middle- and working-class youth felt in the face of Thatcherite austerity, especially as the technological and economic utopias promised by the postwar state failed to materialize.[20]

The post-hippie utopianism of the rave era found another incarnation across the Atlantic as raves became a mass cultural phenomenon in North America, beginning in New York (Storm Rave, 1990) and Toronto (Exodus, 1991). From the outset, these North American rave events tended to attract young, white, middle-class, suburban, and predominantly heterosexual partygoers.[21] This is not to say that these scenes represented hegemonic culture; North American ravers, much like their UK and European peers, self-identified as eccentric outsiders and differentiated themselves from a perceived cultural "mainstream" through a range of aesthetic, discursive, and behavioral means. Ravers were largely part of the "Generation X" cohort, but whereas grunge and alternative rock seemed to channel the malaise of Gen-X directionlessness, raves sought to counter despondency with euphoria.[22] Much like in the United Kingdom, rave events addressed recession-era angst and alienation by offering refuge in collective effervescence.

The acid house / rave narrative may seem to suggest that electronic dance music left North America and returned later in the guise of rave culture, but it never disappeared from the queer nightlife scenes that had served as its crucible. In New York, prominent gay nightclubs such as the Paradise Garage (1976–1987) and The Saint (1980–1988) survived the disco era, serving as incubators for new styles of dance music throughout the 1980s, while newer clubs such as Sound Factory (1989–1995) and Twilo (1995–2001) continued this scene into the next decade and dovetailed with the city's rave scene. Paradise Garage was especially significant as a major "underground" dance music institution, catering to a gay crowd that was predominantly Black and Latinx.[23] Under the musical direction of the resident DJ Larry Levan, the club developed a particular sound—later dubbed "garage" or "garage house"—which rerouted the percussive drive of early Chicago house music back into classic disco, funk, and soul. Instead of the high-tempo, raw, "jackin'" sound of Chicago house, New York garage featured moderate tempos, glossy production, soulful vocal performances, and keyboard riffs reminiscent of gospel and soul. In New York garage music, utopian affect remained closely tied to disco's dancefloor euphoria, to which it added hypnotic grooves such as those in Serious Intention's "You Don't Know (Special Remix)," conveying an ecstatic, expansive, and kaleidoscopic experience.[24] Perhaps more intensely and insistently than disco, garage seemed to imagine the feeling of utopia as musical abandon, "getting lost" in endless dancing.

I end this brief historical sketch of dancefloor utopianism here, conscious of the terrain left uncovered. Much could be said about the utopianism of drag balls and "ballroom culture," for example, which have continued to flourish as an international phenomenon long after *Paris Is Burning*, Judith Butler, and Madonna had their turn.[25] "Trance" could also figure as another thread in this historical account, especially the overlapping substyles of Goa trance and psytrance, with their post-hippie/"freak" inheritance from psychedelic subcultures and "new age" movements, featuring utopian themes that are more introspective, esoteric, and spiritual. Similarly, the dark, machinic but funky techno that was emerging from Detroit during the late 1980s and 1990s is pertinent here, with its paradoxical mixing of dystopian futurescapes and utopian Afrofuturism.[26] In particular, the militant leftist, critically utopian Afrofuturism of the artist collective Underground Resistance (UR) provides a contrast to the more euphoric modes of utopianism that are at the center of this book; I return to UR in the epilogue, where I consider some of its musical output in relation to contemporary experiences of struggle and crisis.

This historical sketch could also jump forward to the events that have unfolded in North America since the end of fieldwork for this book in 2010, when dubstep (a UK substyle of breakbeat, 2-step garage, and "illbient") suddenly exploded in popularity, accompanied by a rapid mainstreaming of EDM in general (as well as the term "EDM" itself, much to the surprise of electronic dance music scholars). The "EDM boom" of the 2010s attracted a new generation of young dance music fans, although they were initially drawn to large-scale festivals rather than urban nightclubs or underground raves.[27] In the wake of the 2008 global recession, it seems that this newer, massive, highly commercialized EDM played a role in North America similar to what acid house played in Margaret Thatcher's United Kingdom: it provided a means of experiencing a sense of collective utopian future at a time when individual life narratives of upward mobility no longer seemed certain.

While it is clear that utopianism runs deep under electronic dance music cultures, the political ramifications of such utopianism is less clear. As illustrated in Dyer's article in defense of disco for the *Gay Left*, criticism of dancefloor utopianism—as naïve, ineffective, or insincere—is nearly as old as disco itself.[28] In fact, this ambivalence toward utopianism has a much longer history, lying at the heart of one of the earliest divisions in socialist political theory: between utopian socialism and revolutionary socialism. Utopian socialists such as Henri de Saint-Simon and Charles Fourier devoted their intellectual efforts to imagining how a perfect socialist society would work in the future, while Karl Marx and Friedrich Engels called for a revolutionary socialism that engaged directly with the actually existing struggles of their time.[29] Marx's refutation of utopian socialism made anti-utopianism the norm within Marxism until nearly a century later, when Ernst Bloch wrote *Das Prinzip Hoffnung* (*The Principle of Hope*), a three-volume treatise on the political importance of hope, daydreaming, and utopia.[30] Writing in the socialist German Democratic Republic (East Germany), Bloch argued that hope contains a "utopian function," playing a critical role within emergent political movements: to dream of utopia is to ascertain what is wrong with the present, actually existing world and to imagine a better one.

In this sense, utopianism can amplify revolutionary politics by creating an imaginative space where the injustices of the here and now can be called out, where a demand for a better world can be articulated. Bloch addresses Marxist misgivings about wasted political energies by drawing a sharp distinction between "abstract utopias" and "concrete utopias," the former referring to escapist, distracting utopias and the latter to utopias that are grounded in real-world, actually occurring struggles.[31] Following these definitions, Teresa's comments at the opening of this section could be understood as imagining a concrete utopia, where the community built through raving served to question the status quo of her everyday American life. Part of utopia's revolutionary relevance is its revelatory access to the Not-Yet-Conscious, Bloch's future-facing alternative to the psychoanalytic unconscious (which he renames the No-Longer-Conscious); the Not-Yet-Conscious represents the impending, soon-to-be-realized worlds arriving at the horizon of consciousness, rather than that which has passed into memory. Bloch thus locates political power in these concrete utopias, doubly grounded in present conditions as well as the near future of the Not-Yet-Conscious.

Bloch's treatise is particularly useful for this book in that he compiled something like an affective-aesthetic catalogue of utopianism. He characterizes hope as the utopian emotion par excellence, a forward-dawning "expectant emotion" that "refers to the furthest and brightest horizon"; in turn, the "wishful images" that arise from hopeful daydreaming take external form "in a better planned world or even an *aesthetically heightened* world, one without disappointment."[32] Bloch's repeated use of dawn as a metaphor for hope and the Not-Yet-Conscious generates a particular affective-aesthetic palette that resurfaces throughout all three volumes: outpouring light, glowing horizons, emerging patterns, approaching figures, swelling feelings, upward and expanding motion. He describes a sense of latency, of something swelling under the surface of the present. Since music unfolds in time and can play with expectation, anticipation, and synchronicity, it seems especially well suited to convey the expectant qualities Bloch associates with hope and utopia. Electronic dance music can project long-spanning structures of expectation through repetition and multimeasure patterning, thus dramatizing movement toward the dawning horizon of utopian yearning.[33] All night long—from track to track, peak moment to peak moment—electronic dance music stages the dawning of a better tomorrow.[34]

Also relevant to this book's understanding of utopian feeling is José Esteban Muñoz's *Cruising Utopia: The Then and There of Queer Futurity*, which combines Bloch's critical utopianism with Jill Dolan's notion of utopian performance to describe how queers make livable worlds for themselves amid suffocating circumstances.[35] For Muñoz, to engage in utopianism is to turn collective longing and shared dissatisfaction with the "quagmire of the present" into something that can put pressure on the real world. I hesitate, however, to follow his rejection of the (purportedly heteronormative) present for a purely queer elsewhere and else-when. His positioning seems to stem from an opposition to a strain of "antisocial"/"antirelational" queer theory that is wary of the violence done to queers in the name of a sanitized collective future ("Think of the children!"). I would rather eschew this temporal binary altogether and focus instead on a horizon that extends spatially, temporally, and socially outward from the dancefloor.[36] Electronic dance music scenes—especially disco, house, and their inheritors—are relentlessly focused on an eroticized nowness that hovers near the dawning horizon: spanning present and future, neither tomorrow nor today but *tonight*.[37]

Utopian dance parties, in any case, are not only dress rehearsals for better days to come; they can also create small, temporary pockets of living utopia—a throbbing future in the visceral present. These fleeting utopian enactments, however, gloss over the pragmatic details of how an ideal society should work, focusing instead on how utopia should *feel*. This focus on the sensory and affective aspects of better living is characteristic of popular culture and leisure. Richard Dyer has argued that much of popular American entertainment is pointedly utopian in its outlook—but rather than presenting a realistic model of how utopia would function, it conveys something about how utopia would *feel*.[38] Surveying mid-twentieth-century American movie-musicals, Dyer compiles a catalogue of the feelings that these films highlight (such as energy, abundance, intensity, transparency, and community), suggesting that these constitute the affective imaginary of utopia for midcentury movie-musical audiences. He also links these feelings to a corresponding set of opposite, negative feelings (such as scarcity, exhaustion, dreariness, manipulation, and fragmentation), which he traces to several widespread, simmering crises in the postwar United States. In this sense, American movie-musicals were not merely escapist, "abstract" utopian films; rather, they gave shape to American worries and dissatisfactions in inverted form.

The same could also be said of post-disco dance music, with its tropes of emancipation, hope, respect, kinship, love, pleasure, fun, ecstasy, and euphoria. In Dyer's attempts to defend disco from leftist critics, he highlights the genre's utopian romanticism as one of its redeeming qualities. He locates the "surging, outpouring emotions" of romantic aesthetics in disco's soaring melodic lines, "heavenly" choirs, sweeping unison violins, and emotive voices, all of which dramatize the "intensity of fleeting emotional contacts."[39] Combined with Bloch's utopian affective-aesthetic vocabulary of dawning, yearning, and intensity, this already provides the beginnings of a hermeneutic lens for reading utopianism in disco's musical legacy. Dyer stresses the political relevance of disco's affective excesses, arguing that:

Its passion and intensity embody or create an experience that negates the dreariness of the mundane and everyday. It gives us a glimpse of what it means to live at the height of our emotional and experiential capacities—not dragged down by the banality of organized routine life. Given that everyday banality, work, domesticity, ordinary sexism and racism, are rooted in the structures of class and gender of this society, the flight from that banality can be seen as—is—a flight from capitalism and patriarchy themselves as lived experiences. . . .

I don't say that the passion and intensity of romanticism is a political ideal we could strive for—I doubt that it is humanly possible to live permanently at that pitch. What I do believe is that the movement between banality and something "other" than banality is an essential dialectic of society, a constant keeping open of a gap between what is and what could or should be.[40]

In conjuring up an alternate world of emotional plenitude, then, disco's romanticism can hold open "the gap between what is and what could or should be"—in other words, a utopian space.

Dyer speaks of disco's romanticism holding open a gap between the lived world and an imagined one, but in this book it may be more fitting to speak of closing the gap. Indeed, one of its key themes is how feelings of vague belonging (awkwardly, tenuously) bridge the gap between utopian aspirations and the not-so-utopian realities of nightlife. At electronic dance music parties, music and dance provide sensory-affective relays between the activity of partying together and the sense of belonging to something larger than oneself, however incoherent or vague that "something" may be. This raises the question of how this sense of belonging can arise from such anonymous, heterogeneous, and yet socially striated environments. This book highlights the important role that stranger-intimacy plays in supporting a vague sense of belonging in volatile and uncertain circumstances.

"In the Field" in Chicago, Paris, and Berlin

Here is an awkward secret: most ethnography is opportunistic. Few (predominantly white, predominantly middle- to upper-class) anthropologists voluntarily disclose whether they "discovered" their fieldwork sites as tourists, missionaries, nongovernmental organization / charity workers, or that special blend of all three often dubbed "voluntourism." For those without the familial wealth, the "good" passports, or the colonially pow-ered expectation of a grudging-but-nonviolent welcome everywhere, eth-nographic sites are more likely to be local, familiar, and low budget. Like most ethnographers, my fieldwork story was very much the latter: I did fieldwork where I *could*, not where I wished. I was continually retrofit-ting my "research design" to my narrowing opportunities. As a foreign grad student studying in the United States, I was disqualified from both kinds of Fulbright fellowships: the ones that send US citizens abroad for a year of fieldwork and the ones that bring foreigners to study in the United States. There was a palpable absence of funding—both external and internal—for extended ethnographic research in domestic locales.

As a result, this research project started as a local, single-site study and only expanded when I succeeded in creating unconventional funding op-portunities. I began preliminary fieldwork in Chicago's minimal techno and house scenes because I was already living there as a PhD student. This became a two-city project when I discovered that my institution was tak-ing applications from graduate students for "assistanceships" at a satellite campus / semester-abroad center in Paris, where the successful applicant would provide technical support and receive a monthly stipend (instead of a salary), along with one day off per week to conduct their own research. Finally, I added Berlin to my project by self-funding short weekend visits while I was working in Paris as well as cobbling together small parcels of internal funding from my home department, which I combined with my own savings to append a pair of two-month visits to my stays in France. Al-though I never experienced the full-year, full-time fieldwork stay that was expected of my cohort at the University of Chicago, the fragmentary fund-ing I collected ultimately enabled me to expand my project across three research sites.

From Chicago through Paris to Berlin, this book is thus a "multi-sited ethnography"; this differs from conventional ethnographic fieldwork by focusing neither on a single site nor on a global system of political and cul-tural flows but instead on the circulation of people, ideas, or things from place to place.[41] This book's multi-sited approach is also *translocal*, based on the view that Paris, Berlin, and Chicago are not three isolated music scenes with comparable parameters but linked nodes in a larger network of circu-lating media and people.[42] There is a great deal of movement and exchange between these scenes as well as significant shared cultural references and practices, all of which contribute to the sense that local techno-scenesters also partake in a transnational electronic dance music scene. Indeed, these shared social and cultural resources support "techno tourism" and "techno migration,"[43] enabling travelers to find their way into the electronic dance music scenes of a new city by drawing on the scene-specific knowledge and social networks they developed in other cities—much as I did during the course of fieldwork for this book.[44] Notably, most of my fieldwork contacts had some experience with this techno-mobility, especially via Berlin: all of my Parisian contacts and roughly half of those based in Chicago had visited Berlin as techno-tourists, and a handful from each city went on to relocate there after I completed my research. Remarkably, none of those who relocated there did so to pursue a career in electronic music, even though they all acknowledged that their previous visits as techno-tourists inspired their migration.

Most cities do not have just one electronic dance music scene; they have many, reflecting the diversity of styles and substyles that developed out of the post-disco era.[45] The internal hierarchies of these scenes do not produce a unified "club culture" in a given city but instead several fragmented clusters that share the same label but maintain distinctive musical genres, styles of dancing, and behavioral norms.[46] Sean Nye, for example, identified four significant electronic music scenes in Berlin during the early twenty-first century: pop techno, techno-house, minimal-electro, and hardcore-noise.[47] Nye provides a useful vocabulary for making sense of similar scenes in other cities; although the clubbing landscapes in Paris and Chicago were not identical, they did tend to group into similar poles. The minimal scenes of each city served as my initial point of entry for fieldwork, although this shifted over time. First, the boundaries between scenes in each city were quite porous; in Chicago, for example, "minimal" tended to be treated as a substyle of techno and house (i.e., minimal techno and minimal house), while in Paris, the subscene boundaries at the time were marked by *minimale* versus *éléctro* (electroclash). Second, the style-specific boundaries of each city's music scenes changed over time; by 2010, when I was completing fieldwork for this book, interest in minimal styles was beginning to wane, with most of my fieldwork contacts shifting their focus toward harder techno on the one hand and "classic" downtempo house and disco on the other. Throughout this book, I treat these scenes as *exemplary*; that is, they serve as a more manageable set of case studies for a broader field of cultural activity. And so, the observations, analyses, and claims I make in this book should be understood to pertain primarily to the continuum of house and techno styles found in each city, with the minimal subscenes of 2006–2010 as the descriptive center of gravity.

Chicago

Active fieldwork in Chicago consisted of two one-year, part-time research phases (2007–2008, 2009–2010), although I had been studying there since 2004. Despite Chicago's pivotal role in the early development of house music as well as its transatlantic exportation to the United Kingdom's acid house and rave scenes, the definitive history of post-disco dance music in Chicago has yet to be written.[48] Nonetheless, most of the local partygoers interviewed for this book were acutely aware of the city's rich musical history, readily naming legendary venues such as The Warehouse and The Music Box as well as DJ/producers such as Frankie Knuckles, Ron Hardy, and Steve "Silk" Hurley as forebears of the city's present-day dance scenes. That said, when the UK rave phenomenon came to the United States with a transformed version of house music, it came to a primarily white, middle-class, heterosexual audience, rather than to the predominantly queer, working-class, Black and Latinx one in which it had originally developed.[49] This racial, sexual, and class divide was still apparent when I was conducting fieldwork in Chicago; upon first arriving to the city, I found a multiethnic but predominantly white and straight techno-house scene (including tech-house, deep house, and minimal), and it was only later that I became aware of a vibrant but less visible Black house and techno scene. Chicago's scenes also reflected the city's history of immigration, and so my immediate network of fieldwork contacts included people of Armenian, Indian, Russian, Ukrainian, Bulgarian, Japanese, Polish, Belarusian, Greek, Hungarian, Chilean, Lithuanian, and Pakistani origins.

Chicago is a particularly decentralized city, with a great deal of its cultural and commercial activity spread throughout the city's numerous neighborhoods. Each neighborhood has a name and a distinctive history, which usually involves several waves of immigration and gentrification.[50] The city is also known for its pattern of racial "hypersegregation," where decades of racist housing policies and urban planning have resulted in the city's Black residents being concentrated in the city's "South Side" and the near-west industrial corridor.[51] Similarly, processes of gentrification continue to push the city's Latinxs out of neighborhoods such as Wicker Park, Logan Square, and Pilsen and toward the southwest quadrant of the city. Many of Chicago's nightlife venues are located in these gentrification hot spots in the city's northwest as well as certain postindustrial zones near the city center (see map 1). The notable exception to this is SmartBar, the city's longest-running dance club, which is located in the northern neigh-

MAP 1 Fieldwork venues in Chicago, 2006–2010. Map by C. Riggio.

borhood of Wrigleyville. Many clubs closed after the financial crash of 2008, although the nightlife industry began to rebound during the rapid popularization of "EDM" in the United States after 2010. During this post-crash fallow period, however, the number of illicit "underground" parties increased, taking place in unlicensed venues and running well beyond the usual hours of operation for nightlife; these locations are scattered around Chicago and include warehouses, artists' studios/lofts, art galleries, and domestic spaces. Many of the ethnographic scenes recounted in this book took place in these informal underground spaces.

Paris

Research in Paris also consisted of two one-year phases, trimmed to the academic years 2006–2007 and 2008–2009 by my service as technical support for the University of Chicago Center in Paris. Discothèque culture in

FIGURE I.1 Entrance to SmartBar (Chicago). Photograph courtesy of Erielle Bakkum (2016) and SmartBar Chicago.

Paris was not subject to the sudden collapse in popularity that occurred in North America in the early 1980s; most discothèques continued to operate throughout that decade, shifting their programming to include rock, Top 40 chart pop, New Wave synthpop, or *variété*.[52] The acid house of the United Kingdom's early rave scenes nonetheless took root in Paris, especially through the influence of Laurent Garnier, who held a DJ residency at the legendary Manchester club Haçienda [*sic*] in 1987. A year later, he brought this sound with him to his residency at Le Rex in Paris, making it the *haut lieu* of French *techno* as well as one of the principal sites for my Parisian fieldwork.[53] Notably, many of the other Parisian discothèques that began to pick up the new *techno* sound were queer clubs, and one of the most prominent radio stations promoting *la techno* was Radio Fréquence Gay. Additionally, many of this burgeoning scene's record stores were located in the queer areas of the Marais and Bastille districts. While the first wave of activity was primarily focused in queer urban nightlife venues, this changed in the mid-1990s with the arrival of English "sound system" collectives such as Spiral Tribe, which were fleeing legislative changes in the United Kingdom that rendered nearly any size of rave party illegal.[54] They organized outdoor/warehouse "free parties" that did not charge admission and espoused a more radically antiestablishment, collectivist, and anticapitalist politics. Primarily held in rural locations in Brittany and the areas surrounding Lyon, Paris, Marseille, and Montpelier, *les free partys*—French open-air raves modeled on British "free parties"—featured harder styles of electronic dance music (such as hardcore, jungle, drum'n'bass) and distinguished themselves sharply from the queerer, urban, house-oriented club scenes.

Giving primacy to rhythm and percussion over melody and lyrics, this cluster of sample-based dance styles ran counter to the aesthetics of middle-class French rock and *chanson* audiences, whom Philippe Birgy describes as prizing "political awareness and a more or less desperate form of gravity"—seriousness and weighty themes, in other words.[55] *La techno* lacked the explicit political lyrics typical of *chanson*, and it was attacked by cultural critics as apolitical—even reactionary—which gave rise to a remarkably strong backlash in public media, law enforcement, and legislative initiatives.[56] But in 1997, the Parti Socialiste (PS, Socialist Party) returned to power in France and saw an opportunity to harness another youth movement for party recruitment, as it did to great success in the early 1980s with the Fête de la Musique.[57] The Ministry of Culture, the Ministry of the Interior, and the Ministry of Youth and Sport all worked under PS direction to reverse the policies that had been targeting raves while also financially supporting the Techno Parade, modeled after Berlin's Love Parade. The Ministry of Culture also sought to sanitize techno's transgressive image through programs of professionalization, both for artists and for event organizers.[58] This strategy has had a lasting impact on Paris's electronic dance music scenes, which became highly professionalized and deeply integrated into the French entertainment industry.[59]

But as *la techno* became a larger and more profitable business sector, nightclubs and promoters felt more pressure to follow market logics and avoid taking risks on less popular styles. As a result, during my fieldwork visits, only a few venues in Paris regularly featured *minimale*-related programming (including minimal house, minimal techno, microhouse, dub house, tech-house), such as Le Rex, Batofar, and La Scène Bastille (see map 2). Smaller-scale *minimale* events tended to take place in bars and cafés with small dancefloors or basements. Geographically, the oldest and largest clubs in Paris were located on the Champs-Elysées and the Grands

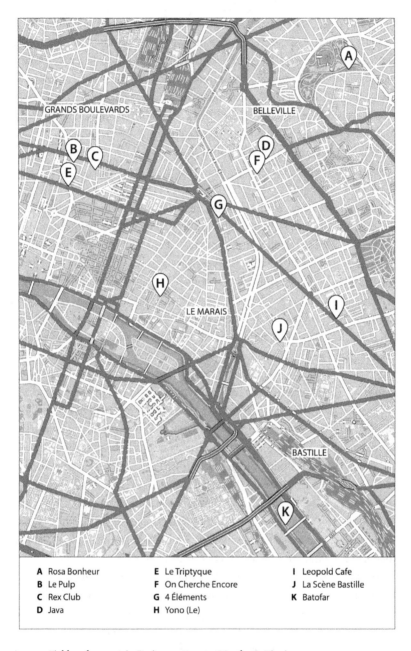

A Rosa Bonheur	**E** Le Triptyque	**I** Leopold Cafe
B Le Pulp	**F** On Cherche Encore	**J** La Scène Bastille
C Rex Club	**G** 4 Éléments	**K** Batofar
D Java	**H** Yono (Le)	

MAP 2 Fieldwork venues in Paris, 2006–2010. Map by C. Riggio.

Boulevards areas, including Le Queen, Le Rex, Man Ray, Le Milliardaire, and Club 79; but, with the exception of Le Rex, my fieldwork contacts dismissed the Grands Boulevards clubs as "mainstream" and "commercial" venues. The smaller, more "underground" venues were located in the northeastern sectors of Paris (such as Le Marais, Bastille, and Belleville). The crowds at these venues were predominantly white and middle class but with a more balanced mix of sexualities than I saw in Chicago; indeed, many of the venues that hosted *minimale* events at the time were located in historically gay districts and catered to queer crowds. Queer women were especially visible in the *minimale* scene as artists, promoters, and venue managers—much of which can be attributed to the legacy of the legendary lesbian club Le Pulp. Its Thursday *électro* nights attracted a crowd of mixed genders, and when it closed in 2007, many former employees and patrons went on to organize their own events.[60]

Berlin

Berlin was added to this project later, near the end of my first year in Paris. As a result, most of the fieldwork was conducted very intensively over the summers of 2008 and 2010. I also made frequent visits to Berlin while living in Paris, and since then I have alternated between living in Berlin full-time and visiting frequently while working elsewhere in Europe. In contrast to Paris, Berlin took to electronic dance music quickly and enthusiastically. In many ways, similar musical styles had been developing in Berlin well before acid house arrived via England in the late 1980s; the city already hosted vibrant scenes for industrial music (especially the Electronic Body Music substyle), Neue Deutsche Welle, experimental rock, synthpop, and noise music.[61] In other words, electronic sounds were already a familiar element in popular music by the time house and techno began appearing in clubs. These experimental and technophilic scenes provided fertile ground for the first generation of clubs in Berlin, which clustered into a sort of *Clubmeile* (club mile) centered on Leipziger Platz in the former East Berlin district of Mitte. Venues such as Tresor, WMF, and E-Werk were located immediately east of where the Berlin Wall once stood, mostly occupying abandoned buildings that were located near the Wall's "death strip" (*Todesstreife*). By the end of the 1990s, these clubs found themselves directly in the path of Berlin's plans for urban renewal; property leases were terminated, tenants were evicted, and the buildings were sold and then either demolished or converted into new commercial spaces (offices, hotels, shops). In the

FIGURE I.2 Entrance to Le Rex Club (Paris). Alain Jocard / AFP via Getty Images.

following decade, a second generation of techno clubs developed in what Tobias Rapp calls "the new club mile" along the eastern banks of the river Spree, stretching along five kilometers between Alexanderplatz and the Oberbaumbrücke.[62] Although numerous clubs opened and closed in this area during the period of fieldwork for this book, the most prominent ones at the time were Berghain / Panorama Bar, Watergate, Bar 25, Golden Gate, the new Tresor (on Köpenicker Straße), and Club der Visionäre (see map 3).

The emergence of these second-generation clubs coincided with Berlin's reemergence as the productive center for minimal styles of electronic dance music, prompted by exceptionally low operating costs and liberal nightlife regulation; this spurred an upsurge in nightlife tourism as well as the relocation of numerous DJs and specialist record labels to the city. Berlin took on a significance for electronic music similar to Nashville's for country music, serving as a center for production, networking, distribution, trade, and career building. This geographic concentration of labor, capital, and bodies could be considered a "creative cluster," although non-nightlife facilities (such as record labels, studios, residences, and the bars and cafés where partygoers gather when they are not partying) are not so tightly clustered as the nightclubs are.[63] Unlike in Paris and Chicago, where minimal subscenes were on the margins of the nightlife landscape, in Berlin it was

A	Tresor 1	**E**	Golden Gate	**I**	Berghain
B	E-Werk	**F**	Tresor Club	**J**	WaterGate
C	WMF	**G**	Bar 25	**K**	Club der Visionaere
D	Weekend Club	**H**	Club Maria am Ostbahnhof	**L**	Arena Club

MAP 3 Fieldwork venues in Berlin, 2006–2010. Map by C. Riggio.

the omnipresent soundtrack to not just nightclubs but cafés, bars, restaurants, galleries, and even supermarkets.

By 2008, Berlin's minimal subscene had become remarkably international, with expatriates and tourists making up nearly half of the crowd at many events that I attended. Rapp corroborates this observation, arguing that, although the "three pillars" of the 1990s Berlin techno scene were *Ossis* (from former East Germany), gays, and creative industry workers, the *Touris* (tourists) became crucial to the post-2000 scene.[64] That said, the scene's demographic profile was more complex than these three or four categories: a substantial portion of the "creative classes" in Berlin consisted of expatriates or domestic migrants, and many travelers to the city would visit regularly and/or stay for longer periods (e.g., one to several months), thus occupying a gray zone between migrant and tourist. Compared to similar events in other subscenes, minimal parties tended to

FIGURE I.3 Exterior of Berghain nightclub (Berlin). Ullstein bild / ullstein bild via Getty Images.

attract a crowd that was evenly mixed by gender and sexuality. The exception to this pattern was Berghain / Panorama Bar, which served a core audience of gay men, although the room that more often featured minimal dance music (Panorama Bar) attracted a straighter crowd than the hard techno downstairs in Berghain. Crowds at most Berliner venues at the time were predominantly middle class and/or white German, with an overlay of cosmopolitan foreigners—whether tourists or relatively privileged migrants ("expats")—while local Berliner minority communities (especially Anatolian, North African, and sub-Saharan African ones) were less visible, although not entirely absent.

Fieldwork Methods and Demographics

My fieldwork moved irregularly among three cities over several years, following the availability of research funding and employment, and so I had to take a flexible and dynamic approach to my methods. In addition to the variable duration, intensity, and regularity of fieldwork visits to each city, their electronic music scenes posed challenges to the ethnomusicological methods in which I had been trained. As a result, I conducted fieldwork as a constant cycle of improvisation, trial and error, and adaptation.[65] In all three cities, fieldwork involved at least two essential activities: participant-observation and one-on-one interviews. Most of the narrative examples (or ethnographic "scenes") recounted in this book are based on field notes from participant-observation, while one-on-one interviews with individual partygoers served as the source for the lengthier direct quotations and dialogues that are woven through each chapter. These two core fieldwork activities fed into ethnography, turning field notes and interviews into an analysis of the lifeways of a group of people; for this third activity, I relied on one additional resource: well over twenty years of personal involvement in electronic dance music as a raver, a dancer, a writer, a DJ, and a promoter. These two decades of knowledge, experience, and relationships informed every aspect of my methods, such as whom I spoke to, what questions I asked, what events I attended, how I behaved, what anecdotes and quotations I chose to highlight as exemplary of broader cultural patterns, and what concepts I used to make sense of my ethnographic data.

Although the dancefloor is at the heart of this research project, it also posed some of the greatest methodological challenges. Admittedly, I conducted interviews well away from the dancefloor (usually at my home, the interviewee's residence, or a quiet café), and the scope of my participant-observation often spilled over to its liminal spaces (the bar, the toilets, a stairway, the entrance). Nonetheless, the dancefloor always remained the primary point of reference for myself and my interlocutors. In common parlance in post-disco dance music scenes, "the dancefloor" frequently serves as a metonym for the audience, the venue, and even the community that animates it; indeed, for those who are immersed in these music scenes, the dancefloor is not just a space but a whole world.

And yet, the dancefloor posed some challenges for these methods, most notably for their documentation. Ethnomusicology imbues photos, audio recordings, and videos with a near-talismanic value, proof that what we are doing is "serious" and "scientific" research. There are, however, factors both practical and cultural that make conventional media capture and note-taking methods inappropriate for documenting electronic dance music events. From a practical standpoint, data collection at a party is awkward for all involved: the crush of bodies and open beverages make it difficult to hold a recording device or take notes; the loud, bass-heavy music drowns out conversation and overloads microphones. From a cultural standpoint, conspicuously taking audiovisual recordings or initiating formal interviews on the dancefloor violates important scene-specific norms regarding privacy, consent, conviviality, and protecting that space as a refuge from "real world" struggles. Furthermore, my object of study, stranger-intimacy, required a light touch when it came to observation and documentation; many factors needed to be in just the right place in order for someone to reach out and open up to a stranger—and my pulling out a notepad or video camera on the dancefloor certainly would not help. Nightlife worlds are meaningful to many partygoers as a "third sphere" separate from work and domestic life, where they strive to create a playful flow of enjoyment in which everyday life seems to recede from view.[66] Deployed at the wrong moment or in the wrong context, recording devices on the dancefloor can be intrusive and disrespectful. Moreover, these modes of documentary capture can easily activate partygoers' anxieties about surveillance—particularly with regard to sexuality, drug use, and political expression. In light of these challenges, I employed a form of "memory work" when I was attending events: I would arrive at the venue, dance, listen, and interact with other event participants, and then write down detailed narrative field notes from memory immediately after returning home.[67]

These same concerns for privacy also prompted me to use a modified "snowball sampling" method for recruiting interviewees. I initially solicited interviews from my network of fieldwork contacts within the local scene, asking afterward for referrals to other potential interviewees.[68] This entailed developing a sort of trust network, cultivated over several months of repeated face-to-face contact at parties. I assigned pseudonyms to all interviewees as a default, although some later requested to use personal names or artist monikers. Admittedly, this method of recruitment does not produce a representative "random sample" of a particular population but rather a portion of an interconnected social web; in this sense, the interviews conducted for this book constitute a window into the music scene rather than a bird's-eye view.[69]

It bears noting that my research contacts were predominantly white, although many of them were also ethnically marked as immigrants (especially in Chicago), and the distribution of gender and sexuality was roughly even. To some degree, this reflects the demographics of the scenes I studied, but I do not wish to erase the contributions of people of color to electronic music—especially Black and Latinx contributions—nor the existence of vibrant dance music communities centered around people of color. The whiteness of my ethnographic archive has much to do with how my own ethnicity intersected with the racial segregation found in all three cities. As a relatively fair-skinned Latino man of mixed ancestry, I was rarely invited to events devoted to dancers of color, and I had trouble finding them on my own. Indeed, in/visibility was a decisive factor here; as I have argued elsewhere, invisibility is an important survival strategy for people of color (especially QTPOC, queer and trans people of color), and party organizers in these communities had several good reasons to restrict their visibility: to avoid the attention of law enforcement (considering the higher likelihood of a violent outcome from a visit from the fire marshal or the police); to filter out "cultural tourists" and other privileged interlopers (who pose a risk of cultural appropriation, violation of local subcultural norms, and oblivious microaggressions); and to avoid overexposure by mainstream media.[70] Although QTPOC electronic music events have become more visible in response to increasing mainstream interest since the mid-2010s, during the time of my primary fieldwork (2006–2010) these minority dance music scenes maintained a lower public profile.[71] In any case, I had more success working my way into white-dominated spaces, where I could inhabit a nonthreatening "vaguely brown" role that I often shared with partygoers of South Asian, Middle Eastern, and North African ancestry. If I conducted my fieldwork now, with the networks I have developed over the years, it would have incorporated more Black and brown perspectives; but since I was new to each city as I began my research for this book, my ethnographic archive reflects the spaces and communities to which I had access at the time.

Also noteworthy is the age of my interviewees, who could be considered either "rather young" or "not that young, actually," depending on how we historicize electronic dance music. If we start with disco, this lineage of dance music has always been supported by multigenerational communities of dancers, with twenty- and thirty-somethings as the "center of gravity." In queer communities, nightclubs were invaluable spaces for intergenerational cultural transmission, the value of which became apparent in absentia, when the HIV/AIDS crisis decimated a whole generation of queer elders and emaciated the clubs, bathhouses, and bars they used to enliven. Queers of all ages are still traumatized by that stigmatized, hidden pandemic; we are still dancing with and for the ghosts of our elders. If, by contrast, we start our history with the rave era of the late 1980s to 1990s, we find contemporary accounts of a youth movement driven by teenaged crowds, which were echoed and amplified by sensationalist press coverage as well as the field of subcultural studies, both of which were focused on revealing youthful deviance and resistance. A similar narrative surfaced during the "EDM boom" of the 2010s, as newer styles of electronic music at large-scale festivals brought in a new generation of teenaged dancers. It is this fascination with youth that prevails in contemporary popular representations of electronic dance music, both in the press and social media. However, viewed from a broader historical perspective—one that connects the moments of mass popularity with periods of "underground" percolation in queer and queer-of-color communities—electronic dance music has been primarily cultivated by young-to-middle-aged adults, while going through periodic cycles of "massification" that have entailed "youthification" as well.

Although the age range of partygoers with whom I regularly engaged during fieldwork was much wider, those who sat down with me for extended interviews and conversations were mostly between twenty-five and thirty-five years old at the time—on the cusp between "Generation X" and "elder millennials" in popular parlance. With regard to life stages, some were still completing postsecondary training, some were beginning to establish themselves in their professions, and others were on the verge of starting families and grappling with how to reconcile those new responsibilities with a life as a devoted raver. Nobody I knew had any plans to retire from these electronic music scenes; some of my contacts took long-term breaks from partying due to health crises or problematic drug use (alcohol included), but almost none of these young adults "grew up and settled down" while I knew them.

It was with this group of dancers that I conducted semistructured interviews (that is, following an outline of discussion topics rather than a rigid set of questions), although these encounters were also decidedly dialogic in style. During interviews, I would solicit narratives relating to specific themes (such as "How did you get into electronic music?" "Tell me about a party where something went wrong"), which were then used as a basis to ask more probing follow-up questions. Since I had already accumulated substantial experience in the field through participant-observation before I began conducting formal field interviews, I often offered my own reflections as prompts for discussion. These reflections included early versions of some of the ideas that run through this book; in fact, well before these formal interviews, I had already begun to discuss these ideas with fellow partygoers in informal conversations during and after music events. Since such dialogue had already been going on informally beforehand, my aim in the interviews was not to collect insider perspectives untouched by ethnographic analysis but rather to engage in a sincere dialogue and collaboration with experts whose feedback I found immensely valuable. This dialogic style of interviewing also served to encourage partygoers to engage in their own analysis and theorization, activities that are all too often reserved as the privileged domain of ethnographers.

Ethnography as Magical Realism

In addition to combining multiple research sites and methods, *Together, Somehow* combines ways of writing at the intersection of music, dance, and nightlife. It blends ethnography, cultural theory, and affect studies, whereas most scholarly monographs on dance music have emphasized either historiography or musical analysis.[72] Throughout the following pages, I draw on a broad range of writing on affect (feelings, emotions, atmospheres), especially from the domains of queer theory, gender studies, urban studies, and anthropology.[73] This book also joins a small but growing cluster of ethnographies that attend to the sensory, emotional, and erotic aspects of dancefloor encounters, each of which approaches its object of study from a different disciplinary perspective.[74] Themes such as stranger-intimacy, texture, fluid belonging, and utopianism are perhaps unusual for music studies, but since strange and unexpected connections are at the heart of this research project, it seems only fitting that this book stages such queer encounters at the conceptual and disciplinary level as well.[75]

Such queer encounters go against the grain of conventional ethnography and its investment in realism; if ethnography is supposed to be a realist genre of writing, this book instead offers ethnography as magical realism. Much like the twentieth-century narrative genre that flourished especially in Latin American literature, *Together, Somehow* palpates the contours of the "real" world, searching for cracks it can pry open to release the strange and wondrous. In *Ugly Feelings*, Sianne Ngai explains how her book is not a history of feelings—despite being historical and focusing on feelings in literature and media—due to her use of "disjunctive alignment" as a method of analysis and theorization.[76] Disjunctive alignment uses juxtaposition instead of relation to find insight, pushing seemingly disparate ideas and objects together and looking for similarities that unlock new, unforeseen ways of understanding them. In a similar vein, much queer theory and queer culture finds perverse pleasure in juxtapositions that violate the "proper" order of things; indeed, nothing is quite so queer as putting things where they do not belong, pressing together things that should stay apart.

This book deliberately and joyfully applies concepts where they do not belong, looking for felicitous alignments and sympathetic resonances. It does so partly in order to unsettle the givenness of the unmagical real in which we toil but also to conjure new and strange things into being—things that might, for once, come from somewhere outside of what Muñoz terms "the quagmire of the present," holding the promise of real change by yanking the real outside the bounds of the normal.[77] This is, for me, the form that Bloch's utopia-without-escapism ("concrete utopias") takes: a spray of deliriously productive joy that spurts forth out of the tectonic pressures of very real suffering.[78] If I am not satisfied with reality as it is—and who is, anyway?—I cannot be satisfied with merely realist ethnographic description, no matter how "thick" (interpretive) it may be.[79]

In This Book

Using ethnographic narratives as well as interviews with partygoers, this book follows three main lines of analysis, which coalesce in the first four chapters and interweave throughout the rest of the book. I first describe a mode of intensified social warmth that can be found on the dancefloors of house, techno, and minimal events in Chicago, Paris, and Berlin; this sociability manifests itself in interactions between strangers that would be unexpected and even inappropriate in "daytime" public life. These intimate encounters with strangers constitute a distinctive mode of togetherness that is vague and underdefined, engendering a feeling of intimacy that supports a sense of cohesion with others, in spite of their strangerhood. The term I propose for this state of affairs is *liquidarity*, a form of fluid solidarity in which vagueness is a crucial condition of its emergence.

The second, sensory claim advanced in this book is that music, dance, and touch are primary vectors for affect at electronic dance music events. Since affect sustains and lubricates liquidarity, the intensified sensory experience of listening and dancing to music on the dancefloor is crucial for maintaining this fluid sense of collective intimacy. This line of argumentation leads to a supporting claim about bodily co-presence: by sharing the dancefloor, partygoers accumulate a shared set of intense experiences—dancing to the same music, exulting at the same musical climaxes, getting into similar states of exhaustion and/or intoxication, witnessing the same moments of surprise and excess—which elicit moments of felt synchrony and convergence.

Finally, this book follows a more explicitly political line of analysis about "the struggle for fun"—the ambivalent bargains we strike with subcultural worlds in order to enjoy them. It argues that this vague feeling of intimacy not only binds a crowd across social differences but also serves as cover for inequity, exclusion, and even forms of violence. The vagueness of liquidarity enables partygoers to bracket out contradictions and power asymmetries by avoiding explicit discussion of topics that would draw attention to such problems. The political implications are thus ambiguous at best: liquidarity risks obfuscating the ongoing reproduction of power and privilege, but it also enables the emergence of collective cohesion in fluid and volatile contexts. In other words, liquidarity makes utopian dancefloor experiences possible by lubricating social frictions, rather than resolving them; furthermore, it may numb us to the damage that these frictions continue to make. This critical angle has long been part of my research project, but since 2016 (in the Global North, at least) the rise of right-wing extremism, populist fascism, and predatory capitalism—all accelerated by a global pandemic—has cast my reflections on the messy utopianism of the dancefloor in a new, pulsating light.

The chapters that follow are organized along these lines of analysis, rather than being sorted by geography, institutions, time periods, or people. The analytic scope also broadens from chapter to chapter, beginning with tactility between dancing bodies (chapter 1) as well as in the sound of electronic dance music (chapter 2), expanding to the dancefloor and its peripheries (chapters 3 and 4), to the narrative arc of "a night out" (chapter 5), and finally to the door of nightlife venues and their patterns of inclusion and exclusion (chapter 6).

Chapter 1 explores the relationship between tactility and intimacy between dancers. It asks how and why tactility intensifies on the dancefloor, turning to interviews with partygoers. On the one hand, many of them valued dancefloor tactility as an embodied expression of intimacy and an antidote to prevailing norms of bodily decorum; on the other hand, they acknowledged that dancefloors can also be spaces of heightened risk for sexual harassment and assault—a risk that women, trans folk, and people of color feel especially keenly. Nonetheless, several women interviewees stressed how beneficial tactile stranger-intimacy could be to their enjoyment, expressing a utopian desire for a world where encounters with strangers could be open to sensual pleasure without being fraught with danger. This spectrum of experience highlights the pleasures, risks, and affective binding potentials of tactility, all of which point toward the ways in which tactility between strangers can offer alternative modes of togetherness and conviviality. In chapter 2, I argue that the tactility of the dancefloor is also evoked in electronic dance music, both thematically and texturally. In particular, this cluster of interrelated musical styles engages tactility through beats, flesh, and grain; that is, it (1) emphasizes percussion (especially at low frequencies and high volume), (2) features sound samples that index fleshy bodies, and (3) highlights sounds that are rich in texture. I support this analysis with close readings of house and techno tracks as well as through a close engagement with the pioneering work of Pierre Schaeffer on "sonic grain." This chapter places sound, vibration, and texture in the interstices of the senses and at the thresholds of perception.

Returning to interviews and fieldwork observations, chapter 3 considers how social warmth arises and endures in contexts of casual contact and anonymity. Although partygoers express desires for belonging to be simple, open, and easy, they nonetheless avoid explicit discussion of who belongs and how they do. I describe this slippery solidarity as a sort of *liquidarity*, a blend of loose stranger-sociability and vague belonging. Under conditions of liquidarity, participants sustain a vague sense of social belonging, recognition, and intimacy while also enjoying the advantages of anonymity, fluidity, and familiar-but-light social contact. I turn to the nexus of sound, feeling, and togetherness in chapter 4, investigating how collective listening and dancing can give rise to a sense of inchoate sociality—that is, something like a "we" coalescing under the surface of shared musical experience. While the idea that "music brings people together" is a common cultural trope that is especially pervasive in electronic dance music scenes, accounts vary as to how music exerts such socially binding force. Partygoers often use the term "vibe" to describe how they understand music to work in these contexts, bringing fellow partygoers into a sort of synchronicity of feeling. This chapter also explores how partygoers' theorizations of the "vibe" and music-driven emotional convergence intersect with scholarship on musical entrainment, emotional contagion, ritual practices, and resonance.

When partygoers recount, plan, remember, imagine, idealize, and nostalgically recall a night out partying, they often articulate a desire for "something" to happen, a yearning for moments of intensity and rupture that make a night out feel special. In chapter 5, I investigate how "rough" experience forms part of nightlife cultures, as well as how partygoers manage its pains and pleasures. A dualism emerges between smooth flow and rough thrills, one that can be found not only in interviews with partygoers but also in the music reviews, sounds, and popular discourses of the minimal-house-techno spectrum. In contrast to psychoanalytic accounts of ecstatic self-shattering and radical transformation (such as *jouissance* and limit-experience), partygoers seeking rough experiences strive for the more modest pleasures of "coming undone": stretching, unspooling, and snapping back together again.

Thinking about belonging means also thinking about exclusion, and although some of the more fluid and implicit modes of exclusion are covered in chapter 3, we should also consider how such exclusions are institutionalized. Chapter 6 profiles the practices of the door staff at Berliner nightclubs, examining how these local leisure institutions may be informed by their broader political contexts. In particular, I examine the ways in which certain aspects of "selection" at these nightclubs bear an uncanny resemblance to national and European debates regarding immigration and cultural policy. Drawing on examples of exclusion at nightclubs in Berlin, I suggest that these nightclubs cultivate *embedded diversity*, that is, a kind of curated diversity that problematically excludes certain "unintegrated" forms of difference, thus presenting a happier and more harmonious image of diversity. The scope of this chapter goes well beyond the "on the dancefloor" focus of this book, but it traces important links between the dancefloor and its wider contexts; furthermore, exclusive door policies are an ongoing concern for partygoers and professionals in these scenes, one that has become even more intense since I first conducted fieldwork for this project.

This book closes with a final ethnographic scene in the form of an epilogue—a brief encounter in the toilets of Berghain—which condenses and illustrates the insights of the previous chapters. This is followed by a more explicit synthesis of the primary arguments of the book, paying special attention to how certain key concepts (touch, affect, texture, intimacy, liquidarity) weave and transform from chapter to chapter. Finally, this book closes with some reflections on the Orlando Pulse massacre of 2016, in which a lone gunman murdered forty-nine people—primarily trans, Latinx, and queer—at a gay nightclub. The online response to this tragedy produced a moment of queer public intimacy, one that was built on sharing memories of queer nightlife spaces as utopian sites of refuge and community. The aftermath of the Pulse massacre suggests how the insights of this book might apply to contexts of overt political struggle, where the "somehow" of togetherness is shaped by oppression and violence.

1 TOUCH AND INTIMACY ON THE DANCEFLOOR

I first met Lola while dancing in front of a set of speakers twice my height. We were both at a sweaty warehouse party in Chicago in the late summer of 2009, shortly after my return from a year of fieldwork in Paris. From the very beginning of our first encounter, tactile contact coincided with social contact: every time we exchanged words or glances, we also touched each other's shoulders and forearms. Twelve hours later, we were declaring ourselves best friends, our arms entwined.

On the dancefloor, intimacy manifests itself in ways that are both strange and familiar. Compared to the prevailing social norms of the surrounding urban environments, partygoers at electronic dance music parties engage in modes of intimacy that seem too intense, too close, too fast, too risky, and too tactile. But such "abnormal" intimacies are hardly treated as aberrations at parties; they take shape within a set of implicit, scene-specific codes and practices that manage stranger-interactions across a variety of electronic dance music scenes, varying from city to city and from subgenre to subgenre. So common are these gestures of social warmth between strangers, in fact, that they reappear in negative stereotypes of clubbers as insincere, shallow, drug-fueled, and libidinally incontinent—in other words, too intimate to be genuine. Particularly troublesome are the tactile expressions of stranger-intimacy, which break the rules of respectability and bodily decorum while also breaking up the story of how intimacy is supposed to develop. The testimonies of participants in the minimal house and techno scenes of Chicago, Paris, and Berlin—supported by my own experiences regularly attending such events—indicate norms, practices, and bodily orientations toward touch that are more intense in comparison to those of everyday public life.

And yet, "more touch" does not always mean "good touch." Although the loosening of corporeal norms and the concomitant intensification of tactility on the dancefloor offer an environment conducive to the cultivation of stranger-intimacy, these conditions also increase the risk of unwelcome touch—a risk that disproportionately impacts women and undermines their sense of full, unalloyed participation in electronic dance music scenes. Several of the women I interviewed nonetheless insisted on the importance of tactile stranger-intimacy to their enjoyment of dance music events, refusing to be passively framed as either victims or sexually available objects. They articulated a desire for such intimacies to be open to pleasure and fun without the threat of harm—all the while remaining aware of how feminine tactility is policed more harshly, especially through stigmatization and punitive gender-based violence. This spectrum of experiences encompasses the pleasures, risks, and affective binding potentials of tactility between strangers, which can offer alternative-but-still-ambivalent modes of intimacy. Given this ambivalence, why rethink intimacy through touch? By beginning with bodily contact, we get a close-up view of how intimacy manifests itself on the dancefloor: primarily between strangers and acquaintances, among bodies dancing in close quarters, and through nonverbal channels.

SOUVENIR 003, CHICAGO; SUNDAY, SEPTEMBER 6, 2009; 2:00 A.M.–2:00 P.M.

During my first weekend back in Chicago—after a year of fieldwork in Paris—I attended a rave organized by my friend Ofelia. The event took place in a disused storefront somewhere on South Michigan Avenue, in a storeroom approximately ninety square meters and six meters high; the sound system, turntables, and makeshift bar were located at the back, near the door to the loading dock. Ventilation in the building was poor, but Ofelia was loath to open doors or windows, worrying that the music's driving bass-drum kicks would waft out to the condominium dwellers who occupied this rapidly gentrifying South Loop neighborhood. The party was unlicensed, illicit, and private, that is, open only to those who had sent an email to an "RSVP" address listed in the event's advertisements.

This was the third installment of Ofelia's "Souvenir" series of parties, which had thus far focused on introducing emergent French electronic music artists to a US audience. That night's headlining performer was Seuil (aka Alexis Benard), a Paris-based producer and DJ whose style ranged from minimal house to those down-tempo edits of '80s pop songs more commonly associated with American labels such as Wolf+Lamb and Visionquest. I was dancing to Seuil's DJ set when a young woman touched my shoulder.

"Hey, are you Luis?"

"Yes."

Her face lit up. "It's so good to finally meet you! I'm really good friends with Ofelia, and I've heard so much about you. I'm Lola." After a brief exchange of pleasantries, we went back to dancing. We crossed paths occasionally throughout the rest of the party, checking in with each other and making inquiries like, "How're you feeling?" while lightly grasping each other's shoulders. All of our interactions were mediated through touch.

I saw her again at the afterparty, which was hosted by another pair of friends who were renting the second floor of a warehouse in the East Garfield Park neighborhood. It began at 7:00 A.M. and continued until around 9:00 P.M. Sunday evening, when the last person gave up and went home. Despite having a great time catching up with friends, I was still marginally jet-lagged, and so by 2:00 P.M. I was running low on energy. I made the rounds of the room, saying good-bye to everyone, and as I was saying good-bye to Ofelia, she saw Lola nearby and asked us both, "Do you know each other?"

"Of course!" said Lola, "We're best friends." Lola's arm came up around my shoulder, and my arm wound around her waist. While still facing Ofelia, we turned to each other, pressed our torsos into a half hug, and reached out with our other arms to rub each other's shoulders affectionately, forming an almost-comical greeting-card tableau of friendship. I turned to give her a kiss on the cheek, and she turned her head toward me. We ended up exchanging a brief peck on the lips.

Ofelia smiled enigmatically and said, with deadpan humor, "Of course."[1]

Lola and I had just met for the first time in our lives a few hours prior, during which we had hardly said anything to each other apart from brief introductions and some "small talk" about travel in Europe. But something about our encounter made it nonetheless possible for Lola to claim that we were "best friends," for me to concur without a second thought, and for both of us to smoothly engage in tactile gestures of intimacy. It was

FIGURES 1.1 AND 1.2 Flyer (front and back) of Souvenir warehouse party,
September 2009. Images courtesy of Koko, 2009.

casual and undramatic, as if we were commenting on the weather rather
than proclaiming a friendship that was both affectively incandescent and
only twelve hours old. In response, Ofelia's wry smile registered the humor
of both transgression and recognition: such short-circuited intimacy was
surely unconventional and yet typical of this milieu. Ofelia's reaction to our
antics represents a moment of bemused recognition, a sort of "cultural intimacy" that recognizes an aspect of group identity that can be a source of
external embarrassment.[2] Read in this way, Ofelia's elliptical "of course" and
her enigmatic smile intimated something about intimacy at such parties:
that it operates in ways that might seem embarrassingly sentimental, su-
perficial, or indecorous to the broader social world outside. In other words,
the practices of intimacy that take place at electronic dance music events
appear to violate broader social norms of stranger-sociability and public
decorum, and the resulting sense of external disapproval also reinforces a
sense of in-group belonging—a "we" for whom such excessively emotional
and tactile behavior is typical and valued.

This is not to say, however, that partygoers' views of stranger-intimacy are unanimous and untroubled. Indeed, although the "easy" intimacy of my encounter with Lola is *exemplary* of how stranger-intimacy unfolds differently in party spaces, partygoers can nonetheless be ambivalent or skeptical about what such intimacy represents. Take, for example, the accounts of two interviewees from geographically distant scenes: Sylvestre and Nick. Sylvestre is a Parisian partygoer in his midtwenties who works as a financial analyst for a music-recording distributor. Nick is a Chicago-based web developer in his early forties. When asked about intimacy on the dancefloor at electronic music events, Sylvestre responded initially with wary skepticism, but he ended up surprising himself by reporting frequent moments of fleeting stranger-intimacy, whereas Nick described an initial flush of stranger-intimacy that was later undermined by doubts about sincerity, only to be ultimately validated by the development of longer-term friendships.

> **SYLVESTRE:** I'm inclined to say that it's a bit fake. . . . At first, people smile, share, and so on, but there are also a lot of people checking each other out, who seem not to be there for the same reason as you and who pay you no attention because you don't have the right look. There's a superficial and artificial side to it. At second glance, though, there are people with whom you develop—over the course of the night—a simple exchange of glances. You start to develop an intimacy. It starts with exchanged glances; from there, you can share your dancing [*partager la danse*] a bit. You might even come and start to chat. That happens pretty frequently, actually; almost every night. (Paris, 2009)

> **NICK:** Is it intimacy, or is it a perceived intimacy? . . . I remember having moments, when you first get into the party scene, where everything's . . . awesome, right? [*laughs*]. Everybody's cool, everybody's fun. And then, I had a few periods of, "Do these people really care about me? Is this really real? Or is this just a role that we all play when we go out to these parties?" But fortunately, in the end, time has proven that a lot of real friendships developed. (Chicago, 2010)

Both Sylvestre and Nick have their doubts about the authenticity of stranger-intimacy on the dancefloor, but they also describe encounters with strangers that lead to something that *feels* real, despite its divergence from societal expectations of how an intimate relationship should unfold. These accounts also highlight how a partygoer's sense of intimacy as a general atmosphere—a "vibe"—can be solidified or eroded by the accumulation of encounters with others, and so this sense of intimacy can change as the night goes on.[3] Furthermore, touch and bodily proximity are central to how these dancefloor encounters play out, giving shape to the intimacy that these encounters sustain.

Through a close reading of ethnographic interviews, this chapter offers an analysis of how participants articulate touch norms at dance events and compare them to other domains of social life. This line of analysis leads to a consideration of unwelcome and stigmatized touch, particularly for women. Personal accounts from partygoers illustrate how the stakes associated with erotic touch impact women differently and disproportionately, thus interfering with their ability to sustain a sense of belonging, participation, safety, and fun on the dancefloor.[4] At the same time, some women interviewees refused this forced choice between safety or fun, recounting experiences in which they actively sought out tactile intimacy with strangers and pushed against the strictures of feminine respectability. All of these factors suggest rethinking intimacy from the perspective of touch, offering a reconceptualization centered on contact and proximity in order to better capture the modes of intimacy at work on the dancefloor.

Touching Strangers

> NICK: I'm definitely, to this day, more intimate with my friends in the techno scene than my other friends in terms of touching, hugging, kissing. . . . Like, me and some of the friends I have through other music scenes, we're great friends—there's no better, higher level of friendship—but they won't stand next to me with their arm around me and talk to me like I would with, like, [our mutual friend] or you or someone at a party. And, definitely, when you're with your friends at a party, you're way more intimate than you are with strangers, or with your friends who are not part of the scene. Does that make sense? . . . Most people like to be touched. It's probably kind of primal. (Chicago, 2010)

At first glance, Nick's claim may come across as a universalizing platitude that erases experiences of unwelcome or violent touch. Indeed, a touch can have many different qualities: nurturing, possessive, annoying, warning, soothing, connecting, consoling, exploring, exciting, imploring, sharing, and so on. Furthermore, the same gesture of touch can convey different qualities to the people involved in the encounter, which makes interpersonal touch such a risky thing to do with those whom you hardly know; this is all the more so when you consider how social class, white supremacy, patriarchy, and other systems of domination can shape our perceptions of it. Nick's claim, however, was uttered not in an effort to universalize so much as to generalize cross-culturally, drawing on his experiences living and working abroad. After growing up in the US Midwest and living in Japan through most of the 1990s, Nick attested to stark contrasts in everyday touch norms between these two locales; and yet, he nonetheless found an underlying desire for touch in both cultural contexts, which led him to conclude that this desire is widespread and probably innate.[5] Earlier in the interview, Nick also compared his experiences in Chicago's techno scene with the city's jazz and noise scenes, noting that he was more open to physical intimacy with his friends in the techno scene. In other interviews, partygoers in Chicago and Paris expressed a range of varying experiences and attitudes toward touch: some spoke enthusiastically of dancefloor intimacy, while some followed a more skeptical or ambivalent line of thinking similar to Sylvestre and Nick. And, as I explore further in the latter half of this chapter, sexual harassment makes dancefloor intimacy more complex and risky for women—trans, cis, and otherwise—to navigate. And yet, everyone whom I interviewed, regardless of their own attitudes toward dancefloor tactility, reported a much higher frequency and intensity of tactile interaction at electronic dance music events in comparison to everyday public life—and even, as Nick claimed, in comparison to other nightlife scenes.

But touch is more than a straightforward vector for intimacy, and its practices are by no means universal. In comparison to other modes of human perception and interaction (especially vision and hearing), interpersonal touch has remained underresearched in fields such as social psychology, cognitive sciences, sociology, or neurosciences.[6] Although much of the earliest research assumed touch to be primarily an expression of warmth, nurturing, or sexual interest, Nadine Henley's work provided a turning point in the discourse.[7] She developed what is sometimes referred to as the "gender asymmetry hypothesis": drawing from Erving Goffman, she hypothesized that touch is a "status privilege"—that is, a gesture that is more prevalent from people in high-status positions toward those in lower ones.[8] Following this logic, she predicted that men are more likely to initiate touch with women than vice versa, due to asymmetries of social status between genders. Since then, the notion that touching encodes messages of power and status has come to be integrated into studies of nonverbal communication. Over the ensuing two decades, most studies assumed either the gender/status/power model or the warmth/intimacy/sex model, rarely considering that it could involve both at the same time.[9] Reviews of the literature nonetheless showed that (North American and Western European) self-report studies mostly confirmed Henley's predictions about touch and gender, that (1) men are more likely to touch women than vice versa, (2) cross-sex touch is more frequent than same-sex touch, (3) touch is more likely to be initiated by higher-status individuals than vice versa, and (4) initiation of touch is evaluated as an indicator of higher status or dominance.[10] Empirical research has shown that, in addition to expressing affection and articulating status hierarchies, informal touch in certain contexts can also improve the receiver's impression of the encounter, create compliance with the touching person's requests, or render the receiver more receptive to persuasion.[11]

Touch norms are likewise impacted by local cultural norms, which complicate the Euro-American universalizing of many empirical studies. Although Anglophone research on interpersonal tactility has tended to focus on European and North American contexts, cross-cultural studies tend to map touch avoidance to northern Europe and East Asia, versus heightened interpersonal tactility in South America, southern Europe, and the Mediterranean Rim, working mostly with the heuristic categories of "contact culture" and "noncontact culture."[12] Such research still risks reducing tactility to nationality and/or ethnicity, but it nonetheless provides some analytic traction for understanding how the interviewees for this book explain their own practices in relation to their broader cultural context. In particular, interviewees with some experience of immigration or long-term travel pointed out that their own tactile behaviors were often thrown into stark relief when they left home. Another benefit of cross-cultural comparative research is its tendency to generate analytic concepts that extend beyond touch, such as interpersonal distance, body orientation, touch avoidance, and body accessibility. These additional factors expand the study of interpersonal corporeal intimacy from tactility to proxemics, thus drawing attention to how embodied behaviors such as posture and positioning may relate to (and cue) touch.[13] In the context of electronic dance music parties, for example, this would suggest that the forced bodily proximity of crowds can create a sense of tactile permissiveness for some and the threat of unwelcome or violent touch for others. Similarly, an individual dancer's bodily orientation toward neighboring dancers can be (mis)interpreted as openness to touch.

Going beyond physical proximity, touch behaviors are shaped by their social settings, such that touch is less likely to be initiated in formal and public contexts than in intimate and familial settings. Notably, recreational or "affiliative" settings such as parties seem to inhabit a vague middle ground, where tactility is slightly intensified.[14] More interestingly, some empirical research has found that tactility between people in an intimate relationship tends to vary according to the developmental stage of the relationship; in particular, the frequency and intensity of interpersonal touch was found to be higher in the "intermediate stage" of a relationship, in comparison with initial or stable stages.[15] This suggests that touch plays an important role in the process of relationship building, which may help to explain the intensified tactility of electronic music parties: perhaps the vague familiarity of belonging to a music scene encourages participants to engage strangers as if they were already in this "intermediate stage" of a relationship—or perhaps it is the forced tactility of a crowded dancefloor that *generates* a sense of a burgeoning intimacy among strangers.

In any case, although everyone has their own unique take on tactility in social settings, this is shaped by the groups to which they belong. This is especially the case in electronic dance music scenes, which cultivate subcultural, "underground" norms and practices that often deviate sharply from what participants understand to be "mainstream" culture.[16] Indeed, as subcultural studies have observed, these social and cultural milieus often distinguish themselves from hegemonic (dominant) culture by in-group norms that are distinctly divergent and transgressive—in other words, norms that are not normal on a broader social scale.[17] Michael Warner's account of discourse publics and counterpublics is particularly relevant here, in that he describes these publics partly in terms of how their norms manage intimacy with strangers. While most publics enforce norms of stranger-sociability that extend dominant cultural norms of civility and respectability, counterpublics arise out of a dominated group's efforts to re-create itself as a (reading, listening, dancing) public, which brings it into conflict both with the dominant social group and with the norms that dominant culture promotes as universal.[18] Counterpublics engage in practices that would be met with hostility or a sense of indecorousness in "polite society," including forms of stranger-sociability and corporeal copresence that violate dominant notions of propriety.[19]

As a relevant example of counterpublic touch norms in queer sexual subculture, "tearoom trade" (United States) or "cottaging" (United Kingdom) employs complex rituals and nonverbal signals to initiate sexual play between men in public toilets, locker rooms, parks, and similar areas. Establishing a space of consent is both necessary and difficult, since erotically engaging with an unwilling or unwitting person risks immediate violence, police brutality, and the various consequences of being "outed" for one's queer desires. As described in Laud Humphreys's pioneering sociological study of tearoom trade, men cruising for sex join this erotic counterpublic by learning a broad set of nonverbal cues that signal both awareness and openness to sexual play; these cues include bodily stances, gestures, and carefully timed eye contact.[20] Notably, these cues are progressive in intensity and overtness: several rounds of subtle cues must be exchanged to "seal the deal" of wordless consent before any contact occurs. Furthermore, participants must also learn and respect a set of cues that signal disinterest and refusal. In this way, cruising counterpublics cultivate subtle systems of nonverbal engagement to navigate consent and tactility under the threat of gender-based violence.

Warner's notion of counterpublics is admittedly dependent on a binary model of hegemony and subalterity, assuming that the social landscape can be sorted out into the dominant and the dominated. In particular, his theory posits two conditions that cannot be safely assumed of most electronic dance music scenes: (1) that the practices of a dominated group, by dint of its domination, will be divergent from and pose a challenge to dominant norms, and (2) that participants in a counterpublic are unambiguously subaltern (dominated) and/or understand themselves as such. First, although the touch norms in effect at electronic dance music parties come into conflict with the predominant societal norms that interviewees describe as "normal" or "everyday," other behaviors at these events may not diverge substantially from prevailing norms or may end up reinforcing dominant ones; for example, a bartender addressing a patron with warm informality can be both a kind of stranger-intimacy and a power-laden commercial transaction. Second, the distribution of power and privilege among partygoers in these scenes is often diffuse and conflicting in ways that make it difficult to claim that any one person is entirely dominant or dominated. Third, these scenes can include more or less marginal subscenes; the social pressures and inequalities that impact a QTPOC (queer and trans people of color) subscene, for example, are greater than those faced by a predominantly straight, cisgendered, and white one. In any case, while electronic dance music scenes are perhaps not as oppositional, marginal, and antinormative as Warner's counterpublics, his concept helps to explain how the "improper" practices of touch on the dancefloor contribute to partygoers' sense of their scene as a crucible of counterculture.

During fieldwork interviews, partygoers described touch at electronic dance music parties in a variety of ways, often seeming to echo research on touch behavior while insisting on the peculiarity of these events. For instance, many made comparisons to other nightlife scenes or to a broader public sphere of everyday interaction, while some also made cross-cultural comparisons. They all drew strong ties between the setting of these events and the intensified tactility they witnessed there, although some placed more of an emphasis on physical-spatial conditions (e.g., a crowded dancefloor) while others highlighted social-cultural ones (e.g., "the scene" and its subcultural histories). Interestingly, several interviewees reported a change in their own tactility during their involvement with underground dance music scenes, sometimes even affecting their touch behaviors outside these settings. These accounts form the basis of a broader "subcultural background," providing an overview of scene-specific touch norms against which the personal experiences of women participants can be compared and contrasted.

Norwood, a freelance graphic designer in his early thirties and a native Chicagoan, described tactility at clubs and raves in terms of openness and acceptability, linking touch with other modes of bodily intimacy, such as proximity and collective dancing.

> NORWOOD: Oftentimes, at techno events, I find that people are much more open to having people close to one another. . . . I think that, in the context of going out to techno events, people are generally open to dancing with one another, maybe standing close to one another, and being more intimate with one another than would be socially acceptable on the street with someone you're not familiar with—or any other public place. . . . It's happened to me I don't know how many times, where people actually start hugging you. And you wouldn't necessarily know the person, but it's, it's . . . perfectly acceptable. (Chicago, 2010)

Norwood illustrates the distinctiveness of these tactile practices by contrasting them with those on "the street," an archetypal place that often served during interviews as a metonym for public spaces, thus referencing a broader public sphere and its prevailing norms. Much like in Warner's formulation of the counterpublic, Norwood's "techno" scene is described in terms of embodied stranger-sociability and in comparison to (dominant) public decorum.

The touch norms of electronic dance music scenes do not differ only from those of the dominant public sphere; they also stand in contrast to other nightlife scenes in the same urban setting. Nick, for example, drew a contrast between the modes of tactility he engages in with his "techno" friends and those reserved for his other friends in Chicago's jazz and experimental music circles: "I'm definitely, to this day, more intimate with my friends in the techno scene than my other friends in terms of touching, hugging, and kissing" (Chicago, 2010). He was careful to point out that this contrast does not represent a difference in the depth of his friendships from one scene to another; when he described his relationship to his friends in jazz and experimental scenes, he said, "We're great friends—there's no better, higher level of friendship—but they won't stand next to me with their arm around me and talk to me like I would with, like, [a mutual friend of ours] or you or someone at a party" (Chicago, 2010). Notably, Nick's list of tactile partners in the techno scene extends to the rather impersonal category of "someone at a party," blurring the lines between friend, acquaintance, and stranger in dancefloor contexts.

Norwood, in addition to being a Chicago native, has accumulated approximately one and a half years of living and partying in Paris, along with several long-term visits to Berlin and London. All of this experience endows him with an illuminating cross-cultural perspective on club cultures. On the topic of Paris in particular, he was "really struck," he said, "by how much more people are willing to accept one another and talk to one another [in a club] than they would on the street" (Chicago, 2010). Affirming my own fieldwork observations, he claimed that the gap between dominant touch norms and those practiced in the local techno scene was far wider in Paris than it was in Chicago. This difference has much to do with the bodily habitus—learned ways of being in the body— of polite Parisian society, which, apart from the ritual kiss of greeting (*la bise*), avoids fleshy contact and emphasizes a physical distance that expresses both respect and restraint.[21] A touch to the hand, forearm, elbow, or shoulder is likely to cause unease except between the closest of friends, while hugging carries an intense erotic charge usually reserved for sexual partners.

Lisette, a Paris-based graphic designer in her early thirties, also attested to this touch avoidance in French public life. A native of Mauritius with French ancestry, raised speaking both French and Mauritian Creole, she identified strongly with her home island's culture, which she described as having vastly different touch norms (to be explored further in the next section). For her, interpersonal touch was the most important index of intimacy—"It's touch, above all else" (*C'est le toucher avant tout*)—and she found herself starved for touch in Paris, where, she said, "we are not at all in the habit of touching" (Paris, 2009). But Lisette also saw herself adapting to Parisian touch norms in a way that disturbed her:

> LISETTE: I'm beginning to be that way myself, I realize. . . . It really bothers me that I've come to be that way. That is to say, when somebody touches me, I'm, like, "Well, what does this guy want?" (Paris, 2009)

Norwood's and Lisette's translocal and cross-cultural comparisons highlight two important points about the minimal house and techno scenes studied in this book: (1) that what counts as "more tactile" varies with the norms of public life in each locale and (2) that the tactile behaviors of individual partygoers also tend to adapt to both scene-specific and local norms—albeit subtly and sometimes reluctantly.

Some interviewees also recounted how their own touch practices transformed during their initial entry into electronic dance music scenes, at times spilling out into their everyday, "outside" lives. Lola, the thirty-year-old Polish American artist and graphic designer featured in the anecdote that opens this chapter, described herself as not very tactile in general, and yet she found that this aspect of her bodily practice had been changing since she began partying in the Chicago scene.

> LOLA: Being in [the scene] has made me feel a lot more comfortable and open and more touchy with people. As a person, in general—with other people or strangers—I'm very reserved. I don't touch people, because I like to respect their space; and I like my space to be respected. However, I feel that, in this scene, it's a lot more invited . . . to be more touchy and friendly and huggy and stuff. Therefore, it's kind of opened me up, personally.
>
> And even outside of [the scene] now, when I meet somebody, after I've talked to them for a few minutes, I want to give them a hug

at the end of the conversation or a peck on the cheek or something. It's kind of changed the way that I approach touch in general. And I think it has to do with the fact that, you know, just being around such warm people and *open* people has made me open and warmer—if that makes any sense. (Chicago, 2010)

Teresa, a DJ, music producer, and flight attendant based in Chicago, was also generally reluctant to engage in physical contact with other strangers, but during our interview, she recounted a more intense and temporally compressed conversion narrative. While in Tokyo some time earlier, she had gone to a nightclub that was overwhelmingly packed with people. Although she was initially uncomfortable with being pushed up against strangers' bodies on all sides, she said, "after a little while, I was able to drop my hang-ups and just sort of enjoy it" (Chicago, 2010). In instances such as these, touch both threatens and promises to rearrange our bodily boundaries; in other words, touch connects bodies while also revealing and reshaping their boundaries, and so tactile experiences have the potential to transform how we feel ourselves, in our bodies, for good or for ill. For Teresa, the constant touch excitation that she experienced while immersed in an overpacked dancefloor environment blurred her body's boundaries and, in so doing, shifted and scattered the norms ingrained in her bodily habitus—temporarily, at least. The crush of bodies in a dancing crowd can thus create a disturbance in dancers' barriers to touch, rendering their boundaries temporarily fluid.

Intoxicants such as alcohol, MDMA/Ecstasy, cocaine, ketamine, and marijuana were sometimes mentioned as contributing factors in intensifying tactility as well as intimacy in general. Marie, a Parisian clubber in her midthirties working at a performing-arts promotion company, suggested that drugs "can explain a lot" about tactility at raves and techno clubs or "at least the acceptance of certain exchanges" (Paris, 2009). Indeed, some substances have effects that blur boundaries and interfere with embodied cultural practices, such as the disinhibiting effects of alcohol or the dissociative effects of ketamine. But other substances can also generate an active desire for touch and not merely an openness to it. The most frequently cited example would be MDMA/Ecstasy, which has among its effects an intensification of haptic sensation, a heightened sense of empathy with others, and a generalized euphoria. Marijuana, as a mild hallucinogen, can also intensify touch, while cocaine and other stimulants engender a combination of excitation, euphoria, and impulsivity that may find an outlet in touch—albeit in potentially more aggressive ways.[22] Many interviewees, however, argued emphatically that they still considered their affective experiences "under the influence" of intoxicants to be genuine and reflective of their feelings in the moment, intensifying rather than falsifying their emotional states.

Sure, touching happens more frequently and intensely at electronic dance music events, but what does touch mean in these contexts? How do different modes of touch signify differently? The term "touch" can refer to a wide variety of gestures and express a similarly broad spectrum of meanings. For example, one study examining the perceived boundaries of appropriate touch in the workplace defined nine modes of touching, while still remaining within a relatively narrow repertoire of upper-body contact: shaking hands, clasping hands, touching a forearm, placing an arm around the shoulders, putting an arm around the waist, touching the face, patting a shoulder, pushing against a shoulder, and not touching (i.e., the control condition for this empirical study).[23] Similarly, a study focused on meaning enumerated twelve distinct meanings—support, appreciation, inclusion, sexual interest/intent, affection, playful affection, playful aggression, compliance, attention-getting, announcing a response, greetings, and departure—along with four further hybrid meanings and several vague combinations.[24] Interviewees also identified a similar range of modes and meanings specific to electronic music events, often generating nonce typologies in order to better distinguish their meanings and consequences. At the same time, they also militated against a simplistic one-to-one mapping between gesture and meaning, pointing out that the same gesture can carry multiple meanings, while the same meaning can be expressed through a range of different (and differently appropriate) gestures. Nick, for example, suggested that touch is sometimes "very functional on the dancefloor. You've got to touch people to get by . . . like, 'Don't step back right now,' for example" (Chicago, 2010). In this context, touch extends beyond a form of communication: it can serve as a form of haptic perception, palpating the mass of surrounding bodies when vision and hearing are limited; it can be the result of an effort to regain one's balance in a frenetically dancing crowd; and it can be an indication of the sheer density of the crowd itself.

Most interviewees nonetheless highlighted expressive modes of touch. Polina, an information systems specialist in her early thirties who emigrated from Belarus to Chicago as a teenager, described herself as not only open to touch but actively in search of it: "When I'm at the party, in the crowd, I like to touch people. I like to hug people. That's how I express my very warm feelings to someone" (Chicago, 2010). Although some scholarship has briefly engaged with nonverbal forms of communication at electronic dance music events, this particular line of inquiry remains relatively uncharted, without published research focusing specifically on touch in these scenes. This gap in research is intriguing, because one of the criticisms frequently leveled at rave culture by critics during the 1990s was that ravers lost the "social" in "social dancing" by facing the DJ (instead of each other) and thus falling into a self-absorbed trance.[25] Despite this characterization, a great deal of interpersonal communication takes place at these parties, especially at the edges of the dancefloor, at the bar, and in line for the toilets. Moreover, touch provides a crowd of strangers with a means to invoke and accelerate intimacy. On the dancefloor, a casual and undramatic hand on the shoulder can allude to a familiarity that did not exist before but instead emerges out of the encounter itself.

Several interviewees also described touch as transitive, as a mode of physical encounter that shares and passes something between bodies. For Lisette, for example, a large part of touch's significance is its capacity to transmit energy between bodies: "It's touch that passes on energy, and that's really important. When you touch somebody, you feel energy. I really need that" (Paris, 2009). Lisette's notion of energy resembles the central object of affect theory—particularly in the stream that follows Spinoza's *Ethics*—that is, an increase or decrease in the capacity to act and be acted on that arises from the encounter of two or more bodies.[26] Lisette's touch-energy, if we understand it through Spinozan affect, increases her capacity to act, registering as an expanded sense of possibility and an intensified sense of presence in the world. As I argue in later chapters, the transmission of affect is central to the sense of intimacy within crowds at electronic dance music parties. But energy is not the only thing that is shared through body contact—or, more precisely, there are more concrete ways in which the energies of dancing and partying are shared across bodies. "You're sharing sweat!" exclaimed Keiko (Chicago, 2010), a Japanese translator in her midthirties living in Chicago. A high-level practitioner of martial arts, she likened the casual tactility and camaraderie of the city's techno parties to that of a sports team, suggesting that the physical exertion and close bodily contact of both activities break down social boundaries and create intimacy. Following this notion of athletic intimacy, contact between sweaty bodies can also serve as a means of sharing the energies of intense experience by mingling the body's external indicators of physical exertion. This could extend to other haptic modes as well, such as the feel of evaporated sweat against the skin in the form of humidity or the feel of heat generated by a mass of moving bodies in close quarters. Beyond the haptic, one could also follow the transfer of affect through olfactory modes such as the smell of sweat and pheromones; indeed, Teresa Brennan's *The Transmission of Affect* has already considered the sense of smell as a vector for affect, although more research remains to be done. This line of analysis locates touch within a larger system of affective transmission that would include such bodily processes as sweating, odor, and heat production—all of which are potent indices of excitement. It is difficult to imagine that these sensory factors would not have an impact on partygoers' bodily experiences of intimacy and collective feeling.

Touch norms in the minimal house and techno scenes of Chicago, Paris, and Berlin are thus distinctive across several axes of comparison, enabling more intense forms of tactility than would be acceptable in most public settings. This contrast is particularly evident in instances of tactile interactions between strangers, much of which would count as flagrant violations of decorum in public spaces. Indeed, the contrast between predominant and scene-specific touch norms seems to be wider in locales where prevailing touch norms are more restrained, such as Paris. The touch norms of electronic dance scenes, while still more intense and permissive relative to their local contexts, can vary enough from city to city to cause problems for travelers and migrants. Furthermore, many interviewees attested to the capacities of recreational substance use to intensify haptic experience, to weaken the force of dominant touch norms, and even to heighten the desire for touch in some cases. Spending time in these scenes can also affect partygoers' tactility, as some interviewees recounted finding their own patterns of tactile intimacy shifting both in the scene and beyond it. Here, touch plays multiple roles, including communicating sociability, transmitting affect, and both sensing and navigating a crowded environment.

"I'm Not a Prude, But . . ."

Privilege manifests itself in interpersonal touch as "the right to touch" and "the right not to be touched." First, it is a privilege to be able to presume that your touch will be well received, welcomed, tolerated, or at least endured without comment. Second, if you can go about your daily life unworried about unwelcome and potentially violent touch, you enjoy another kind of touch privilege. In turn, disempowerment takes tactile form when these privileges are turned into prohibitions, when you are forbidden to touch or when you are forbidden to refuse others' touch. These two kinds of touch disempowerment might seem contradictory, but they are almost always found together, such as in the way that the roots of anti-Black racism in slavery manifest themselves in tactile ways, across a long history of violently enforced taboos against interracial touch as well as in the treatment of Black bodies—especially Black women's bodies—as the rightful domain of white hands. Rather than undermine each other, "the right to touch" dovetails neatly with "the right not to be touched," in that the former gives access to pleasurable experiences of touch, while the latter affords some control over unpleasant ones. Since having agency in determining experiences of touch (yours as well as others') indexes social power, it should come as no surprise that the risk of disempowerment through stranger-tactility is most keenly felt among marginalized and stigmatized groups: people of color, queers, trans and nonbinary folks, women, people with disabilities, and so on. Indeed, partygoers' ambivalence toward touch on the dancefloor can be diagnosed as a symptom of underlying patriarchy, white supremacy, and classism—the "unfinished business" of electronic dance music's utopianism.

In addition to privilege and agency, social inequalities become apparent on the dancefloor through risk—who is expected to take risks and who is expected to manage them. In Fiona Hutton's study of risk-taking and pleasure among women clubbers, she points out that much scholarship on this topic assumes that women want to avoid risk, thus reproducing broader social norms that stigmatize women who seek it out while admiring and rewarding masculine risk-taking. "It is assumed that women will want to avoid risk, and risk is seen in very narrow, negative ways. . . . Women who engage in risk-taking behaviour, such as female clubbers, are seen as being responsible for managing themselves and are consequently blamed when things go wrong."[27]

The heavier consequences and stigma of risk-taking for women clubbers influence their relationship with touch—especially with strangers. Stranger-intimacy involves taking risks with expectations and boundaries, such as opening oneself to touch or reaching out to others, but these risks weigh differently on women; in addition to contending with a greater likelihood of violent outcomes in these situations, women are judged more harshly for taking risks at all.

In a similar fashion, women are expected to do most of the "risk work" around tactility at electronic dance music events. This is apparent in how rarely sexual harassment has been addressed in popular electronic music media (such as magazines, online discussion boards, blogs), leaving women partygoers to grapple with these issues alone, invisibly, and/or on the margins, all the while enabling men to avoid awareness of and thus accountability for this struggle. Sexual harassment in dance music finally became an issue of general concern in the mid-2010s, manifesting in discourse (including magazine articles, blogs, vlogs, and audio podcasts) as well as in practice (such as nightclubs adopting antiharassment / "safe(r) spaces" policies, sensitivity training for venue staff, and harm-reduction measures around drug use and sex).[28] This public discussion was still rare during the time of my fieldwork (2006–2010), but the nuance and force of women partygoers' responses during interviews indicated that they were nonetheless thinking and talking about sexual harassment on the dancefloor.

"Being a woman," Teresa said pensively, with frequent pauses, "I find I enjoy myself more when I'm at a party where I am, for the most part, left alone, versus going to a party where I'm constantly warding off guys that are trying to make advances" (Chicago, 2010). In this context, "to make advances" referred primarily to unsolicited and unwelcome touch, although Teresa did not exclude other forms of intrusive courtship. For her as well as for many other women interviewees, the tactile attentions of some male partygoers feel sexually predatory and thus reduce their sense of security in a crowd while also undermining their enjoyment of the party—all of which carries an emotional impact that can range from irritation to profound violation. When such attention persists, it can drive women away from the dancefloor and even out of the party space entirely, thus hampering their access to the dancefloor as a site of (uncomplicated) pleasures.

Cultural differences in touch norms and bodily habitus can make navigating dancefloor harassment especially difficult. For example, when Lisette moved from Mauritius to Paris, she was puzzled and upset to suddenly find herself on the receiving end of unexpected sexual advances.

> LISETTE: I had this problem when I moved here. I'm a girl. I got here, and I had a lot of problems because everybody—well, I couldn't talk to someone for even an hour without him wanting to kiss me. And I just didn't get it. (Paris, 2009)

According to Lisette's Parisian friends, she was "too close" to other people. As mentioned earlier, Lisette grew up in Mauritius, where she was raised with body norms that were more open to tactility than those in Paris; and so, her orientation toward touch tended to be more casual and receptive. Eventually, a native French friend who had lived and worked in Mauritius suggested that Lisette was sending confusing signals, since she showed interest in conversation by meeting a man's eyes, touching his arms or shoulders, and leaning into the space around his body—all of which her friend characterized as legible gestures of feminine sexual interest in Parisian nightlife contexts. Although this explanation gave Lisette some useful clarity, she nonetheless pushed back against the implication that she was responsible for attracting these advances through her tactility; during our interview, she exasperatedly refused to accept Parisian codes of body language, saying, "That's a language for *him*. Me, I just can't . . . [*sighs*]." Notably, Lisette did not consider herself especially "tactile" before leaving Mauritius; upon moving to Paris, however, tactility became an identifying personality trait.

The preceding accounts might give the impression that women are constantly being assailed at dance events, but interviewees described it otherwise. Experiences of tactile harassment appear to be context specific: when women partygoers complained about intrusive sexual touching, they did so while speaking of mainstream clubbing or urban nightlife in general. But when it came to the music events that they attended as part of their own particular subscene, they found such problems to be much less present— although not entirely absent. Lola, for example, illustrated this distinction clearly, in the context of Chicago's electronic dance music scenes:

> **LOLA:** I love this question [about touch], because I actually think that touch in the techno scene in particular is a lot more respectful, but it's also a lot more . . . it's a much more friendly thing. Now, let me explain what I'm saying, because it doesn't make sense, but once I get through it . . .

> **LUIS:** Go for it.

> **LOLA:** When I used to go to Vision for trance shows and progressive [house] shows, there would always be somebody trying to get up on your ass and be in your space; completely disrespectful, whether you wanted them or not. And I *hate* that. I really hate that. Not that it's inappropriate, because I'm not a prude, but at the same time, it's just kind of unwanted touch.
>
> I find that in the techno scene, there is almost none of that. And half the time, if it is somebody, you just go, "Hey, step off." And they respect it. . . . So, I find that, in the techno scene, touch is a lot more

respectful, and it's also a more friendly thing. I don't find it to be as sexual, I guess, or as *desperate* as some of the other scenes [*laughs*]. (Chicago, 2010)

For Lola, Vision nightclub represents a "mainstream" club scene from which she distanced herself as she became more involved in the minimal-house/techno "underground" scene in Chicago. She clarifies that she does not see all forms of touch as inappropriate to the context—disidentifying from conservative sexual mores in the process—but she takes issue both with the failure of some people to understand the terms of the encounter and with their subsequent disrespect when she refuses their advances. In Chicago's underground techno scene, however, she finds a lower frequency of unwelcome touch accompanied by greater respect for the bodily boundaries that she sets. Notably, she also makes a distinction between friendly and sexual touch, implying that she is more inclined to perceive touch as nonsexual when attending electronic dance music events in her subscene. Teresa also described the difference between mainstream clubbing and this subscene by indicating that touch rarely raises anxious questions for her at underground parties: "You don't have to analyze it and think, 'Oh, well, what does *that* mean? Does that mean they like me? Are they trying to put the moves on me? Am I trying to put the moves on *them*?'" (Chicago 2010). Like Lisette, Teresa is concerned with both sending and receiving the wrong nonverbal cues, but she finds that she does not need to worry about them as much in this subscene. Despite being generally disinclined to touch, she experiences touch in certain contexts as undramatic.

How might women like Lola, Lisette, and Teresa gauge their safety in nightlife settings? According to Hutton's *Risky Pleasures?*, women clubbers take *attitude* into consideration when distinguishing between nightlife spaces.[29] In particular, they are attentive to sexist and "macho" attitudes in these spaces, which they associate with potentially exacerbating factors such as the type of drugs commonly used (especially stimulants like amphetamine and cocaine), the consumption of alcohol, the style of music played, and the sartorial styles of the people in attendance. These indicators of gendered attitude are often mapped across a distinction between "mainstream" and "underground" club spaces, where underground clubs are seen to be less likely to foster sexist attitudes because there are fewer exacerbating factors at play, while other factors are understood to mitigate the likelihood of aggression, such as the use of the empathogen Ecstasy (MDMA). This, in turn, feeds into their sense of safety at electronic music parties, which hinges on how they perceive the collective attitude of the venue, the event organizer, the artists, and the attendees. This is not to say that underground clubs are free of sexual harassment; rather, women report experiencing a "toned down" version of what they experience elsewhere. Notably, their "experience in underground spaces is seen as *relative* to mainstream 'meat market' club spaces."[30] In any case, this constant assessment of party spaces for indicators of gender-based violence is an example of the "risk work" that is disproportionately placed on the shoulders of women partygoers, as part of a broader pattern of self-protective hypervigilance.

This contrast between various music subscenes and venues raises questions about how one can manage stranger-tactility in an environment where touch norms are vague, inhibitions are lowered, and partygoers have divergent attitudes toward touch. It may be that the enveloping, already-tactile environment of the nightclub encourages openness to touch, thus making stranger-touch seem less dramatic. But it also seems that, at such events, there is a tacit expectation that one will be gentle with unwelcome touch—that one will not "overreact." This, in turn, complicates the ethics of proximity by placing the burden on the recipient of unwelcome touch—most often women—to absorb, deflect, or otherwise manage it in ways that do not disrupt the festive atmosphere of the dancefloor. This expectation to "not make a big deal about it" is another example of risk work for women partygoers, imposing both docility and conflict avoidance. For those women who already endure unsolicited touch in the workplace or at home, these expectations can seem unfair and retraumatizing. Furthermore, the distinction between welcome and unwelcome touch becomes even more fraught when the gap between these categories is harnessed for profit or survival.[31] Imogen, a Detroit native in her early thirties living in Chicago, felt this pressure at her workplace (at the time of our interview), where she worked as a server and bartender.

> IMOGEN: I've had instances where somebody that I've been waiting on—or bartending for—has touched my arm. And it makes me feel uncomfortable, but you can't say anything in those situations. You just smile, and you go, "OK, no problem." You know? So, I feel that [when I go out dancing]. (Chicago, 2010)

These workplace pressures inform Imogen's attitudes toward stranger-tactility in nightlife spaces; of all the interviewees, Imogen was the most vociferous in declaring her boundaries: "If you don't know me, *don't touch me*." But she immediately qualified this statement by saying, "That's depending on who you're with. If a friend of a friend is standing by and happens to be, like, 'Oh, hi' [*placing her hand on my shoulder*], I won't think anything of it" (Chicago, 2010). Imogen's attention to networks of friends and acquaintances is yet another way in which women partygoers engage in risk work on and around the dancefloor. In general, most interviewees described themselves as being more tactile with their friends than with strangers at electronic dance music events, while also feeling more open to touch from strangers at these events than in everyday public life.

In some cases, this intensified intimacy between friends blurs the boundaries between platonic and sexual intimacy. Lola, for example, described a level of tactile intimacy with "certain friends," an intimacy that she suspects would be inappropriate outside the minimal-house/techno subscene of Chicago. She takes pleasure from it and finds it valuable, but she also takes pains to distinguish it from a sexual encounter. In the following quotation, note the way in which the norms of sexual propriety that she invokes at the beginning of her account begin to exert pressure on her as she describes her own intimate practices. Recounting her experiences in a forum that she knows will circulate in channels outside the scene (i.e., an interview for an academic publication), she becomes nervous and uncertain.

> LOLA: There are levels of intimacy and touch that, I think, people who are not in [the scene] would find kind of disturbing.
>
> I mean, personally, I'm never that girl who goes around and makes out with the whole friggin' party. However, there are certain friends that I know that are always, like, "Oh my God, let's make out!" And I'm like, "Yay!" That's cool. I don't have any problems with it because I know it's not some drunken or fucked-up act. It's just that we're friends and we love each other. I don't even mean, like, groping each other or anything—just being intimate, you know? Like, face-to-face, person-to-person. To me, that's not sexual at all. It's not desperate. It's like a different level of friendship, kind of . . . I think . . . maybe [*pauses*]. I feel like I'm saying too much! [*laughs*]. (Chicago, 2010)

The effusiveness with which Lola begins this statement quickly transforms into defensiveness, producing a proliferation of explanations and qualifications. In seeking to protect her reputation, her wording anticipates patriarchal norms that stigmatize feminine sexuality ("that girl"; see also

Polina's use of "whore" later). This defensiveness is understandable in light of how patriarchy only promises to protect "respectable" women from violence. Hutton argues that, in nightlife spaces, women contend with constraints on their behavior that are "still very much based on respectability and the performance of acceptable forms of femininity."[32] She describes heterosexuality and feminine respectability as "part of a whole package of behaviors that are defined by the values of a patriarchal society. . . . If women do not conform to this 'package,' they are punished for their transgressions by the threat of violence."[33] To the extent that feminine respectability in club contexts is tied to the avoidance of touch, women who open themselves up to tactile pleasure risk losing social protection from violence, as punishment for their transgressive femininity. As a result, women partygoers often end up policing their own tactile behaviors as yet another form of risk work.

Polina finds herself in a similarly defensive position, being one of the few female interviewees to unambiguously articulate an active interest in tactile intimacy with strangers.

> POLINA: One moment you meet someone, you're on the same page, and you think, "That's the person!" You completely understand each other! So many times, especially with guys, it's *pure*; nothing dirty about it.
>
> I've had so many encounters like that with guys—even with girls sometimes—that were just pure *love*. And I would never consider myself dirty or a whore who makes out with everyone. Absolutely not! These types of connections, they're different. I don't know, maybe my counterpart would perceive them in a different way. Maybe they were hitting on me sexually, whatever. . . . But, for me, in that moment, that person is the *one*. So many times, stupidly, I just fall in love with someone from the first glance. But I will never, ever in my life regret it. (Chicago, 2010)

For Polina, stranger-tactility is part of an accelerated narrative of romantic intimacy. What is interesting here is that she recognizes a certain ambiguity in her connection to an unknown counterpart while remaining committed to her own sense of intimacy. Polina is also unique in considering that her counterpart's perceptions and motivations may be different from her own—unreadable or perhaps ambivalent. By contrast, most of the other women partygoers I interviewed either did not address the intentions of tactile strangers or assumed them to be a priori sexual. Interestingly, Polina's acknowledgment of the opacity of others' intentions and perceptions does not undermine her own sense of intimacy; she is certain of the specialness of these instances of connection but also blasé about their reciprocity.

Through their experiences at these dance events, women like Polina and Lola relate experiences of intimacy that bring touch to the forefront of the encounter. In Michael Warner's terms, these constitute a "counterpublic" form of stranger-sociability that violates dominant regimes of decorum by mixing stranger-sociability with bodily intimacy.[34] On the dancefloors of these parties, intimacy can arise without familiarity, without talk, and without prior relationships; and in this mix of strangers and acquaintances pressed together on the dancefloor, touch provides a way of short-circuiting the usual narrative of intimacy. This creates openings for moments of intense stranger-intimacy that some participants value precisely because they would not be possible in other contexts. But women in these scenes continue to be subject to unwanted touch in ways that can be distressing, violating, and infuriating—especially when such boundary violations dispel their fantasies of participating in a utopian, inclusive, and energetic dancefloor. Furthermore, these women find themselves burdened with the "risk work" of handling unwanted touch, and those who wish to keep tactility and eros in their clubbing experiences (like Lola and Polina) also feel the looming threat of punitive violence as they tentatively flaunt feminine respectability. Indeed, while tactile stranger-intimacy can be a risky endeavor for any person, these women strike an especially uneasy bargain between pleasure and protection, discovery and distance.

Rethinking Intimacy

> POLINA: Yeah, someone might judge, "This is not how you meet people!" [*laughs*]. But this is how it's been working for me. Not dating, not slowly, gradually sliding into intimacy, kissing on the third date. No, it's *immediately* on the dancefloor. [It's] the convergence of these crazy emotions and powers that just *overwhelm* you both. So, yeah, it's . . . it's like instant love. Like instant coffee: instant love [*laughs*]. But sometimes . . . sometimes, it's just single-serving love. (Chicago, 2010)

The term "intimacy" circulates widely in a variety of contexts, appearing on talk shows, internet dating sites, self-help books, sex-toy packaging, and restaurant reviews, to name just a few examples. This leaves the underlying idea of intimacy both undertheorized and difficult to define in terms that capture its varied range of meanings. Under the heading of "intimacy," one can find references to long-standing relationships, affective attachments, warm feelings, mutual knowledge, daily routine, tacit communication, trust, marriage, risk, vulnerability, closeness, sex, contact, consent, and disclosure. Some scholarly research on the topic has been explicitly normative and therapeutic in aim, usually promoting some model of "healthy" intimacy.[35] Some scholars take a more descriptive approach, such as Karen Prager, whose social-psychological framework helpfully distinguishes between intimate interactions and intimate relationships; this distinction enables her to imagine and analyze intimate encounters that are not necessarily based on a preexisting intimate relationship.[36] In other words, her definition of intimacy reserves some conceptual space for stranger-intimacy. Further examples of descriptive research into intimacy can be found in such fields as history, literary studies, anthropology, sociology, and music studies. While descriptive projects perhaps risk perpetuating and naturalizing dominant cultural norms about intimacy, some projects—mostly linked to queer, antiracist, and anticolonial activism—aim instead to make critical interventions by focusing on nonnormative intimate practices.[37]

Many of the qualities conventionally associated with intimacy become unlikely if not impossible in the circumstances of a nightclub dancefloor. The fluid, anonymous, and unpredictable aspects of crowds displace the conventional social structures of intimacy (such as spouse, lover, parent, and sibling) and replace them with strangers and acquaintances. Consequently, many of the assumptions about knowledge, duration, stability, vulnerability, and consent that are often made about intimate relationships do not pertain to the forms of intimate encounter that can take place on a dancefloor. Furthermore, these assumptions serve to support a normative discourse of intimacy that easily dismisses such fleeting encounters as false, insincere, or inadequate. The pressure of these broader cultural norms was hard to miss during fieldwork; in conversation with those who were *not* involved in the electronic music scenes of my respective fieldwork locales, similar doubts were often raised. It also had an impact on those scene participants whom I interviewed—Lola and Paulina, for example—who were often anxious to anticipate and address these critiques.

Nonetheless, one conventional mode of being intimate applies well in electronic dance music contexts: touch. Engaging in intimacy can be touching in both senses of the term, both tactile and emotional. Following the titular wordplay of Eve Kosofsky Sedgwick's *Touching Feeling*, I echo her insistence that the intersection of these two meanings in one term is not happenstance: both being touched and being "touched" have to do with registering a kind of impact, and these two events often meet on the social horizon of comfort, care, and conviviality.[38] One can also find support for a nonverbal but nonetheless expressive notion of intimacy in the definition of the verb "to intimate," which Lauren Berlant glosses as "to communicate with the sparest of signs and gestures," bestowing on intimacy the "quality of eloquence and brevity."[39] Touch is also clearly important to partygoers, both as a corporeal practice of intimacy and as an index of intimate feeling. Many stressed this importance during interviews—most strongly by a subset of women interviewees including Lisette, Lola, and Polina. Polina provides an especially clear articulation of tactility's value to her as both a pleasurable experience and an index of others' feelings toward her.

> **POLINA:** It's *amazing*. I mean, it's such a warm feeling. It actually gives me a lot of emotional fulfillment—from touch, from the physical [aspect]. In addition to the beautiful music that you hear and all of the fun that you have, you get this emotional fulfillment from hugging in a very friendly, intimate [way]. Every moment that you touch or hug someone, it kind of . . . makes you closer, in a way.
>
> Immediately, for me, I can see—I can almost *feel* how the person feels about you by how they want or don't want to give you a firm hug. (Chicago, 2010)

Following Polina's description, touch not only provides a sensory basis for an emergent feeling of intimacy but also provides a medium for conveying intimacy in its myriad modalities: care, desire, warmth, familiarity, openness, vulnerability, trust, and sincerity. In a mix of strangers and acquaintances pressed together both physically and affectively on the dancefloor, touch provides a way of short-circuiting normative narratives of intimacy.

Touch can also provide a conduit between sound and intimacy, between moments of musical intensity and the affective experience of closeness. In nightclub settings in particular, sound's haptic aspects provide an experiential basis for the emergence of a sense of proximity, contact, and/or solidarity. Following both Berlant and Sedgwick, a sense of intimacy can arise from relations that have an impact on us, and I would argue that intimacy can also arise from relations surrounding or emerging from impact. Thus, if haptic impact can provide an index for an unfolding intimate relation, the impact of sound-waves on the body could be understood as having an iconic relationship to intimacy—an imitation of intimacy by means of tactile excitation.[40] Reconceptualizing intimacy through touch also gives purchase on other modes of doing intimacy: its vocabulary of impact, proximity, transfer, contact, and texture open up new ways of describing and conceptualizing intimacy as an unfolding encounter. Moreover, this focus on physical contact provides a means of engaging meaningfully with affect, the body, music, and dance in a collective setting.

Touch serves as a powerful vector for engendering intimacy, but it is also charged with the potential to disturb and violate bodily boundaries. These risks are keenly felt by some participants in nightlife scenes, where anonymity, excitement, and an atmosphere of permissiveness can blur the norms that manage the risks and pleasures of touch. For women especially, this destabilization of conventional touch norms can result in increased exposure to unwelcome sexual touch. And yet, some female participants insist on the importance of such fluid stranger-tactility to their enjoyment of electronic music parties—as well as to their sense of belonging to something larger than themselves. More broadly, interviewees of various genders and backgrounds describe tactile stranger-intimacy as a prominent and important aspect of the music scenes in which they participate. Not "just" physical intimacy, touch is also a powerful index for closeness and connection across corporeal, affective, and imaginative registers. To rethink intimacy through touch, then, is to think of intimacy as a perpetually emergent quality of interactions between bodies—patterns of proximity and contact that sustain a sense of entanglement beyond the encounter.

2 SONIC TACTILITY

Feeling is everywhere in electronic dance music, especially in those styles that draw on disco, gospel, and soul.[1] From "Feeling You" to "You Make Me Feel (Mighty Real)" to "I Feel Love" to "Push the Feeling On" to hundreds of other permutations, dance music's track titles pun endlessly on feeling's double meaning as both emotional experience and tactile perception (that is, to feel by touching).[2] Notably, this emotional-sensory wordplay riffs off the nuanced meaning of the verb "to feel something/someone" in Black poetic and vernacular speech; expressions such as "I feel you" or "I felt that" or "that got me feeling some kinda way" can convey an affective epistemology, a deep understanding that arises from compassion, intuition, and shared feeling. In post-disco dance music production, however, track titles tend to remain ambiguous about the content of feeling itself: what or who we are supposed be feeling. For example, the question "Can you feel it?" has served as the title for at least three well-known tracks, while the imperative phrasing "feel it" appears with even more frequency.[3] The content of "it" remains unspecified, and no distinction is made between touch and affect—palpation versus palpitation—leaving it up to the listener to surmise from context, innuendo, and the sound of the track itself. Indeed, perhaps this "it" is to be found in sound, rather than text. For example, the sound of John Tejada's 2008 minimal-techno track "Feel It" is dominated by a resonant bass kick drum with a thudding attack, seemingly aimed to puncture as much as punctuate. As the track progresses, the sparse and asymmetrical loop comes to be filled out with a range of sounds that evoke scraping, rubbing, crackling, snapping, and so on. From beginning to end, "Feel It" is rich in sonic texture. Listening to this track, we may not know what "it" is, but we learn how it *feels*.

If, as chapter 1 illustrated, electronic dance music scenes such as minimal house and techno cultivate spaces of heightened tactility at their parties, it should not be surprising that their musical aesthetics also highlight touch. Sound is by no means an intangible phenomenon; it involves impacts and vibrations that are perceived not only through the ear but also through the skin, flesh, and bones. Sound is also strangely tactile in how timbre and sonic texture can evoke tactile experience by conveying something about how touch *feels*—in both senses of the term. Within the broader context of this book's investigation of what music and affect have to do with intimacy on the dancefloor, this chapter examines the *tactilization* of sound in electronic dance music, which offers an important sensory-affective bridge between touching, feeling, hearing, and a more expansive sense of intimacy in crowds. The aim here is to go beyond the representation of dancefloor tactility in lyrics and visual imagery, turning instead to the *sound* of electronic dance music, which foregrounds percussion, texture, grain, and other sonic elements that resonate with how we experience touch. Indeed, this genre of music excels at creating multimodal, trans-sensory resonances between the aural and the tactile, offering a sonic surface that is rich in texture and timbre.

More precisely, the niche substyles of minimal house and techno that were ubiquitous during ethnographic fieldwork for this book are especially effective in invoking touch. They do so in a number of ways, of which three will be the focus of this chapter: (1) the aesthetic convention of foregrounding *beats*, that is, percussion sounds that index real-world objects coming into forceful contact, thus activating a sense of physical impact through amplified bass frequencies and sharply sloped amplitude envelopes; (2) the use of timbre to evoke vibrant and vibrating *flesh*, especially in certain substyles that frequently sample the sounds of the body as part of an extended sonic palette; and (3) the intense focus on sonic *grain*, which enables a cross-modal sensory mapping of texture between the microstructures of sound and surface. This chapter relies less on ethnographic data (such as interviews and field notes) and engages instead in a form of genre analysis, tracking tactility in electronic music's sonic conventions by drawing on musical/sonic analyses of tracks encountered during fieldwork, sound studies literature, and the scholarship of electroacoustic and acousmatic artists.[4] Notably, my discussion of sonic grain engages with Pierre Schaeffer's treatise on "sound-objects," Curtis Roads's work on granular synthesis, and Laura U. Marks's notion of "haptic visuality." To trace the connections between touch, texture, and affect, I close this chapter with a turn to the queer theorists Eve Kosofsky Sedgwick and Renu Bora, who associate texture with multiple thresholds that border affect: between the senses, between pattern and form, between activity and passivity, between sense and impact, between feeling and narrativizing, and between the actualized and the virtual. In turn, texture's perceptual reverberation between pattern and form resonates with Gilles Deleuze's distinction between molecular and molar levels of order, suggesting new ways of understanding Shaefferian texture-as-microstructure, building a sonic bridge—both sensory and symbolic—between individual bodies and a sense of vibratory collectivity.

Beats: The Sound of Impact

Beats beat not only time but surfaces, bodies, and crowds. Dance music highlights impact and physical contact through its preponderance of percussive sounds, which serve as sonic indexes of real-world objects striking, rubbing, and vibrating. This is especially the case in the bass register of most electronic dance music tracks, where kick-drum samples and other low-frequency percussive sounds dominate the overall sound profile, providing a driving stream of regular pulses usually grouped into sets of four.[5] The ubiquity and fundamentality of the bass kick can be seen in its vernacular nomenclature, as "the beat" or "beats," ascribing structural and metric qualities to a single layer of musical texture. Indeed, a common criticism of popular electronic dance music styles is that it is "just beats," prioritizing sonic elements that would be usually relegated to merely functional roles in most Euro-American popular and art music traditions, at the expense of privileged musical "content" such as melody and harmony.

And yet, what signals this genre's emptiness to some critics is also what conveys a sense of fullness to its adherents. The core of most electronic dance music tracks is composed of multiple layers of percussion distributed across a wide range of frequencies. Take, for example, the Parisian DJ/producer Jef K's remix of The Gathering's "In My System (Jef K SystemMix)," a downtempo deep-house track by a Chicagoan producer that was ubiquitous over the summer of 2010 in Berlin, played almost weekly at minimal-oriented clubs like Club der Visionäre (Club of the Visionaries).[6] The midrange percussion is relatively spare throughout the track, and its central motif is made up of a string synthesizer playing a four-bar chord progression under a short loop of a male voice singing, "You're in my system / And you're in my life tonight." The entire bass register is repeatedly filled out by a bass kick with a rounded attack enriched with "subbass" harmonics (that is, below 90 Hz). Played on a high-powered sound system like those found at the nightclubs I visited for fieldwork, this track produces a visceral sense of impact even at moderate volumes.

Another instructive example is the Italian producer Davide Squillace's "The Other Side of Bed," a tech-house track that features not only a resonant bass kick but also a melodic loop pitched down to subbass frequencies (beginning at 2:34), where it takes on percussive qualities.[7] The percussion samples used in the midrange frequencies are notable, in that they feature acoustic percussion instruments (hands, tom-toms, cymbals) that have been compressed and "gated" to heighten their impact and lend them a "punchy" quality. In sound-engineering parlance, a gated sound is one that has been routed through a *noise gate*, which is a circuit that blocks an incoming signal until it exceeds a particular decibel threshold; it opens to let the signal through and then closes shortly after the signal drops below the threshold. This effect was originally developed to "clean up" recordings of instruments by cropping out low-level background noise—especially sonic "bleed" between microphones placed close together on a drum kit— but when the threshold is set high, this creates a short but powerful percussive sound that is often described as "punchy" for its abrupt attack and brief duration. Similarly, "compression" refers to a signal-processing algorithm (dynamic range compression) that reduces the volume of loud sounds while amplifying quiet sounds. This has the effect of narrowing the dynamic range of the signal, thus reducing fluctuations in volume and enabling the producer/audio engineer to place the sound "high" or "low" in the mix (that is, loud or soft compared to the rest of the mix) without risking distortion, overload, or loss of detail. Compression is often used in popular music recordings to create a sense of sonic fullness and intensity usually described as "loudness."

As these examples suggest, beats do not only play an associative or representational role in relation to touch; they are impactful and tactile in themselves. In a Berlin-based documentary film, *Feiern*, the DJ Nick

Höppner (who is a resident DJ at Berghain / Panorama Bar as well as the former manager of the club's label, OstGut Ton) describes the experience of techno music as being "about volume and bass. Not only do you hear the music, but it also has a direct, bodily impact. Your trouser legs vibrate when you're standing in front of the bass speaker."[8] For Höppner, the experience of techno is multimodal, perceived not only through hearing but also through his sense of touch; he grounds this claim in his experiences of low frequencies played at high amplitudes (volume), which impact, penetrate, and resonate in his body. More precisely, beats in electronic dance music not only index the event of forceful contact but also enact it sensorially and non-representationally through the intensity and sharpness of their amplitude envelopes. In other words, beats do not just sound like impact; they *are* impacts.

But what makes beats so impactful? Or, more precisely, what makes percussion sounds percussive? The answer lies in their *amplitude envelope*, which is a line that traces the contours of a sound's waveform. In its simplest form, one can draw an amplitude envelope by joining the peaks of a waveform to create a silhouette, which indicates how a sound's amplitude (volume) evolves and fluctuates over its duration. As sound-synthesis technology was being developed throughout the twentieth century, the amplitude envelope came into use as a paradigm for controlling the output of synthesized sound in response to a trigger event (such as a key on a keyboard being pressed and later released). Using a preprogrammed amplitude envelope, a synthesizer would shape the amplitude at the beginning, middle, and end of the sound event to resemble the amplitude envelope of various instruments. Over time, people working with sound synthesis schematized the shape of this envelope into a set of variable durations and amplitude levels, which could be used together to plot out the curve of amplitude envelopes.

By the mid-1960s, Vladimir Ussachevsky (the director of the Columbia-Princeton Electronic Music Center) and the engineer Robert Moog developed the four-element ADSR envelope (attack, decay, sustain, release), which became the industry standard for audio engineering.[9] "Attack" refers to the time it takes, beginning from when a key or other trigger is activated, for a sound's volume to increase from zero to its peak. "Decay" designates the time taken to decrease from this peak level to the level it will maintain for the duration that the trigger remains activated; this element is particularly important for accurately representing/reproducing percussive sounds, since these always have a prominent *transient*—that is, a brief, spectrally rich burst that is substantially louder than the rest of the sound. "Sustain" then specifies the maintenance level for the remaining duration, until the trigger is released; notably, "sustain" is the only element of the four that specifies an amplitude level rather than a time duration, since time will vary according to how long the user "holds" the triggering mechanism. "Release," finally, indicates the time taken to decrease the sound's volume from its "sustain" level down to nil, once the trigger has been released.

While the contours of ADSR envelopes vary greatly from instrument to instrument, a few archetypes can be ascribed to instrument families (see figures 2.1–2.4). Woodwind instruments, for example, usually have a gradual and linear attack curve, followed by little to no decay, high sustain, and a gradual release. Brass instruments produce a plosive transient at their onset, which is reflected in a short, angular attack, a brief decay leading down to a relatively lower sustain, and a more gradual release. Bowed string instruments tend to have a short, rounded attack, a brief decay leading to a relatively high sustain, and a gradual release. By contrast, percussion instruments are composed almost entirely of a prominent transient with variable amounts of resonance; that is, they have a sharp and loud attack, a sharp and deep decay, no sustain to speak of, and a release that can be abrupt or gradual, depending on how resonant the instrument is (for example, a woodblock versus a gong).

Since electronic dance music scenes developed in close contact with synthesizers and other sound-studio technology, the ADSR envelope has become an important compositional paradigm, employed by producers and other technologically literate actors to make sense of the microcontours of the sounds they employ. Especially since DAW software (digital audio workstations, such as Logic Audio, Cubase, ProTools, Ableton Live, Fruity Loops) became widely available in the early 2000s, producers have been able to visualize, shape, and trim amplitude envelopes with millisecond precision. And, whether sculpted "by hand" or selected from an archive of sampled sounds, the percussive amplitude envelope is by far the most prevalent one in most styles of electronic dance music. Indeed, the sonic textures of most tracks are dominated by layers of sounds with percussive envelopes, characterized by sharp, high-intensity fluctuations of air pressure that can be registered as impact across several of the human body's sensory organs. At high volumes, these sonic spikes *strike* the body in a very concrete way, eliciting sensations not only in the ear but also in the body's skin, flesh, viscera, and bones.

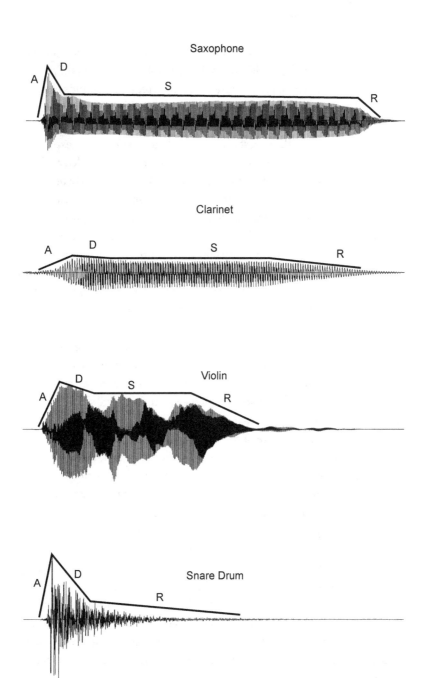

FIGURES 2.1–2.4 Waveforms of sample instruments with their ADSR envelopes traced and labeled: (1) saxophone, (2) clarinet, (3) violin, and (4) snare drum.

Spiky amplitude envelopes are not the only factor that makes dance music's beats so tactile; in addition to the high-volume transients of percussive sounds, the overall preponderance of low-frequency sounds contributes to electronic dance music's tactility. The beat in particular—the regular pulse that provides both metric organization and kinetic energy—is almost always to be found in the lowest register of a dance track's sonic texture. On most audio-engineering equipment, the frequency range labeled as "bass" usually extends from 150 Hz (cycles per second) down to 60 Hz or 40 Hz; this is the range of frequencies that give the "thump" to kick drums and similar bass percussion. But, since the sound systems of nightclubs and concert venues are capable of reproducing a much wider range of frequencies, it is common for producers to bolster the impact of their beats by employing percussive sounds pitched in the "subbass" range, which extends down beyond the threshold of human hearing (20 Hz). Sound cannot be heard below this threshold, but it can still be *felt* through the flesh as vibration and impact.

Steve Goodman, a theorist of affect in sound studies (as well as a dubstep DJ/producer working under the moniker Kode9), notes that sound "dissolves completely into tactile vibration at frequencies around 20 hertz."[10] He highlights how low-frequency sounds "bleed" across a range of sensory modes such as hearing, touch, and proprioception (the sense of the position and posture of one's own body), which undergirds his notion of *bass materialism*: "the collective construction of vibrational ecologies concentrated on low frequencies where sound overlaps tactility."[11] In this sense, low-frequency beats can produce a sense of material presence and fullness, which can also serve to engender a sense of connection and cohesion. Notably, Goodman develops this notion while conceptualizing a "planet of drums," a "subpolitical" global assemblage of the dispossessed, bound together through the beats of various bass-oriented and primarily Afrodiasporic genres such as dancehall, reggae, baile funk, crunk, reggaetón, kwaito, kuduro, and so on. For Goodman, the materiality of bass beats provides a concrete basis for new political and subpolitical formations. In a similar fashion, an important dimension of electronic dance music's affective impact is the felt materiality of its beats, which can be experienced as energizing, oppressive, driving, disorienting, and so on. Through volume, bass frequencies, and a preponderance of percussive sounds, electronic dance music's beats constantly engage the body's haptic senses during listening and dancing.

Flesh: Bodily Timbre

Considering the visceral dimension of loud, low-frequency beats—impacting the body's skin, flesh, bones, and viscera—it should come as no surprise that electronic dance music often dramatizes the corporeality of its own aesthetics by making sonic reference to the body. Dance tracks often evoke tactile experience through the use of sounds that are recognizable as originating from a fleshy body, such as prominent (and realistic) hand claps, breathing, humming, rubbing, crackling, and so on. In contrast to the nonrepresentational tactility of beats, this evocation of tactile experience functions primarily through association, relying on the ability of listener-dancers to associate certain sounds with an enfleshed sound source.

A classic example of this fleshy compositional style is Matthew Herbert's concept album *Bodily Functions*, which makes exclusive use of sounds emanating from fleshy bodies to compose an entire album of minimalist house music.[12] Although this album was released well before the period of fieldwork for this book, its subsequent success continues to resonate into the present day; retrospectively, it came to be considered by music critics as a foundational work of the "microhouse" substyle, while also remaining well-known and oft-played among my ethnographic contacts. Indeed, it remained relevant enough throughout the first decade of this century that it was rereleased on Herbert's own label, Accidental, in 2012 as a double album containing a full set of remixes.[13] Across all of his musical output, Herbert's compositional process shows clear influence from *musique concrète*, eschewing synthesized sounds altogether and focusing instead on the transformation of recordings taken from real-world objects and events. Herbert makes this explicit in his compositional manifesto "PCCOM" ("Personal Contract for the Composition of Music [Incorporating the Manifesto of Mistakes]"), which lays out ten rules for studio work. Of particular relevance here is his first rule: "The use of sounds that exist already is not allowed. . . . No drum machines. No synthesizers. No presets."[14] In doing so, Herbert denies himself some of the most widely used compositional resources among house music producers. As a result of these self-imposed constraints, most of his album-length productions are centered around thematically unified archives of self-made recordings, meticulously annotating in liner notes the tracks compliant with his manifesto with the phrase "Written according to the rules of PCCOM." Despite his idiosyncratic approach, he uses this unconventional and restrictive set of tools to craft dance tracks that remain true to the aesthetics and conventions of this genre; indeed, many of his tracks can be smoothly integrated into DJ sets alongside conventional minimal-house and deep-house tracks.

While the entire album features recognizably embodied sounds, "You're Unknown to Me" and "Foreign Bodies" are the most remarkable tracks in *Bodily Functions*, with regard to their sonic figuration of flesh. The opening track, "You're Unknown to Me," functions like an overture for the rest of the album, laying out compositional procedures, formal patterns, and aesthetic orientations that reappear in the tracks that follow. The track begins with a slow, four-beat loop of a piano alternating between two open-spaced tone clusters pitched roughly a major seventh apart. After two iterations, this piano loop is layered with a series of mouth noises—the sounds of swallowing, teeth sucking, sighing, breathing—that continue for two more iterations without settling into a predictable pattern. When Dani Siciliano's voice enters at 0:15, the teeth-sucking noise rises in register and becomes an ersatz hi-hat sample, ticking away the backbeat (i.e., the "twos" and "fours" of a four-beat cycle) of this languorous track while a bass clarinet enters with a descending, slowly unfurling bass line. As the track progresses, the initial mouth noises return in slightly altered form as percussive elements. During the bridge (1:15–1:32), two very short samples of a baby's gurgling and gasping begin to mark the backbeat, one immediately after the other so as to approximate a descending minor sixth. As for the source of these mouth noises, the album's liner notes credit "Sunray Star" for "percussion," adding that these samples were recorded both before and after her birth on October 12, 2000.

The second track, "It's Only," follows with a placid, "downtempo house" ballad that provides a stylistic and affective bridge between the album's contemplative opening and the more energetic tracks to follow. But it is the subsequent title track, "Foreign Bodies," that most audibly implements this album's body-focused concept, assembling its sonic palette out of digestive gurgling, blood, toothbrushing, popping joints, hand claps, speech, nonverbal vocalizations, and singing. The track conveys intensity and effervescence through constantly bubbling percussion patterns as well as staccato chord loops that coagulate into a rhythmic ostinato, mirrored later by Siciliano's similarly staccato singing. The "preverse" introduction (0:00–0:27) begins with a stream of dripping, bubbling sounds, which settles into a loop incorporating more percussive popping noises, bouncing between the left and right audio channels and filling the "mid" frequency range. Strewn atop these layers are the chopped fragments of a muttered conversation between a male and female voice, just below the threshold of intelligibility and punctuated by a sharp intake of breath, a fleshy slap, and a moan (0:15–0:17). After eight four-beat cycles (0:28), the lower-frequency range of the track fills out with a bouncing bass line and chords in syncopated counterpoint, composed of resonant, soft-edged sounds that resemble a low-pressure pipe organ. This multilayered groove continues in various permutations throughout the rest of the track, evoking Afro-Brazilian styles such as samba and bossa nova through its asymmetrical division of the sixteenth-note pulse layer (i.e., 3+3+3+3+4), polyrhythmic layering, and the use of sound samples that approximate typical samba percussion instruments. Of particular note is the pitched bubbling sound that emerges early in the track (0:10), which evokes the *cuica*, a friction drum used in samba ensembles that produces a squeaking sound alternating between usually two or three approximate pitch levels. In the album notes, the sound sources that provide this effervescent, samba-inflected percussion are described as "Bodily Function Sounds kindly donated by Strangers"—who are listed by name in the credits for the track, along with Siciliano's digestive sounds and the blood of Martin Schmidt from the electronic music duo Matmos.

While nearly every track on the album features Siciliano singing intelligible lyrics that adhere to jazz and pop forms, I am deliberately deprioritizing them here. I do so partially as a counterbalance to the tendency in popular music studies to focus on the analysis of lyrics at the expense of musical materials but mostly because I wish to train our analytic focus on the sonic, nonverbal evocation of flesh. Nonetheless, it is notable that Siciliano's vocal lines are always embedded in a lush sound world of nonsensical vocalizations, breathing, and other mouth noises, thus undermining the distinction between the voice as medium of symbolic communication and the voice as enfleshed sound event. In *Bodily Functions*, the human voice plays multiple roles, as the reciter of text, the singer of music, the producer of sound, and the audible trace of the body.

Although this sonic evocation of flesh is mostly representational and associative, it operates primarily through sonic *timbre* rather than linguistic cues; that is, it has to do more with recognizing certain qualities in acoustic phenomena that reference the presence of a fleshy body. Timbre, however, is one of the most difficult sonic concepts to define—not least of all because it has often been used as a shunting ground for any aspect of sound not adequately described by pitch, duration, and volume. Ironically, this situation has not been helped by the increasingly fine-grained visibility of sound made possible by technological advances such as Fast Fourier Analysis and spectrography, which not only provide overwhelming amounts of data that are difficult to parse but also often fail to show stable relations between what is acoustically present and what is psychoacoustically salient—in other words, *human hearing parses sound in ways that do not line up neatly with how sound recording technologies process it.* As the "spectromorphological" composer Denis Smalley suggests, "we now know too much about timbre," in the sense that sound spectrography has made a mess of traditional distinctions between sonic phenomena, which all now seem to be continuous with each other through frequency harmonics.[15]

Despite this gap between human hearing and computer-assisted analysis, Smalley identifies four definitional clusters for timbre. The first he describes as the "negative" definition used by most traditional musicians: everything that remains of sound when pitch, duration, and volume are already accounted for. In other words, timbre is what enables a listener to distinguish one sound from another, when they are otherwise equivalent in pitch, duration, and volume such as a violin and a saxophone playing the same note. The second definition he attributes to "spectral" composers, who treat timbre as an extension of harmony through the use of spectrography, allowing for the creation of relationships between pitch and other sound qualities. The third he associates with electroacoustic composition and research, in which timbre is seen as a multidimensional phenomenon that is determined through a range of different variables (e.g., transient attack, iteration, harmonics, noisiness, and fluctuation)—albeit with an awareness that the relation between these variables and human auditory perception is often nonlinear, messy, counterintuitive, and sometimes undefinable. Finally, Smalley points to the term's colloquial use in everyday language, where it is intelligible to nonspecialists; the vernacular use of "timbre" often references the synaesthetic materiality of sound to make timbral distinctions easily comprehensible, using terms such as "bright"/"dull," "compact"/"spread," "dry"/"wet," and "hollow"/"dense."

Across all four of these definitions, the primary perceptual dimension of timbre here remains its capacity to imply a sound source through the qualities of the sound itself. This characteristic forms the center of Smalley's generalized definition of timbre: "a general, sonic physiognomy through which we identify sounds as emanating from a source, whether that source be actual, inferred or imagined."[16] Understood in terms of Peircean semiotics, timbre's relation to its source of emanation is *indexical*, in the sense that what underwrites the relation between sonic signifier and corporeal signified is neither likeness (icon) nor habitual association (symbol) but trace (index).[17] In Herbert's "Foreign Bodies," for example, the sonic events of breathing, bones crackling, joints popping, skin rubbing, fingernails flicking, and teeth biting all index the presence of a fleshy body as their sound source. Furthermore, sampled sounds imply a cause-effect relation to physical objects in that their sounds index an event and object of emanation—such as the clapping of hands—albeit temporally and spatially separated from their original occurrence. Thus, the evocation of flesh in electronic dance music has much to do with how the timbral qualities of its of sound samples index a fleshy sound source—which may or may not have a "real" relation to an actually existing body.

As a "concept album" that restricts itself to body sounds, Herbert's *Bodily Functions* is admittedly something of a boundary case for the aesthetics and practices of electronic dance music, but the sonic evocation of flesh made so explicit here is nonetheless a prominent aspect of most styles in this metagenre. In particular, Herbert's musical output is particularly relevant to the minimal spectrum of electronic dance music, which shows a similar proclivity for "found sounds" and field recordings. Perhaps the most common example of electronic dance music's fleshy evocativeness would be the use of "acoustic" hand claps (instead of the synthesized approximations available on most drum machines such as the Roland TR-808) or fragmented vocal samples. This fleshy aesthetic is especially salient in the minimal-spectrum substyles prominent during the first decade of this century, where the exploration of nonconventional, noninstrumental sound samples has encouraged the use of a wider range of sounds emanating from the body. In a manner similar to the development of "extended instrumental techniques" in twentieth-century avant-garde composition, electronic dance music producers since the genre's first emergence have been continually extending, deconstructing, reconfiguring, modifying ("modding"), and creatively misusing audio technology to expand their range of available sounds. And, much like the more recent generation of "spectralist" composers, their innovative efforts have been primarily devoted to the extension of timbre. For producers associated with the glitch, microhouse, and minimal substyles of the early 2000s, for example, this creative work has included expanding electronic music's sonic palette in a manner somewhat orthogonal to the metagenre's conventional tendencies toward either "realist" instrument sampling or futuristic, "pure" sound synthesis.[18]

The use of flesh as a sound source in these substyles can be illustrated with two brief examples taken from tracks that were in heavy rotation during fieldwork for this book. M.A.N.D.Y. and Booka Shade's collaboration "O Superman feat. Laurie Anderson (Reboot's 20 Cubans Rework)" samples heavily from Laurie Anderson's 1981 recording of the same name, which features Anderson singing and speaking through a vocoder that alternates between two chords.[19] The German duo Booka Shade is known for combining prerecorded, sequenced loops with "live," onstage percussion performance on standard drum sets; this is clear in this track, which is saturated with richly variegated acoustic drums and hi-hats. Reboot's "20 Cubans Rework" of the track adds an ostinato loop of layered hand claps—slightly out of phase and out of tune with each other, in order to create the psychoacoustic impression of a group of clapping performers—which are recognizable through their timbre as acoustic samples, foregrounding the sound of skin hitting skin. The robotic "ha" by a female voice that marks time in Anderson's original song also reappears here but as a part of a syncopated percussion loop rather than as a steady four-four pulse. At important structural points in the track, especially moments of suspense preceding a salient change in musical texture, the track's sonic surface is often stripped down to the hand claps and the syncopated vocal "ha" loop, thus making fleshy sounds the core of this track.

But sounds do not need to be sampled directly from the body in order to evoke flesh. A particularly striking example of this is the Berghain resident DJ Ben Klock's remix of the legendary New Jersey house producer Kerri Chandler's "Pong," retitled as "Pong (Bones and Strings Rework)."[20] What do the "Bones and Strings" of the remix's title refer to? The strings are relatively easy to identify, as Klock takes the melodic loop of string instruments from the original track and makes it more prominent in the mix (starting at approximately 2:00), both by increasing its volume and by stripping away many other layers from the original version. One might identify the "bones" with the sparseness of the track (that is, a "bare-bones" arrangement of the original), but that would ignore the crackling sounds that emerge early in the track (1:14) and remain a salient element throughout. Taking the rhythmic place of hand claps, these sounds are composed of clusters of high-pitched transients that clot together to create a bright crackle, evoking the sounds of joints popping and bones cracking. In contrast to the "chorused" effect of the hand claps in Reboot's remix of the Anderson/M.A.N.D.Y. collaboration, here the clustering of sonic "pops" is smooth enough to create a more sustained, aggregate sound with a crisp, brittle texture. In other words, it is the *microstructure* of this cloud of clicks that lends it a granularity that is both evocative of the body and rich in textural, tactile detail. Not only does this track reference the body through its timbral approximation of bones, but the *grain* of its samples affords a tactile, embodied engagement with sound.

Grain: The Matter of Sound

In addition to the tactile impact of beats and the timbral evocation of flesh, electronic dance music engages tactility through sonic texture itself. In particular, it does so by favoring granular sounds and complex sonic textures, which sonically index (that is, act as a trace of) tactile encounters with similarly textured objects. By "granular" sound, I refer to the notion of "grain" as developed by the *musique concrète* composer Pierre Schaeffer and later expounded by Michel Chion.[21] In contrast to Roland Barthes's more poetic use of the term, Schaeffer's definition is quite precise: it is the "microstructure of sound," in the form of irregularities in a sound's sustain, such that it gives an "overall qualitative perception of a large number of small irregularities of detail affecting the 'surface' of the [sound-]object."[22] Highly granular sounds thus have rapid groupings of sonic impacts, which may sound like a sequence of discrete attacks (such as the teeth of a zipper clicking together), a cluster of smaller sounds (the grains of sandpaper brushing against a surface), or something "noisy" with sonic interference (white noise or distortion from a waveform "clipping" as it exceeds the limits of an audio channel). By contrast, "smooth" sounds of low granularity either have little surface fluctuation (such as an oboe) or have regular fluctuations of pitch with smooth transitions (such as the use of vibrato on many instruments). Notably, most smooth sounds have a clear pitch that emanates from sustained vibration, while coarsely granular sounds are usually indeterminate in pitch, harmonically complex, and composed of percussive impacts.

In *Traité des objets musicaux* (*Treatise on Musical Objects*), Schaeffer developed a rich but also highly schematic vocabulary for sonic grain. His sonic explorations were very much grounded in the epistemologies of laboratory science, conceptualizing sonic events as "sound objects" on which he would conduct experiments through the manipulation of sound recordings in systematized ways. For example, book 5 of his treatise (which contains most of his definitional and schematizing work) is titled *Morphologie et typologie des objets sonores* (*Morphology and Typology of Sound Objects*), borrowing the term "morphology" from the natural sciences to describe a classification of objects according to their perceptible form and structure (rather than function). Book 6, which contains his definition of "grain," is titled *Solfège des objets musicaux* (*Music Theory/Grammar of Musical Objects*), suggesting that he understood his work as forging new analytical tools for this expanded world of sound. One outcome of Schaeffer's scientistic approach is that his elaboration of grain is lavishly taxonomic, seemingly determined to fit all of his musical "criteria of musical perception" into each of the nine columns of "qualifications" and "evaluation" in his *Tableau récapitulatif du solfège des objets musicaux* (*Summary Diagram of the Theory of Musical Objects*), a classification-matrix for the entire sonic universe.[23] While this leads to a baroque surfeit of terminology that undermines the utility of his analytic scheme in sound studies, his terms for grain are intuitively descriptive, providing useful heuristics for organizing a large field of difficult-to-describe phenomena.

Since Schaeffer considers grain to be an aspect of the sound object's sustain, he first organizes sonic grain by the manner in which it sustains itself, distinguishing between nonexistent sustain (*entretien nul*), continuous sustain (*entretien soutenu*), and iterative sustain (*entretien intératif*).[24] He equates sustain with the microtemporal organization of attacks, thus positing three corresponding types of grain: resonance grain (*grain de résonance*), rubbing grain (*grain de frottement*), and iteration grain (*grain d'itération*). Resonance grains consist of the shimmering harmonic vibrations that follow a percussive attack, rubbing grains are composed of completely random of attacks, and iteration grains have a relatively regular microstructure of attacks. As examples, Schaeffer tentatively classifies the sound of a flute as a very gentle rubbing grain, while he considers woodwinds to have a gentle iteration grain, based on how the striking of the reeds "crenelate" its dynamic profile. He also notes how the human voice tends to transition from rubbing to iteration grain in its lowest registers, where the beating of the glottis becomes perceptible (see also "vocal fry").

Schaeffer renames these grains as "pure types" and then combines them into three mixed genres of grain, which provide more descriptive detail (see figure 2.5). Thus, resonance grain becomes *harmonic* grain, associated with the sonic quality of shimmer (*scintillements*); rubbing becomes *compact* grain, associated with friction (*frottements*); and iteration becomes *discontinuous* grain, associated with impact strikes (*frappements*). The combination of the first two pure types of grain produces compact harmonic grains, composed of resonant scrapes (*frottements résonants*) that would include squeaking (*crissement*) and buzzing (*bourdonnements*). The first and the third combine

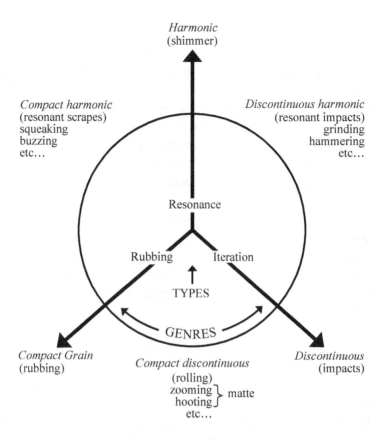

Harmonic
(shimmer)

Compact harmonic
(resonant scrapes)
squeaking
buzzing
etc…

Discontinuous harmonic
(resonant impacts)
grinding
hammering
etc…

Resonance

Rubbing   Iteration

↑
TYPES

GENRES

Compact Grain
(rubbing)

Compact discontinuous
(rolling)
zooming ⎱ matte
hooting ⎰
etc…

Discontinuous
(impacts)

FIGURE 2.5 Author's translation of figure 39 in Schaeffer, *Traité des objets musicaux* (1966), 553.

to form discontinuous harmonic grains, which consist of resonant impacts (*frappements résonants*) associated with grinding (*grincements*) and hammering (*martellements*). Finally, compact discontinuous grains combine the second and third of the pure types, such as the rolling sounds (*roulements*) found in "zooming" (*vrombissements*) and hooting (*hululements*). Schaeffer stops at this sixfold permutational classification but suggests that the three pure types could be further combined and recombined in varying proportions to create more fine-grained distinctions between sounds.

In the interest of filling out all of the columns in his *tableau récapitulatif*, Schaeffer attempts to identify different "species" (*espèces*) of grain on the basis of its location and extension in auditory space.[25] He thus assigns to grain a kind of pitch placement (*site:tessitura*) along with pitch thickness (*calibre:écart*); with regard to intensity, he classifies grain by its relative weight (*site:poids*) and amplitude of variation (*calibre:relief*). He does not take this line of nomenclature very far, however, finding that these criteria cannot be measured with much precision and do not help distinguish between grains as they are perceived. Instead, Schaeffer proposes an empirical, morphological, and thus psychoacoustically centered approach that would capture some of these qualities through degrees of granularity. Resonance/harmonic grains, for example, could then be described as quivering (*frémissant*), shimmering (*fourmillant*), and limpid (*limpide*); rubbing/compact grains would be either rough (*rugueux*), matte (*mat*), or smooth (*lisse*); and iterative/discontinuous ones would be coarse (*tremblé/gros*), medium (*serré/net*), or fine (*fin*).

Based on auditory experience rather than sonic waveforms, this final set of nine terms for sonic grain is also the closest to describing sound as tactile experience, using adjectives that are usually applied to surfaces and fluids. For Schaffer, this analogical usage extends from his treatment of sound objects as tangible, real-world objects: "To speak of a sound as rough or matte, velvety or limpid is to compare it to a stone, a skin, a piece of velvet, or a flowing stream."[26] Although these terms describe perceptions that seem to be disconnected from tactile and visual modes, he argues that the underlying analogy is well founded and intuitively convincing, because "it is not the objects of vision or hearing that are important in themselves, but rather their assemblage."[27] His analogy is structural, in the sense that aural, visual, and tactile perceptions of grain all refer to the way that small elements combine to form a textured surface.

These similarities in microstructure also lead Schaeffer to understand grain as a perceptual phenomenon that functions across sensory modes, suggesting that tactile, auditory, and visual experiences of texture are not only comparable but intersecting and concretely interconnected. This can be seen in the way that sonic grain can provide information to the listener about the texture and physical state of the object(s) used to produce it. An example relevant to electronic dance music would be the "scraper" family of percussion instruments, such as the guiro found in many traditional Latin American percussion sections; this instrument consists of a hollowed-out gourd (or another object of similar shape and rigidity) with parallel ridges carved into one side. The performer uses a stick-shaped tool to play the instrument, scraping the stick along these ridges and thus using the surface irregularities of the instrument to create an iterative/discontinuous grain that consists of a relatively regular succession of attacks. The frequency, regularity, timbre, and intensity of these attacks are all directly related to the spacing, regularity, substance, and shape of the guiro's ridges, along with the force with which it is being scraped. In this sense, sonic grain not only resembles material grain but also has a direct, indexical relation to real-world textures, allowing the ear to perceive physical textures that are usually associated with tactile experience. Thus, the perceptual mapping between sound and touch that Schaeffer achieves through the use of adjectives like "rough" and "smooth" is not arbitrary; rather, it is a descriptive tracking of how the perception of texture arises across multiple modes at once.

Grain is also a phenomenon of perceptual thresholds: for Schaeffer, grain is the middle ground between a singular, smooth tone and multiple separate attacks, where microtemporal attacks are perceived to coagulate into a single but variegated sound event. Other scholars, composers, and music critics have accorded grain a similarly liminal status, although they more often use the term "texture" instead of Schaeffer's more specialized usage of "grain." Denis Smalley locates grain in an "attack-effluvium continuum" that spans from discrete impulse attacks through iteration, grain, and finally to an "effluvial state."[28] Notably, he diverges slightly from Schaeffer's definition of grain by differentiating between iteration and grain; the former refers to the stage where "linked attack-impulses are perceived as a unified object," and the latter occurs only "once individual impulses have lost any vestiges of separate identity," thereby drawing a line between what Schaeffer would consider iteration/discontinuous and rubbing/compact grain.[29] The electronic-music critic Philip Sherburne, in the liner notes for the glitch-music compilation *Clicks & Cuts 3*, places sonic texture in a continuum with rhythm rather than regular iteration: "Rhythm is texture writ large, peaks and valleys turned to pulse. Texture is rhythm rendered microscopic, (ir)regularity encoded and impressed upon the surface of sound."[30] Sherburne's formulation is particularly well suited to electronic dance music, in that it links together two essential elements of the metagenre by positing them as parallel phenomena running on differing timescales. In these examples as well as in many others, the notion of sonic grain functions as a slippery placeholder for the thresholds of human perception: registering across hearing, touch, and vision; functioning in the border zone between unified and disparate sound events; conveying information about objects, real or imagined; and unfolding as a temporal "microstructure" that can be registered as an information-rich surface. In so doing, it troubles distinctions that have historically been made between sound and hearing.

Although the impact of much of Schaeffer's sonic solfège did not extend beyond his immediate circle of collaborators, the concept of sonic grain continued to be of importance throughout the twentieth century, particularly for electroacoustic composers specializing in granular synthesis. Granular synthesis is a method of sound synthesis that works with what Curtis Roads terms "microsound," that is, "grains of sound" that have a duration "near the threshold of human auditory perception, typically between one thousandth of a second and one tenth of a second (from 1 to 100 milliseconds)."[31] Notably, in contrast to Schaeffer's definition, "grain" here is not a quality of sound but a rather a thing: a sonic building block as well as a unit of measurement. Nonetheless, the results of granular synthesis do tend to be rich in Schaefferian sonic grain. Whether sampled from preexisting sources or synthesized using oscillators, these grains of sound are played back at varying time points, speeds, frequencies (pitch), and amplitudes (volume), such that they perceptibly fuse into composite sounds with novel timbre and rich texture, which can be manipulated in ways that are difficult or impossible to achieve with conventional meso-temporal sampling (that is, over 100 milliseconds). Much like cinema's illusion of movement arising out of a rapid succession of still images, granular synthesis exploits the perceptual phenomenon of temporal continuity in hearing (often termed the "forward masking effect" in psychoacoustics), where one sound masks the perception of a sound following closely thereafter (below a threshold of 200 milliseconds), thus creating the impression of one continuous sound.[32] Since this usually requires the placement and mixing of thousands of grains across multiple parameters to create an audible composite texture, most composers working in this method have a methodological and aesthetic preference for using statistical algorithms to redistribute these grains across time, frequency, and amplitude fields in ways that result in complex clusters, producing textured masses of sounds that are sometimes described as "clouds" (in analogy with "particle clouds" in physics).

Although the notion of "sonic grain" used by granular synthesis artists diverges from Schaeffer's, they have remained keenly aware of the tactile qualities of the sounds they produce, usually discussing them in terms of "texture" or "timbre." For example, Roads's magisterial tome *Microsound*— which has granular synthesis as its core compositional process—shares with Schaeffer a focus on the "microstructure" of sound. Here, the Schaefferian notion of sonic grain reappears as "texture," the qualities of which Roads defines as a function of "grain duration and density combined," ranging from continuous/opaque to sparse/transparent textures.[33] Through experimentation, he notes textural shifts that are dependent on the frequency bandwidth of grain density: narrow bands (from unison on a single frequency to one or two semitones) produce tone streams that have an audible pitch center; medium bands (spanning several semitones) result in "turgid colored noise"; and wide bands (an octave and beyond) generate atmospheric soundscapes and "clouds" of sound. Much like Schaeffer, Roads locates sonic grain—both as a general quality of sound and as a compositional building block—at the threshold of human auditory perception, where individual sound events blur into a unified stream. He also describes sounds resulting from synthesis as having varying degrees of "granularity," which echoes Schaeffer's framing of grain within a continuum from coarse to fine. In any case, the theoretical framework of granular synthesis and its compositional applications preserve the liminal status of sonic grain, in which the tactility of sound emerges from the murky perceptual zone where solid sound masses dissolve and individual sound particles melt together.

Using these notions of grain and granularity, all electronic dance music—or even all sample-based music—seems to be saturated with granular sounds. With this genre's tendency to prioritize rhythm and timbre over melody and harmony, this observation may be broadly accurate in comparison to other styles of music; indeed, to the extent that sonic grain is an aspect of timbre that has inherently rhythmic properties (that is, fluctuations of regularity and frequency), it makes sense that granular sounds would play an important role in the aesthetic appeal of electronic dance music. This is all the more so for an array of substyles that cluster around particular compositional practices, such as the postdigital "glitch" styles that were in ascendancy during the turn of the twenty-first century as well as the 1980s-nostalgic, low-fidelity "electroclash" that emerged at roughly the same time. During fieldwork for this book (2006–2010), however, it was the minimal spectrum of electronic dance music that magnetized the local scenes I studied, especially where those substyles overlapped with glitch aesthetics (such as microhouse, minimal house, and minimal techno).

A clear example of heightened granularity can be heard in the German producer Oliver Hacke's "Millepieds (SLG Remix)."[34] The title refers to the French word for the millipede, which translates literally as "thousand feet"; millipedes move about by advancing each pair of their numerous legs in rapid succession, and this conjures up a sonic image of an unbroken stream of footsteps—which seems, in turn, to inform the remix of Hacke's minimal-techno track by SLG (Łukasz Seliga). SLG fills in the track's texture with a proliferation of granular sounds, from coarse to fine grained, with a particular emphasis on tight iteration grains (that is, rasping and grating sounds) and short, shimmering resonance grains (rattles and closed hi-hats). From the beginning of the track, one can hear a rhythmic, three-fold back-and-forth scrubbing/rattling sound that evokes coarse sandpaper (on the third beat of every four-beat cycle), a zipper-like rasping sound (extending over the third and fourth beats, starting around 0:30), a short hissing sound (from 0:30, at the end of every eight-beat cycle), a lower-mid-frequency rumble (marking a 4+3+3+2+4 = 16 subdivision of the four-beat cycle, most noticeable when the other layers are briefly removed for thirty-two beats, 0:13–0:29), and a wide array of other pops and crackles that mark longer metric cycles. By contrast, Martin Stimming's remix of the Berlin-based British producer/DJ Lee Jones's minimal-house track "Safari (Stimming Remix)" provides an example of granularity that focuses less on regular, iterative grains.[35] Stimming, whose own production style has often been described as "lush," enriches the texture of Jones's original track with a plethora of "noisy" resonance and continuous grains, including chorused hand claps, shakers, heavily gated tambourines, closed hi-hats, rasps, and the occasional use of long "reverb" effects at transitional points to create sonic "clouds" that dissipate as a new loop configuration emerges. All of this is held together with a rolling loop of pitched bass kicks, framed by short melodic fragments.

The minimalism of electronic dance music's minimal continuum tends to be reflected both formally (through slow, gradual changes) and texturally (sparse, thin layers). But despite this spartan aesthetic, minimal tracks can still feature an overall sonic texture that is quite complex, especially through the layering of contrasting sounds spread across a range of disparate frequency bands. This juxtaposes variations in sound envelope (i.e., attack, decay, sustain, release), tone, color, grain, and other aspects of timbre to create a richly textured sonic surface across the entire track—rather than just across a particular layer. Although it is difficult to describe this in detail, some examples of minimal tracks with complex overall textures would include Niederflur's "z.B." and Martin Dawson and Glimpse's "No One Belongs Here More than You."[36] Both tracks combine sustained and sharply punctuated sounds, as well as smooth synths or strings with coarse hand claps and crackles; tracks such as these evoke a rich, variegated tactile experience and thus encourage a similarly tactile engagement with sound.

This sonic evocation of touch in electronic dance music could be understood to evoke *haptic aurality*, a term that I adapt from Laura U. Marks's notion of "haptic visuality."[37] In her study of touch in film, Marks defines haptic visuality as a mode of seeing that also attends to texture in an image, where the eyes register information about texture, which in turn activates our fleshy senses. The haptic gaze, then, "tends to move over the surface of its object rather than plunge into illusionistic depth, not to distinguish form so much as to discern texture."[38] While Marks locates haptic visuality in a viewer's inclination to see texture—one might speak of an especially haptic filmgoer, for example—she also identifies haptic images, which invite an attention to texture through parameters such as framing, zoom, motion, and detail; heavily textured images, in other words, encourage the viewer to engage in haptic visuality. In a similar fashion, the musical examples examined in this chapter demonstrate the centrality of haptic aurality to electronic dance music, in that these tracks feature richly textured, granular, embodied sounds that draw attention to haptic experience. On the dancefloor of parties especially, the experience of listening and dancing to electronic dance music invites an engagement with sound that is alive to texture, touch, and other fleshy excitations. Through granularity, powerfully percussive samples, and sounds that index the body, the rich sonic textures of tracks such as "Millepieds," "Pong (Bones and Strings Remix)," and "z.B." might encourage partygoers to experience the entire event as intensely tactile.

Hearing is, after all, a kind of touch sense. The eardrum and its cilia register varying impacts of air molecules as they move and are compressed and rarefied, reading the texture of these impacts in the way one might run a finger over the surface of an object.[39] But vibrations can also be "heard" as much on the skin as in the ear, as evidenced by the generation of tactile hearing aids developed before cochlear implants became the dominant prosthetic for hearing loss.[40] This is particularly noteworthy in the context of a nightclub, where powerful sound systems are usually employed to project sound at such high decibel levels that sonic vibrations become quite literally tactile: "beats" beating on the body. These tactile vibrations can also be experienced as an enveloping touch, partially because low-frequency vibrations like subbass tend to propagate through a space in a more omnidirectional way than high-frequency ones do—but also because clubs almost invariably choose immersive, surround-sound arrangements for their speakers; indeed, sonic immersion or envelopment is a design goal of electronic music venues. This aesthetic of envelopment continues across several experiential modes on the dancefloor: the absence of windows, dark interiors lit in oblique or disorienting ways, smoke machines filling empty space and shortening the field of vision, the press of other bodies in the crowd, and a combination of heat and humidity that can make the surrounding air feel dense and palpable.

Feeling Together

> A particular intimacy appears to subsist between textures and emotions.
> EVE KOSOFSKY SEDGWICK, *TOUCHING FEELING*

As helpful as the concept of sonic grain can be to the analysis of tactility in electronic dance music, the term recedes from view the further one moves away from scholarship on Schaeffer, granular synthesis, and electroacoustic music. Instead, it is more often under the rubric of "texture" that one finds the most fruitful explorations of the relationship between touch and affect; this relationship, in turn, offers a basis for understanding how the tactile aspects of listening and dancing to electronic dance music connect to the sense of diffuse, collective intimacy that lies at the heart of this book. Paraphrasing Renu Bora's essay on the queer resonances of texture in Henry James's *The Ambassadors*, Eve Kosofsky Sedgwick suggests that "to perceive texture is always, immediately, and de facto to be immersed in a field of active narrative hypothesizing, testing, and re-understanding of how physical properties act and are acted upon over time."[41] In this account, touch is an inherently interactive mode of perception that not only involves physical contact with its object but also opens up a field of potential action, both past and future.

Bora and Sedgwick both describe textural perception as narrativizing, in that it addresses two questions about/to the object: What happened to it? What can I do with it? In other words, tactile experience provides potential insight into how an object came to possess a particular texture, as well as what kinds of interaction the object affords. This hearkens back to the analysis of fleshy timbres earlier in this chapter: much like surface texture can have an indexical relation to the "life story" of the object being palpated, the timbre of many sounds used in minimal dance music indexes bodies by evoking micronarratives of striking, slapping, snapping, squishing, sucking, and so on—which in turn conjure up potential future narratives of action and interaction. Texture, Sedgwick argues, thus belongs to a category of "intrinsically interactive properties" called "affordances," defined by James J. Gibson as the properties of an object (or environment) that provide opportunities for action.[42] How these opportunities are felt and embodied can be understood in terms of Spinoza's *affectus*, that is, as the variation in the capacity to act or be acted on; moreover, this sense of multiple, superimposed, latent action resonates with later theoretical elaborations on the virtuality of affect.[43] The texture of an object (or sound object) can thus be understood to carry the affective resonances of its past encounters while also conveying a sense of encroaching virtual, potential, desired, and/or expected encounters. All of this resonates with the reconceptualization of intimacy that this book undertakes, in that intimacy is also a phenomenon that unfolds between bodies—through proximity, contact, and impact—which can be registered as a sense of both closeness and expansiveness, of expanded possibilities, and of latent connection.

Both Sedgwick and Bora note that texture is not limited to touch but can also be transmodal, multimodal, or even synaesthetic. For Bora, texture is registered liminally, "on the border of properties of touch and vision," while Sedgwick expands this to include hearing, providing as examples "the brush-brush of corduroy trousers or the crunch of extra-crispy chicken."[44] But perhaps texture should instead be understood as an *amodal* phenomenon, providing a field of experience that extends beyond the remit of any particular sense organ; Steve Goodman makes a similar argument for rhythm and vibration, in which he defines "amodality" as "ontologically preceding the designation of a sensation to a specific exteroceptive sensory channel (the five senses)."[45] This leads him to posit a "vibrational substratum" out of which the experience of sound as a specific sensory modality emerges. If we follow Goodman in not assuming that vibrational phenomena (such as the vibration of air particles) correspond exclusively to specific human sensory channels (hearing), then we could understand texture as a property that does not simply map from touch to other senses by analogy; instead, it is an aspect of the microstructuring of the lived world that can be simultaneously registered across a range of sensory channels. This level of presensory abstraction helps us to understand how the sonic "feel" (texture) of electronic dance music can simultaneously entail "feeling" (tactile perception / physical contact) and "feelings" (affect).

Here again, as with Schaeffer and Roads, texture remains closely associated with the thresholds of perception. While Bora grounds this relationship in etymological similarities between "texture," "threshold," and "limen," Sedgwick provides a general definition of texture centered around a threshold: "Texture, in short, comprises an array of perceptual data that includes repetition, but whose degree of organization hovers just below the level of shape or structure."[46] Similarly, sonic grain is also a threshold phenomenon—both in the Schaefferian sense and in that of granular synthesis—where sound events coagulate together but do not yet form a continuous whole. In Deleuzean terms, sonic granularity could be said to make the "molecularity" of sound apparent, in contrast to the "molar" wholes of smooth tones; it renders the particularity and dynamism of sonic aggregates perceptible, without losing a sense of cohesion.[47] In a more abstract sense, then, texture can be understood as a blurring, fluid phase situated between atomized individuality and collective mass.

For Pierre Schaeffer, sonic grain emerges from the microstructure of sound objects, but could its affective and symbolic resonances not carry further? Perhaps we could also understand grain and texture in terms of a microstructure of belonging. With an aesthetic foregrounding of sonic grain, electronic dance music seems to draw attention to the vague terrain between molecular and molar modes of organization. And, following the Deleuzean notion of becoming, could its granular aesthetics reveal something about the affective experience of becoming-group or becoming-crowd? We will return to these questions from a rather different angle in chapter 4, where ethnographic interviews and scene-specific musical practices provide a path from sonic vibration through affective contagion and toward an emergent sense of social cohesion. But for now, it suffices to suggest that the fascination with sonic grain in electronic dance music draws the listener-dancer's attention to the perceptual border zones between granular individuals and aggregated wholes; it aestheticizes the in-betweenness of microstructure through its engagement with touch and "feeling it"—whatever "it" is in the moment. All of this will come to seem ironic in light of chapter 3's examination of vague and fluid belonging in electronic dance music scenes, where participants avoid discussion of precisely these border zones between the individual and the collective, in an apparent effort to preserve their experiences of loose social cohesion.

3 LIQUIDARITY

Who can you count on when you go out dancing? What is your responsibility to fellow partygoers? Do you belong to something by sharing a dancefloor? With *whom* and *how*? Nightlife scenes are simultaneously social realms, leisure sites, and entertainment industries, wherein partygoers share an interest in cultivating atmospheres of suspended responsibility and enhanced conviviality between strangers—or "relaxed and friendly vibes." And so, a desire prevails among partygoers for social encounters to be *smooth*, to be simple, open, and friendly, which contrasts puzzlingly against the conspicuous lack of clear community guidance about how such interactions should occur in an anonymous crowd. In spite of this lack, partygoers often remember parties filled with chance encounters, surprising stranger-intimacy, conviviality, and the diffuse glow of social warmth. In the minimal electronic dance music scenes of Paris, Berlin, and Chicago, partygoers seemed to avoid the sort of questions that open this chapter; and this, in turn, raises questions about why they avoid explicit talk of belonging in music scenes that have historically valued openness to difference.[1]

The puzzle of this chapter is how gestures of warmth, care, and support arise from a context of casual contact and vague interpersonal knowledge. The account developed here highlights a combination of loose stranger-sociability and vague belonging that I call *liquidarity*: a fluid togetherness that manages to hold the shape of a heterogeneous and unconnected crowd. Under conditions of liquidarity, participants maintain a vague sense of social belonging, recognition, and intimacy while also enjoying the benefits of anonymity, fluidity, and a certain lightness of social contact. In other words, this is a form of belonging that *feels* firm enough to support social cohesion while remaining fluid enough to accommodate a wide range of ideas about what such cohesion entails. Liquidarity also captures an important aspect of public culture that extends well beyond electronic dance music scenes: it identifies the affective relationships that can arise between people who are not bound to one another by traditional ties of kinship and affinity. The term "liquidarity" also suggests the precariousness and volatility of such underdefined relationships, as became apparent through my fieldwork in all three cities.

In this chapter, I develop the notion of liquidarity by engaging with three archives—ethnographic anecdotes, interviews, and relevant scholarship—across several analytic axes. First, an encounter that took place at the front door of Berghain (Berlin) provides framing for an initial conceptualization of liquidarity, which also takes its shape from interviewees' comments regarding solidarity at electronic music parties. Following this, another anecdote/interview cluster focuses on vagueness and its importance to stranger-sociability in these contexts. In analyzing the discourse of scene participants, I identify two streams of thought on crowd cohesion, which I characterize as additive and subtractive. This structures the following two sections, which analyze musical taste and nighttime as additive and subtractive factors, respectively. These analyses trace linkages with past and current scholarship on taste, ritual, reading/viewing publics, and other theoretical accounts of collectivity.[2] Finally, encounters with Lauren Berlant's "intimate publics," Byron Dueck's "indigenous intimacies," Zygmunt Bauman's "liquid modernity," and Nigel Thrift's "light-touch intimacy" all bring this chapter to a close with a consideration of the broader political implications of liquidarity as an analogous concept to solidarity.

Is This Togetherness?

BERGHAIN / PANORAMA BAR, BERLIN; SUNDAY, AUGUST 17, 2008; 1:00 A.M.

"Hej, bist du allein?" [Hey, are you alone?]

   "Ähm, nee . . ." [Um, nope . . .]

I have a split second to finish my sentence, and the outcome of the rest of my night (and probably that of my friends) hangs in the balance. I am certainly not alone; I came with my friend Fantômette, her girlfriend (Noëlle), and a friend of theirs (Lisette), whom I have met only once before, more than a year ago.

Fantômette is a DJ, producer, and event organizer in her late thirties, primarily involved in the *minimale* subscene of Paris but also active as an organizer in the city's larger house and *éléctro* scenes.[3] In mid-2007, she left her job at a financial consulting firm and threw herself completely into a musical career, increasing her profile as a performer and launching an event-promotion collective named La Petite Maison Éléctronique. Lisette is a native of Mauritius in her early thirties who was based in Paris as a graphic designer at the time. Lisette had come to Berlin for this weekend as a surprise, to celebrate Noëlle's birthday along with Fantômette.

This scene takes place in front of Berghain, a nightclub that has become an institution of the Berlin techno scene while also taking on mythical proportions in global electronic dance music discourse. The club is in fact a reincarnation of an earlier Berliner nightclub, Ostgut (1998–2003), which was located in the empty Güterbahnhof railway-shipping warehouse near the Ostbahnhof station in Berlin's Friedrichshain district (former East Berlin).[4] Ostgut closed and was demolished in 2003, and the vacant space became part of the construction site for the multiuse sports and entertainment arena O_2 World, the naming rights of which were bought by the mobile telecommunications company Telefónica O_2 Germany in 2006. With some support from municipal government and outside investors, Ostgut reopened as Berghain in 2004, in an East German–era electrical plant on the other side of Ostbahnhof's railway tracks. The new name, Berghain, is a portmanteau taken from the final syllables of the names of the two districts that flank the location: Kreuzberg and Friedrichshain (former West and East Berlin, respectively).

Ostgut, Berghain's precursor, began as an itinerant gay fetish event called "Snax," which eventually found a permanent home at Ostgut in 1998. Although much has changed since these first Snax parties, fetish-focused gay men remained a core clientele at Berghain during my fieldwork, and these queer, sex-positive origins continue to inform the behavior of other patrons.[5] On a regular night/day at Berghain in 2008, the escapades of the darkrooms (unlit spaces for anonymous sex) would often spill over to the bathroom stalls, the half-lit alcoves lining the hallways, and sometimes right to the middle of the dancefloor or at the bar. It has become something of a cliché in firsthand accounts of Berghain to claim that one witnessed some form of sex act in a well-lit area of the club—and this cliché is not complete without insisting that none of the surrounding partygoers were at all fazed by these antics. This is not to say that such clichés are false: while the sensational framing of these stories may present a distorted picture of the typical practices of the club's patrons, it nonetheless speaks to the hedonistic permissiveness of the space. This permissiveness also extends to the consumption of illicit substances, an undeniable part of the marathon partying that takes place at Berghain and other Berliner clubs. There seems to be a tacit understanding between the club's staff and clientele that, so long as partygoers make a credible effort to hide their drug use in toilet stalls, the security personnel will not sanction or eject them. It is a common and unremarkable sight, for example, to see four or five clubbers spill out of one bathroom stall.[6]

While all of these practices and discourses perpetuate Berghain's reputation as a site of excess, experimentation, unraveling, and freedom, this club also has a reputation as a global epicenter for techno and house music—especially the minimalist substyles that became the musical "brand" of Berlin in the early 2000s. Philip Sherburne, an electronic-music critic and contributor to *Pitchfork* and *Resident Advisor*, suggested in 2007 that Berghain "is quite possibly the current world capital of techno, much as E-Werk or Tresor were in their respective heydays."[7] The readers of *Resident Advisor*, a long-standing online media and ticketing platform for electronic dance music, voted Berghain / Panorama Bar the best club in the world in 2008, while readers of *DJ Mag* voted it best club in the world in 2009.[8] Most profiles of the club echo Sherburne, praising the booking policy (a mix of high-profile DJs, legendary veterans, and rising talent), the appreciative and engaged crowd, the powerful Funktion One sound system, the marathon DJ sets (usually four hours or more, giving DJs more freedom to range widely in style and mood), and the relatively low cost to visit (compared to clubs of similar caliber in other European capitals).

All of these factors help to explain why Lisette and Noëlle had flown in from Paris to celebrate Noelle's birthday—as well as why we spent nearly an hour waiting in line in the wee hours of the morning—but they do not explain why a bouncer's simple question, "Are you alone?" had filled me with anxiety. Along with Berghain's reputation for being a space of freedom, hedonism, musical connoisseurship, and intense experiences comes a reputation for being severely, inscrutably, and at times arbitrarily selective at the door. The club's bouncers are notorious for enforcing a stringent but elusive door policy, the precise parameters of which are never divulged by the staff and can be inferred only from observing the fate of those who are ahead of you in the queue. Online and face-to-face, there is a constantly churning discourse within clubbing networks about how to avoid being turned away at the door: don't look too glamorous; look queer; don't act like a tourist; don't look too young; don't show up as a group of straight men or women; dress eccentrically; look like a hipster; *don't* look like a hipster; go alone; if you don't speak German, avoid speaking your native tongue in the queue; learn how to say "hello" and "one, please," in German; and so on. At least one of these unspoken rules is widely known and broadcast among all Berlin clubgoers: *no groups*. During my time going to Berghain nearly weekly during the summers of 2008 and 2010 (as well as during all of 2012), I regularly saw groups of four and even three turned back at the door—although sometimes there were exceptions. These exceptions seemed to be people whom the bouncers recognized, as if they were "regulars" who had been in some sense preapproved for entry.

"Bist du allein?" On previous visits to the club, I had seen the bouncer ask this same question to other people, usually regulars at the club, and then bring them to the front of the line; in other words, it seemed that I had been recognized as a regular and was about to be offered immediate and guaranteed entry. But I was not alone; I was here with Fantômette, Lisette, and Noëlle, two of them having traveled all the way from Paris for the sole purpose of celebrating Noëlle's birthday at this club. Sensing that a group of four would almost certainly be refused entry, we had split into two pairs, with Fantômette and Noëlle standing several feet ahead of us and Lisette at my side. And so, given the complexities of Berghain's door policy as well as its importance to my companions as a nightlife destination, I was presented with a difficult choice: either I claim that I am alone and gain quick and certain entry for myself, or I admit that I am actually in a group of four and risk having all of us refused entry. In the split second given to me, I decide to split the difference.

"Ich bin mit diesem Mädchen hier." [I'm with this girl here.]

Fantômette and her girlfriend are about ten people away from us, pretending to be a lone couple, while Lisette is right next to me, watching the exchange but unable to follow the conversation unfolding in German. Fantômette, like me, has been living in Berlin all summer and going to Berghain with regularity, so I am reasonably certain that she can get in with her girlfriend. Lisette, however, just flew in from Paris, and I feel as though her entry has been entrusted to me.

"OK, kommt mit." [OK, come along.]

I immediately regret not bringing in all four of us at once, and I cast an apologetic glance at the other two as the bouncer pulls Lisette and me out of the queue. By the time we submit to a frisking and pay the entry charge, I am drenched in a mixture of relief and guilt, and so I decide to do a sort of penitence by waiting for the rest of the group at the coat check, nervously checking my mobile phone for news of their entry or refusal. About fifteen minutes later, Fantômette and her girlfriend emerge from the box office and breezily dismiss my apologies. Nonetheless, the guilt lingers all night.

This scene relates an encounter in which the aspirational utopian together-ness of post-disco dance music is called into question. It is part of a much larger archive of anecdotes that involve a cast of friends, acquaintances, contacts, and strangers, all of whom are thrown into situations in which they must translate their vague sense of fellowship into concrete ethical action. During an interview with Teresa, we came to the topic of exclusive door policies in Berlin, which prompted her to consider the implications for friends going out together:

> TERESA: Let's say you get in, but one of your friends doesn't get in. I mean, how does that feel? How does that leave you feeling? Can you still carry on like it's a good night? I don't know. (Chicago, 2010)

Teresa expressed ambivalence at the prospect of parting ways with one's partying companions when they are refused access to the venue, implying that she would rather forgo entering that space out of solidarity with her companions. Although her rhetorical questions refer to solidarity among friends, they echo broader questions about ethical responsibilities to fellow partygoers. How much care and support is expected of you, and how much can you expect from others? How serious should you be about solidarity, anyway, when "it's all in fun"?

Such questions of ethical entanglement are already complex in any so-cial context, but they seem impossible to pin down in the loosely tethered and largely anonymous social worlds of underground electronic music events. And yet, participants frequently navigate such fluid situations, in which decisions about belonging and responsibility are made with scarce interpersonal knowledge or institutional guidance. And, as long as such encounters resolve smoothly, little attention is paid to the underlying ambiguities and contradictions. The fellowship of fellow revelers remains underdescribed, and yet individual actors act *as if* their understanding were more complete, using partial knowledge, intuition, observation of others' comportment, and a vague sense of the surrounding affective atmosphere. Throughout my fieldwork, I encountered a form of togetherness that found expression in actions without being verbally articulated; in particular, it was a form of social cohesion in which constituents avoided talk about what made them cohere. The anecdotes and interviews analyzed here describe a vague togetherness that feels solid enough to support gestures of care and recognition but melts into incoherence under scrutiny—a liquid solidarity, in other words. I call this *liquidarity*, a state of fluid cohesion that generates a sense of inclusion uncoupled from identity or kinship. Vagueness is crucial to sustaining this sense of solidarity in spite of potentially divisive differences; it comes with its own costs and risks, but it seems adaptive to the volatile conditions of contemporary urban life.

In any case, the tactical vagueness underlying this cohesion made it difficult to bring the topic into explicit discussion during interviews. When I raised the topic of belonging or solidarity with my fieldwork contacts, they were often hesitant to make any firm claims regarding electronic dance music scenes in general, unsure of how to describe it, and ambivalent about its effects. Polina, however, was absolutely certain that solidarity existed at parties, although she also thought that it operated through a diverse mix of ideas about what such solidarity would entail. She described solidarity in this context as a set of tacit rules that are nonetheless followed collectively. But she also thought that, since these rules are never discussed, there is considerable unacknowledged divergence between partygoers regarding what grounds their collective revelry. In these few sentences, she encapsulated the concept of liquidarity as I develop it here.

> **POLINA:** There definitely is solidarity and certain unspoken rules that everyone follows—although I think various people might have various ideas about what those rules are. Sometimes, when I talk to people they have—well, everyone's got their own little idea of what an underground scene is! [*laughs*]. I think I have a pretty good idea, but I might be wrong in the end, you know? (Chicago, 2010)

Polina shares with other interviewees an uncertainty in articulating the terms and conditions of belonging to a nightlife crowd. Most interviewees described a feeling of togetherness that sometimes emerges in gestures of care, trust, and respect but does not seem to function according to conventional notions of solidarity. Imogen, for example, took pains to limit her claims of dancefloor intimacy to particular social surroundings and venues:

> IMOGEN: I think that there's definitely intimacy. I think that there's definitely intimacy on the dancefloor. I think that . . . uh, how can you not? But there's times that it's not a constant; it happens at some events, and it depends—for me—on the surroundings, when you have something that's more of an intimate surrounding. Like, there's no way I'm feeling intimacy on the dancefloor that much when I'm at Vision [a mainstream Chicago dance club]. (Chicago, 2010)

From chapter 1 we can also recall Sylvestre's concerns about the apparent superficiality of dancefloor intimacy. Partygoers such as Polina, Imogen, and Sylvestre recognized dancefloor intimacy as part of their experience, but they struggled to describe and delimit it. How, then, does a loose assemblage of partygoers manage to socialize, feel connected, and even support each other when the conditions of belonging are so vague? If a crowd cannot rely on preexisting social ties, if it deflects acknowledgment of conventional categories of belonging (such as ethnicity/race, nationality, gender, sexuality), and if it avoids explicitly articulating a unifying agenda or ideology, how does this crowd cohere at all? This is the problem that the concept of liquidarity is meant to clarify.

Vagueness

Vagueness is a supporting factor for dancefloor intimacy; in fact, I would argue that it is *productive*, in that it enables partygoers to project their own ideas of social cohesion and conviviality onto fellow dancers while reducing the chances of these ideas being undermined by the messy complexity of the underlying social relations. The socially lubricating effects of this vagueness is apparent in the triptych of fieldwork encounters related below, buttressed in turn by excerpts from interviews with partygoers who highlight the potential perils of overfamiliarity on the dancefloor.

While the scene that opened this chapter occurred at the door of Berghain, the following three shorter narratives occur in the interior of the same club;

its architecture and interior design thus merit some further description here, as the layout and décor of the club impact stranger-sociability by creating a particular atmosphere and providing numerous opportunities for a wide range of encounters.[9] The former East German electrical plant that houses Berghain was built between 1953 and 1954 in the socialist-neoclassical style, with alternating pilasters and lattice windows running the height of the building, underlined by a band of rusticated masonry around the base.[10] Although there are essentially three levels to the building, each level has a height of approximately nine meters (thirty feet).[11] The ground floor includes a relatively small ticket booth area followed by a large entry hall and coat check, featuring *Rituale des Verschwindens* (Rituals of disappearance, 2004), an art installation by the Polish artist Piotr Nathan composed of 175 one-square-meter aluminum tiles. Suspended steel stairs lead up to the former turbine room that serves as the main dancefloor—also named Berghain—with eighteen-meter-high ceilings (sixty feet), a capacity surpassing five hundred people, and seven massive FunktionOne speaker stacks. The second floor also holds two bars, another darkroom, a mezzanine with an ice cream bar, and large unisex bathrooms. Another set of steel stairs on one side of the main dancefloor leads to Panorama Bar, a second dancefloor located in the former control room of the electrical plant. This space includes a wrap-around, rubber-coated bar and walls bedecked with several large-format prints of photography by Wolfgang Tillmans, including two from his abstract "Freischwimmer" series and one of a woman sitting on a chair, naked below the waist, with her legs spread to expose her shaved vagina with pink, engorged labia.[12] The DJ spins at a table suspended by chains from the ceiling, separated from the crowd by a railing of steel tubing decorated with worn-out dials and needle meters (left over from the room's previous life), which also serves as a shelf for drinks. The floor-length windows running one side of the room are covered by mechanized metal blinds, which the bar staff opens during moments of musical climax to allow the morning sun to wash over the crowd. The rest of this upper floor includes another set of unisex bathrooms, another bar, several alcoves (old storage lockers that have been modified and cushioned), and a smoking area. A door on the eastern side of the ground floor opens out onto a patio space (another bar, a dancefloor covered by netting, and plenty of cushions and alcoves), which opens up from midday until dusk of the following day, weather permitting. Throughout the club's interior, couches have been fashioned out of 1,462-kilogram (3,223-pound) concrete channel sections. All of this space, which has a capacity of 1,500 people, occupies only half of the building; part of the remaining space is dedicated to a fetish-focused gay sex club, called the Lab.Oratory, while the remaining space is occasionally used for concerts, art exhibits, and private functions—although some of these spaces have become formalized as regular "chillout" / sound installation spaces in the years since my fieldwork, such as the "Halle" space. It is in this postindustrial, labyrinthine club space that three memorable encounters took place in the same night.

BERGHAIN / PANORAMA BAR, BERLIN; SUNDAY, FEBRUARY 15, 2009

ABOUT 6:00 A.M.

On my way up to Panorama Bar from the Berghain dancefloor, I decide to take the less noisy, less crowded path through the club's smoking area, which consists of a glass-enclosed external stairway between the two floors. As I walk out of the darkness of Berghain into the mottled gray light of a cloudy Berlin morning, a young man heading in the other direction stops me.

"Hey, don't you know Natalie?"

"Yeah, I do! I rented a room in her apartment last summer."

I didn't recognize him at all, but admittedly Natalie and I only spent a couple of weeks socializing together before she left for the United States. I apologize to my interlocutor for not having recognized him, claiming that I had a poor memory for faces. He informs me that Natalie is now living in Lichtenberg, which strikes me as odd, considering that I know she has gone to the US Midwest to spend time with her grandfather while he undergoes a medical operation. When I mention this, he insists that she is in fact still living in the Berlin suburbs. I bring up the possibility that we're talking about different Natalies, but he will hear none of it: he recognizes me; we both know the same woman; and that makes us friends.

After trying a few more times to explain that our stories of Natalie are irreconcilable, I eventually acquiesce, tell him that it was nice to meet a friend of Natalie's, and move on. Still, I am impressed by how assertive he was in recruiting me to his intimate world, exerting considerable social force to conjure a relationship into existence.

ABOUT 8:00 A.M.

I am up in Panorama Bar, right next to the DJ booth where Matthew Styles is currently spinning. Dancing next to me is a young man in a white tank top, of stocky build, with a "fauxhawk" (a less dramatic version of the classic punk

"Mohawk" haircut) and glitter on his cheekbones. He makes eye contact with me while we are dancing, and we spend a moment mirroring each other's gestures—fist pumping, finger pointing, hand clapping—and exchanging expressions of pleasure and approval, as if we were bringing ourselves into affective alignment through our response to the music. There is something about this scene—dancing to house and techno for hours on end, in close confines, crossing glances, in comparable states of physical exertion, and with particular moments of musical intensity synchronizing our gestural responses—that prompts my neighbor to reach out to me. He grabs his beer, takes a swig, and then offers it to me. I take it and thank him, and he leans in and says, "Trinken ist wichtig!" (Drinking is important), and goes back to dancing. About four hours later, I will offer him my own drink and repeat the same phrase back to him.

AROUND NOON

As I'm passing through the smoking area again, two young men strike up conversation with me. One has long blond bangs falling over one of his eyes, a small lip ring, cargo pants, and heavy yellow boots. The other is wearing similar pants and boots but instead has a large tongue piercing and an unspiked Mohawk lying flaccidly across his scalp. Judging from their half-lidded eyes and their grinding jaws, I presume that they are high on ecstasy, or MDMA, which also goes some way toward explaining their insistent friendliness. They introduce themselves as recent transplants to Berlin from a small town in Bavaria. Then they listen patiently as I slowly tell my own story, frequently pausing to search for the right word in German or to calculate the right declination of articles and adverbs. It is often hard to practice one's German in the Berlin techno scene, as many young Berliners will switch to English at the first sign of difficulty. These two, however, let me work it all out in German, suggesting vocabulary when necessary and speaking to me in moderately paced, clearly articulated phrases. Not only are they patient, but they exert a real effort to sustain and support the conversation where others might have switched into English for expediency (or simply abandoned the conversation entirely). Considering the transience of most contact in a nightclub context, I am struck by their commitment to sustain this conversation—or, considering the state they are in, perhaps it is merely inertia.

In the first encounter, my interlocutor was relentless in pushing past the apparent contradictions between our accounts of an allegedly mutual friend, insisting that we were socially linked; it was as if his initial sense of recognition and connection overrode the factual inconsistencies that surfaced as we picked away at the vagueness between us. In the second encounter, a moment of shared musical enjoyment prompts us to exchange gestures of care and resource sharing with surprisingly familiarity, without introductions or the exchange of names and pleasantries. And the final encounter relates a moment of remarkable friendliness, as two partygoers demonstrated a surprising commitment to sustaining friendly interaction, despite laborious communication. There is a kind of cohesiveness apparent in "that intimacy of not knowing each other, but still having something to say to each other" (Lisette, Paris, 2009).

As places of leisure, nightclubs offer a zone of escape from everyday societal control through an atmosphere of relaxed rules, suspended responsibilities, expanded possibilities, and pleasures unburdened by guilt or sanction. But these refuges are both socially fragile and vulnerable to violence, and so they often employ exclusionary practices that, under the guise of protection, run counter to the ethos of inclusivity and equality that has been historically important in popular electronic dance music scenes.[13] This ethos came partly from the continuities between disco in the 1970s and the early "garage" and "house" scenes of the 1980s, which not only thrived in the same communities but also absorbed themes of love, liberty, and transcendence from disco's gospel-inflected songs.[14] An overlapping set of ideals also came to post-disco dance music from the echoes of "hippie" psychedelic counterculture that resonated in British "acid-house" scenes during the late 1980s, carrying into the more global "rave" scene of the 1990s.[15] In fact, contemporary commentators dubbed the 1989 explosion of rave parties in the United Kingdom the "Second Summer of Love," explicitly drawing ties to the hippie "Summer of Love" of 1967–1969.[16]

This tension between ethos and practice has the potential to create awkward moments of dissonance. And so, partygoers tend to avoid explicit discussion about norms and belonging, which in turn affords an optimistic or "reparative" reading of this avoidance as tacit consensus about a shared code of ethics.[17] In other words, there is a sort of feedback loop of conflict avoidance and wishful thinking, where the latter encourages the former, and the former makes the latter tenable. This self-amplifying loop could be dismissed pessimistically as hypocrisy or false consciousness, but that would overlook the ways in which such strategic vagueness can make the seemingly impossible fleetingly possible. Such vagueness provides cover for a risky performance of community across diversity; and it works like a charm—until it doesn't. This much is clear in the words of Norwood, who points to shared norms in electronic music scenes while also asserting that this sense of consensus cannot withstand much scrutiny.

> **NORWOOD:** I think, with certain people . . . they shouldn't fill in the blanks. They assume that similarity goes beyond the particular context. . . . In the broader context of social interaction with one another at a rave or a techno party, people just assume that the people they associate with share some kind of—I don't know, what do you want to call it?—social norms or similar ideas about the situation, whatever it may be.
>
> It's about being satisfied with just the contact and not pushing this need to know more than what the situation is going to allow. Going with it. Going with the flow [*laughs*]. (Chicago, 2010)

During this interview, Norwood reached back to the early disco era to trace a legacy of dance music parties that, in his view, provides sufficient cultural scaffolding to serve as a basis for social interaction without explicit instruction. But he was also quick to point out that this implicitness leaves "blanks" in one's knowledge of fellow partygoers and, furthermore, that these blanks are best left unfilled. Hailing from the same Chicago techno scene as Norwood, Nick reflected on stranger-intimacy by recounting how his perception of it shifted as he became more socially engrained at techno parties:

> **NICK:** I remember having moments, when you first get into the party scene, where everything's, like . . . awesome, right? [*laughs*]. Everybody's cool, everybody's fun. And then having a few periods of, "Do these people really care about me?" You know, "Is this really real? Or is this just a role that we all play when we go out to these parties?" But, fortunately, in the end, time has proven that a lot of real friendships persisted and developed. But there were moments—especially when you're in a crowd of mostly strangers, where, at first, you feel like, "Yeah! Even though we're all strangers, everyone's cool!" But then, when the veil gets lifted a little further, you realize, "Well, there is some politicking going on. . . ." You know, "That guy . . . he's kind of taking advantage of people a little bit" or "This person, they're not actually that super; they're not as friendly as they seem." (Chicago, 2010)

Nick highlighted the fragility of felt intimacy at Chicago techno parties, as strangers become acquaintances and the messy complications of "real life" seep in. It seems as if avoiding "filling in the blanks," as Norwood put it, protects stranger-intimacy from some of this corrosion. By leaving these gaps in place, he believes, partygoers are able to project their own identities and values outward onto the surrounding crowd, thereby presuming more commonalities than probably exist in reality. In describing the sociability of dance music scenes in this way, Norwood also revealed a crucial insight about liquidarity: partygoers avoid explicit talk of norms not only because doing so postpones dealing with awkward contradictions but also because this reticence allows them to build a sense of vague belonging *on top of* these contradictions. In this context, vagueness figures less as an absence of something than as a blurry, shifting, coalescing semipresence. The practice of liquidarity, then, is the use of such fluid conditions to support social interaction. This definition also foreshadows the importance of atmosphere: liquidarity sustains an intimate world on the merest whiff of sociability.

Additive Taste

> **NICK:** We're in the scene, and we know the people we know because we like the music. And that's how we've made the connections we've made. It's not because we wanna go to cool parties. It's not because we wanna find drugs. It's because we like the music and we meet people who also like the music that we like. And from there, everything grows. (Chicago, 2010)

During interviews, I asked partygoers first to provide an example of an event where they experienced a strong sense of cohesion and then to give their thoughts on what contributed to that sense. Their examples and hypotheses were diverse, but they tended to cluster around two models of collective cohesion, which I characterize here as *additive* and *subtractive*. What I mean by "additive" is that some explanations posited a common factor, like musical taste, that sutured the crowd together. "Subtractive" explanations, on the other hand, credited the removal or occlusion of factors that would hamper the cultivation of solidarity. Both of these modes of explanation resonate in turn with several streams of scholarship on collective life. Most anthropological/sociological accounts of collectivity—such as taste communities, tribal totems, and group leaders—could be described as additive, in that their explanatory power rests on the addition or presence of a unifying element.[18] Conversely, theories that emphasize the dissolution of social bonds and hierarchies, such as ritual *communitas* or anonymity in crowd behavior, align well with subtractive theories.[19]

Although Norwood's and Nick's reflections on social vagueness could stand as an example of a subtractive account of crowd cohesion, the most widely repeated theory of dancefloor collectivity among interviewees was in fact an additive one: musical taste. Maintained by nearly everyone I interviewed, this hypothesis assumed that a shared taste in music indexed other commonalities and similarities—or at least it assured a degree of compatibility in face-to-face interactions. During interviews, partygoers were unanimous in prioritizing music and musical taste as an additive factor for social cohesion at parties. For them, "our music" attracted people of a particular sensory, corporeal, and aesthetic attunement, and this shared attunement would ensure a degree of deep similarity, despite apparent differences—kindred spirits, in other words, where musical taste represents something essential and ineffable about mind, body, and soul. There is undoubtedly some selection bias at work here: in interviewing people who identify with a particular music genre and whose social networks have largely developed through music scenes, it is hardly surprising that they would all consider music as the foremost factor of affinity in their social worlds. This could be understood as a musically specific version of a pattern that Sarah Thornton observes in UK clubbers' accounts of "the rightness and naturalness" of those crowds to which they feel they belong, where "the experience is not one of conformity, but of spontaneous affinity."[20] Fantômette, for example, sees cohesion on the dancefloor as a matter of self-selection along lines of musical taste:

> **FANTÔMETTE:** The tribes that listen to rock, pop, and other such concert genres . . . aren't the same as the tribes that listen to electronic music. And so, they don't have the same lifestyles, they don't have the same codes; and so their behaviors are distinct, too. (Paris, 2009)

While there may be overlap between these audiences, Fantômette emphasizes the power of musical taste to sort and group identities. Later in the interview, when we returned to discussing music's relationship to dancefloor intimacy, she rearticulated this view in stronger terms, while clarifying that these affinities may attach to particular locations or fine-grained distinctions between substyles, drawing a contrast between the typical *minimale* establishments in Paris at the time (such as Le Rex, Batofar, Le Léopard) and the more upscale clubs that played more mainstream "techno" (such as Le Showcase, Social Club, Paris Paris).

> LUIS: In your opinion, what sort of role does music play on the dancefloor? What are its effects?
>
> FANTÔMETTE: In my opinion, the first effect happens upstream, that is, according to the music—the artists who are chosen to play at a party that features music. That brings out a certain category of people, primarily folks who listen to electronic music. [Our group of friends] tend to hang out in relatively specialist music circles—that's what I know the best; that's what I can tell you about—and so this attracts that population. In my view, [music's] first effect lies therein.
>
> LUIS: A form of self-selection, then?
>
> FANTÔMETTE: Voilà. At first, selection comes into play through music—well, through musical tastes. . . . Take a party playing *électro minimale*, the sound we listen to, and you'll see the kind of person that it attracts; you'll see the behaviors—you'll see, more or less, the sociocultural milieu. You'll see the level of wealth, the clothing. You'll see all those things. When you go to a party at Social Club or Showcase, for example, they're still playing electronic music, but it's not exactly the same sound; and so you'll notice that.
>
> LUIS: The crowd changes, in any case.
>
> FANTÔMETTE: Voilà. The crowd changes. At different sociocultural levels, the behaviors are different. And you'll find your tribe based more or less on the sound that you choose. (Paris, 2009)

You "find your tribe," according to Fantômette, by choosing your sound. "Sound" (*le son*) is a metonym for musical style in this instance, and yet she clearly explains how it also functions as a synecdoche for a whole sociocultural world of class, clothing, and comportment. Electronic music's "sounds" serve as portals into *soundworlds*: realms of feeling, aesthetics, lore, and rituals organized around a shared affinity for particular kinds of sounds. Layered and interpolated together, niche soundworlds like minimal techno or dubstep or nu-disco combine into a dynamic system that could be considered an electronic dance music *scene*, which combines in turn with other coexisting music scenes (such as salsa or dancehall) to constitute a given city's nightclub *ecology*. Soundworlds help us understand why the seemingly slender differences of musical style matter so much to partygoers, who by identifying themselves with a particular sound can also associate themselves with complex configurations of social status and cultural identity, *but without having to discuss them explicitly*. Notably, although Fantômette's account is exceptional for how clearly she links musical taste to sociocultural milieu, she nonetheless stops short of specifying *which* social class corresponds to each style of music. Sound-as-style thus serves as a conveniently fluid placeholder for soundworlds that remain underdefined and in flux, enabling partygoers to lay claim to a sonic community that is aspirational and always in the making. This also helps to understand the constant proliferation of new, niche styles of electronic dance music—especially during "boom" cycles of increased popularity—where each new "sound" signals an opportunity to reframe and reshape an emergent soundworld, along with the people who call it home.

Over in Chicago, Polina also noticed correlations between shared taste and a range of possible commonalities that indexed class, mobility, and cosmopolitanism. While recounting how she found and joined a network of "minimal techno" and "deep house / minimal house" fans—her "tribe," in Fantômette's terms—she described a moment of recognition: "I was, like, 'Woah! There are people who are actually smart and worldly and know so much and [are] well traveled . . . and just like me.' And, just like me, they love electronic music" (Chicago, 2010). Nick told a similar "find your people" narrative, although he placed less emphasis on specific musical styles mapping to sociocultural niches and more on his enthusiasm for music in general, his "music geek" identity. Notably, he described how his musical tastes evolved as his life circumstances changed and his musical connoisseurship deepened, thus drawing him into new soundworlds:

> **NICK:** Well, it started from music, just being a music fan and a music geek. It was kind of a natural [process] for me, a natural evolution of going from college house parties, when there were punk bands and local bands, to getting old enough to go to bars, where there was music, to then eventually meeting more people and getting to know where the better parties were [*laughs*] and better music. As my taste in music evolved, so did the types of parties and events that I went to. (Chicago, 2010)

Although the accounts of Nick, Polina, and Fantômette are remarkable for the connections they trace between taste, identity, and belonging, similar narratives are extremely common across all of the interviews I conducted (as well as in the countless informal conversations I had with partygoers at parties). The following three interview excerpts are presented together as a representative cross-section of these narratives, sharing themes of music-driven discovery and subcultural recognition—albeit with some ambivalence in the final example.

> TERESA: Most of the people in my high school had no idea that it was going on; they didn't know about it or didn't care about it, whichever it was. And, all of a sudden, I'd find myself amongst another forty or fifty people who kind of felt the same way that I did about the music, and I just loved that sort of . . . small community. . . . Maybe these aren't people you're going to keep in really good touch with, but you still kinda look forward to seeing them in that sort of situation in the future. And it's a sort of relationship that exists that—you know, it's not really maintained in any other way but through the parties. (Chicago, 2010)

> LOLA: Honestly, I feel like the first thing that always brings us together—whether it's on the dancefloor in a completely different city where you don't know anybody to where you know the people and you see them every weekend—it's the music. And I think that music is the first kind of binding element that brings people together. And then you look around, and everyone's having a good time, and I really—I can't tell you the number of times that I would leave [a well-known Chicago club] being, like, obviously rolling [high on ecstasy] and all happy: Wow! You love everybody! (Chicago, 2010)

> FRANCK: I think that I don't party because I like to, but because I ended up doing it. That is to say, at the beginning, I didn't go clubbing at all, because I always preferred places where people could get a bit closer, like after-work drinks at a friend's place, that sort of thing. But it turned out that—well, I always loved the music. I discovered that, in the club, I could play it, and that's how I wound up going out clubbing. It was when I started playing records, which I loved doing, that I had to start going out. Things went in that direction. I didn't devote myself to music because I liked nightclubs; I came to like nightclubs because I loved the music, and I loved to play records. (Paris, 2009)

Sounds may be portals to soundworlds, but they are not open to everyone. In Franck's case, he loved the sound but not the soundworld, and yet he eventually adapted to it. In other cases, someone may love the sound *and* the soundworld but find themselves excluded from the latter, whether through barriers to entry (such as high entry fees) or a hostile environment (such as classist and racist microaggressions). First-person narratives of such exclusion were largely absent from interviews, perhaps due to the overall whiteness of the interviewees I managed to recruit for this project and probably due to employing "snowball sampling" from *within* music-scene networks and thus selecting those who had already succeeded in accessing these soundworlds. Nonetheless, these interviews provided some enlightening examples of how partygoers' accounts of musical taste as an additive theory of social cohesion can be as much about attrition as it is about attraction.

Musical taste, according to some interviewees, has the benefit of filtering out undesirably undercommitted partygoers when combined with certain obstacles to entry. Such obstacles might include an elevated entry fee, a remote venue, a secluded or hidden venue, admission restricted to personal acquaintances and/or "regulars," event promotion restricted to word-of-mouth and social networks, and unconventional or inconvenient operating hours. When I asked these interviewees to describe how this process of taste-based filtration worked, they suggested that partygoers with a stronger affinity to the particular style of music offered at a party would be more likely to dedicate their resources to attending than those whose interests and motivations were focused elsewhere. Allegedly, only dedicated fans of such music would value the anticipated musical experience over the costs of attendance. Fantômette, for example, credited both the remote venue and the inclement weather for the cohesion she felt among the crowd at Mobilee Records' "Summer Soirée" party (August 27–28, 2008). Located at the now-defunct Funkpark Rechenzentrum in Rummelsburg (an eastern suburb of Berlin), the weekend-long event was far removed from the city's usual nightlife districts. Fantômette spent nearly an hour biking in the rain, getting lost several times before finally reaching the venue.

> FANTÔMETTE: When we went to Rechenzentrum, in Berlin . . . it was really far away; getting there was a bit of an ordeal. You really had to be motivated. And once you're there, a sort of *écrémage* [skimming] has already taken place. This makes it such that the only people one finds there are those who are there for the music, who are motivated,

who are in a special state of mind, which in principle brings them together—well, ultimately, everyone there was close to one another. (Paris, 2009)

This process of *écrémage*, of social filtration through inconvenience, may contribute to stranger-intimacy, but at the cost of inclusivity. In fact, it ends up encoding many factors of privilege in the process of excluding those who are deemed likely to behave in antisocial ways. First, financial obstacles are a very blunt instrument for filtration, prone to selecting for socioeconomic class as much as taste-based "motivation." The effectiveness of financial barriers to entry as taste-based *écrémage* is limited by the financial resources of each individual partygoer; for example, an elevated admission price may present no obstacle at all to a wealthier casual partygoer while at the same time proving insurmountable to a poorer but nonetheless passionate music fan. Second, the reliance on social networks to avoid high-profile public advertising and/or to decide who gets in provides an advantage to those who are well connected socially, even if they do not share the passion for the local scene's music that interviewees considered so important; in other words, social networks can override musical taste. Third, the same applies for people who may not feel drawn to a minimal party by their musical tastes but whose entry is nonetheless facilitated by scene insiders due to other forms of social capital (such as connections to important record labels or booking agencies, perceived coolness or attractiveness, access to materials/venues for holding future events, or access to drugs). Finally, this model assumes that musical taste would be the only force driving a potential partygoer's desire to attend a party, but this ignores other factors that may drive attendance, such as the soundworld's "mainstream" exposure (that is, how discoverable it is for casual partygoers), "buzz" within the scene (such as overexposed venues/events that become "victims of their own success"), performing artists who have developed a high profile (like "superstar" DJs such as Ricardo Villalobos or Richie Hawtin during the early 2000s), and the increased motivation *and* budgets of out-of-town visitors (such as "techno-tourists" in Berlin).[21]

Nearly all of these mitigating factors are at play in Berlin, and it seems hardly coincidental that the city's club scenes have developed forms of filtration that are more conspicuously exclusionary than in Paris or Chicago, such as door staff running a "hard" or "tight" (that is, exclusive) door. In addition to the aforementioned "soft" obstacles to entry, many interviewees credited nightclub bouncers with providing a final layer of "hard" exclusion for undesirable partygoers. Bouncers and nightclub door policies remain uncomfortable topics for most of my fieldwork contacts; since participants in contemporary electronic dance music scenes tend to see themselves as inheritors of the 1990s rave movement and/or 1970s disco, an ethos of egalitarianism and open access still remains important to them. This ethos comes into direct conflict with the exclusionary practices of many nightclubs, and this contradiction tends to be buried in silence, circumlocution, and ambivalence. None of my contacts broached this issue on their own during interviews; and when prompted by me, most discussed it with unease: some derided and rejected the entire system, some defended it, but most expressed ambivalence. Ambivalent respondents argued that, when done "well," it kept out disruptive partygoers, but they were uncomfortable with the fact that such judgments were usually made on appearances.

Marie, a Parisian clubber in her midthirties working at a performing-arts promotion company, was active in the final years of the rave scene in the south of France. She suggested that bouncers and door policies have come to replace a subtler means of selection from the rave era. "The selection is 'Who knows?' It's the person who'll follow the flyers, who has a car—I lived through that, and it was great" (Paris, 2009). The use of alternative media channels for advertising, obscure locations, and complicated directions ensured a certain degree of (self-)selection for those who successfully found a rave party. During the 1990s, most events were advertised solely through the distribution of flyers at community record shops and word of mouth. They were located in remote, hidden, and often illicit venues that were usually disclosed only hours before the event to those who called a phone line or met at an intermediary location for directions or communal transport. As with Fantômette's earlier anecdote about going to Funkpark Rechenzentrum, exclusivity was built on inconvenience as a litmus test for musical affinity and commitment to "the scene."

While the implications of "door work" are examined in more detail in chapter 6, afterparties and "underground parties" serve as interesting examples of collective selection that further complicate this commonly held belief in musical taste as an additive factor for social cohesion. In Chicago, for example, private "loft parties" and illicit events in temporary-use commercial/industrial spaces were common around the end of the first decade of this century, especially since most clubs would close around 2:00 or 3:00 A.M. News of afterparties was usually disseminated by word of mouth through organizers and their friends, on the dancefloor or near the exits of established venues like SmartBar, and in the final hour before closing.

Souvenir, the minimal party series featured in the opening anecdote of chapter 1, was a more public-facing underground party that was promoted through printed flyers, but there were also several semiregular loft after-parties that acquired nicknames like "Club Regret," where the access to the hosts' private parties was managed through social networks and vouching. At Club Regret, for example, admission was initially based on whether the hosts recognized you as a friend when you knocked on their door at the appointed time; friends could bring one or two companions (and were responsible for their behavior at the party), but unaccompanied strangers would be turned away. In such cases, selection was not a matter of either/or but both/and: in the moment, at the door, access was only obtained through social connections, and yet those who had such connections cultivated them through sustained participation in the wider music scene. That said, building such social connections can be a difficult task for partygoers who are already marginalized in these contexts; despite their best efforts, their peers may be reluctant to forge bonds of trust with them, due to latent prejudices (such as misogyny, racism, transphobia, ableism). There is a way in through music, sure, but it is not smooth for everyone.

Thus, selection by musical taste ultimately provides a convenient but troublesome mode of passive social sorting, which can be easily subverted by other factors that, in turn, prompt "harder" and more conspicuous exclusionary practices. Both this logic of filtration and its resulting inequities bear a resemblance to the process of distinction as described by Pierre Bourdieu, where the divisions of social class are signaled and reproduced through "cultural capital" (or "subcultural capital" in this instance)—that is, education, styles of dress, modes of speaking, and behavioral codes that can provide privileged access to exclusive social worlds.[22] In the context of Bourdieu's work, "taste" becomes more than an ineffable faculty of appreciation and affection; it also encodes one's upbringing, influences, capacities, and resources. And so, if taste is imparted and cultivated along lines of social class, then filters of musical taste can also function as subtle, surreptitious filters of class.

The additive models of taste put forward by my fieldwork contacts have much in common with scholarship that theorizes the interconnections between taste, consumer culture, and identity formation. For example, the notion of "taste communities" emerges out of a line of research that traces the ways in which taste and class are socially articulated, such that "personal" preferences also serve as a powerful index of class, whether through "high"/"low" distinctions or "omnivore"/"univore" distinctions.[23] But rather than treat taste as an expression of class—as a sort of coded language or symptom of socioeconomic hierarchies—the analysis of taste communities focuses on how taste also expresses and generates new categories of belonging. More precisely, this scholarship tends to emphasize how the social clustering made possible by shared taste can forge identities that do not conform to conventional notions of class.[24] This focus on the socially binding and identity-shaping capacities of taste closely resembles the accounts that many of my interviewees made, with one exception: these partygoers never spoke of identities in more specific terms than "music lover" or "fellow fans." For them, musical taste instead produced cohesive crowds and a sense of belonging without a clear sense of group identity. Furthermore, accounts foregrounding identity formation through taste risk endorsing a fantasy of consumerist self-fashioning, where one can "buy in" to identity at will, whereas, in light of my earlier critique of the filtration-through-inconvenience model, the lines of division created by patterns of shared taste sometimes follow very familiar class striations—particularly with regard to financial, cultural, and social capital.

A pattern emerges through these accounts of belonging through musical affinity: details about the means and conditions of membership are avoided or downplayed, while vague and primarily aesthetic-affective accounts provide more satisfying narratives of open belonging. In general, interviewees preferred to discuss vaguely inclusive models of shared musical taste rather than more explicitly exclusive practices that often hinged on appearances, privilege, social capital, or identity-class. All the while, such vagueness nonetheless permits these distinctions to operate unnoticed and largely undisturbed. There is a conflict here between an ethos of inclusivity that has been historically important to post-disco nightlife scenes and a desire to gather a crowd that is somehow harmonious and compatible. This tension between desires for inclusivity and intimacy—for a space both welcoming and protected—is apparent in my interviews with scene participants, whose aspirations for simple and unproblematic belonging seem to discourage a more deliberate consideration of the messy and often discomfiting details of such belonging. Instead, interviewees preferred vague explanations that preserved a sense of ethical coherence: vague conflations of shared musical taste and compatible social norms; vague notions of how affective attachments to music engender affinities with people who have similar attachments; and a vague calculus of motivation, effort, resources, and obstacles that justifies why some people never make it (in)to the party. This vagueness is thus operative, productive, and perhaps necessary for the maintenance of a sense of "easy" belonging in heterogeneous crowds; here, vagueness is not so much a loss of coherence but rather a condition of cohesion's imaginative possibility. In other words, rather than vagueness being seen as merely a lack of information that hinders togetherness, it should also be understood here as a productive tactic that supports aspirations toward a wider, more open belonging.

Subtractive Nighttime

While many interviewees explained the coherence of crowds at minimal parties by positing a common factor such as musical taste to bring them together, some also pointed to the removal of something that would normally hinder cohesion. Most of these subtractive theories had to do with nocturnal settings and their tendency to relax inhibitions, blur hierarchies, and suspend some of the antagonisms of daytime life. For many of the partygoers whom I interviewed, nightlife settings (even when they extend into daylight hours) somehow liquify the self-protective carapace of polite distance that impedes stranger-intimacy in everyday life. This phenomenon was often described in terms of "barriers" that fall away in nocturnal settings, such as in the following interview excerpt from Lisette, who began with an additive account of musical taste and then pivoted to a focus on nighttime and its subtractive capacities:

> LISETTE: There's already a coming together through the music; the fact that we choose the same dancefloor, we like the same music, that already shows that people are coming together—already a point in common. Generally speaking, I find that people come together at night. The barriers really fall at night. So, on the dancefloor, it really is much more flagrant, in terms of "intimacy on the dancefloor." (Paris 2009)

> MARIE: Another reason [for intimacy on the dancefloor] is that techno parties, by the hours of operation, the venues—well, these are the circumstances where you'd want to meet people who love this music; you already want to meet people that you wouldn't meet in another context, I think, or an exterior context. . . . Well, the fact that it's nighttime and . . . well . . . all of the substances that you might be familiar with, I think that makes for a sort of collective atmosphere that is general. . . . Imagine: you look at your watch—compared to

your normal schedule—and you're dancing and drinking and so on. You're already in a truly open disposition of mind; and so, you can talk much more easily to people, to everyone. (Paris, 2009)

Marie also claimed that something about nighttime creates an *ambiance collective*, an atmosphere of collectivity, suggesting that the temporal dislocation of being awake and active at night dislodges daytime mentalities while also creating social openings. Marie coyly referenced intoxicants along with nighttime as factors that contribute to this collective atmosphere. Perhaps Marie understood these two factors to operate in similar ways or to have comparable effects. Indeed, if alcohol and "club drugs" (such as MDMA/ecstasy or ketamine) impart an altered state of consciousness on partygoers that enables more adventurous socializing and intimacy, perhaps nightlife settings (as functionally designed spaces and subcultural worlds) impart their own subtle altered states, as they pleasurably disorient partygoers through sensory overload and flipped temporalities.

Such accounts suggest that the everyday conventions of stranger-sociability loosen or dissolve in nightlife contexts, thus creating a space where intensified and riskier forms of stranger-intimacy can be ventured. For many interviewees, the sense of freedom and possibility that they associate with electronic music venues also extends to nightlife in general, with its promise of release from the strictures of one's daytime identity—however partial and fleeting they may be. Imogen highlighted how the stresses and frustrations of everyday life can be alleviated at nightlife events:

> IMOGEN: When I'm feeling frustrated or feeling just not . . . not *happy* with my surroundings, it's good to know you can meet up with your friends—on the dancefloor in particular—and you don't have to ask how my shitty job is going. You don't have to ask about how my failed relationships are going. You don't have to ask about how my parents' health is doing. All that kind of evaporates, and it's just, "How are *you* doing, in general?" "So good to see you." "Let's get it out of our systems." (Chicago, 2010)

For Imogen, this repertoire of dancefloor sociability avoids bringing up one's "real" life, focusing instead on the affective pleasures of the moment: social warmth, companionship, collective catharsis, and intimacy—a sense of emotional closeness *without* detailed interpersonal knowledge.

In addition to blurring socially prescribed norms of casual contact and self-presentation, then, nighttime is also subtractive through its association with at least partial anonymity—some of which is actively cultivated through participants' avoidance of "personal" or "real-life" topics in conversation. Here we see the social vagueness described earlier by Norwood and Nick being characterized as a virtue of nightlife contexts, enabling partygoers to project a sense of belonging and communion onto a crowd of strangers. It would seem that the biographical vagueness Imogen described allows partygoers not only to temporarily ignore those life circumstances that hinder their efforts to have fun but also to overlook the personal details that could be a source of antagonism and alienating difference. Although several interviewees hinted at this in various ways, Fantômette explicitly argued that the lack of detailed interpersonal knowledge among partygoers serves as a way of forestalling recognition of differences that might undermine a sense of intimacy and belonging on the dancefloor.[25] In a manner similar to Imogen, she enumerated the gaps in knowledge that partygoers have about their fellow dancers:

> FANTÔMETTE: When you look at the majority of people you'll encounter on a night out, you know their first names, [but] you don't even know their last names; you don't know about jobs; you don't know their brothers and sisters—you don't know. As a result, you have fewer of those social barriers that you might have in the daytime. Or, in any case, you don't self-impose these barriers because of social or cultural differences or money. (Paris, 2009)

For Fantômette, such biographical details prompt people to put up interpersonal barriers based on sociocultural differences, and so their absence enables partygoers to more easily reach out and connect with each other. Notably, she characterized most social contacts in nightlife as *embryonnaire* (embryonic), suggesting that these connections feel like they are still developing, although they may not develop into the more conventionally intimate relationships they seem to promise. Her word choice suggests an important affective aspect of these vague relations: they provide a feeling of an emergent, more stable, more enduring, more deeply entwined relationship that may never materialize.

Such avoidance of explicit personal discourse has also been described as an adaptive strategy for diversity in Kiri Miller's study of North American shape-note ("Sacred Harp") singing conventions. Miller describes participants as representing a wide range of political, religious, and socioeconomic affiliations, and some of them are staunch political opponents: "the active-duty troops in the 'culture wars.'"[26] To some extent, this is managed by a shared narrative both of resistance to a perceived mainstream and of homecoming among fellow outsiders; but these narratives "tend to essentialize both mainstream society and marginal communities," which creates space for a broader sense of belonging—so long as the details of what counts as "mainstream" and "margin" are not openly discussed.[27] In a similar fashion, public discourse at shape-note conventions avoids discussion of politics, religion, and class; indeed, there is a socially enforced "separation of spheres" at these gatherings, which is doubly articulated as a separation between activities (singing and speaking) as well as between social realms (shape-note gatherings and "private" life).[28] Similar norms and boundaries are at play at minimal parties—albeit perhaps not so sharply and viscerally enforced as Miller describes them to be at shape-note gatherings—where the focus on music, dancing, and embodied copresence keeps fellow partygoers from discovering too much about each other.

This attempted erasure of social hierarchies through collective musical activity resonates with the notion of *communitas* as it has been developed in anthropological scholarship on ritual.[29] *Communitas* is associated with the middle, "liminal" phase of transformative ritual, after initial social ties have been unraveled but before new ones have been fastened. During this phase, ritual participants form a kind of unstructured community that is de facto egalitarian due to the dissolution or suspension of socially legible identity; in other words, the unraveling of identity also undoes hierarchies, albeit temporarily. *Communitas*, in turn, is the feeling of this kind of untethered collectivity, its affective shape. For Victor Turner, to be in this second phase of the ritual is to be in a state of liminality, where *communitas* takes the form of a structurelessness ("anti-structure") that allows for the reorganization and renewal of society. Considering that ritual was a central concern of subcultural studies—which in turn was one of the first disciplines to study electronic dance music scenes in the late 1980s and early 1990s—*communitas* has a strong precedent as an analytic framework in electronic dance music studies.[30]

Despite this trend, however, I have reservations about its applicability to the minimal parties studied in this book, based on two aspects of *communitas*: first, its theoretical grounding in transformative life-cycle rituals ("rites of passage"); and second, its presumption of internal egalitarianism. A night out at a minimal party rarely results in a radical transformation of social role, and it rarely involves the high stakes of life-cycle rituals, such as those that accompany birth, adolescence, death, adulthood, religious initiation, or marriage. With regard to egalitarianism—and despite participants' efforts to downplay inequities and awkward differences—minimal parties are undeniably striated by hierarchies of scene-specific capital (e.g., coolness, social connectedness, esoteric musical knowledge, DJ and music-producing proficiency, attractiveness, wealth), so it is not clear that these events enact the consensual and "joyful" leveling of social structure that is supposed to arise in liminal activities.[31] Nonetheless, this paradigm explains how the nocturnal slackening of social structure allows for the enactment of fantasies of community and the feeling (if not always the practice) of *communitas*. In the archetypal ritual envisioned by ritual studies, such slackening usually occurs through some ritualized and symbolic stripping of social caste; at minimal parties, however, similar effects are achieved through mostly anonymous crowds and their capacity to temporarily release partygoers from their own identities.

For Fantômette, Imogen, Marie, Lisette, and several other interviewees, it is not so much what nighttime adds to a party that makes a crowd come together but rather what it subtracts: inhibition, identity, responsibility, polite distance, formality, and the habitual patterns of everyday life. In this sense, nocturnal settings dissolve blockages in the flow of affect and the cultivation of intimacy on the dancefloor. Here, a lack of interpersonal knowledge blurs differences, loosening normative social bonds articulated around difference and thus clearing the way for other forms of togetherness. It is worth noting the seemingly contradictory link that interviewees make between structural disruption and socioaffective cohesion, a sort of inverse relation that also surfaces in ritual studies. In their accounts, the social solidification of crowds occurs when some of the more restrictive structures of "normal" life slacken or disappear from view. These metaphorical collisions of fixity and mobility, apparent in these accounts from partygoers, support my choice of "liquidarity" as a term that combines both solidity and fluidity. It is this counterintuitive association of melting social structure with thickening sociality that is at the heart of what I understand to be liquidarity.

Ambivalent Liquidarity

Reliant on vagueness and laden with affect, scenes of liquidarity could be considered "intimate publics." In *The Female Complaint*, Lauren Berlant defines an intimate public as a public sphere where participants presume that they "*already* share a worldview and emotional knowledge that they have derived from a broadly common historical experience."[32] Berlant develops this definition from a study of "women's culture," which they frame as a scene of cultural production and consumption—a scene to which its participants expect to belong, based on their belief that the affective shape of women's lives are generic enough to be shared.[33] They use the term "generic" here to recast femininity (and identity in general) as a genre, that is, as a structure of expectation that absorbs details and differences to present a more stable singularity through its generality. In other words, genres are bundles of conventions and expectations that subsume divergence as variations on a generic scheme. An intimate public based on generic womanhood thus has "porous boundaries and complex attachments," which make it possible to imagine belonging to a larger world—but which also serve to obfuscate the underlying antagonisms and contradictions that would otherwise endanger this fragile sense of community.[34] Indeed, with Berlant's focus on the complex intersections between gender, sexuality, race, and class in early American melodramatic film (i.e., "women's films"), they find ample evidence of how social inequities and asymmetrical relationships can be folded away under the generic solidarity of womanhood.

What is germane to the concept of liquidarity here is that Berlant's intimate public does not exist in spite of its own incoherence about what makes it cohere but rather *thrives* on it. Like the fluid forms of solidarity attendant at minimal parties, an intimate public produces scenes of recognition and feelings of belonging without providing the details of how such recognition and belonging could come to be; counterintuitively, this lack of detail is actually what makes such experiences possible for their consumers. Indeed, it seems that the interpersonal vagueness of dancefloor settings prompts partygoers to rely instead on intuition and inference when deciding how to engage with others, as a means of managing social uncertainty. During an interview with Franck, as we were discussing how "party friends" manage to cultivate a sense of ethical responsibility to each other without discussing it explicitly, he stressed the importance of intuition in guiding our interactions with others:

FRANCK: All that, it's suggested. It's suggested by attitudes. But I think that's what makes us continue to see each other—us and not others—for the time being; and afterwards, there'll be others who come along. . . . One doesn't just set out rules; there is no table with numbered rules. There's just a culture of each person that we suggest to each other through our behavior, through our manner of speaking; through all that, which is why we feel closer to one another . . . than to others. It's very simple. Well, all of that converges with what we were saying a moment ago about intuition at soirées, which will lead us to approach one person more than another. Ultimately, it's the same thing! . . . It's vague, but it's not random, . . . nor is it predestined. (Paris, 2009)

As with Berlant's intimate publics, feelings play a critical role in how party-goers build a sense of belonging to a larger, underdefined public of fellow dancers.

Berlant's analysis suggests that explicit talk about belonging risks turning scenes of recognition and solidarity into ones of disillusionment and repudiation; and this, in turn, casts some light on why participants in minimal electronic music scenes seem to studiously avoid discussing the specificities of belonging. Berlant also alludes to the connection between vagueness and intimacy when they define the verb "to intimate" as "to communicate with the sparest of signs and gestures," thus characterizing intimacy as having "the quality of eloquence and brevity."[35] Part of what makes a public "intimate," then, is its use of indirect, laconic language to inscribe a space of belonging, relying on an intimate logic of affinity and shared affective experience to fill in the gaps. An intimate public is thus easy to join but difficult to delineate: to be part of an intimate public, one requires only a sense of belonging, regardless of how or why. Notably, Berlant's definition of an intimate public combines subtractive and additive logics: implicit subtractive processes (i.e., messy incoherence, vague communication, fragmentary epistemology) help make an explicit additive process possible (i.e., positing generic womanhood as a basis for belonging). A similar combination of additive and subtractive processes is at play on the dancefloor at minimal parties. While I understand liquidarity to be essentially a subtractive mode of crowd cohesion, it also combines with additive factors such as musical tastes and sound-based affinities, which provide *real but vaguely defined* points of commonality in support of liquidarity's fragile sense of belonging beyond identity. Both Berlant's "intimate publics" and liquidarity describe a collectivity that coheres—loosely but powerfully—at the level of affective attachment, all the while being incoherent at the level of explicit discourse and social structure.[36]

In a similar vein, Byron Dueck's conceptualization of "indigenous intimacies" has much in common with liquidarity. Focusing on Indigenous popular music practices in the Canadian province of Manitoba, Dueck develops several terms to examine the interactions at these events, three of which are relevant here. Imaginaries are "social formations that come into being through the circulation of mass-mediated performances and publications," such as "the aboriginal community" or "the Paris minimal techno scene."[37] Imaginings, in turn, are such collectivities imagined as an abstract whole, "a relationship, facilitated by mass mediation, between people who, though unknown to one another, understand themselves to have something in common."[38] If liquidarity provides an imagining, in Dueck's sense, of minimal electronic music scenes, then their intimacies are the face-to-face interactions on their dancefloors that build up into prevailing imaginaries of belonging. Dueck defines intimacies as "engagements between known and knowable persons, especially those that involve the 'interaction rituals' . . . of 'face-to-face' social and musical contact."[39] Notably, his notion of intimacies does not include stranger-sociability, which he frames in terms of strangers addressing an unknown audience through mass-mediation, rather than face-to-face. In this sense, our theoretical frameworks perhaps differ in that my focus here is on intimate engagements that arise from stranger-sociability. Nonetheless, this focus centers on face-to-face interactions, which Dueck associates with "intimacies"; furthermore, partygoers may be unknown to each other at the moment of interaction, but they are potentially knowable over longer time spans. Indeed, in Dueck's terms, the intimacy of liquidarity arises from partygoers engaging with unknown persons as if they were not just knowable but already somewhat known, inferred by the environment in which they encounter each other.

Liquidarity, in any case, is not without its problems. To intimate is not only to communicate with economy and eloquence but also to leave a vast margin for error. Liquidarity entails a wishful "overstanding" of underdefined and volatile conditions, and while this can contribute to stranger-sociability, it depends on partygoers' ability to hold awkward contradictions in abeyance. Indeed, although the proliferation of late twentieth-century cultural theories foregrounding movement and fluidity were welcomed for their ability to describe the conditions of globalization and neoliberal capitalism, some scholars are skeptical about the promises that fluidity seems to offer.[40] Zygmunt Bauman provides an example as both theorist and critic, since he applies liquid metaphors to his analyses of contemporary modernity while also warning against the developments that such metaphors describe.[41] He proposes the term "liquid modernity" to describe the state of affairs at the turn of the twentieth century, arguing that global flows of capital, culture, and bodies are destabilizing and melting the seemingly solid social forms of early modernity (e.g., the sovereign nation-state, work, community, home, family). Not only do liquid-modern subjects have to contend with the problems of earlier modernity, but they must also adapt to a new world order, where stability has been replaced by uncertainty, precariousness, and incessant mobility; a "good life" is no longer measured by settled security but rather by "lightness," agility, and the ability to adapt to constantly changing circumstances.[42] Under conditions of liquid modernity, human relationships are a potential liability to this "keep moving or perish" mentality, which prompts people to eschew deep, stable relationships in favor of shallow, easily replaced ones.[43]

For Bauman, it seems, liquid modernity threatens more than it promises. And yet, I am not convinced that this state of affairs is either so new or so purely deleterious. While Bauman's focus on fluidity highlights the ways in which travel, trade, and communication have all expanded and accelerated in recent decades, this should not lead us to believe that such changes are entirely unprecedented. Indeed, it is hard to believe that modernity's social forms have ever been as solid as Bauman remembers, especially considering the upheaval and transformations of colonialism, the French Revolution, the wider European uprisings of 1848, the industrial revolution, the world wars, the Cold War, the disintegration of colonial empires, and postcolonial struggles for independence and decolonization. When were social structures ever standing still? Also, with the emergence of massive multinational corporations and supranational economic bodies, one must consider that liquefaction in one level of activity may in fact be complemented by solidification elsewhere. But at a broader level, in any case, it remains difficult to argue with Bauman's characterization of life under globalized capitalism as especially fluid and volatile.

It is also far from self-evident that the conditions that Bauman describes as "liquid modernity" only signify a turn for the worse, not least of all because the prior status quo may not have been ideal in the first place. Ethnic minorities, for example, may hold little nostalgia for the modern nation-state form and its origins in ethnonationalism. Sexual and gender minorities may see in the destabilization of traditional family forms the possibility to develop and recognize forms of kinship beyond the heteronormative nuclear family; indeed, campaigns to legalize same-sex marriage have been criticized by some queer activists as a loss of fluidity in queer intimate life-worlds.[44] To be sure, as with any kind of broad social transformation, one must be attentive to the ways that change may also permit further exploitation, marginalization, inequality, displacement, violence, and exhaustion. But while Bauman's critical voice is invaluable as a reminder not to mistake the symptom for the cure, these risks should not prevent us from recognizing the opportunities that also arise as new social forms emerge out of new conditions.

But for all that liquidarity enables and sustains, its power to bracket and neutralize antagonism is also its greatest risk. As theories of "agonistic" politics would argue, *agonism* (conflict that does not aim to annihilate one's opponent) is an important resource for political change, providing the impetus to identify injustices and demand their resolution.[45] To blur difference is also to hinder the detection and recognition of asymmetries that stem from difference; and so, what allows a crowd of strangers to come together can also be what allows it to ignore—and thus perpetuate—its own inequities. Ultimately, it is perhaps unwise to frame liquidarity as a political strategy, an adaptation to dissolving modernity, or an approach to urban communal life. To do so would risk reductively instrumentalizing a form of stranger-sociability that seems too ephemeral to hold any shape for very long. After all, liquidarity—as I found it operating at minimal electronic music events in Paris, Berlin, and Chicago—arises out of nocturnal worlds of fun, companionship, retreat, release, and survival. As such, it is a way of life aimed at the prolongation of fun, the success of a party, a memorable "night out," the warmth of companionship, and the temporary release from the strictures of everyday life. Much like Warner's "counterpublics," these parties often enact idealized notions of conviviality, stranger-sociability, cosexuality, corporeality, discourse, affectivity, and decorum—all of which can be intensely political categories with urgent stakes.[46]

4 THICKENING SOMETHING

NICK: I think it's music's job to make you feel something. That's its role. Or to communicate something—and it doesn't have to be something deep. Its role is to pull people together. (Chicago, 2010)

Nick assigns a heavy responsibility to music, especially for a dancefloor full of strangers and acquaintances. He charges music first with arousing affect ("to make you feel something"), then with transmitting something not yet known or specified, and finally with drawing people together. At that moment in the interview, Nick did not specify if music was supposed to create social or physical togetherness, but in the broader context of our conversation about stranger-intimacy on the dancefloor, it seemed that both meanings were intended. This chapter draws from interviewees' narratives of intense experience and collective communion to examine how music accomplishes these tasks at electronic dance music events, paying particular attention to the role that affect plays in this process of social binding. Extending the tactile metaphors developed in previous chapters, this process is described here as a *thickening* of the social, in which the circulation and intensification of affect adds density to an emergent-but-evanescent sense of crowd solidarity (that is, liquidarity).

The undefined nature of Nick's "something" will come to be just as analytically important as vagueness was in chapter 3's elaboration of liquidarity, in that it helps to understand how this sense of thickening sociability may be difficult to describe and identify, while nonetheless being broadly shared among fellow partygoers. Somehow, this "something" signals the impending coalescence of a social formation, all the while hovering at the horizon of actualization.

Chapter 3 described the coherence of crowds—those gathering on the dancefloors of minimal parties, in any case—as fluid and shifting, characterized by a vague sense of belonging and by messy, incoherent identifications. I argued that, in fact, it is precisely this messiness that enables crowds to cohere across an incoherent range of identities, providing its members with a sense of social solidity despite the underlying fluidity. This line of analysis continues in this chapter, looking for the sensory, affective, and sonic basis for the felt texture of liquidarity. While chapter 3 described collective intimacy in terms of fluid-but-sticky structures lubricated by strategic vagueness, this chapter aims to account for the conditions of emergence for such collective intimacy. Nick's tripartite analysis serves as an organizing principle in this chapter—albeit in a different order—exploring first how music mobilizes and articulates affect, then how affect circulates through a crowd of dancers, and finally how this transmission of affect generates a thickening sense of the social. That exploration is prefaced here with a brief analysis of narratives from partygoers who relate moments of collective communion on the dancefloors of minimal parties. Significantly, these memorable moments of coming together usually feature sharply intensified affect, in which music seems to play a pivotal role.

Narratives of Intensity

At the opening of Maja Classen's documentary on the Berlin techno scene, *Feiern*, she presents a montage of first-time arrival narratives. Before identifying any interviewees by name, she pieces together accounts of their first moments at techno parties, reassembling sentence fragments to create a composite narrative. This modular assemblage suggests a certain common, almost interchangeable quality to these experiences and their recollection by interpolating them into a dense succession of affective spikes: gasps, doors opening to a dramatic "reveal," friends propelling each other into the fray, pounding bass, and scenes of collective excitement and tense anticipation. These narratives are generic and conventional but also shared and intimate. José Mari, for example, describes the scene of his arrival in terms that resonate with affect theory: "And then we noticed this flow of energy coursing through us." For Inga, who has the longest uninterrupted contribution to this montage, music plays an important role in this scene: "There was tinsel coming down from the ceiling, and a really emotional song was playing, which almost made me cry. And then the whole place was glittering, and everybody flipped out—seven thousand people or something. And I just stood there and got goose bumps, and I thought, 'Oh, madness! This is what I want to experience from now on. I want to experience only this kind of party.'"

Inga's narrative, like many others in Classen's montage, is one of feeling overwhelmed, but in a way that ignites in her a desire to feel that way again and again. It is interesting to note what details merit inclusion in her description of the event. In her recollection, a salient part of what made the moment impactful was the copresence of vast numbers of people, all of whom she perceived to be in similar states of extreme excitation. Read next to her narrative, José Mari's brief comment suggests that part of what gave Inga goose bumps was a torrent of affective energy passing through people—impersonal energy that belonged not to any particular person but to the dancefloor environment as a whole. The glittering tinsel falling from the ceiling was also important to Inga, representing a source of visual overstimulation that was part of a larger process of excitation. But what about the music? Why did Inga almost cry in reaction to the music playing at the time? She does not address this directly in the film, but the aggregate testimony of other interviewees in the film suggests that music must have played a role in intensifying the affective impact of this kind of moment.

Many of the partygoers I interviewed similarly recounted their most memorable moments at parties in terms of music and felt intensity. One of the standard prompts I used in every interview was, "Tell me the story of a party where you felt that everyone really came together; describe when and how you felt it." Everyone had stories to tell, many clearly relishing the opportunity to relive such moments. Some interviewees had trouble choosing one moment to recount, while others had difficulty recalling any of them in precise detail. In any case, partygoers had inexhaustible archives of such moments, which they often termed "peak moments," "collective moments," "special moments," "climaxes," "high points," or simply "rushes." Notably, they often described these moments as both intensely intimate and collective, what Polina termed "the one rush of hearts, the one rush of feelings" (Chicago, 2010). But what is the musical content of these moments of collective communion, this "one rush of feelings"? Since the long-form interviews I conducted took place outside of minimal parties, it was difficult for interviewees to recall precisely which piece of music was playing during a specific moment of coming together. Lola, however, was remarkably precise in her recollection. She described a particular musical moment at an afterparty following "Souvenir 03," an underground warehouse party held in Chicago in 2009.[1]

> **LOLA:** When Seuil [the headliner at the main party] came on, he played fucking "Bakerman"! That was the first person I ever heard play "Bakerman."[2] And I remember how that song made everybody feel. . . . It was, like the . . . [*deep inhalation*] you felt the [electric] fans throughout the room [*pauses*]. It was the perfect sound for that moment. He did well. (Chicago, 2010)

For Lola, the arrival of "Bakerman"—a relatively tranquil, down-tempo track by the 1980s Danish band Laid Back—in the midst of DJ Seuil's minimal-house set was a catalyst for this moment of convergence. As she reached this moment in the storytelling, she closed her eyes, tilted her head back slightly, lifted her hands with her fingers somewhat splayed, and inhaled deeply; the gesture indexed both exhilaration and bliss, much like Inga's goose bumps in *Feiern*. Furthermore, Lola's juxtaposition of this musical moment with the haptic excitation of electric fans blowing in a hot environment—since the afterparty was in a warehouse loft, without air-conditioning, during a hot, humid summer morning/afternoon— suggested heightened tactility as well as the start of a "cool-down" period after an overheated moment of emotional intensity. In Lola's case, the moment of peak intensity came with a drastic reduction of tempo and intensity, but other interviewees described moments of climax or sustained high intensity. In any case, the accounts related by partygoers (including those featured in the opening montage of *Feiern*) locate a sense of communion, convergence, and burgeoning collectivity in dramatic moments of affective intensity. This intensification is both driven and expressed by dancing, rhythmic entrainment, crossed glances, altered bodily states, and the music that seems to bring everything into alignment—feelings included. Affect as it is described here is impersonal and transmissible, wherever it may originate; it streams through bodies and, in doing so, generates ephemeral connections. This emergent sense of collective connection seems to come at moments when the flux of affect traces a spiked contour, pushing shared aesthetic experience into the realm of communion and social convergence. The question remains, however, of what these moments are in sonic and musical terms.

The Musical Articulation of Affect

> **LOLA:** Music in general, I cannot live without. Not at all. Because music has been a huge, huge part of my life since I was a child. And, you know, once I started experiencing music in a crowd scenario, I noticed how it really, really bonded people.
>
> I feel like it's the music that binds all of us together, but it comes into the scene in particular stuff. Like, not to lessen the whole . . . but, you know, the truth is, a lot of the times we feel close to people or we do feel more intimate because we're fucked up, you know? So, it's just feeling, like, "Oh my God! I love, love, love this track! I love you! You're beautiful!" You know what I mean? So, some of it is maybe a little artificial on the outside, but deep down, you know that you're experiencing this awesome moment, this awesome track, with people who feel the same way about it, . . . who are, like, "I love this music. I love being here. I love the people who are here." (Chicago 2010)

Chapter 3 noted how most interviewees identified music as the primary factor that held people together—an "additive" theory of social cohesion—serving as a common basis for partygoers' understandings of shared taste, affinity, and scene-specific cultural capital. Here, in contrast, the focus turns to the sensory-affective experience of dancing to music in bodily co-presence with others, exploring the ways in which that experience provides a basis for a sense of collective intimacy. This analytic framing has its basis in my fieldwork, where interviewees often placed shared musical experience at the heart of their stories of dancefloor intimacy. In addition to Lola, several other interviewees highlighted the importance of music in engendering a sense of collectivity at parties. For example, as the Parisian *minimale* producer Franck recounted how he gradually learned to write tracks aimed at moving a dancefloor—both physically and emotionally—he stressed the importance of *ressenti* (inner feelings) in guiding his compositional decisions as well as determining how dancing crowds respond to music:

> FRANCK: I eventually started to compose. And there I found myself using a new approach to music. That is, as I was listening to it, I would occasionally tell myself, "Wait, that's probably this or that instrument; this or that machine." For other tracks, it would be, "Wait, I've got the feeling that this guy or girl felt this or that thing [when composing this track]." No matter if I was right or wrong, by the way. It's *ressenti*. What I mean by that is that music, as far as I'm concerned, always has a role during a night out because that's the thing through which everything moves. (Paris, 2009)

When I asked Nancy, a Parisian public-relations consultant and event planner, what role music played in her experiences of partying, she immediately replied, "Well, music is the vector. It's the trigger [*déclencheur*] for the whole thing" (Paris, 2009). Similarly, Polina described the "beats" of electronic dance music as a force of pleasure-inducing embodied movement: "I just can't comprehend how is it that this repetitive electronic beat makes my body want to move! And I experience so much happiness from it" (Chicago, 2009). Franck, Nancy, and Polina's linking of feelings to motion through music suggests an understanding of musical affect as a kind of force or vector for energy—a kind of vernacular affect theory that informs my analysis here.

While the term "affect" rarely surfaced in interviews—least of all in its specialist scholarly sense—many of my interlocutors explained the binding capacities of music to me through the notion of *vibe* (vibration), referring to a collectively experienced affective tone or atmosphere that is shaped by sonic experience.[3] For these partygoers, "vibe" is not only a metaphor for an affective state or atmosphere; vibration is also a fundamental aspect of the embodied experience of sound. As discussed in chapter 2, the percussive "beats" of electronic dance music can have a tactile impact on the entire body, especially at the extremes of frequency and intensity. Depending on these extremities as well as context, this sonic impact can elicit a range of positive and negative feelings, such as excitement, distress, pleasure, dread, or pain. Suzanne Cusick, for example, describes a form of this in her work on the use of music as torture on detainees at the United States' Guantánamo Bay detention facility; she argues that the reduction of music to sheer sonic force short-circuits conventional modes of listening and similarly reduces the perceiving, aesthetic subject to aching flesh and ringing bones, all the while shattering shared cultural fantasies about what music is—and might be good for.[4] Similarly, Steve Goodman explores "sonic warfare" across a wide range of modalities, including audio-assault weaponry (real as well as imagined by military researchers), dub "dread bass" (subbass frequencies), Afrofuturist "audio viruses" (earworms), and the martial sounds of "dubstep" (a substyle of breakbeat descended from British 2-step).[5] Both Cusick and Goodman attest to the affective power of sound as an overwhelming force.

Although an analytic turn to the violent uses of sound renders the affective force of music all the more clear, partygoers in minimal electronic dance music scenes tended to describe the experience of being caught up in powerful sound as a pleasurable one. Nick, who is also a multi-instrumentalist and composer of experimental electronic music, developed his own theory of music, vibration, and embodied listening. When I asked him about the role of music in bringing together a dancefloor, he launched into an improvised lecture on embodied listening, sympathetic resonance, and attunement.

> NICK: You notice that sound moves in waves, and bass waves are further apart. And high tones are very close together. So, the further-apart waves can move through walls; that's why, when a car goes by, you hear the bass and you don't hear anything else, because it can move through walls. It can move through things, and it can also move through your body that way. It travels *through* things. Higher/faster wavelengths will get blocked and stopped and bounced off, whereas lower/slower wavelengths go through things. (Chicago, 2010)

In reframing sound as vibration and distinguishing between different frequency ranges, Nick resonates with the work of Goodman as well as my previous reflections on sonic tactility in chapter 2. Nick described vibration as transmissible across matter—both living flesh and "vibrant matter"—thus characterizing sound as impersonal in a sense similar to the way other interviewees described musical affect as impersonal and transpersonal.[6] In other words, sound may emanate from a singular body, but once put into motion, it fills a space and strikes all objects as its waves propagate. Nick went on to describe how vibration might engender sympathetic vibrations in other objects, using a model of sympathetic resonance:

NICK: Everything has a vibration, has a frequency. And then there's the music of the spheres (in space), you know: "The planet is in tune." And I think that's a part of it; you just hit those frequencies, and they hit your body, and it's *in tune*.

Have you ever been near a big bell [*strikes large gong nearby*] and then tried to hum the note? You can feel the sound! If you can hit that note in your chest, you all of a sudden feel in tune to the room or the space. It goes from being inside of you to being . . . *you*, right?

Yeah, I think that's why people love bass [*laughs*].

There's something just very physical about sound. And everything vibrates; everything has a pitch that it can tune to. Everything. And so, I think techno does a very good job of hitting those frequencies deep inside you. (Chicago, 2010)

Every body, fleshy or otherwise, has a resonant frequency (or "natural" frequency) at which it responds to external vibrations. When an oscillating force (vibration) strikes a body (physical object), some of its force is retransmitted as kinetic energy, but the inefficiency of this conversion results in a loss of energy, thus dampening the resulting reflections. When this force is oscillating at a body's resonant frequency, the energy loss during conversion approaches zero, and the body vibrates with increased kinetic energy: *sympathetic resonance*.

As Nick's comments indicate, this notion of sympathetic vibration already undergirds the discourse of "vibe"; furthermore, it suggests that certain levels of intensity and certain patterns of fluctuation have the capacity to excite bodies and to incite them to move, respond, express, and/or retransmit this energy. Although Nick is something of a specialist practitioner, a more general notion of vibe is widespread among partygoers, within electronic dance music scholarship, and in nightlife cultures more broadly.[7] I would argue that Nick's account of vibratory affect provides a model of electronic music events as scenes of social, sonic, and affective *attunement*—that is, of coming into (or falling out of) sync with the vibe of others and/or the surrounding environment.[8] For example, Nick suggests that, through sound, one can come to feel in tune with a space or a "room" (i.e., a crowd, since "a room" can also mean "an audience" in the context of nightclub events). In keeping with the vague, nonidentitarian forms of belonging described in chapter 3, "being in tune" with a space or a person need not be predicated on identity: vibrating in tune with another body does not necessarily mean that one identifies with that body or that one has the same understanding of what this attunement even means.

Nick's account of sympathetic vibration, electronic music culture's vernacular uses of "vibe," and partygoers' accounts of music's emotional impact all find resonances in a particular notion of affect that has its roots in the writings of the seventeenth-century philosopher Spinoza.[9] Promoted and further elaborated by Gilles Deleuze in the twentieth century, Spinoza's notion of *affectus*, defined as the variation of a body's power to affect and be affected, has been central to much scholarship on the role of "feelings" in culture and society.[10] Notably, Spinozan affect arises from the interaction of bodies, as a kind of emergent phenomenon that provides a way of linking feelings and emotions to sensory experience. In the introduction to *Parables for the Virtual*, for example, Brian Massumi metaphorically describes the body as a hollow resonator in order to develop an acoustic account of sensation and affect. He traces sensation to bodily intensity (the variation of which forms the basis of his notion of affect) by turning the body into an echo chamber. Like sound waves, sensations enter through and then bounce off the body's various "sensory surfaces," which in turn create an "interference pattern" of self-relation that Massumi dubs "intensity."[11] Notably, his resonance model frames affect as impersonal, which bears a resemblance to the way in which partygoers, during interviews, described musical affect and collective emotion as coming from somewhere outside the individual dancer.

The connections between tactile experience and affect are to be found everywhere in everyday language as well as in specialist scholarship. Indeed, much of Spinoza's affect theory is elaborated in terms of impactful encounters between bodies, whereby the kinetic energy of touch can elicit fluctuations of affect. It is a more complicated task, however, to conceptualize the sonic transmission of affect, especially with reference to specific sonic events or musical techniques. While the use of vibration as a metaphor is often deployed to conceptualize affect as a state of excitation, more recent scholarship on sound and affect has emphasized the way in which physical vibrations also constitute real states of excitation, which register in the body as affect. Goodman, for example, develops a "nonrepresentational ontology of vibrational force," by examining instances when powerful (sonic) vibrations have been used to manipulate affective tone (his term for collective affect) and physically impact the lived world.[12] He posits a "vibrational substratum" that is both amodal and nonsensory, in the sense that it is not exclusively addressed to a particular sensory or perceptual mode a priori but rather registers across the entirety of the body's sensorium before being perceived as "sound"; and due to its qualities of movement, force, and action, vibration becomes a potent vector of affect.[13] Goodman's notion of an amodal vibrational substratum is useful in providing a theoretical account of how sound can transmit affect transpersonally and nonrepresentationally, providing a sense of shared affective experience even when it is emotionally perceived in divergent ways by co-listeners. In other words, Goodman's vibrational substratum lies below the semiotic tangle of representation, language, and communication, thus providing a model for "subterranean" connections between differing subjective perceptions of shared affective experience. Although primarily focused on violent uses of sound and "bad vibes," Goodman also insists on the "subpolitical power of music to attract and congeal populations," which he dubs—with a twist on Marxist theory—"bass materialism": the capacity for organized vibration to occupy space-time and galvanize collectivities.[14] This vocabulary of sonic social thickening ("to attract and congeal") closely resembles the tactile metaphors developed here and in previous chapters: it describes the capacity of sound to articulate affect in a way that engenders an emergent sense of the social.

While these approaches to sonic affect go beyond conventional models of emotion (as personal, private, internal, and nameable) and potentially ascribe some agency to sound, we should be careful not to underestimate the agency that listeners and dancers have in directing their own affective experiences, assigning meaning to them, and expressing them outwardly. Imogen framed music as a screen on which she can project a variety of affects, describing how electronic dance music's tendency to avoid lyrical reference to specific emotions allows her to embody it according to her own affective state:

> IMOGEN: The importance of music for me: it's very physical. I like to express my body, and with electronic music, you have such a wide spectrum to do that, because it's such tone-based—or rhythm-based—[music] that you can set your own tone or emotion to it. You know what I mean? It's not like with lyrics; they kinda set the pace, whether it's gonna be a love song or a hate song.
>
> I can take whatever beats and manipulate that into my body movements; it's how I'm feeling that night—whether it be sexual, whether it be angry, whether it be frisky [laughs], whether it be silly . . . you know what I mean?

And then other times, if you're pissed, or fuckin' . . . you know,
you're feeling frustrated—maybe there's somebody there that's making
you feel uncomfortable—you can just put your fist up and say, "Fuck
it," you know? Get it out of your system. (Chicago, 2010)

Here, Imogen characterizes (electronic) music as a moving and polyvalent
phenomenon that allows her to channel, express, and purge her own feelings through dance. Her account reminds us to avoid imagining bodies on
the dancefloor as passive and empty vessels to be filled with affect. Affect
can originate from a particular person (or linger from a previous encounter), but it is not confined to that person; affect is contagious. An affect or
mood might be brought onto the dancefloor by somebody, and yet it may
also spread to other bodies and the environment. On the dancefloor at minimal parties, then, partygoers should be understood as both contributing
their own affective dispositions, moods, and emotions to the dancefloor and
being exposed to the affective tone of others, their surroundings, and the
sound that envelops them.

But how can sound shape affect, beyond the mere fact of vibration? Electronic dance music partygoers, performers (DJs), and writers all frequently
trace a causal connection between DJ performance and crowd affect, which
raises questions about power and control while also providing examples of
how particular musical techniques articulate affect. Teresa spoke from her
long experience as a DJ, noting how certain musical moments induced a convergence of feeling as well as a synchronization of responses from the crowd.

TERESA: [Being struck by the same musical moment] is something
that happens quite a lot. I think that's why there are these sorts of
general reactions that happen when a DJ does something like *drop the
kick* [drum] and build it back up. Everybody reacts the same way, for
the most part. They maybe throw their arms up in the air, they start
jumping, they're yelling, and that kind of moment when [*laughs*] the
DJ—which can get a little cheesy if it's done throughout the night—
but there's something about that. It's this moment where there's this
sort of little, mini-anticipation that . . . you know, it's kind of an
example of a moment when everybody is excited at the same time,
feeling that same feeling, and reacts . . . very similarly.

I think it's interesting, and I think there are moments like that,
too, when somebody's maybe playing a certain sound for a long time,
maybe something really *dark and heavy,* and then they change to

something, you know, maybe a little more *uplifting* or giving a *feeling of light*, and you notice that people kind of react in a similar way, and, and . . . it's kind of a joyous moment.

I always loved moments like that at parties, when you just felt like, even though you didn't know most of the people there, *there was sort of a connection being made*. (Chicago, 2010; emphasis added)

Although she did not seem to be certain as to what sort of togetherness was emerging at these points, Teresa nonetheless identified a "connection" in the making between strangers on the dancefloor. Interestingly, she did not locate these moments of musical communion exclusively at points of high intensity but instead located them at points of sharp variation; for her, it was when there was a significant change in texture, mood, or theme that these moments of social solidification would take place.

In electronic dance music performance practice, there is a rich repertoire of musical techniques that producers and DJs such as Teresa employ to articulate affect, forming a vernacular music-theoretical vocabulary that is being increasingly studied by popular-music scholars.[15] Many of these techniques are recognized and explicitly discussed by both performers and

FIGURE 4.1 Dancers and DJs as well as sound/lighting technicians working together to articulate musical affect. Interior of Watergate nightclub (Berlin); Carsten Koall / Getty Images News via Getty Images.

dancers alike, using vernacular terms or ad hoc descriptions. One notable example of this can be heard—and narrated—in a remix of Roland Clark's "I Get Deep," by the Australian producer Late Night Tuff Guy, which was in wide circulation during the fieldwork period for this book.[16] This track was first released in 2007 as a limited-edition vinyl "edit" (which implies a rearrangement of the original track's elements without introducing new elements or making radical changes) before being framed as a remix when it was picked up for global digital distribution by Get Physical Music in 2012. But the track is closer to the "mash-up" format popular in the early 2000s, in that it combines the spoken-word vocal track from Clark's original "I Get Deep" with the opening loop of Rework's "Anyway I Know You"—both releases from the year 2000—without substantial alterations to either source recording.[17] Nonetheless, the combination of the bass-heavy loop with Clark's spoken performance makes the latter much more clearly audible than in its original deep-house setting, where a very "busy" midfrequency layer tends to mask the voice. In any case, Clark's vocal performance rhapsodically relates a scene at the New York City club The Shelter, as he sinks deeper and deeper into a musical-kinaesthetic experience. After complaining about strutting, inauthentic poseurs who "don't know what is what" cluttering the dancefloor and then describing his sweaty state of abandon (to be discussed in chapter 5), he turns to the music:

> *I get deep, I get deep, I get deep, I get deep*
> *When he takes all the bass out the song*
> *And all you hear is highs*
> *And it's like: oh . . . shit!*
> *[moan] I get deep*
>
> *I get deep, I get deep, I get deep, I get deep*
> *and the rhythm flows through my blood like alcohol*
> *and I get drunk*
> *and I'm fallin' all over the place.*
> *But I catch myself*
> *right on time*
> *right in line with the beat,*
> *and it's so sweet, sweet, sweet, sweet.*[18]

Clark's narrative describes something similar to what Teresa called "dropping the kick," although in this case, the entire bass-frequency range is filtered out and then later returned. Here, this change in texture elicits a thrill that Clark conveys in a falsetto exclamation, "Oh *shit!*" followed by an audible release of breath. He then describes how the music's rhythm penetrates and flows through his body, creating a feeling of intoxication that impacts his movement. And yet, he manages to use "the beat" to stabilize and bring himself back into synchrony, which brings with it a feeling of sweetness that he expresses with the same fourfold intensifying repetition that opens each stanza of his recitation. Notably, Late Night Tuff Guy's musical setting mirrors Clark's narrative: the bass-frequency range of the Rework loop is cut out in a gradual "filter sweep" as Clark describes the self-same technique, losing most of the midfrequency layer as well by the time he flips into falsetto; and then the bass gradually returns as he narrates "catching" himself, filling out the full frequency spectrum as he repeats the word "sweet" four times. The time span between the release of the sample sources (2000), the vinyl pressing of this mash-up (2007), and its rerelease in digital format (2012) provides a historical dimension to the performance practice described here, demonstrating continuities in DJ technique that span decades.

Both Teresa and Roland Clark describe a technique that has been dubbed "withholding the beat" by Mark J. Butler, who has extensively studied and codified the repertoire of performance/composition techniques in techno.[19] Working in consultation with techno DJs, Butler identifies and describes a number of techniques used by producers in the composition of individual tracks as well as by DJs during their performances. Most of these techniques cluster under the heading of *breakdowns* and *removals*.[20] Breakdowns involve a noticeable reduction in musical texture—almost always including the bass kick—which tend to go on for a substantial duration of time, usually long enough to fill a set of sixteen- or thirty-two-bar cycles of four beats each, if not more. The return of the full texture at the end of the breakdown is usually accompanied by a climactic buildup, and this technique most often appears in fixed form on a recorded track. Removals or "cuts" involve the removal of a textural element, most often the bass kick but sometimes also elements in the treble register. These cuts are usually executed by a DJ during performance and rarely last longer than a few beats. Butler describes most of these cuts as "anacrustic," the formal equivalent of an "upbeat"; in other words, brief cuts are often introduced just before a significant moment in the track's musical form (a "structural downbeat") to heighten the impact of its arrival. Anacrustic cuts can begin at any point beforehand, but they are always timed to end at the arrival of a structural downbeat. Although DJ-performed cuts are usually quite brief, Butler considers "withholding the beat" to be a special case of bass removal, the definition of which merits quoting in its entirety:

> Withholding the beat occurs when the DJ removes the bass drum during a live performance. Audience interplay is an essential part of this phenomenon. The crowd seems to actively anticipate the return of the beat: during its absence, they look toward the DJ as if to see what will happen next, and their dancing becomes tentative or breaks off. When the bass drum comes back, however, they dance with greater energy than in any other portion of the track, while enthusiastically expressing their appreciation to the DJ. Furthermore, as the term suggests, withholding can involve an element of teasing between DJ and audience. The DJ heightens the audience's desire for the beat, which represents the music in its most essential form, by taking it away and giving it back at carefully controlled intervals.[21]

Not only is this form of removal longer and more complex than a generic cut, but it also involves intense interactivity between DJ and audience, a push and pull of desire, control, and pacing. In comparison to the rest of Butler's book, the affective vocabulary deployed here is also remarkable; his description of a typical audience reaction focuses primarily on the DJ–dancer relationship, but this can also impact how dancers express themselves and interact with each other. Nancy, in a manner similar to the narrator of "I Get Deep," described her experience of the "buildup" (French: *la montée*), connecting it to an explosive sense of embodied affective intensity that surges through multiple lines of flight. By comparison, Marie described a broader category of musical "key moments" (*moments clés*) with a similar narrative of collective excitation and synchronization, but with a greater emphasis on stranger-intimacy.

> **NANCY:** A vibration, for me, it's—by the great wizard, the great DJ—it's letting yourself be tamed and waiting a bit to know where he wants to take you, where he wants to go. So, already, there's a bit of suspense. So you dance, you wait, you're in suspense, you listen, you're attentive, you try to find out where he wants to take you, et cetera. And the buildup [*montée*] arrives, which is what you've been waiting for. So you start to explode, because you're happy. And that's a vibration for me, which comes from the bottom of my belly . . . and that you want to expel by throwing your hands in the air, screaming,

kissing your friends, and—voilà. Vibration is primarily a satisfaction; it's an auditory satisfaction. (Paris, 2009)

MARIE: Well, I believe that it's magic [*laughs*]. But it's true! You see, that moment, I think that—talk to any fan or person who listens and dances to techno—really, there are these key moments [*moments clés*] in tracks, or in DJ mixes or during parties, which create, as they say, "a grand collective communion." And people are able to sense that. You can find yourself next to a stranger, and as soon as you look at them and they look back at you, and since you're both hearing the same thing, you feel the same thing in the body. It's as if they were someone you knew from—or in—complicity. And that's really rare; at least, it's rare in daily life. (Paris, 2009)

Contrasting in execution and yet similar in their affective contours, these accounts of music driving affect highlight the role of the DJ in precipitating these moments of intensity, while at the same time placing them in a dialogic relationship with the dancing crowd. But as powerful as these techniques might be in shaping and guiding the flow of affect through a crowd, the testimony of some interviewees challenged this narrative by suggesting that performers must also contend with a sort of affective inertia or resistance from partygoers. Norwood, for example, described the musical articulation of affect at parties as "really contextual," noting that multiple factors determine how effective these techniques will be—not least of all the mood of the crowd itself.

NORWOOD: I think the DJ plays a role in kind of shaping attitude, depending on the way people are behaving. You can't go completely off in left field, but you can feel out the crowd and push it in a certain direction. . . . [DJs] can kind of push the mood, the feeling in a general direction. But you can't go completely against it; otherwise it'll blow up in your face. (Chicago, 2010)

Norwood's comments provide an important intervention in the widely repeated trope of DJs "working the room" and single-handedly controlling the dancing crowd's emotional responses. It is for this reason that the title of this section uses the term "articulation" rather than "manipulation" or "modulation" of affect. Sound, individual bodily experience, and collective mood are separate systems that interact with each other at various points of articulation. This same dynamic of articulation pertains between sonic, bodily, and collective affect as well: DJs articulate their sets by using mixing techniques, giving direction to the flow of sound, shaping high points and low points, and lending the entire set an episodic structure, but these articulations do not determine dancers' affects so much as provide them with a kind of affective scaffolding on which they can build.[22] In other words, the power of DJs lies more in their capacity to crystallize affective dispositions that are already latent among dancers and to afford them opportunities for collective expressions of affect, using techniques that articulate and shape the flow of affect across the space of the dancefloor. And, from the perspective of the DJ, successful moments of affective attunement and rhythmic entrainment can nonetheless provide intense pleasure and satisfaction. Teresa, for example, explained, "One of the reasons I love to DJ is because I love looking out and seeing people dancing and just . . . completely in a moment of joy and enjoying themselves. And it's when they're feeling that moment in the music the same way that I am, it's just . . . it's just a perfect feeling" (Chicago, 2010).

In addition to sensing and responding to the mood of the crowd (as well as to many other factors), DJs must also contend with genre-specific performance patterns and expectations, which inform dancers' reactions. Much like social norms, most of these patterns remain implicit until they are in some way violated, but from my own fieldwork observations, I can enumerate four examples that are widely observed. First, textural removals such as "cuts"—however brief—are expected to happen in anticipation of structural downbeats, with their ends (and possibly their beginnings) coinciding with dominant beat cycles, that is, multiples of four, eight, sixteen, and so on. Second, the technique of "withholding the beat" should not undermine the sense of meter or larger multicycle patterning ("hypermeter"). Third, a crowd has several modes of expressing its dis/satisfaction—including applause or booing, rushing to or leaving the floor, standing conspicuously still or dancing more vigorously—and a DJ is expected to understand and respond to these signals. Fourth, in addition to the removal and return of textural elements, a DJ is expected to make use of a wide range of articulating techniques, such as (1) manipulating the equalizers (EQs) to focus on particular elements in the musical texture or to change the overall sound profile; (2) using "EQ sweeps," in which an increasingly wide swath of frequencies are either dampened or amplified; and (3) using "effects" devices, such as echo/delay, reverb, and flanging.[23] These patterns do not constitute a set of hard and fast rules but rather point toward a constantly evolving bundle of genre-specific expectations, which DJs can affirm, violate, or transform as they work to keep dancers engaged.

In any case, most of these performance practices govern the maintenance (and occasional troubling) of rhythm and meter, thus seeming to value a certain amount of elastic play in how easily dancers can synchronize their movements to the music—in other words, they all play with *entrainment*. Much like vibration, entrainment is defined abstractly in terms of oscillating forces: it occurs when one cyclical process is captured by and set to oscillate in rhythm with another process—that is, a process of phase shifting and phase locking. In the context of musical hearing, Justin London defines metric entrainment as a "phase locking of the listener's attentional rhythms with the temporal regularities in the musical surface," which is often matched with gestural regularities from the listener—such as the rhythmic and synchronized dancing "to the beat" that electronic dance music partygoers accomplish to varying degrees.[24] Interestingly, London uses the term "attunement" almost interchangeably with "entrainment," which suggests a common thread between Nick's earlier theorizations of vibrational attunement and London's sensory-cognitive account of entrainment. London describes a process that is at once mostly unconscious and very complex. It requires attention, sure, but a form of attention that is more diffuse and indirect than the sort of analytic focus usually assumed in studies of musical listening. Although it may not be immediately clear what effect entrainment has on people, aside from bringing them into relatively synchronized action, one can imagine how successfully achieving collective coordination could generate pleasure and contribute to a sense of "flow" or optimal experience.[25] Furthermore, some form of entrainment is common to nearly every neuropsychological account of emotional-musical response, suggesting that rhythmic entrainment is closely bound with *emotional* entrainment.[26]

Thickening the Social

What effect can entrainment have on bodies, aside from bringing them into relatively synchronized movement? How can entrainment shape affect and generate a sense of the social? In studies of organizational behavior, researchers have shown that groups share affect through a range of implicit and explicit processes: implicit processes include emotional contagion, the vicarious experience of others' affects ("modeling"), and behavioral entrainment; explicit processes include "impression manage-ment" and the intentional induction of affect.[27] Of these, the processes of emotional contagion and behavioral entrainment are the most useful in understanding the convergence and transfer of affect at electronic dance music parties.[28]

Emotional contagion is a process of affective transfer, in which an in-dividual's emotions and mood are propagated to nearby individuals. This process is described as a relatively automatic and unconscious tendency to "mimic and synchronize facial expressions, vocalizations, postures, and movements with those of another person and, consequently, to converge emotionally."[29] This model has been supported by research that shows a human tendency to mirror and synchronize with the manifestations of emotional behavior in others.[30] The model for how this mirroring leads to emotional convergence is called "afferent feedback," which pro-poses that, when people reproduce bodily expressions of affect, they expe-rience the emotion itself through physiological feedback from muscular, visceral, and glandular responses.[31] Notably, these exchanges of emotional expression are often cross-modal, where a vocalization of enjoyment, like laughter, elicits a facial expression or gesture as response, suggesting that behavioral entrainment involves not only mirroring but also a *translation* of emotional expressions and perceived feeling states.[32] Behavioral entrain-ment is similar to metric entrainment in principle but focuses on the syn-chronization of behavior between members of a group rather than between a listener and sonic stimuli. Imogen, for example, provided an example of emotional contagion through behavioral entrainment during our inter-view, as we discussed stranger-intimacy on the dancefloor:

> **IMOGEN:** There's certain people that, when you get into a tangle with them, when you get into a really good "eye-lock," you're just laughing and smiling. I think that that can totally be heavier than a conversa-tion sometimes. It can bring you closer. (Chicago, 2010)

Imogen finds intimacy in these moments of sustained eye contact, coor-dinated dancing, and the mirroring of both facial and vocal expressions of emotion. Notably, entrainment of this kind may entail behavioral mir-roring, but it can also involve the sequential coordination of action, such as a conversation that "flows" well or a series of interlocking dance moves. In this sense, the affective convergence of behavioral entrainment is also a *rhythmic* entrainment of sorts, since expressions of affect are not just shared simultaneously but exchanged over time.[33] Such rhythmic-behavioral entrainment not only encourages affective mirroring between participants but leads to a more positive experience of interpersonal interaction.[34] As a result, successful entrainment tends to generate positive affect merely from people's experiences of being in behavioral synchrony.[35]

In any case, researchers have linked the convergence of mood in a group to a number of factors, including stable group membership, a sense of interdependence, and engagement in collective activity.[36] Given the fluid and often-anonymous membership of crowds at electronic dance music events such as minimal electronic music parties, it is unlikely that the stability of membership is a decisive factor in this context; the other two factors, however, provide potential explanations for how affect comes together on the dancefloor, since the experience of liquidarity described in chapter 3 includes a sense of interdependence (however vague) and the primary activity at these events is a collective one: social dancing. Admittedly, the differences in objects of study do limit the explanatory power of these models: most of these researchers are studying relatively small and stable groups, usually in the context of the workplace. The patterns they identify have not yet been systematically described in large, anonymous crowds in leisure settings (and such a laboratory setting is far from feasible), but there is nonetheless a striking resonance between these theories of mimetic emotional contagion and the nineteenth-century crowd psychology of Gabriel Tarde and Gustave Le Bon, as well as between this scholarship and other writings that engage with crowds and coordinated movement.[37]

Despite the gap between the research of (small, countable) group affect and that of (large, uncountable) crowds, most of the accounts of social convergence that I collected from partygoers during interviews made frequent reference to the same processes of mimesis and affective attunement. Lisette, for example, described emotional convergence in terms of nameless energies that circulate between people, while Polina explained her notion of dancefloor solidarity in terms of synchronized actions and convergent feelings:

> **LISETTE:** There's energy that circulates and that passes through
> people. That's what I feel. When I go out with a bunch of people,
> when I wait in the queue and all that, . . . there are these energies
> that develop, good or bad, and they'll influence your own behavior.
> Me, I really work with energy. I'm a sponge, in fact; I take on a lot of
> energy. All it takes is to be surrounded by stressed-out people and my

behavior changes; and, inversely, if everyone is friendly, it'll change [accordingly]. I find that it's really a question of energy that brings all of this about, for good or ill. It really brings about a . . . collective behavior. (Paris, 2009)

POLINA: I think the way that solidarity is expressed is when, for example, we all really like the track, we're dancing, and everyone would go, like, hands up in the air and look at each other and be, like, "Yeah! Oh my God, what's this track?" and just look at each other and dance together and do those similar kinds of gestures. . . .

For me, solidarity is there when you're dancing, and you can look at anyone and smile at them and they will smile back at you understandingly, like, "Yeah! This is amazing! We're all in this, we're all *feeling* it." (Chicago, 2010)

Lisette and Polina described these moments of solidarity in terms that recall much of the foregoing scholarship on affective convergence in groups. In Polina's account, emotional contagion seemed to take place in the exchange of glances and especially in the exchange of smiles, both of which suggest a process of expressive mimesis. These exchanges might also partake in behavioral entrainment, as would the synchronous "hands up in the air" and the side-by-side dancing. Notably, the sentiment she expressed at the end of this sequence is, "We're all in this, we're all *feeling* it." In other words, she articulates a sense of belonging that coincides with a shared feeling; even if these feelings are not explicitly identical from person to person, the intensity of the moment provides a ground for fellow feeling. Polina thus engaged in a kind of *affective epistemology of solidarity*—a way of almost-knowing through feeling—in which the perception of affective attunement supports a sense of the social. This use of affective experience in order to affirm perceived social bonds is a crucial part of what makes it possible for partygoers to report a sense of belonging among strangers.

Although Émile Durkheim's account of ritual belonging is less invested in processes of mimesis and entrainment, it nonetheless provides some insight into the role that affective *intensity* plays in the affirmation and reproduction of social bonds.[38] In his work on sociological method as well as on religion, Durkheim imagined the massive surges of mood attendant to group gatherings as arising not from individual or aggregated consciousnesses but rather from society itself or, as Sarah Ahmed puts it, "from the thickness of sociality itself."[39] For Durkheim, society owes its continuity to this collective ritual, in which the intensification of emotional energies leads to a "collective effervescence" that both reaffirms and instantiates social structure. If we read Durkheim's "collective effervescence" as a kind of affect, we can understand his account of ritual as establishing a connection between intensified affect and the revitalization of society. And yet, it is important to note that the minimal electronic music parties studied here present a situation in which this collective effervescence occurs outside of (but adjacent to) the kind of stable, clearly demarcated social order that Durkheim assumed in his colonial-era account of tribal life. Membership in electronic dance music scenes is voluntary, casual, relatively open, fluid, and mostly anonymous; and so, it may seem like these scenes generate collective effervescence without stable collectivity as such. But the ethnographic data presented here and elsewhere in this book suggest that Durkheim needs to be read backward in order to make sense of this: one of the main claims of this chapter is that the intense collective experiences at minimal electronic music parties engender a sense of a burgeoning community that is not yet there but could be. Much in the same way that the phenomenon of "afferent feedback" can induce an emotion in a body that mimics its expressive indicators, the collective enactment of affectively effervescent rituals can give rise to a sense of a social structure that was supposed to precede it. In other words, dancing together can make social worlds out of shared feeling.

Durkheim's account of ritual and affect has had a profound and long-lasting effect on anthropological theory, which in turn has informed ethnomusicology's ethnographic and theoretical investments. Ethnomusicologists have paid great attention to the collective performance of music and its capacities to affirm, contest, and negotiate social relations.[40] Thomas Turino provides a particularly compelling account by drawing from the work of Edward T. Hall, who argues that "being in sync" (that is, engaging in collective synchronized activity) is crucial to feelings of social belonging—thus prefiguring much of the scholarship on behavioral entrainment and affect discussed earlier.[41] Turino expands this account to the musical rituals of Aymara-speaking residents of the *altiplano* of Conima, Peru, where this "being in sync" involves "moving and sounding together."[42] Musical and gestural repetition is particularly important here: "The possibility of 'being in sync' is extended and the social union is intensified, leading to an affective intensity."[43] Furthermore, repetition has been shown to play an important role in emotional responses to music, especially when it is coordinated with bodily gestures.[44] Given the predominance of repetition in dance music as well as its association with collective dancing as its idealized mode of enjoyment, one could expect electronic dance music parties to be especially conducive to this process of affect-led sociability.[45] More broadly put, the activities of both "musicking" and dancing afford a wide range of ways to "be in sync" with others, which sustains a sense social cohesion that can endure beyond the moment of performance.[46]

Turino goes further with repetition, however, noting that it does not lead to satiety or boredom but rather provides a basis for what he dubs "aesthetic power." Not only does the synchronized, repeating performance of sound and movement accumulate power, but its use also harnesses this power to generate real social relations: "During special moments, culturally specific rhythms and forms of movement are not merely semiotic expressions of community and identity; rather *they become their actualization*."[47] For Turino, Aymara rituals are not merely expressive but also productive of sociality; in other words, the totality of relations and interactions in ritual performance *is* society, if only for that moment. Here, Turino converges with Stanley J. Tambiah, who argues that ritual is *performative* in the sense first developed by J. L. Austin: particular acts have the power to enact what they name or express.[48] Thus, he argues, rituals are constitutive of the transitions that they mark, which means that looking for cause-and-effect relations inside ritual is to miss the point: "simply by virtue of being, [they] achieve a change of state, or do something effective."[49] In this sense, the ritualized aspects of electronic dance music parties can be seen as not only performing utopian aspirations of participatory belonging but also conjuring them into existence.

If Durkheim's analysis of ritual grounds collective effervescence in the "thickness of sociality itself," while Turino sees social structure arising from collective participation in musicking, then we can also imagine a sense of the social coalescing out of the thickness of musical participation itself. Steven M. Friedson also employs metaphors of sonic thickening in his analysis of the repeating "riff" in the musical ritual of *Brekete*, a *gorovodu* religious practice of the Ewe-speaking people of Ghana and Togo.[50] Focusing on the asymmetrical patterns of the *agbadza* drums as they explore cross-rhythmic possibilities in "a standing field of intense motion" sustained by repetition, Friedson describes a "stacking effect of the riff, [where] there is both a thickening and simultaneously an opening up of sonic space."[51] Notably, he sees this as not only an acoustical phenomenon but also a "bodying-forth-into-the-world," which seems to imply that these processes also engender a sense that something "real" is emerging out of the repetition of drum riffs.⁵² Although Friedson does not explicitly tie his account of thickening sonic space to sociality, his analysis usefully suggests a way in which ongoing musical repetition might generate a sense of accumulation and thickening.

For all of these tactile-sonic accounts of collective musicking, the identity of what thickens out of this musical-affective experience remains unclear. With what forms of collectivity does this incipient sense of solidity resonate? Sianne Ngai provides a potential analytic foothold through her exploration of resonance and affective shape in *Ugly Feelings*, a study of the "minor affects" (such as irritation, anxiety, envy, paranoia) in literature, film, and television.⁵³ In a way that resembles Nick's ontology of affective transfer as sympathetic vibration, Ngai employs the concept of resonance as a useful way of imagining the relationship (and interaction) between artificially fabricated and subjectively experienced affect. Working from Silvan Tomkins's clinical-psychological notion of affect, she characterizes affects as analogous to the shape of the stimulus they are assembled with, such that they have some sort of felt, recognizable resemblance to a broader nexus of experience.⁵⁴ Ngai suggests that resonance can occur between loosely organized feelings or ideas about feelings ("ideo-affective postures") and highly organized ideologies or political agendas ("ideological postures") when they have a similar shape. In the context of the minimal electronic music parties studied in this book, Ngai's model offers an account of how "vague" feelings (such as shared excitement on the dancefloor, musical transport, a sense of sociality and connection) can resonate with a particular ideology that has a similar shape (such as "underground"/"subculture," a community of music lovers, "techno family," "house nation," and so on). But there is also a crucial difference: my ethnographic fieldwork at electronic music parties does not reveal a one-to-one mapping of feelings to specific ideologies but rather a whole range of vague (but at times very urgent) feelings whose shapes seem to resemble a corresponding range of ideas about collectivity. Indeed, my analysis in this chapter does not describe resonance with a specific model of togetherness but rather describes resonance with the idea of togetherness *as such*. Nonetheless, both Ngai's and Tomkins's accounts of affective-ideological resonance serve as important reminders that this music-affect-collectivity model need not be automatically associated with utopian or altruistic agendas: similar dynamics could be at work in musically mobilizing fascist/reactionary "hate politics" or authoritarian states, for example.

Thus far, I have argued that the moments of affective communion described by interviewees in minimal electronic music scenes are primarily precipitated by the musical articulation of affect, eliciting an intensification of affect among partygoers on the dancefloor, who in turn engage in processes of emotional contagion and musical/behavioral entrainment. These moments of affective convergence, described by many interviewees as "feeling it" or "feeling the same feeling," come to serve as an experiential basis for a sense of social convergence, which in turn provides the imaginative ground for those practices of heightened intimacy and vague solidarity that lie at the center of this book. I have characterized this process of social convergence as a kind of social thickening, which extends the tactile metaphors of previous chapters while also highlighting the way that these moments of shared intensity seem to cause a nascent sense of the social to congeal. In other words, the intensification of sonic affect on the dancefloor engenders an emergent sense of *something*, and this thickening "something" provides a shared point of reference for a sense of communion among a crowd of strangers. Up to this point, I have been employing terms such as "community," "collectivity," and "the social" as placeholders for this "something," but the fieldwork sites of this ethnographic project do not center on a well-delineated identity group or a stable social organization. If a stable social order is not being produced here, what *is* being brought into being?

Something Coming

> There's something about that environment and all the different pieces coming together—with the music and the drugs and just that feeling of freedom that exists in that space—to just sort of let yourself go, and maybe have a conversation that you wouldn't dream of having with your sister or your coworker or somebody else that you talk to on a day-to-day basis.
> TERESA (CHICAGO, 2010)

> This kind of thing happens all the time. It's a kind of experiment that starts with sheer intensity and then tries to find routes into a "we" that is not yet there but maybe could be.
> KATHLEEN STEWART, *ORDINARY AFFECTS*

The testimonies of minimal-scene partygoers that fill this chapter describe a sense of a burgeoning collectivity where there had been little or none before. There seems to be a sort of social-sonic-affective logic at work, in which moments of musical intensity drive moments of affective convergence on the dancefloor, which are in turn taken to signal a thickening of the social fabric between strangers. A well-timed return of the bass kick drum, for example, can elicit simultaneous cheers and fist pumping and frenzied dancing and elated eye contact, all of which contribute to a sense of becoming collectively "in sync." This chapter is replete with narratives of sonic-social thickening, whereby the liquidarity described in chapter 3 takes on a certain density at these moments of intensity. But what kind of social formation does a crowd of strangers produce in these circumstances? What emerges out of these encounters, as the sense of stranger-intimacy intensifies?

Like Teresa in the quote at the beginning of this section or Nick at the beginning of the chapter, most of the interviewees from these scenes frequently used "something" as a placeholder for this emergent sense of the social, without detailing what this something represented. Perhaps there was a sense that, since something was emergent, it was still inchoate and could not be identified. Perhaps there was a worry that, should a term like "community" or "society" or "family" be attached to this something, it would collapse under the weight of the expectations that those terms carry with them. But perhaps their descriptions of this burgeoning sense of the social were vague because their perception of it was also vague. As a kind of social convergence that is enacted through moments of sonic affective convergence, the sociality that emerges here seems to hover at the horizon of perceptibility and description. It is a sense of the social that is shared at the level of affect (e.g., "we're feeling it!"; "feeling the same feeling") and through expressive activities such as listening and social dancing, and yet it is difficult to express in explicit discourse. Ultimately, the partygoers I interviewed struggled to describe a potential, virtual, not-yet-fully-there sociality arising out of shared moments of intense experience.

This sense of an emergent collectivity throbbing under moments of affective intensity has been described eloquently in Kathleen Stewart's *Ordinary Affects*, in which she bundles together fragmentary fieldwork anecdotes and conceptual asides to provide a fine-grained view of affect in ordinary, everyday life. The passage in the epigraph comes from Stewart's analysis of an anecdote regarding a death under the wheels of a railway train, tracing the traumatic echoes it left among the survivors; the train itself, in turn, becomes magnetized with the affective force of this memory, which comes to represent the promise of a life that is not this (exhausted, marginal, striving, flat) life. Alluding to Deleuzean notions of assemblage and lines of flight, Stewart depicts the affective surge that the train brings as a burgeoning sense of collectivity spilling out of the virtual and into lived experience.

This "we" that is not yet there (but maybe could be) is analogous to the "something" that thickens during moments of intensity and affective convergence on electronic dance music's dancefloors. Despite the stark differences between these scenarios, they both present moments when the sheer force of experience gives rise to a sense that something is coming—notably, a "something" that promises to include the one who senses it. In both cases, this "something" is an emergent effect of a situation charged with affect. In systems theory, emergence is a property of complex systems: an accumulation of small, relatively simple interactions produces patterns at a larger level of complexity.[55] In a similar way, dancefloors and the crowds that fill them can also be understood as complex systems out of which a sense of collectivity can emerge, without being deliberately induced by any particular participant. And much like the emergent effects described by systems theory, no one knows what shape this solidifying "something" will take before it emerges. Crucially, I argue that what matters is not so much the precise form or name of this "something" to come but rather that its incipience is felt and shared among members of a crowd. For many of the partygoers whom I interviewed, it was the event of "feeling it together" that generated a sense of the social, and the process of its emergence was more significant in their recollections than the precise form of what eventually coalesced. For Teresa, this emergent "something" enabled partygoers to "let themselves go," to open themselves up to new and adventurous encounters. Chapter 5 focuses on how partygoers talk about letting themselves go while partying, considering the risks and rewards of "coming undone."

5 THE SWEETNESS OF COMING UNDONE

During the Silvester (New Year's) party at Berghain / Panorama Bar in 2013–2014, resident DJ Virginia played Dominica's "Gotta Let You Go," a mid-1990s vocal dance track that was a crossover pop hit of the rave era.[1] This track marked a high point in her set, eliciting a shared moment of surging affect on the dancefloor: the audience sang along, hands in the air, to the lyrics of the chorus-like buildup and exploded in euphoric dancing when the track's core groove of drums and melodic synth bass line followed immediately afterward, marking a thunderous and collectively articulated "structural downbeat." I was there, in the throng of dancers pressed close to the DJ booth; in the wake of this moment, I had the opportunity to discuss it with several friends, acquaintances, and strangers. For many longtime "regulars" of the club, Virginia's musical selection in that moment was understood to be a loving tribute to Prosumer (Achim Brandenburg), a former resident DJ of the club for whom "Gotta Let You Go" served as a "signature track" frequently played in his own DJ sets.

These conversations extended into social media over the following days, such as the "Panorama Bar Music" Facebook group, where partygoers would post YouTube links to tracks they had heard at the venue the previous weekend.[2] A few days after Virginia's New Year's set, a friend of mine posted a link to the Dominica track, describing Virginia's selection as a "shout-out to Prosumer." In April of the same year, as I was working on another part of this book, I sought out that link on the Panorama Bar Music page and reposted it on my own Facebook wall with a heart-shaped emoji as my only comment. Another friend immediately posted a comment on the link in a mixture of English and French: "So many souvenirs . . . *pincement au coeur.*" Translated literally as "a pinch to the heart," their "pincement au coeur" served as a somatic articulation of affect that conveyed poignancy, bittersweet feelings, pain, and a tugging at their heartstrings.

The poignancy of "Gotta Let You Go" was never more intense than when Prosumer played it during his farewell DJ set in Panorama Bar. Prosumer left the roster of resident DJs in 2012, allegedly due to an irresolvable conflict between his booking agent (who had left the club's booking agency and record label OstGut Ton) and the club's own "360-degree artist management" policy, which required resident DJs to have their bookings, musical releases, and publicity managed "in house" by OstGut Ton. In June of that year, during the weekend of Berlin's "Christopher Street Day" gay-pride events, Prosumer played his last set as a resident DJ in Panorama Bar. Tama Sumo (Kerstin Egert), a fellow resident DJ and longtime friend of Prosumer's, handed out more than two hundred button pins with an "I ♥ Prosumer" design reminiscent of the iconic "I ♥ NY" logo. Two friends of mine brought Prosumer flowers and orchestrated a surprise tribute to him, where, toward the end of his set, "sparklers" were lit and distributed to people near the DJ booth while everyone in the room sat down on the dancefloor in a gesture of both deep respect and deep sorrow. Prosumer wept openly throughout most of his four-hour set—wiping tears from his eyes as he wiped dust from his records—and he was not alone: friends, strangers, fans, bartenders, and dancers were all caught up in the vortex of affect.

The party was saturated with the affects of slow-motion rupture: sorrow, love, pain, uncertainty, bitterness, helplessness, consolation, and—at moments—grace. Lauren Berlant defines *cruel optimism* as an attachment to an object that obstructs your flourishing but also sustains your sense of being in the world.[3] If Prosumer was breaking with a dynamic of cruel optimism by leaving the world-famous OstGut Ton roster after nearly a decade, the affective intensity and collective distress felt at the occasion illustrates how destabilizing such a departure can be. And yet, another Facebook comment to the same video link by another regular patron and mutual friend read, "Oh I remember when Achim played it, [it] was sooooo sweet!" Indeed, as painful as Prosumer's farewell set was to experience, it was remembered fondly afterward by many who were there as a moment of profound sweetness.

This chapter works toward a better understanding of musical-affective moments such as these, when things seem to come undone but also to come together. Drawing from interviews and musical analyses as well as fieldwork observations, it considers how intense experiences figure in festive narratives as well as how partygoers manage both their destructive and vitalizing potentials. In contrast to chapter 4's focus on the thickening of collectivity through shared affective experience, here narratives of unraveling and crisis are examined in light of the value they hold for partygoers. Continuing on with the textural metaphors of previous chapters, "rough" experiences play a prominent role in these narratives, where they are valued for adding richness and vibrancy to these musical outings. The resulting dynamics of *coming undone*—of finding pleasure and relief in unraveling—provide a combination of roughness and sweetness that addresses the dissatisfactions of partygoers' everyday lives.

I argue, however, that the rough experiences of coming undone do not aim toward the sort of self-shattering and radical transformation associated with psychoanalytic concepts of *jouissance* and limit-experience but rather to the smaller-scale, incremental, and iterative pleasures of stretching the self apart and snapping back together again. In contrast to the collective and impersonal aspects of affective experience explored in earlier chapters, here my focus is on how practices of unraveling impact the self, the person, the subject. But, in keeping with previous chapters, theory emerges out of engagement with ethnographic materials, following narratives in which the self seems to come undone at the seams. These analyses are buttressed at various points by Kane Race's queer-critical work on the politics of drug use, particularly his exploration of experiential states that go outside the realm of self-control and intention.[4] By identifying the potential pleasures of unpredictability and serendipity through drug-induced self-derailment, Race provides a means of understanding why and how rough experience and coming undone can be desirable, despite the risks and strains they entail. In this sense, the practices gathered under the heading of "coming undone" seem to be aimed at creating openings in and for the self, a place where one can sustain a utopian hope for feeling (and being) otherwise than ordinary—or at least for a temporary reprieve from the exhausting work of maintaining a coherent self under everyday regimes of normalcy. This dynamic emerges in partygoers' accounts of "a good night out," which eschew heroic/melodramatic narratives of self-shattering in favor of more ambiguous and variegated ones, blending enjoyment and ordeal.

Compared to earlier chapters in this book, the conceptual work here is grounded in a more dialogic style of interviewing, in which I shared my preliminary concepts and analyses with interlocutors at the time of the interview, inviting comment and collaboration. As such, this chapter includes voices that extend, complicate, and sometimes challenge the ideas developed within, thus providing an opportunity for interviewees to intervene in the development of analytic concepts that bear on the musical and social world in which they are stakeholders. During my fieldwork, partygoers often expressed ambivalence about what one should want from a night out partying. Do you go out for thrills or relaxation? Do you want to enjoy control or abandon? Should the night go smoothly or be full of surprises? This ambivalence played out between two extremes of experience that my interlocutors often articulated using pairs of terms describing contrasting qualities, such as "intense"/"relaxed," "ordered"/"chaotic," "hot"/"cool," "wild"/"tame," and "smooth"/"rough." Since my preliminary research had already been taking a tactile and textural turn, I found myself focusing increasingly on the terms "smooth" and "rough." Many aspects of a night out might be usefully described in terms of texture, such as music, affect, social contact, space, and the flow of events. Much of the ambivalence underlying the questions about a "good" night out could arise from conflicting desires for the flow of the night out to be both richly textured and frictionless. Affectively, smoothness provides stability and comfort, while roughness generates excitement, novelty, and a whiff of danger. Each offers its own kind of pleasure.

And so, I decided to disclose my own preliminary ideas about textured experience during one-on-one interviews with partygoers. When broaching this topic, I first asked my interlocutors to describe a "good night out" without any conceptual framing or prompting beyond the request that they begin by "telling a story" from their own experience. After this first round of storytelling, I offered a preliminary reading of their narratives through my own theoretical lenses, highlighting notable moments and outlining my tentative ideas about rough/smooth experience. Continuing in a dialogical fashion that invited feedback and revision, interviewees' responses indicated that the use of texture as a metaphor to describe nightlife experience was both an apt and useful means of articulating their own take on an otherwise nebulous topic. Interviewees first engaged with these concepts by using them to reinterpret their own stories, which then prompted them to speak in more general terms about the role of rough/smooth experience in a night of dancing to electronic music. These storytelling sessions and subsequent conversations provided the primary materials for this chapter's conceptual work.

One of the risks of effectively "beta testing" one's own preliminary concepts in ethnographic interviews is that they could override those that interviewees may already have developed about a given phenomenon. It was due to these concerns that I chose to wait until after the first round of storytelling to introduce my own analytic concepts. Also, I took pains to present my own conceptual framework as tentative and subject to revision, explicitly asking for their opinions and suggestions. Fortunately, as their quotations throughout this book attest, my interlocutors were not shy in sharing their own interpretations of dance music culture. In any case, I was struck by the lively engagement these textured metaphors elicited during interviews, seeming to provide a handy heuristic that facilitated a more productive discussion of their experiences. As soon as I had briefly proposed "rough" and "smooth" as descriptors of textured experience, interviewees seized on them and put them to use, illustrating them with personal anecdotes while also refining and/or extending their conceptual scope. The concepts introduced in this chapter have thus arisen from a multithreaded dialogue with actors in the field, functioning as a sort of feedback loop in which they were able to intervene and collaborate in the process of theorization.

This chapter is organized into two ethnographic sections focusing on the roughness of partygoing experience and the sweetness of coming undone, both of which frame an intervening musical analysis of three minimal-house tracks by Ricardo Villalobos, a German Chilean electronic dance music producer who has enjoyed both critical acclaim and wide popularity since the beginning of the twenty-first century. His influential dance music tracks serve as examples of musical unfurling and shifting sonic textures, indexing the practices of psychic unraveling that are presented in the ethnographic portions of this chapter. Diverging from the hyperbolic trajectories of self-shattering usually associated with the quest for extreme experience, partygoers' accounts of coming undone suggest a different set of stakes, aims, and potential consequences, which are the subject of a brief reflection on "openings" in the closing section.

Roughness

Although the bittersweet moment at Prosumer's farewell performance arose from a unique confluence of circumstances, it is also emblematic of a broader pattern in electronic dance music scenes, where ordeals are endured but also enjoyed as productive and potentially transformative. During her interview, Fantômette remarked, "J'aime bien quand il se passe des choses dans la soirée," translating roughly to "I like it when things happen during a night out" (Paris, 2009). When partygoers plan, imagine, idealize, and recount a night out, they often articulate a desire for something to *happen*, a yearning for moments of intensity that make a night meaningful and memorable. Notably, the textures of these festive narratives often alternate between smooth flow and jarring rupture, which also manifest themselves in the sonic textures and figurations of the music circulating in these scenes. Here, the vocabulary of sonic texture and grain developed in chapter 2 provides a useful heuristic: smooth experience is stable but flat, whereas rough experience is richly textured but risky and destabilizing. In interviews with partygoers, they cherished memories of "a good night out" enriched by the textures of rough experience, although they were usually sustained (and contained) by a frame of smooth experience.

For example, when I asked Lola to describe "a good night out" partying, she related several narratives full of crises, surprising reversals, and narrow escapes. In particular, she highlighted the second and third installments of the Souvenir parties, which were a series of minimal-house-music parties organized in Chicago by a mutual friend, Ofelia, and her husband in 2009. Souvenir 03, in fact, has already appeared twice in this book: as the vignette of tactile stranger-intimacy that opened chapter 1 and as Lola's "musical moment" related in chapter 4. Although Lola and other members of the Souvenir collective remember these parties fondly, they were also marked by memorable adversity.

A Good Night Out

Lola played an important supporting role in the Souvenir series, helping with organizational tasks as well as displaying her paintings at the party as a "resident" artist. The night before Souvenir 02 was to take place, she received a call from a distraught Ofelia: the venue owner had changed his mind and broken their verbal agreement to rent the building for the event. The headlining performers, Masomenos (Adrien de Maublanc and Joan

Costes, a creative duo from France who ran their project as music producers, performers, a record label, and a graphic-art conceptual "brand"), had already been flown into town, the sound and lighting equipment had already been reserved with security deposits, the refreshments had already been purchased, and advance tickets had already been sold.[5] A day later, after making frantic phone calls, Ofelia announced that she had secured a new location: it was "perfect" in size and dimensions, located in an industrial zone that was away from prying eyes (and ears), and well suited for creative decoration as well as an exhibition of Lola's artworks.

Lola arrived at the venue early with the rest of the Souvenir crew and spent well over four hours transforming the space. It was a vast warehouse space with a set of large reinforced-concrete pillars about halfway between the walls and the center of the room, creating a rough rectangle. In order to create a more intimate dancefloor without sacrificing the rest of the space, they spent hours winding and taping clear plastic sheeting around all of the pillars well above head level, creating translucent walls with a "door" between two pillars. The outer "gallery" area was host to the rest of the party's infrastructure: box office, refreshment booth, art exhibition, and seating. Lola and a few other visual artist friends also took masking tape in fluorescent colors to the black walls of the space and re-created several of the cartoon-like animal figures that are part of the Masomenos visual concept.[6]

By all reports, the party was a success—until the police showed up. Attendance was substantial but not overwhelming, and the atmosphere was both exuberant and intimate. As Lola related, however, at 4:00 A.M., "the fucking cops come in, just right as Adrien [of Masomenos] was playing. And, within a half-hour, I saw hours and hours of hard labor being . . . taken to shit, basically" (Chicago, 2010). But all was not lost: two friends from the Souvenir crew had recently moved into a "true warehouse loft" (that is, an industrial space not officially converted to residential use), in an isolated industrial zone of the East Garfield Park neighborhood of Chicago. They offered their new apartment as an alternate venue, word was spread to relieved partygoers, and the party crew spent the next hour cleaning up and moving to the new space. During our interview, Lola identified this afterparty as the first occasion where she felt "a real kind of connection" with the Souvenir collective.

> **LOLA:** The party, Souvenir 02, was such a struggle. Losing the space, then finding the space, then getting it all together and people *loving* the space, loving the party, . . . then it all getting broken down, us

tearing it down in a half hour—the hours and hours and hours of labor going down. And then, going to [our friends' place] and just kinda being, like, "*Pshhh* . . . here we are now!" (Chicago, 2010)

The warehouse-loft apartment would become the weekly destination for bacchanalian afterparties for the rest of 2009 and the first quarter of 2010; my friends and fieldwork contacts dubbed the loft "Club Regret," with a mixture of irony and shared embarrassment that evinced a sort of "cultural intimacy" of their local music scene through an ambivalent mix of affective resonances.[7] Souvenir 03, as described in more detail in chapter 1, was held in a disused storefront in the South Loop neighborhood, with the Paris-based DJ and music producer Seuil (aka Alexis Benard) as the headliner. The space was underventilated and close to freshly gentrified condominiums, which created a great deal of tension, considering the organizers' experiences at the previous Souvenir party. Although the party finished without interruption by the police, the night was not devoid of excitement for Lola.

> **LOLA:** [A fellow artist, Craig] and I were splashing paint on the wall and we had to clean it up.[8] Oh my God! I didn't realize until recently how much cleaning there was to be done, because what happened that morning, at eight in the morning, is, um . . . Jim's girlfriend got extremely ill, and I was like, "I will drive them home." I was fine. What's really interesting about that morning is that I had *just* taken a pill, and I willed it to not kick in.
>
> [Anyway] me and Craig sprayed paint all over the wall, and then we tried to clean it up [with a fresh layer of white paint]. And people came up to us and were like, "Don't use that paint because it's smelling up the whole place, and there's no ventilation in here! What the fuck are you guys doing?" You know, we had people yell at us, "Stop using the paint to paint over it!" I see a lot of people are leaving to go to [another friend's place], and I really, really felt like leaving, but I'm like, "I can*not* leave here! I'm invested in this." I always am, you know? I always feel bad leaving; even if Ofelia and her husband are gonna leave five minutes later, I feel a little weird leaving.
>
> The next thing I know, Jim's girlfriend is pale and blue, like . . . just sitting there, and everybody's trying to make her come back alive. Ofelia's husband asks, "Who can drive them home right now?" And I had just taken a pill, *just* taken it. And I'm like, "I'm OK to drive. Let me

do this." And I go to Craig, I'm like, "Look, this girl is sick. I need to get them home, like, now." Me and Margaret, we go around the back. We pick them up from the loading dock. She's looking all pale; she looks like she's about to die, and I'm thinking to myself, "Holy fuck! I am high, and this girl might die in my car right now." But I'm like, "I don't care, I don't care, I don't care, I don't care." I'm like, "I will try to get her home OK."

So, yes, we're at [an intersection near the couple's home], and Margaret is trying as best as she can; she's studying to be a nurse, so she's trying to make her breathe; she's making her take deep breaths. Once we're on Grand Avenue, I see Jim's girlfriend go, "Ahhh, I'm better!" And all of a sudden, the color comes back into her face, and she's like, "I'm way better now." And I'm like, "Oh, thank God, thank God." And she starts smiling, and Margaret is making her do breathing exercises. We get to her house, and they get out of the car. And Jim's bicycle is parked outside, and it's bright orange with a bright-orange chain to it. . . . And I'm like . . . I just felt so good about doing this for them. And she's like, all in tears, "I'm so sorry! I'm so sorry!" And I'm like, "You have nothing to be sorry about. Nothing at all."

But we get back to the space, and then there's more drama because I guess, like, John was leaving and Kate wanted to stay [both DJs from another town, both had performed that night, and both were in the process of ending a romantic relationship with each other]. So, she thought they were leaving, and she seemed all unhappy. And I was like, "Come with us! Come with us! We're going to [our friends' apartment]!" And she gets there, and she starts playing hard techno because she's *pissed*. And then, you know, John ended up showing up anyway, and, oh . . . just so much, so much. (Chicago, 2010)

Note how Lola recounted both of her nights out almost entirely in movement from crisis to crisis; the smooth and untroubled intervals barely merited a mention, despite making up a much larger proportion of the duration of these two Souvenir parties. Furthermore, it was during these moments of high intensity that she recalled sensory details, such as the orange of Jim's bicycle as she drove them back home or the paint vapors as she and Craig struggled to cover their paintings while dancers complained of the stench. Lola's account highlighted moments of struggle and surprise—both collective and personal—that became temporal markers for the evening, serving both as mnemonic "bookmarks" for recollection and as moments of intensity that lent phenomenological thickness to the whole night out. While her conflict-focused storytelling is not unique to electronic dance music scenes or especially atypical of narrative form in general, what is of interest here is how rough experiences dominate Lola's recollection of these specific parties, eclipsing parts of the evening that went more smoothly.

Lola was certainly not alone among my interlocutors in foregrounding difficult moments of intensity; nearly every person I interviewed included stressful and destabilizing events in their accounts of a successful night out. Taken as a sort of oral archive or repertoire, these accounts share certain tropes of rough experience that tend to arise at different points in their festive narratives. Polina, a Chicago-based systems analyst in her early thirties, provided a vivid example of one of the most common narrative tropes, in which challenges are overcome at the beginning of the night—especially getting to or into the party. She had traveled to Berlin a few years before our interview to visit a romantic partner and spend some time partying with him. One of her favorite memories of that visit was when the two of them successfully entered Berghain by pretending to be on the guest list, all the while being very high on MDMA. This was no small feat, considering the severity of the door staff at the club.

> POLINA: I don't even know how it can make someone so happy and passionate to remember a moment like this! Five o'clock in the morning, and we had just gotten out of some drama—we had to send someone home [*laughs*]—and I'm with this guy. I'm completely fucked up, with my pupils like this [*gestures to indicate dilated pupils*]. We come up to Berghain, and my knees are just *shaking*. We see a crowd of people, and he's telling me, "Wait, OK, you gotta be strong! You gotta act cool, OK?" And we started walking past the crowd, past the line. And we come up to the door and we say, "We're on [a certain DJ]'s list." And I'm about to fall over and *collapse*, because, like, we have several hundred people looking at us, like, "Who the hell are *you*?" And then [the bouncers] are like, "Yeah." They let us in. That moment: "Oh my God, we're in Berghain!" (Chicago, 2010)

Polina's narrative illustrates a powerful trope of difficult beginnings, in which an initial ordeal serves multiple narrative ends as a rite of passage, a dramatic transition to an extraordinary setting, and a means of "earning" the fun and pleasure that follows. But another common trope highlights crises that happen during the party itself, where some form of challenging experience "makes the party," in the sense of making perseverance itself a victory to be celebrated. For example, the Detroit native and Chicago resident Imogen, who works primarily as a restaurant server and bartender, told a tale of inclement weather at the outdoor "piknik elektronic" event as part of Montréal's digital arts and music festival MUTEK:

> IMOGEN: I never had so much fun with a group of strangers—and wanted to get so tight with them—than when we were at MUTEK [2009] and it started to rain. Everybody put their blankets over their heads, and we had a big party underneath there. We probably had, like, sixty people we didn't know underneath there, crouching in together, *laughing* about the rain, just enjoying it. You know, at one point we were bummed that it was cold; at the same time, though, it really made the moment, and it really brought everybody closer together. So, that's a great example of intimacy and how even bad things become good—and how . . . one big piece of fabric can change the entire vibe of a party. (Chicago, 2010)

Although cold weather and rain would normally put a significant damper on an outdoor dance party—as Imogen initially admits—the efforts made to mitigate this setback create a sense of camaraderie and adventure for her, illustrating how "even bad things become good." Notably, the two foregoing tropes conclude in some form of positive resolution, allowing these rough experiences to be assimilated into a larger narrative of "good times." By contrast, a more ambivalent trope sometimes occurs toward the end of partying narratives, when the party ends adversely and the struggle to cope eclipses earlier revelry. Polina, for example, attended a large rave in 2005 in the suburbs of Chicago, which was dangerously overpacked and doomed to be shut down by the police—while she and other partygoers were still high.

> POLINA: We went, and it was . . . fuck, that huge factory warehouse building in Chicago. It was like 2005 or something, and for some reason a lot of people showed up. I'm, like, "Oh my God, yes!" You walk in, there's this huge industrial space, several rooms. I took a pill, I met a guy, and, uh . . . [*laughs*]. things like that, you know? And the party got shut down, and . . . the whole, the *affect* of it: "Oh my God! It's so illegal!" They were trying to keep the cops at the door for a while, and finally they somehow got in. And then, all of a sudden, the music stops, the

light turns on, and all these crowds of people! We start going out, and I'm like, "Oh my God, what do I do? Like, I'm still rolling!" [i.e., high on MDMA/Ecstasy]. So much excitement! (Chicago, 2010)

Polina exclaimed, "Oh my God!" three times during this anecdote: expressing excitement to see the gritty industrial location and above-capacity crowd, expressing titillation at the illegality of the rave, and expressing a mixture of confusion and panic as she found herself still high while having to deal with the abrupt termination of her night out. And yet, the distressing situation indicated by her final exclamation was immediately followed by another—"So much excitement!"—which she delivered with a tone of voice and facial expression that conveyed sweet memories rather than distressing crisis. Beyond the tropes illustrated in the foregoing anecdotes, interviewees fondly recounted other small-scale dramas of loss: losing belongings, getting lost in transit, unraveling in extended states of intoxication, and so on. Notably, all of these tropes of rough experience are related as moments rather than ongoing states; conversely, when an unpleasant situation becomes an ongoing condition that must be endured without reprieve, the pleasurable interplay between roughness and sweetness seems to be lost.

Managing Roughness

Indeed, the pacing, rhythm, and proportion of rough experience all factor into how partygoers assess electronic dance music parties—both retrospectively and prospectively. This concern for the ebb and flow of nightlife outings repeatedly came up in conversations with my fieldwork contacts and especially so during one-on-one interviews. Notably, every interviewee had strong—if sometimes divergent—views about the optimal balance and flow of rough and smooth experience. Among them, Nancy's clearly articulated comments bear citing at length:

> NANCY: I think that when you arrive at a venue and you're immediately hit with rough music, that doesn't put you in very good condition. I think that I need something more gradual, that is to say, something that, at the beginning of the night out, lets you have a drink with friends, chat, put yourself a bit in the groove, do your warm-ups—your stretches on the dancefloor. That can quickly become boring, so there needs to be something a bit more impactful and

omnipresent during the night, that is, music that is a bit rougher. That's my point of view. Otherwise, I don't really see myself doing a totally smooth night out, all night long.

On the other hand, a night where it does nothing but slam away all night—only rough—poses the same problem. If there isn't a moment of punctuation, if there isn't a moment of respite, breathing, and oscillation between different emotions. . . . You can't stay endlessly in the same emotion and at the same intensity; it's just not possible. (Paris, 2009)

Slipping fluidly between music, dance, socializing, and consumption as indexes of affective texture, Nancy employs elements of dramatic narrative form to limn the contours of her night out, beginning with a low-intensity introduction into the nightclub space followed by gradual escalation. But rather than treating rough experience as the teleological endpoint of a singular narrative climax, she instead invokes articulation and repetition to describe an ongoing play between rough and smooth. In doing so, she also refers back to the extensible, modular temporal cycles of electronic dance music that facilitated affective entrainment in chapter 4. Several other interviewees also characterized the affective flow of a good night out as an oscillation between rough and smooth experience, highlighting the importance of pacing. Notably, for Nancy as well as for many other interviewees, this oscillation is shaped to a great degree by DJs, party organizers, venue staff, and other nightlife workers who have a hand in shaping the flux of intensities during the party.

Rather than alternation, some interviewees spoke in terms of layering, preferring to have rough experience embedded within a broader frame of smooth experience. In contrast to Nancy's comments, Franck initially claimed to appreciate both rough and smooth experience equally, but he ultimately professed a predilection for more intense, rough experience.

FRANCK: Well, I like both [rough and smooth experience]. I like things that flow. The problem is that the rougher nights out that you were describing are more difficult to . . . well, not to manage, but they require many more favorable factors in order to go well. You see, that means that I do indeed like it when things are much more extreme, but nothing can go wrong. You can be pushing towards something good, but as soon as something goes wrong, you can derail real fast. (Paris, 2009)

Franck saw the potential fun of a very rough night out as perhaps more intense and gratifying but also much more precarious. For him, rough experience was only enjoyable when everything else went smoothly, when stabilizing layers of smooth experience prevented rough experience from veering off into catastrophe. Imogen, by contrast, seemed at first to have an inverse perspective on this layered approach: in principle, she preferred an evening of smooth experience, but she acknowledged that some of her most fondly remembered moments came from facing and overcoming a crisis with her friends. As an example of this, she recounted a tale from the last of the Souvenir parties in Chicago:

> IMOGEN: My idea of a good time, or a smooth show or a smooth party, is no problems, no fights, lots of cold drinks, not running out of drinks, awesome music, great lighting, killer dancefloor, everybody happy, and a fun afterparty. Part of the fun, though, of a good party is when something goes wrong and you fix it really, really fast, you know?
>
> Prime example: last Souvenir, the speakers went down. Me and Ofelia [the party organizer], I look at her, and I'm like, "You still got JBLs [monitor loudspeakers] at your house?" She goes, "Let's go. And we'll need some boys to carry it" [laughs]. It made for a good story, and it was really funny that she said that. We fixed it, and then we partied on. (Chicago, 2010)

Although contrasting, Imogen and Franck both describe situations where rough and smooth experience happen at the same time; or, to be more precise, one is embedded in another. For Franck, rough experience in one aspect of the evening is only sustainable to the extent that other aspects remain smooth; for example, getting very drunk or high can go well only so long as you have access to water, you can find a taxi to go home, your friends are willing to play a caretaker role, nobody tries to take advantage of your intoxication, and so on. For Imogen, rough experience is not so much sustained as absorbed: jarring experiences irrupt into the scene of smooth experience and then dissipate. Interestingly, it is the moment of rough experience's neutralization that makes a good night out for her, providing welcome focal points for her energies as well as the satisfaction of overcoming them. Although Imogen and Frank differed in how they envisioned mitigating rough experience, they both understood it to be embedded in smooth experience, as if the latter provides a stabilizing scaffold for the pleasurably destabilizing effects of the former.

Precisely because of its perceived predictability, smooth experience risks engendering boredom, and boredom is an affective state (or an attenuation of affect) for which partygoers have little tolerance. All of my interlocutors, at one point or another during their interviews, characterized feeling bored as the telltale sign of a failed night out. For example, when Polina described her notion of "a good night out," her first move was to forbid boredom and gesture toward unpredictability: "It can't be boring. It should be adventurous, and it should be something unexpected" (Chicago, 2010). Similarly, Lisette described herself as "easily bored," during a night out: "even *smooth, cool*, and all that . . . sure, great. But, if I go out, I want things to move. I want things to *happen*" (Paris, 2009). For Lisette, there is a sense that things do not "happen" with smooth experience—or, rather, that smooth experience does not leave behind affective echoes of impactful "happening" in the way that rough experience does. Georges, a midthirties Parisian working in the culinary arts, went further, making an explicit connection between smooth experience and boredom:

> **GEORGES:** If everything were smooth, sooner or later, it could become repetitive, and then you'd get bored. It would be a bit flat, ultimately. Whereas, when it's a bit more rough, when things happen—whether they are negative or positive—that's the best. It's about going to extremes; it's about living intense moments. (Paris, 2009)

For Georges, there was no ambiguity about which mode of experience he prefers for a night out; regardless of other factors that may constrain his choices, he prized the rougher experiences as most valuable—whether positive or negative—and devalued smoother experiences as trending toward boredom. In doing so, he set up another binary opposition, in which one kind of experience approaches extremes of arousal and another flatness.

In contrast to those like Nancy, who prioritize a balanced mix of smooth and rough experience, Georges, Lisette, and several others conceptualize their ideal night out in terms of maximizing the proportion of rough experience while maintaining only as much smooth experience as necessary to mitigate the risks and costs of rough experience. Crucially, their perspective transforms the apparent dichotomy between smooth and rough into a dialectic of regulation and mutual mitigation. Rather than smooth and rough experience being mutually exclusive, these partygoers see them as managing each other in some fashion. Rough experience provides a sort of insurance against boredom by injecting unpredictability into the situation, while smooth experience stabilizes precarious acts and partially absorbs their consequences.

Smooth and rough experiences each furnish the conditions of (affordable) perpetuation of the other, thus making a night out as much a project of synthesis as one of pleasure. There remains, however, the question of why one would devote leisure time and resources to a festive experience tinted with ordeal. Polina raised this question while reflecting on her desire for darkness and difficulty during a night out dancing:

> POLINA: It's not interesting when it's all good and just, you know, just happy thoughts and nothing's going on, you know? It's gotta be a little . . . it's gotta be a little shady. And it's weird. Why would I . . . why would I like that? (Chicago, 2010)

The rest of this chapter addresses Polina's question: Why would a partygoer seek out difficult experiences? How are such experiences fun, or is there more to fun than distraction and release? In order to better understand the sweetness of roughness, I turn to an analysis of musical examples from the oeuvre of the DJ and producer Ricardo Villalobos, tracking how both smooth and rough experience are figured musically in electronic dance music. The musical processes involved will in turn provide the basis for understanding the dynamics of "coming undone"—or what it means to put oneself through rough experience.

Musical Unravelings: Three Tracks by Ricardo Villalobos

> POLINA: Stretching yourself, and coming undone . . . and undone and undone [*laughs*]. Coming undone and getting back, going to the place and getting back . . . without electronic music? Would I think that it would be possible? There is a magic, that hypnotic something that makes it appropriate for activities like that. And when everything is just right, you see every minute from an absolutely different perspective. (Chicago, 2010)

Many of the themes evoked in this chapter coalesce sonically in the music of the minimal electronic music producer Ricardo Villalobos. In many of his most popular tracks, smoothness and roughness are aesthetically figured in textural, metric, and vocal registers. The manner in which the (musical-*cum*-psychic) "subject" of each of these registers dissolves and coalesces provides a music-theoretical framework for engaging with ethnographic accounts of the sweetness of rough experience. In particular, this sweetness seems to arise out of a process of *coming undone*, a sort of unraveling under stress that generates pleasure and drives subtle transformations. In other words, the trippy textures of Villalobos's tracks can help us understand the appeal of coming undone.

References to mental and emotional unraveling abound in electronic music cultures: in published reviews of dance music tracks and parties, in promotional copy for these same recordings and nightlife events, in intimate conversations between partygoers on and off the dancefloor, in the titles of dance tracks, in the semantic content and sonic treatment of vocal samples, and even in the wordless textures of the music itself. Nowhere is this clearer than in the music (and persona) of Ricardo Villalobos. The following ethnographic vignette provides a small taste of how some fans respond to the musician and his music.

LE REX CLUB, PARIS; SUNDAY, NOVEMBER 2, 2008; 1:30 A.M.

The atmosphere is somewhat tense in the guest-list line. Tonight is a showcase event for the Cologne-based Kompakt label, and everyone seems to have underestimated the sheer size of the crowd that this would draw. The guest list is set to close at 2:00 A.M., and there are still at least fifty people waiting in the guest list line at 1:30 A.M. To add to the tension, latecomers are cutting the line to join friends near the front (or pretending that they have friends near the front), much to the disgruntled muttering of those around me.

I am distracted from the shenanigans of line cutters by a conversation that begins just behind me. A young woman and a young man, apparently strangers, introduce themselves and launch into the most important sort of small talk: comparing taste in music and recounting vivid tales of their most memorable nights out.

At first, I am struck by their detailed knowledge of DJs and producers in the minimal-techno/house circuit; back in Chicago, this level of connoisseurship is rare except among a small community of aficionados. Then I am struck by the way in which they describe the emotional character of their attachments to the music they like. The woman is particularly passionate when she describes her favorite DJ and producer, Ricardo Villalobos, whose music she claims "gets into [her] head" and overwhelms her. And then, this: "The last time I saw him, I didn't know whether to dance or cry or scream or whatever. I was thinking: What do you want from me?"

As she continues to talk, she repeatedly describes an intense musical excitement that is polyvalent or ambivalent. It's not clear to her, even in hindsight, whether that excitement was euphoric, distressing, shattering, or enraging; she feels disorganized, she comes undone—at least a little bit. Of course, if she loves Villalobos's music as much as she does, the excitement that his music engenders in her must feel like some sort of pleasure more often than not. But it seems nonetheless possible that coming undone gave her a kind of pleasure, too.[9]

It is perhaps unsurprising that two fans of *minimale* would end up bonding over Ricardo Villalobos; his international profile as a celebrity DJ and minimal-house/techno producer makes him an inexhaustible topic of conversation among fans. Since the early 2000s, he has enjoyed something resembling superstar status within the global networks of electronic dance music, frequently appearing at or near the top of "World's Best DJ" lists and performing internationally nearly every weekend at the height of his career.[10] When he works as a studio producer, his musical releases are always eagerly awaited and frequently "charted" by prominent DJs.[11] Rumors and underground lore also abound about his hard-partying lifestyle, particularly his alleged propensity to indulge in intoxicants (especially the dissociative drug ketamine) while performing. These rumors are often repeated or obliquely referenced by music critics to explain the strange, surreal, or psychedelic qualities of his music. In reviews of his albums and releases (singles, EPs), critics often use a vocabulary of extreme mental states and psychic breakdown: "trippy," "mind-melting," "hallucinogenic," "addled brainsoup," "devastating," "entropic," "demented," "skull-crushing," "freaky," and so on.[12] In fact, Villalobos's idiosyncratic style has sometimes been dubbed "ketamine house," drawing comparisons between psychic dissociation and the sparse, shifting, unraveling textures of his music.

The approaches to sonic texture developed in previous chapters provide an analytic starting point from which to make sense of the layered minimalism of Villalobos's tracks, which feature a variegated mix of textures. For example, "Que Belle Epoque 2006" begins with a smooth surface, including syncopated synth loops with rounded attack envelopes and watery, harmonized resonance; tightly compressed bass kicks with similarly rounded attacks but also a very short decay; and samples of rhythmic "ahs" by a breathy feminine voice (fading in from 05:13), eventually opening up into a sighing refrain supported by syncopated woodwind riffs.[13] And yet, the momentum of this sustained flow is punctuated by hi-hats and hand claps—crisply compressed and noise-gated—that create momentary gaps in the otherwise reverb-heavy middle frequencies, as well as the female vocalist's shift from soft vocables to nasal shouting and cry breaks (for example, at 05:30 in the recording).[14] "Easy Lee" and "What You Say Is More than I Can Say" are both built around masculine voices drowned in effects—pushed through a vocoder in the former track, through a harmonizer in the latter—drifting in and out of aural and semantic intelligibility over percussion loops that seem to alternate between precarious staggering and driving, flowing movement.[15] This play between smooth and rough sonic textures echoes interviewees' narratives of "a good night out"; and these narratives, in turn, tell a story about release and reshaping in the register of excitement and escapade.

Villalobos's treatment of vocal samples and meter, as well as the interplay he creates between voice and percussion loops, indexes coming undone by staging the human voice as a subject that is continually unraveling. In most of his tracks featuring vocals, Villalobos places various forms of pressure on the human voice, such as chopping it into nonlexical vocables, submerging it in "reverb" or distortion effects, and attenuating its volume until it blends into the rest of the musical texture. "Que Belle Epoque 2006," for example, begins with what sounds at first like a midfrequency synthesizer stab on offbeats (see figure 5.1); but once a breathy feminine voice begins to sing a sixteen-beat melodic pattern (05:30), her voice lines up rhythmically with the synthesizer stab, and it becomes clear that the stab had actually been a chopped, compressed sample of the woman's voice. This voice later changes to a sighing, murmuring eight-beat pattern, providing the closest thing this track has to a refrain (06:01); her voice projects a relaxed, low-affect, "smooth" mood here, not only by the contour of the melodic pattern but also through her use of a low vocal register (which requires less air pressure and thus less strain) and low volume. This eight-beat sighing pattern returns repeatedly throughout the rest of the track, always accompanied by a short, four-beat, polyphonic woodwind sample that interlocks rhythmically with her pattern (its point of repetition is on beat 2 rather than beat 1).

"Que Belle Epoque" (2006), Partial Transcription
Ricardo Villalobos (trans. Luis-Manuel Garcia)

FIGURE 5.1 Ricardo Villalobos, "Que Belle Epoque 2006," partial transcription by the author; music engraving by G. Galindo (2021).

Throughout the track, this driving percussion loop interlocks with a bass synth pattern that crosses the bar line (starting a sixteenth note before beat 3 and ending on beat 1 of the next bar, coinciding with the woodwind sample), thus giving the impression of forward momentum. This momentum, however, is interrupted at several points in the track through a temporary destabilization of meter. One instance occurs on the fourteenth iteration of the opening four-beat loop (at approximately 0:23), when the hand claps shift from offbeats (beats 2 and 4) to downbeats (1 and 3). Since the hand claps were the only element with an attack at the beginning of beat 2, this shift creates a silence on beat 2 that breaks the flow of the loop and gives the impression that the downbeat of the metric cycle has shifted by one beat. Eight cycles later (at 0:38), the hand claps return to beats 2 and 4, the full loop is restored, and the sense of meter snaps back into place. This metric diversion, which repeats at 01:33 again, is a transient instance of what Mark J. Butler calls "turning the beat around," where a conflict between metric layers renders the overarching meter ambiguous, only to be resolved by a "reinterpreting" layer that endorses one of the layers.[16] In this case, the shifting of one layer and the cutting of one beat are together responsible for both creating metric dislocation and later resolving it. This temporary dislocation provides a mininarrative for the listener-dancer: one of entrainment, then surprise and disorientation, and then re-entrainment; it dramatizes a falling out of sync that is followed by a resynchronizing "click."

Released together on the album-length *Alcachofa* (2002), both "Easy Lee" and "What You Say Is More than I Can Say" feature masculine vocalists who seem to be drowning under the sonic weight of their own voices. In "Easy Lee," the first forty-six seconds of the track are bereft of percussion, featuring only a lone voice that has been run through a vocoder, producing a "harmonic" voice that is both split into separate pitches and yet moving as a single, complex singularity. The heavy vocoder effect obscures vowel color and blurs consonants, making his lyrics barely-but-not-quite intelligible. Is he singing "Easy Lee" or "easily"? Is the second phrase "chemical" or "telephone" or "kill the phone" or "cut the cord"? Sounding like speech but remaining bare sonority, this voice is eventually joined by a simple, austere, alternating kick drum–snare pattern, which builds a twenty-four-bar metric structure around this forty-six-second vocal sample. Upon each iteration of this long cycle, a new layer is added, slowly building in complexity and density while the human voice continues to bleed and thin out across the track's sonic surface. A full percussion loop is thus gradually built up around this vocal sample, but it is only when the voice disappears entirely that the percussion loop takes on the driving momentum that is characteristic of minimal techno (07:52).

In "What You Say" (see table 5.1), after sixteen bars of a skeletal percussion loop consisting solely of bass drum, hand claps, and bass synth, a masculine voice that has been run through a harmonizer enters, singing, "And it's time to loo—" (0:29); he never completes his first utterance, as the sample is seamlessly reversed and run back to the beginning of the phrase, creating a sonic palindrome that also makes the singer "unsing" his entrance onto this musical scene.[17] For the rest of the track, this voice repeatedly sings the phrase "What you say is more than I can say" over a long eight-bar period (thirty-two beats), bathed in heavy reverb and swaying between major and minor sonorities, falling slightly in and out of rhythmic synchronization with the underlying beat. As with "Easy Lee," the primary percussion loop only solidifies when the voice has dissipated (02:50), although in this case, the voice does eventually return to sing over the complete groove. In this sense, this track adheres more closely to the "accumulative form" common in electronic dance music, in which the primary musical subject is first presented in fragments before coalescing into a complete whole (labeled "full loop" in table 5.1) later in the piece.[18] Before the voice returns after this break, however, a flute-like sample appears in the upper-middle frequency range, panning rapidly between left and right with heavy flange effects, which lend a whirling, dizzy feel to the entire piece. If there ever were a track that represented Villalobos's "ketamine house" style, this dizzy, kaleidoscopic horizon of shifting layers would be the one.

In both of these tracks, there is a diastolic/systolic play between unfurling voices and tightening beats, intimating an indexical relation between vocal/musical coherence and psychic coherence. In my reading of these tracks, Villalobos figures subjective unraveling by blurring or effacing verbal comprehension; these voices remain at the horizon of intelligibility, constantly wavering in and out of understanding—as if vocal intelligibility were an index of psychic coherence. These tracks also highlight cyclic processes of unraveling through moments of metric dislocation and contrasting sonic textures. Ultimately, however, these tracks never disintegrate completely but rather gently approach and retreat from entropy, holding it in abeyance at a distant horizon.

Villalobos deploys processes of unraveling and rebinding across all three tracks examined here, in both the metric cohesion of percussion loops and the verbal coherence of vocal samples; at the same time, he also creates

TABLE 5.1 Structural Analysis of "What You Say Is More than I Can Say" (Villalobos, *Alcachofa*, 2002)

TIME	BARS (4 BEATS)	ELEMENTS/LAYERS
0:00–0:29	16	Skeletal loop (bass drum, bass synth), gradually stripped away
0:29–0:37	4	No loop; harmonized voice: "And it's time to lo—*ol ot emit s'ti dnA*"
0:37–1:06	16	Skeletal loop
1:06–1:36	16	Skeletal loop + harmonized voice: "What you say is more than I can say"
1:36–2:06	16	Skeletal loop + harmonized voice + hi-hats and hand claps
2:06–2:16	6	Skeletal loop + hi-hats and hand claps (no voice)
2:16–2:31	8	Skeletal loop + hand claps (—**hi-hats**) + new bass synth pattern
2:31–2:43	6	No loop; harmonized voice: "And it's time to lose my mi—*im ym esol ot emit s'ti dnA*"
2:43–2:50	4	Bass synth pattern + hand claps only
2:50–3:19	16	Full loop (skeletal loop + hi-hats and hand claps + mid-range flute stabs on offbeats) *Note:* four-bar bass drum removal starting at bar 12 (3:12)
3:19–4:19	32	Bass drum return; full loop (—**flute stabs**) + flanged flute pattern *Note:* four-bar bass drum removal starting at bar 28 (4:11)
4:19–4:48	16	Bass drum return; full loop (flute stabs return) + flanged flute
4:48–4:56	4	Full loop (—**hi-hats and hand claps**, —**bass synth**) + flanged flute
4:56–5:10	8	Full loop returns
5:10–5:25	8	Full loop (—**flute stabs**)
5:25–5:52	15	Full loop (—**flute stabs**, —**handclaps**)
5:52–6:21	16	Full loop (—**flute stabs**, —**hand claps**) + harmonized voice ("What you say . . .")

TABLE 5.1 *cont.*

TIME	BARS (4 BEATS)	ELEMENTS/LAYERS
6:21–6:36	8	Bass synth and hi-hats only + harmonized voice *Note*: four-bar hi-hat removal starting at bar 4 (6:30)
6:36–6:52	8	Bass synth + hi-hats and hand claps + harmonized voice
6:52–7:09	8	Full loop (—**flute stabs**) + harmonized voice
		Note: four-bar hi-hat removal starting at bar 4 (6:59)
7:09–7:51	24	Bass synth "cadenza"; bass drum and hand claps *Note*: hi-hats return at bar 12 (7:30)
7:51–8:02	8	Bass synth + harmonized voice ("What you say")

Note: text set in **bold** indicates sonic elements that have been temporarily removed from the track's overall texture.

textural contrasts between musical layers, which I read here as contrasting "rough" and "smooth" textures. The figurative musical-human subject never completely shatters but instead oscillates in a constant flux of greater and lesser entropy. Read in the light of fieldwork observations and interviews with partygoers, these tracks provide a sonic figuration of "coming undone," a festive practice of the self that holds special significance for partygoers.

Sweetness

> I get deep I get deep I get deep I get deep
> when he takes all the bass out the song
> and all you hear is highs.
> And it's like: oh . . . shit!
> [moan] I get deep.
>
> I get deep I get deep I get deep I get deep
> and the rhythm flows through my blood like alcohol
> and I get drunk
> and I'm fallin' all over the place.

But I catch myself
right on time
right in line with the beat,
and it's so sweet, sweet, sweet, sweet.
I get deep.
I get deep.
I get deep.[19]

What is the sweetness of this moment, when coming undone becomes enjoyment? In chapter 4, we encountered Roland Clark's spoken-word, stream-of-consciousness recounting of a night dancing at New York City's legendary club The Shelter as a narrative example of the musical articulation of affect. In the context of this chapter, however, the whole track can be reread as a story of coming undone. After describing the surroundings and atmosphere earlier in the track, he focuses on a moment of musical intensity on the dancefloor, when night becomes morning and the dancing becomes more frenetic. In the verse just quoted, music elicits a sense of precarious unraveling described in terms of intoxication, followed by the sweet pleasure of reintegration and resynchronization. As the narrator's ecstatic transport abates, he repeats the phrase "I get deep," three times, as if panting with satisfied exhaustion. The sweetness described in this track resonates with the analyses of Villalobos's tracks in the foregoing section, where the repeated unraveling and reraveling of the musical subject plays out within a sonic landscape that is both blissful and kinetic.

Narratives of coming undone surfaced repeatedly across all three fieldwork sites, whether in my own observations of electronic dance music parties, in conversation with fieldwork contacts, or in more focused interviews. These narratives all involved situations in which rough experience placed pressure on partygoers and created openings for a different version of themselves to emerge—however briefly. The self-transformation that coming undone enables, however, is rather incremental; it offers not radical reinvention but a subtle unfolding, untangling of the self. Despite the similarities to psychoanalysis-informed concepts such as *jouissance* and limit-experience, coming undone is "sweet bliss" with a remainder: the experience does not end in total shattering, annihilation, or derailment but instead ends in exhausted afterglow. But this is also a process that is not equally accessible to all partygoers, as the concomitant loss of bodily sovereignty poses increased risks for members of marginalized groups (such as women, queers, trans folk, and people of color). And yet, the sweetness of unraveling is all the more precious to precarious partygoers, for whom it provides the utopian affects of release from stricture, new openings, and alternate enfoldings.

My notion of "coming undone" arose out of preliminary fieldwork in Chicago and Paris, where I encountered common expressions among partygoers that employed similar metaphors, such as "cutting loose" or "letting go." Among my Francophone contacts, similar expressions included *se mettre la tête (à l'envers)* (putting your head on [backward]), *se déchirer* (tearing yourself up), and *se laisser aller* (to let yourself go). Many of these expressions connect unraveling with some form of release, echoing Kane Race's suggestion that the pleasurably destabilizing effects of drug use are bound up with a release from intentionality and normativity.[20] In similar fashion, Lisette had an especially interesting expression for coming undone, which she used repeatedly while explaining to me why she so enjoys rough experiences during a night out:

> **LISETTE:** It's especially in the cities, where we're pushed to take on stress, to work in stressful jobs. On the weekend, we have a desire to go entirely in the other direction. It's about not even knowing your name. If I've had a stressful week, I want to lose my mind [*me mettre la tête*], to no longer know my own name. Because we're forced so much to hold everything together during the week, to know everything, to . . .
>
> **LUIS:** Yeah, to be boxed in.
>
> **LISETTE:** Voilà. To know everything, to do everything, to know how to do everything.
>
> **LUIS:** To handle everything.
>
> **LISETTE:** To handle everything. When the weekend comes around, we want to go to the other extreme—in the desire to not know anything anymore, not understand anything anymore. (Paris, 2009)

Lisette expressed a desire to come undone in terms of a cascade of cognitive losses: a cathartic, stress-relieving night out involves forgetting one's name, erasing one's knowledge, losing one's capacities to comprehend. She went on to describe this process as a reversal of (cultural, normative) learning: "It's about really forgetting everything you learned during the week" (Paris, 2009). On one level, Lisette was describing her loss of identity—her name, her knowledge, her coherence—as a tactic of escape from the constraints and pressures of everyday (urban, capitalist) life. Considering the effort that can go into maintaining a consistent and coherent identity, especially one that counts as "normal," it is not surprising that some people might feel anonymity to be a release rather than a loss. Lisette, however, went beyond anonymity, insisting on a form of self-erasure that not only suspended her social legibility but also inhibited her capacities to comprehend and interact with the world. Her perspective framed cognitive absence as a relief, a return of the desire for disappearance that troubled some early scholars of electronic dance music, particularly in subculture studies.[21]

Lisette, however, saw her practices of coming undone as more than escapism. She described them as part of a process that reversed the workings of the everyday world on the individual—or, to be more precise, the self-refashioning you feel compelled to do in order to remain on the inside of productive normalcy: "It's a certain way of undoing what you've done to yourself all week" (Paris, 2009). She also saw the inhibition of cognitive capacities as a form of resistance within the context of a knowledge economy. Her frustration was evident as she searched for the right words: "Since we're in a society [where] we already need to know everything, this is a way to say, '*Fuck off!*'" (Paris, 2009).

Lisette found political agency in "no longer knowing [her] own name," fulfilling her aim to undo the effects of normative life, especially those associated with intellectual capital and properly ordered subjectivity. One might ask, however, what is at stake in putting oneself radically in question—and who can afford to undergo such a self-imposed destabilization. For example, Lisette's claims about the power of cognitive unraveling and nonknowledge bear a striking resemblance to claims made by Maurice Blanchot about "limit-experience." Drawing from Georges Bataille's concept of "inner experience" as well as the writings of Marquis de Sade, Blanchot describes limit-experience as "the response that man encounters when he has decided to put himself radically in question."[22] Within limit-experience, there occurs a loss of knowledge, a nonknowledge that he characterizes as ecstatic, as "the grasping seizure of contestation at the height of rupture and dispossession."[23]

The stakes of such ecstatic dispossession, however, can vary widely for partygoers. Writing about female subjectivity in rave culture, Maria Pini warns against framing ecstasy as a form of desubjectification (undoing the self), which sacrifices the identity category of "woman" just at the moment when women need it as a base for political agency in a male-dominated subcultural sphere.[24] Instead, she promotes an alternative reading of ecstasy as resubjectification (rebuilding the self), in which women use these moments of dancefloor intensity to reaffirm womanhood on their own terms. Fiona Hutton, in her study of feminine risk-taking in Manchester's club scene, argues that "female clubbers do not lose their identities, they consolidate them when out clubbing, and for clubbing women their pleasure is in consolidating identities that challenge traditional stereotypes of what they should be."[25] Extending this argument to other marginalized identities, perhaps some of the sweetness of coming undone for marginalized partygoers is the opportunity to consolidate different, less suffocating identities. They might even seek out experiences in which they can feel released from the identity categories of their own marginalization—however briefly. The sweeter the reward, the greater the risk, it seems. As discussed in chapter 1 in light of Hutton's work, women and marginalized partygoers are exposed to greater risk of harassment and violence in club spaces, their behavior is policed more closely, and the consequences for failing to maintain "respectability" are more dire.[26] Thus, women, queer, trans, gender-nonconforming, and nonwhite partygoers can ill afford the slackening of self-control and the blurring of situational awareness that coming undone entails. There is a cruel irony in considering how, although coming undone may promise a special sweetness for those who suffer marginalization, the opportunities are fewer and the risks higher.

Lisette nonetheless valued the attempt to suppress cognitive function as a means of resisting everyday life under a knowledge economy. The resonances between Blanchot's notion of limit-experience and her account of coming undone suggest two propositions: first, that part of the allure of coming undone is the diffuse glow that ecstasy casts from the radical Outside of knowledge; and second, that ecstatic states can be understood as expressing contestation against hegemony by targeting knowledge. This comparison only carries us so far, however, because the scene of limit-experience described by Blanchot is one of violent self-shattering and near-death, while such scenes are rare in nightclub contexts; indeed, none of my interlocutors described their aspirations for a night out in such radical terms. The process of coming undone usually encountered in electronic music scenes is nonradical and thus subject to reversal. That is, one might throw off the reins of respectable, working society on the weekend, but most partygoers still return to that world on Monday, with those same relations of power and normative force mostly (but perhaps not completely) undisturbed. As a project of self-fashioning, coming undone is a process that creates openings for something else, for incremental, subperceptible transformation. Thus, although coming undone as a political act may be a moment of small-scale rebellion that leaves larger lines of force mostly undisturbed, it also creates potential lines of flight. One can nonetheless retain the notion that coming undone offers a refracted and diffused version of the blinding light that ecstasy is supposed to offer, which in turn provides, to those who stand in its glow, a feeling of escape from and resistance to the hegemony of everyday life.

Not every interviewee was so eager to endorse coming undone, however, especially in the strong terms Lisette used. When Nancy and I began discussing rough experience, she first valorized it as a means of dismantling the self in terms similar to Lisette's. She described it as "a form of rupture of my person, because there are no longer the constraints of the everyday, the constraints of work, the constraints of who you are, of what you represent at that moment" (Paris, 2009). She later evoked destruction and constraint again, describing rough experience as "a form of destruction of what you are, of the straitjacket that society imposes on you" (Paris 2009). Nancy was careful, however, to specify that she was describing a social undoing of the self rather than psychological "self-destruction" (*autodestruction*). Further into our conversation, after I had outlined my own concept of coming undone and the connotations of the expression in English, Nancy began to distance herself from the idea, which led to a moment of insight into her own history of partying.

> **NANCY:** So, to *come undone*, that's not a term that applies to me. To be completely torn up, turned inside out, that doesn't speak to me. That's not my goal. Although I think that, last year, I was sort of searching for that, because I . . . I went there several times. So, that must mean that, at some level I . . . I expected it, I desired it. (Paris, 2009)

"I didn't want it but found myself there anyway" encapsulates the sort of oblique and suspended intentionality that Kane Race describes as the "incidental subject."[27] When using drugs, he argues, events veer on the edge of accident, which is an incident that "evades the scope of intention" but remains available to insight and reflection—that is, unexpected and unintended things may happen, but they may turn out to be revelatory or otherwise provide access to a different kind of knowledge.[28] This rush toward the unexpected and the volatile can be felt as a relief for those who find the societal pressure to be a thoroughly intentional, sovereign subject limiting and exhausting. Rather than maintaining a rigid mapping between will, decision, and action, this incidental subject takes drugs and is released from—or forcefully ejected out of—the zone of pure intentionality. This release takes the form of incidents that were not completely expected—nor entirely willed—and Race suggests that "the recognition of these moments of unpredictability can be one of [drugs'] pleasures."[29] When engaging in practices of coming undone, then, the mutually mitigating dynamics of smooth and rough experience may distort one's perceptions of the risks one takes. As Franck observed earlier, the stakes are high with rough experience, and a small mishap could derail everything. Thus, you may begin a night out with a desire only to be in a vague proximity to roughness and nonetheless find yourself dragged farther along than you had intended. Indeed, a partygoer's partial loss of control over the flow of events is part of what makes rough experience rough, and so coming undone involves a loosening of the personal controls that brought them there in the first place.

The combined loss of control and escalation in intensity associated with rough experience raised concerns among interviewees as to the physical limits and bodily costs of such pleasure-seeking. As Norwood put it, "sometimes, things get too fun" (Chicago, 2010). This expression invites comparisons with the Lacanian notion of *jouissance*, the experience of pleasure beyond the limits imposed by the Symbolic Order, where unbearable pleasure overlaps with pain.[30] Indeed, the overlay of pleasure and pain appears in many accounts of partying that I collected, especially with regard to extremes of experience. Polina, for example, valorized the lingering pains of a night out as a bodily trace of a passage through an ordeal, one that reminded her of past pleasures and engendered a sense of fulfillment and positive memories:

> POLINA: [Doing] things that you feel entitled to do, that . . . you've never felt entitled to—that's the most fun. And then you come back, and the next day, you feel really bad physically, but you feel fulfilled. You feel like you've experienced something that's gonna stay with you forever and that made you so happy, yet it's so wrong! [*laughs*]. It's so wrong, but it's so good, you know? (Chicago, 2010)

For many of the partygoers I interviewed, the search for extremes of experience generated pleasure and left reminders of their passage in aches that were painful but sweet. For Polina especially, the transgressive aspect of partying played an important role in a symbolic-moral economy of hedonism. She felt that she allowed herself access to morally sanctioned experiences (e.g., illicit pleasures, indulgence, excess) and that this transgression of the social boundaries of respectable fun created the mental and bodily cost that she feels in the days that follow. These lingering costs in turn become remembrances of the "so wrong," illicit, naughty fun she had.

While much could be said about the convergence of pleasure and pain at the extreme ends of experience, the dramatic terms of *jouissance* do not square well with the more modest practices and aspirations of most partygoers. *Jouissance* entails unbearable pressures/pleasures animated by a nostalgic fantasy of a presubjective bliss that could only be approached— but not ultimately reached—through a violent shattering of the self. Conversely, most partygoers do not express a sincere desire to destroy themselves or their subjectivity, nor is complete mental disintegration a common occurrence during a night out. Nonetheless, coming undone obtains its experiential sweetness from its proximity to *jouissance* while retaining the ultimate coherence of the subject as a transformed remainder.

For similar reasons, coming undone is not the same as a commitment to the sustained deterritorialization of the self that has been described in other electronic music subcultures, such as psychedelic trance.[31] While the comments of some interviewees like Lisette and Nancy certainly resonate with the tactics and goals of deterritorialization, "a night out" provides only momentary temporal and spatial pockets for deterritorializing activity, embedded in the heavily striated bedrock of the workweek. This sporadic temporality also contrasts with Anthony D'Andrea's work on the "global nomads" of the Ibiza-Goa-Pune techno/neo-hippie circuit, the participants of which he describes as engaging in "neo-nomadism," a sustained, lifelong practice of self-deterritorialization.[32] While coming undone could certainly be imagined in Deleuzean terms of "becoming" or even "unbecoming," neither of these terms captures the oscillating motion described by interviewees; coming undone entails an unfolding of the self with an expectation of an eventual refolding—albeit perhaps incompletely or differently.

In any case, the subtle stretching of coming undone can be easily absorbed back into a regular routine that does not radically alter one's everyday subjectivity. Despite the heroic aspirations sometimes ascribed to house, techno, rave, club, and other nightlife scenes, most revelers go home, sleep, take a shower, and go to work or school. This is not to dismiss the transformative potential of a good night out or the political agency of risk-taking and pleasure-seeking as practices of transgressive enjoyment but rather to propose an alternate, nonheroic, less totalizing narrative for the intensities of "a (good) night out." Nick, for example, restaged the excesses of the weekend as a small diversion from the everyday: "I danced for, like, an hour and it was great. I cut loose, . . . and then I got some stuff out of my system, and then I went home and I went to bed" (Chicago, 2010). Even Polina, who was one of the strongest proponents of extreme experiences and subjective unraveling, described her return to normalcy:

> POLINA: I've done some crazy stuff, you know. I've done things that are not so good for me. I've, ah . . . I've kinda done too much sometimes. I managed to go back to normal, and I think I'm still [*laughs*] doing just fine, you know? (Chicago, 2010)

Openings

Coming undone creates an opening—and nothing more. It requires an application of pressure that forces an opening in the self and enables partygoers to stand and bask in the halo of possibility that it casts. Maybe you will step through, maybe not. The narrative of a good night out focuses primarily on loosening the knots in the self; thus, the consequences of this unraveling remain undetermined, and "no change" is always a possible outcome. Self-transformation is not a necessary element of coming undone, but the glow of it on the horizon certainly is. Notably, the nonheroic aspirations of coming undone provide an important counterweight to the insights of previous chapters; with the use of liquid metaphors to describe group cohesion and the conceptualization of crowd intimacy as engendered and driven by impersonal affect, one might expect that I would characterize electronic dance music parties as aimed toward self-liquefaction or depersonalization. Instead, I suggest here that they aim toward a wider range of pleasures and kinks, foremost among them being a sort of psychic torsion.

Moving from the individual subject to the collective crowd, coming undone evinces a longing that can be understood as utopian, in the sense that it calls on a world or a way of being that is not yet here.[33] It creates openings where things might happen, folds where something might emerge or take root; in this sense, it is an open-ended utopianism that is not explicit about what form a utopian world might take, focusing instead on how it might feel.[34] If part of what I described in chapter 4 was an affective registration of a "we" that is not there but could be, then coming undone and the cultivation of smooth/rough experiences address a longing for a different future, a "then" and "there" that is not yet here but could be.

6 BOUNCERS, DOOR POLICIES, AND EMBEDDED DIVERSITY

Many clubbers talk about the rightness and naturalness of the crowds in which they have had good experiences. They feel that they fit in, that they are integral to the group. The experience is not one of conformity, but of spontaneous affinity. "Good" clubs are full of familiar strangers.

SARAH THORNTON, *CLUB CULTURES*

The spontaneous affinity with familiar strangers that Sarah Thornton refers to in the epigraph provides a glimpse into the experience of what I have dubbed *liquidarity*, the sense of loose sociability that undergirds stranger-intimacy at electronic dance music parties. In these contexts, this feeling of belonging arises less from identification through mirror-like sameness than from the recognition of compatibility, affective resonance, shared (sub)cultural references, common festive practices, and a broadly shared, historically rooted ideological commitment to conviviality across difference. As one of the first scholarly monographs to examine electronic dance music through an ethnographic lens, Thornton's *Club*

Cultures presents an analysis of UK club culture in the early 1990s; on the topic of crowds and belonging, however, the participant perspectives she relates closely resemble the views I encountered in my own fieldwork in Paris, Chicago, and Berlin more than a decade later. Thornton summarizes the discourse of clubbers who have had "good experiences" within clubbing crowds—that is, those who succeed in gaining access to the dancefloor and sustaining a sense of loose belonging there. For them, the composition of the crowd to which they belong feels right and natural. However, those whose entry is challenged or refused at the doors of dance music venues bear witness to the deliberate stage management behind these scenes of spontaneous affinity.

Electronic dance music parties offer a curated microcosm of cosmopolitanism: a selectively multicultural field of "familiar strangers" who incarnate a collective aspiration to postidentitarian ecumenical belonging. Vaguely defined but strongly felt, this fluid belonging constitutes a core value of most electronic dance music scenes, reflecting the genre's emergence out of queer, urban, ethnically marginalized communities and into a globalized "rave" phenomenon. Notably, this multicultural mix does not come about spontaneously—even if a sense of spontaneous affinity may be part of how this mix is experienced; a great deal of effort goes into the planning and execution of dance music parties, both to attract the "right" crowd and to exclude those who are deemed somehow unassimilable to these festive microcultures.

In an essay on the techniques of early disco DJs in New York, the ethnomusicologist Kai Fikentscher describes the scene at the disco megaclub Studio 54 as marked by an "intentionally monitored heterogeneity," relying to a large extent on the "selection" (that is, permitting or refusing entry, based on a mixture of explicit and tacit principles) provided by the door staff.[1] Even at The Loft (David Mancuso's members-only party in the Lower East Side of Manhattan and the earliest crucible of disco), measures were taken to carefully select and filter a crowd of dancers that reflected contemporary ideals of progressive cosmopolitanism. "It's not the mix, it's the selection," writes Fikentscher, quoting the Studio 54 veteran DJ Kenny Carpenter, who was in turn invoking a motto attributed to Mancuso.[2] Although this motto refers to the relative importance of two core DJ skills, it also serves as a useful starting point for a critical rewriting of club culture's utopian narratives of inclusive dancefloors, encouraging us to focus on the processes of selection at work behind the apparently spontaneous and effortless mixing of partygoers at these events. In particular,

Fikentscher's quotation alerts us to the impact of "the door" on collective intimacy at dance music parties.

Where there's smoke, there's fire. But where there's diversity, is there inclusivity, too? Dancefloor heterogeneity is often celebrated as a small-scale enactment of EDM culture's utopian ideals of capacious inclusivity, but venues/promoters rely on various exclusionary practices to curate the crowds that perform these scenes of "happy" diversity. Thornton, reflecting on the varying histories of exclusivity in disco and rave scenes, considers it a "classic paradox that an institution so adept at segregation, at the nightly accommodation of different crowds, should be repeatedly steeped in an ideology of social mixing."[3] In a study published nearly two decades later on the (in)visibility of ethnicity in door work, Thomas Friis Søgaard rearticulates this paradox at the level of urban cultural policy, suggesting that "urban regeneration and cosmopolitanism as political projects are often coupled with intensified policing and exclusion of 'differences' categorized as disturbing otherness."[4] This chapter does not try to "solve" these paradoxes—in fact, it goes some way to suggesting that these circumstances are not so much contradictory as mutually enabling; instead, it sets out to better understand how the tension between exclusionary practices and utopian aspirations is navigated by various actors in these music scenes. Using interviews, ethnographic vignettes, media coverage, and online discussion, this chapter presents an analysis of the "selection" that takes place at the doors of dance music parties, paying particular attention to how such selection manages and monitors difference. Whereas chapter 3's account of liquidarity touched on some of the passive mechanisms of social filtration that produce crowds of culturally compatible partygoers, this chapter turns to the more active and explicit modes of selection that take place at the doors of clubs and other nightlife venues.

Berlin's music venues predominate in this chapter, since they are more reliant on discretionary door policies than are similar venues in Paris or Chicago. This stems partially from the larger scale of Berliner nightlife as well as the greater presence of nonlocal "techno-tourists," who render the process of selection at the door more visible, since door staff openly scrutinize partygoers in the queue and often refuse entry to a substantial proportion of them. Also, the overt and deliberate selection of guests is a long-established practice in the entire Berlin nightlife scene—not just "techno" clubs—and so door policies are a common topic of discussion there. Local authorities in Berlin also give more autonomy to private venues to control access to their spaces and demand less transparent accountability, and so they are rarely called on to justify their decisions to patrons or external parties; the process remains conveniently opaque. In Paris and Chicago, by comparison, there is a sense that any potential patron has by default a right to entry—as long as one can pay the entry fee and observe publicly posted codes of dress and conduct. Partygoers there mostly feel entitled to an explanation for exclusion, even if the reasons proffered function as de facto proxies for bigoted discrimination (such as dress code, apparent intoxication, rude behavior, age, "no unaccompanied men," and so on). And, finally, there is a sense within the local electronic music community (notably shared by interviewees from Paris and Chicago who have traveled there) that the door selection in Berlin is more successful at creating the sorts of optimally sociable crowds that Thornton describes in the epigraph to this chapter. All of these factors make Berlin a privileged site for the investigation of door policies. I nonetheless include perspectives from Paris at various points in this chapter, since some of the most interesting comments on Berlin's door policies came from Parisian interviewees interpreting their experiences of partying in Berlin through the lens of their own local nightlife scenes as well as through national debates about cultural integration.

Indeed, the debates around diversity, integration, and multiculturalism figure prominently in this chapter—particularly the European debates—providing a framework for making sense of how nightlife venues attempt to balance social cohesion with diversity.[5] This framework draws comparisons between "door policy" and cultural policy, building on a homology between the nightclub and the nation-state: both are institutions where designated bodies make decisions about membership, shape communal life, and strive to manage difference while presenting a coherent and cohesive image of the groups they enclose. Of course, nightclubs and nation-states are not identical, nor are there simplistic causal relationships between these institutions (such as "A is reflected in B" or "A predicts changes in B"); rather, both enact a politics of belonging that, despite their differing scales and degrees of formalization, permit mutually illuminating comparison. Echoes of national debates on cultural policy resonate at the doors of nightclubs and in scene-specific discourse, while the attitudes and practices present at these venues may shine new light on cultural policy. Moreover, the tensions and contradictions apparent in national debates on immigration and cultural diversity are useful in providing a vocabulary for the underlying tensions and contradictions of nightlife belonging.

Much in the way that the term "multiculturalism" stands in for a wider field of discourse around managing belonging in diversity, "bouncers" should also be understood as a synecdoche for the entire *door apparatus*. A full complement of door staff will often include not only a handful of bouncers but also personnel running the box office and the guest list as well as an event-specific "host." Depending on the size of the venue, the involvement of external event promoters, and local practices, these roles may be shared across several people or consolidated into one person. In those cases in which an external promoter is curating a particular event, the bouncers may be the only staff at the door directly employed by the venue. The bouncers' role nonetheless differs crucially from others in that only they are expected to use coercive force and violence in the execution of their work; they serve a policing role as a privately contracted security force, primarily tasked with the maintenance of safety and order. But whereas the police have an overarching mandate to enforce the law, a bouncer "operates according to a highly ambiguous cocktail of extralegal maxims, occupational codes, and personal discretions, underpinned by an interpretation of what is good and what is bad for business."[6] This ambiguity nonetheless has high stakes for venues, clientele, and staff, and so bouncers learn to constantly manage legal, physical, and financial risk.[7] It is through their police-like role that bouncers are assigned to negotiating and physically enforcing selection at the door. If an event-specific host is present, the power of selection is usually entrusted to that person, but in their absence, this usually falls to the bouncer. And even in cases in which a host is present to make a selection based on some other measure of "subcultural capital," bouncers usually provide a preliminary screening for security concerns—that is, assessing partygoers for their potential for violence or disorder inside the venue.[8] In Berlin, it is common for bouncers to be entrusted with the entire selection process, although they are usually briefed before their shift by venue management or event promoters, who describe the kind of crowd they would like on their dancefloor.

In contrast to other ethnographic research on "door work," which has concentrated on ethnographic engagement with door staff, this chapter approaches the door apparatus from the perspectives of partygoers standing in the queue.[9] This is partly due to the overarching scope of this book project, which largely focuses on the experiences of partygoers rather than those of nightlife workers—which could easily fill another book.[10] But this also stems from practical limitations, in that it was very difficult to secure interviews with bouncers to discuss the intricacies of their work; in Berlin, bouncers were protective of the veil of professional discretion that shielded them from scrutiny, in their navigation of legal and moral gray areas. Furthermore, many venues explicitly forbade employees from speaking to external parties about door selection and other behind-the-scenes activities. Some researchers have succeeded in obtaining candid disclosures from bouncers, but only through very long-term ethnographic immersion in their professional world; for example, the coauthored book *Bouncers: Violence and Governance in the Night-time Economy*, resulted from more than three years of deep, narrowly focused participant-observation among bouncers, working with them as well as going through training and certification.[11] Nonetheless, my time in Berlin as a frequent visitor (since 2008) and as a resident (2011–2014) has provided several opportunities for informal, "off-the-record" conversations with door staff; although these exchanges were understandably guarded and at times elliptical, they have furnished useful insights that enrich the partygoer interviews, participant-observation vignettes, and online discourse that form the core of this chapter.

In contrast to the affective tone most often associated with electronic music's dancefloors, this chapter begins with a moment of discontent and ambivalence in the Berlin scene, which provides a point of departure for a brief historical excursion through Germany's and France's prevailing models of civic belonging, with a focus on their ramifications for cultural policy in former colonizer nations characterized by immigration and growing diversity. This excursion provides a preliminary framework for an analysis of the door policies of Berliner electronic music venues, based on the examination of fieldwork vignettes, interview data, and online discourse. The concluding section turns to the notion of "embedded diversity," demonstrating how cosmopolitan scenes of joyous diversity find themselves embedded in larger systems of exclusion and enforced (sub)cultural integration.

"Promote Diversity": *Leitkultur* and *citoyenneté*

Many electronic dance music venues proudly highlight the relative diversity of their dancefloors, and yet their parties have not been free of controversy regarding lingering suspicions of bigoted discrimination. In the early autumn of 2013, several prominent clubs in Europe, North America, and Israel hosted "Promote Diversity," a coordinated series of dance music events that served as fundraisers for All Out, an LGBT+ rights organization with a global scope. The event was initially organized in response to new legislation passed in the Russian parliament that June, which sought to prevent the "promotion of homosexuality" by outlawing the distribution of information relating to nontraditional sexualities to people under eighteen years of age. The campaign to pass this legislation was accompanied by street violence in Moscow as well as a sharp upsurge in homophobic rhetoric and violence across the nation. In the weeks that followed, several other high-profile instances of intensified homophobia—such as the surprisingly strong and vitriolic opposition to same-sex marriage in France or the (temporary) recriminalization of gay sex in India—created a palpable sense of cultural crisis within electronic dance music communities.

Berghain hosted the Berlin edition of "Promote Diversity," for which it booked thirty-eight high-profile DJs to play over a span of approximately fourteen hours (all of them performing "back-to-back" in pairs). In coordination with other participating venues, Berghain posted a three-paragraph statement (in English and German) about the fund-raising event on its website, on social media channels, and in the corresponding event-listing on *Resident Advisor*. However, some readers accused the venue of hypocrisy in the ensuing comment thread on *Resident Advisor*, skeptically comparing Berghain's notoriously exclusive door selection to phrases such as "Equality on all levels and tolerance are basic values that the club and music scene has always supported."[12] "So Berghain stands for diversity all of a sudden?" wrote user elektro_joe acerbically. "Berghain is pro-gay and that's why they support [Promote Diversity], but self-labeling 'tolerance and diversity' is totally hypocritical." This reignited a debate that had been unfolding across the comment threads and discussion forums of this electronic music platform for several years: Berghain has always steadfastly refused to publicly disclose the criteria that its door staff use for their door policy, and this has enabled no small amount of speculation about the role that racism, classism, and subcultural elitism play in selection. Although this reticence is common practice among Berliner nightlife venues, the international renown that Berghain had garnered in the preceding five years brought increased scrutiny from beyond the microcultural frame of the city's music scenes.

Rather surprisingly, one of the only public statements made by Berghain's door staff about its selection process appeared in *GQ* magazine in 2015, in an interview with Sven Marquardt, the club's head bouncer.[13] Greeting guests at the door of the club since its opening in 2004—usually framing his numerous facial piercings and tattoos with goth-dandy variations on men's formal wear—Marquardt has long been the de facto "public face" of Berghain. The interview is enticingly titled "How the Bouncer of Berghain Chooses Who Gets into the Most Depraved Party on the Planet," although well over half of the interviewer's questions are directed at Marquardt's efforts to relaunch his career as a photographer. When the line of questioning finally turns to the decision-making process of door selection, Marquardt replies directly, "It's subjective." He goes on to note that he carefully selects the selectors: only a limited set of bouncers who "understand what Berghain is all about" are allowed to select guests at the door. Throughout the rest of the interview, he repeatedly deflects attempts to draw out the sartorial, behavioral, linguistic, and/or corporeal criteria used in selecting guests. "There are no set rules," he insists, thus shielding the inner workings of Berghain's door apparatus from outside scrutiny by weaving a veil of professional discretion out of the implied ineffability of both personal judgment and intuitive understanding. "You always want friction, though," adds Marquardt, conceding at least one explicit axiom of selection. "That's the theme in any good club: diversity, friction."

It is notable that Marquardt mentions diversity and friction in the same breath—rather than harmony, for example—considering the revival in previous years of debates about cultural diversity in a migrant, culturally diversifying Europe. As a form of cultural policy intended to deal with the diversity of a globalizing world, multiculturalism has faced criticism and resistance ever since it was first proposed in the 1970s; but the debate took on renewed significance at the end of my active fieldwork in 2010, when the leaders of both Germany and France proclaimed the failure of multiculturalism (as cultural policy) within a few months of each other. German chancellor Angela Merkel, during a speech that October to a youth conference of her Christian Democratic Union, derisively characterized "that *Multikulti* thing" as having "failed, utterly failed" in Germany.[14] These comments were an implicit response to doubts about her conservative leanings within her own party, but they should also be understood as a form of political triangulation toward resurgent anti-immigrant sentiment in Germany—a resurgence that was making headlines at the time through the surprising popularity of Thilo Sarrazin's explosively controversial book *Deutschland schafft sich ab* (Germany does away with itself). Sarrazin's book proclaimed the failure of Germany's postwar immigration policy, bemoaned falling birthrates among white Germans, described Turkish and Arab immigrants as work shy and unwilling to integrate, referred to their daughters as "little headscarf girls" (*Kopftuchmädchen*), associated Islam with increased criminality—and sold more than 1.1 million copies.[15] In July of that same year, French president Nicholas Sarkozy launched a campaign to demolish Roma encampments and deport their inhabitants by giving a speech in Grenoble, wherein he blamed "fifty years of insufficiently regulated immigration" for a "failure of integration" among the nation's postmigrant populations. This speech accompanied a number of changes in law enforcement and integration policy that impacted immigrants, and the efforts of investigative journalists later revealed internal communications that targeted the Roma as an ethnic group.[16] In both countries as well as in several other nations within the European Community at the time, a turn to more forceful integration policies seemed to be on the horizon. Looking back after the close of the 2010s, this lurch toward xenophobic nationalism in Europe at the start of the decade was merely a faint prelude to the resurgent white supremacism, populist fascism, and anti-immigrant violence that intensified from year to year throughout the next decade.

What is this multiculturalism that has so failed the white leaders of an increasingly ethnically diverse Europe? Broadly speaking, "multiculturalism" can refer to existing circumstances or to a body of public policy; in other words, it can describe a plurality of cultural groups living together, or it can refer to an array of public measures that are oriented toward fostering cultural diversity.[17] A city, for example, may be multicultural in its demographics and everyday experience without the municipal government implementing any multicultural programs. As a political stance, multiculturalism concerns a commitment to supporting cultural diversity and the belief that valuing cultural difference will make for a more harmonious society; as public policy, multiculturalism entails addressing the question of how to implement such a commitment. Multicultural policies usually begin with an official recognition of cultural groups as such, which serves as a basis from which to provide other forms of support and accommodation. These can range from financial or logistical support for cultural clubs to the provision of state services and documents in multiple languages to the accommodation of dress codes, gender-specific practices, religious observance, and so on. State multiculturalism rarely exists as a fully integrated, monolithic, coherent regime of incorporation; instead, one usually finds "ramshackle, multifaceted, loosely connected sets of regulatory rules, institutions, and practices in various domains of society that together make up the frameworks within which migrants and natives work out their differences."[18]

According to the anthropologists Steven Vertovec and Susanne Wessendorf, most of the public measures that appear under the rubric of "multiculturalism" aim at one or more of the following objectives: reducing discrimination; promoting equality of opportunity; removing barriers to full participation in society and/or helping people overcome them; providing unconstrained access to public services; avoiding forced assimilation; and fostering the acceptance of ethnic and cultural pluralism.[19] They argue further that there has been criticism of these policies since the 1970s, when they were first being implemented in several nation-states. This resistance was relatively sporadic until the turn of the millennium, when critical voices seemed to converge on a set of common arguments. Often casting multiculturalism as a singular, fixed doctrine and overstating its predominance in state policy, these arguments accused multiculturalism of: stifling debate and silencing grievances through a "tyranny of political correctness"; fostering separateness between groups, leading to social breakdown and separatism; undermining common societal values by prioritizing particular cultural values; condoning reprehensible practices—most of these being gender specific—such as gender inequality, forced marriages, honor killings, and genital mutilation; and providing cover for terrorism, where the terrorists are always assumed to be immigrants, rather than "home-grown" nationalists and fascists.[20]

Nation-states develop their own stance toward multiculturalism, influenced by their respective national histories as well as notions of nationhood and citizenship. Both Germany and France have avoided official policies of multiculturalism—even when such policies were being adopted elsewhere—mostly due to concerns about how the recognition of minority ethnic groups might contribute to cultural separatism within their borders. In Germany, this concern has been associated with the notion of *Parallelgesellschaften* (parallel societies), in which immigrant groups retreat into ethnic enclaves and avoid contact with wider society, thus preventing integration and undermining notions of German nationhood.[21] For France, multiculturalism threatens the republican model of *citoyenneté*, wherein each citizen encounters the state as an individual *without* any group affiliation; this atomistic model of citizenship does not extend official recognition to cultural or ethnic groups, and the dominant public discourse about multiculturalism expresses fears of *communautarisme* (communitarianism) and state-sanctioned racism.[22] Throughout the 1990s and the early 2000s, the preferred paradigm for the incorporation of immigrants and other minorities into national society was "integration," although what this term meant and how it was distinguished from "assimilation" varied from country to country.[23]

Angela Merkel's comments about the failure of multiculturalism in Germany may seem odd to historians of German public policy, since there has never been an official public policy of multiculturalism at the federal level. Certain demographically multicultural cities and city-states, such as Stuttgart and Frankfurt am Main, implemented programs that were described as multicultural or intercultural—and calls for multiculturalism sometimes came from political groups that welcomed immigrants—but Germany has never officially taken up the concept as a leading paradigm for managing cultural diversity.[24] This is probably due to the guest-worker paradigm that was established in West Germany during postwar reconstruction, which focused on temporary migrant labor rather than long-term immigration and resettlement.[25] These *Gastarbeiter* (guest workers) were expected to work for one or two years and then return to their home countries to make space for more workers.[26] While many of these guest workers did indeed return after the end of their terms of labor, a significant proportion of them remained and were eventually joined by their spouses and other family members.[27]

Since the guest-worker program was based on the assumption that residence would only be temporary, there was no coherent program for conferring citizenship on those workers who remained in West Germany.[28] Additionally, West Germany had a *jus sanguinis* (Latin: "right of blood") citizenship policy, which granted citizenship based on the nationality of one's birth parents rather than on the place of one's birth (*jus soli*, "right of soil"), thus preventing the children of guest workers from attaining citizenship.[29] Beginning in 1973 with a ban on further labor recruitment, the West German government's policy on immigration remained focused on stemming the inflow of further immigration, encouraging guest-worker families to return to their home countries, and preventing the permanent settlement of former guest workers.[30] After German reunification in 1990 and under the conservative chancellorship of Helmut Kohl, this policy of settlement prevention was abandoned, and through several incremental changes in immigration policy, cautious first steps were made toward recognizing former guest workers as permanent residents and recognizing permanent residents as German citizens.[31] At the turn of the millennium, a modified form of *jus soli* was introduced by a coalition of the Social Democratic Party and the Green Party, and efforts were made to open German borders to new immigration.[32]

In response to the long-term settlement of Germany's guest workers, its immigration policy came to be directed toward "integration" programs for settled immigrants, which placed an emphasis on adaptation to and adoption of German culture.[33] It is in the context of debates about these cultural integration efforts that the notion of *Leitkultur* (leading culture) arose around the turn of the millennium, which posited a core set of values and practices that represented what it meant to be German. Although the concept of *Leitkultur* was and remains controversial—particularly due to potential implications of cultural supremacy and monocultural nationhood—integration programs still focus on language acquisition and the inculcation of German constitutional values and cultural practices. Immigration policy was often conceptualized in terms of the slogan *Fordern und Fördern* (challenge/demand and support)—a phrase that also appeared in Merkel's memorable speech—which indicated that immigrants would be supported in their efforts to integrate but were in turn called on to demonstrate their willingness to learn and adapt. Merkel's comments on multiculturalism, then, speak less to a specific history of public policy than to contemporary debates about how to repair a situation of cultural estrangement that was already in place well before multicultural policies could have been instituted. In any case, the notion of *Leitkultur*, as a socially recognized set of values and practices that can be leveraged for access to institutions, will serve as a useful analytical tool later in this chapter.

In contrast to Germany, France's ambivalence toward multiculturalism arose from a strong aversion to the recognition of difference by the nation-state, which undermines its republican model of abstract citizenship (*citoyenneté*). France has been described as an archetypal "assimilationist" country, owing much to its history as a republic and as a colonial power.[34] In particular, a French republican policy of individualist, undifferentiated citizenship combined with a policy—both domestic and colonial—of monocultural assimilation created a situation in which one did not need to be ethnically French to gain citizenship *and yet* the cultural and legal expectations of such citizenship had been set by the French ethnic majority. A citizen of the French Republic is supposed to belong individually to the republic, without any other group membership intervening in the relationship between state and citizen; as such, this relationship is at once profoundly universalizing, abstracting, and atomizing. The state recognition of identity-based groups thus poses a threat to French *citoyenneté* that is at least twofold: first, that these group identifications could compete with individual citizens' "republican" identification with the state and thus erode social cohesion; and second, that it could be used to endorse racial logics of difference, which could then be harnessed to target and exclude citizens on the basis of race or ethnicity. The French anthropologist Jean-Loup Amselle provides one example of this line of critique against multiculturalism, calling it a form of "affirmative exclusion": in recognizing a multiplicity of ethnic groups within a nation-state, multiculturalism reduces citizens to their ethnic belonging and "offers ideal conditions for the rise of racism."[35] In his view, this creates a contradiction between France as a liberal state and France as a "racist communitarian" state, violating a fundamental republican principle of equality through undifferentiated citizenship.

Amselle's rather sensational arguments emerge out of a broader political backlash beginning in the 1990s against what was perceived as a shift toward multiculturalism in the previous decade. The pre-1980s French policy of assimilation, which promised full and equal citizenship rights in exchange for the adoption of French culture and values, shifted in the 1980s toward a policy of "integration," which had some multicultural aspects. In particular, this integration involved immigrants being permitted to retain their distinctive norms and traditions, so long as they abided by French law. In the late 1980s, the increasing push by minority groups to gain recognition by the state and popular media, however, met with resistance both by traditional liberal republicans and by a rapidly expanding right-wing populist movement under the banner of Jean-Marie Le Pen's Front National.[36] Both sides of the political spectrum converged on the idea of a nonnegotiable "national identity," although one group saw this tied explicitly to (white-European) French ethnicity and its cultural superiority, while another drew this from an abstracted set of "republican values." This debate led to the development of a "French model of integration," which attempted to balance assimilation with diversity by emphasizing citizenship as a commitment to civic values. The French government framed the citizenship process as an individual and transformational one that allowed for benign forms of cultural difference, provided they did not conflict with these civic values. By the early 2000s, increasing tensions around immigration—especially the increasing capacity of right-wing voices to promulgate an "unintegrated immigrant" archetype and associate it with crime—led to a revival of the notion of assimilation, despite the official term for France's immigration policy remaining "integration."[37]

This debate echoed in the words of my French interlocutors, as they discussed the politics of inclusion and exclusion in electronic dance music scenes. Franck, for example, was initially uncomfortable with my project's focus, as he saw it, on groups and crowds rather than individuals; this uneasiness crystallized when I asked for his thoughts on the politics of exclusion at the doors of nightclubs:

> FRANCK: There's the problem. It's that, when you started, you were speaking about groups. I really have a problem with the principle of groups. A group is constituted out of individuals; and the problem is that, when we speak of groups, we forget the individuals. . . .
>
> When you talk to me about the problem of groups being refused entry at the doors of clubs, the problem is right there. It's that you can't refuse—you can't turn away a group at a door. . . .
>
> What we're saying when we turn people away because of their color, their clothes, their attitude, their social class—at first glance—that means that we're completely forgetting the individuals. . . .
>
> Turning away people because they're too drunk, and we feel that they're spoiling for a fight, asking them to wait: OK. Because the goal of a club is that there's a good atmosphere and there isn't someone fighting every two minutes. So, indeed, [for] someone who looks a bit trashed at the door, I can understand telling him to wait. But for other things, no. (Paris, 2009)

For Franck, the collective and cultural dimensions of a person have to be separated from their status as an individual applicant for entry; someone is evaluated solely on the likelihood of respecting the rules and norms that are enforced inside. Franck thus rearticulated the "French model of integration" in explaining his unease with my focus on groups.

And yet, there are problems with prioritizing the individual here, particularly in relation to abstract citizenship. The French republican notion of *citoyen* is posited as a "color-blind" (and more generally identity-neutral) construct, which is supposed to maximize freedom and minimize discrimination.[38] But it also covers over the discrimination that takes place interpersonally and structurally by rendering identity-based aspects of life illegible to the state and thus also to the state's instruments for ensuring justice and equality.[39] For example, if it is illegal to collect information on race in police records, how can activists, scholars, and policy makers demonstrate racism in policing? Does the absence of this data collection prevent police officers from engaging in racial profiling? Additionally, the civic duties that one is expected to fulfill as a citizen are left vague, and yet they are structured and enforced by an ethnic and cultural majority that has the power to universalize its own traditions and values as unproblematically "republican."[40]

Rooted as they are in their own national histories and juridical frame-works, Germany and France have developed different policies with regard to immigration and citizenship, which are reflected in the differences between *Leitkultur* and *citoyenneté*. These two models have informed correspondingly contrasting approaches to dealing with cultural diversity, with one positing a Germanic "leading culture" that functions as a supercultural frame of reference while the other offers an abstract set of "republican values" intended to transcend cultural difference. Borrowing from Michael Ignatieff's work on nationalism, one might see in these policies a contrast between a sort of ethnic nationalism and civic nationalism.[41] I employ the term "nationalism" here to refer to both the state's and citizens' deployment of "nation" as a concept to organize belonging and to accumulate political power, rather than as a shorthand for authoritarianism and xenophobia. For Ignatieff, ethnic nationalism assumes that a "person's deepest attachments are inherited, not chosen," and so the nation coheres around bloodlines, while civic nationalism envisages a state of rights-bearing citizens who are united around a shared attachment to political practices and values.[42] In both cases, a dominant cultural paradigm is promoted as a framework for facilitating belonging across difference, but it is also used as a benchmark for assessing cultural integration. Knowledge of and adherence to German *Leitkultur* or French "republican values" become important factors in gaining access to society, the state, and its institutions. Nonetheless, whether it is leading culture or abstract republican citizenship, both forms of national belonging create a space that is supposed to be capacious and capable of absorbing difference, and yet they also relegate certain kinds of unassimilated difference to their peripheries.

The *Leit(sub)kultur* of Berliner Clubbing

WATERGATE CLUB, BERLIN; SATURDAY, JULY 12, 2008; 1:30 A.M.

On a brisk early Saturday morning in mid-July 2008, I made some new acquaintances in the queue for Watergate nightclub. Located on the southern bank of the river Spree near the easternmost border of the Kreuzberg neighborhood, Watergate sits in the shadow of the Oberbaumbrücke, a red-brick, double-decked, listed landmark bridge. The club occupies two levels of a former office building, including a main room at street level and a "Waterfloor" directly underneath, at level with the river. The main room is a long hall, with the DJ booth and toilets at the far end and a wrap-around bar near the entrance. Running behind the bar, along the ceiling, and back down behind the DJ is a massive panel of LED lights that displays moving, multicolored patterns synchronized to the music. The Waterfloor has more seating, a smaller dancefloor, lower ceilings, and floor-to-ceiling windows across the entire length of the room, looking out over the river Spree. The windows are kept unobstructed, allowing the morning sun to spill in as the party continues. In addition to these two floors, a small door on the Waterfloor leads out onto an outdoor deck that is moored in the river itself, which serves as a smoking area and "chill out" space. Watergate began as a drum'n'bass- and breakbeat-oriented club in the early 2000s but moved toward "minimal" (i.e., minimal house and minimal techno) as the subgenre became the emblematic sound of Berlin in the latter half of the decade. On that night in 2008, the party was headlined by Kiki, a Berlin-based Finnish DJ and producer affiliated with the Berliner label bpitchcontrol, which was known at the time for producing primarily minimal house.

Despite 1:30 A.M. being a rather early time to go out clubbing in Berlin, the crowd in front of Watergate was already remarkably large. As I joined the queue, a clot of five young British men formed behind me, dressed in collared shirts and leather shoes, beers in hands, joking loudly with each other in English. They would have not looked at all out of place in the entertainment district of a midsized British town, but this was hardly to their advantage here. Like most clubs in Berlin, Watergate implemented a stringent door policy that contrasted sharply with what one would encounter in most other large European cities. In Paris or London, for example, men could increase their likelihood of accessing most nightclubs by dressing in midrange prêt-à-porter fashion (collared shirt, designer jeans/chinos, no sneakers) and appearing in the company of at least one woman; in Berlin in 2008, male clubbers were more likely to have punk-inflected, asymmetrical hair, some conspicuous piercings or tattoos, some sort of printed T-shirt or plunging V-neck tunic shirt, scuffed sneakers, and a relatively muted performance of masculinity. In any case, the men behind me were well outside the range of sartorial expectations for Berlin nightlife. To make matters worse for them, they were young, exclusively male, and numerous. The combination of these three factors functions as a bright red flag for door staff in any European city, who associate such groups with an increased potential for violence and sexual aggression. Although young men often comprise the majority of guests in nightclubs in Berlin and elsewhere, they are more likely to be admitted alone, in pairs, or in mixed-gender groups.

FIGURE 6.1 Entrance to the Berghain nightclub, an example of the metal barriers frequently used by Berlin nightclubs to monitor and filter partygoers while queueing. Sean Gallup / Getty Images News via Getty Images.

If there is one universal axiom for getting into nightclubs, it is to avoid resembling a bachelor party. Furthermore, my neighbors in the queue were speaking English, which—combined with their attire—made them easily legible as tourists.

By 2008, Berlin's techno scenes had already developed a reputation for being ambivalent at best about tourists; the city's nighttime economy had come to depend on tourist revenues to maintain its size and intensity of activity, but local music-scene stakeholders were increasingly worried that a saturation of tourists (and their "foreign" nightlife cultures) would dilute Berlin's nightlife microculture and erode what made it special (and, ironically, attractive to tourists). As a result of these dynamics, appearing to be a tourist reduced one's chances of getting in; relatively more welcome, however, was the tourist who could somehow demonstrate some degree of adaptation to local nightlife culture. This was, essentially, what I was planning to do. It was only my second weekend in Berlin, having moved there for the summer; I had not yet been to Watergate often enough for the door staff to recognize me, and so I was thinking strategically as I stood there in the queue. I had come alone, dressed in loose-cut jeans, Adidas shell-toe sneakers, a T-shirt, and a light, zippered black track top with minimalist contrasting bands of color at the shoulders. I showed up to the club alone partially because I already knew that bouncers tended to turn away groups, but I also did so because it allowed me to stay silent in the queue, thus preventing the door staff from hearing me speak either a foreign language or German with a foreign accent. If my verbal interaction with them remained limited to answering "Wieviel seid ihr?" (How many are you?), then I still stood a chance of passing as a vaguely brown, postmigrant Berliner; but if I had to be more verbose in German, I hoped I could still pass as the "right" kind of tourist.

So there I was, feeling anxious but also mildly superior in my ability to blend in, when I felt a tap on my shoulder. I turned to see one of the British men leaning into me, trying to ask a question in broken, unintelligible German. Now, if I had been able to understand him, I would have answered in the most authentic-sounding German I could muster and then left it at that, as I did not want the bouncer to assume that I was part of this group of partygoers whose likelihood of entry I had already assessed myself. There was a significant possibility that they would not get past the door, and this inspired me to treat their disqualifying difference—their perceived incompatibility with the hyperspecific context of club, music scene, and city—as something contagious. But I had no clue what this man was trying to say to me, so I grudgingly "came out" as an Anglophone.

"Try that again in English," I said.

"Oh. How much does it cost to get in?"

"I'm not sure, but it's usually around ten euros."

Feeling uncharacteristically antisocial and trying as best as possible to make it clear to everyone watching (especially the bouncer standing nearly within earshot) that I was merely being informative but would never even imagine being socially burdened with this lot, I cut off further conversation by briskly turning my back on them and conspicuously busying myself with deleting old photos on my digital camera. (In 2008, Berghain's "no photo" policy had not yet become a citywide practice.) The self-appointed spokesman of the British blokes, however, was having none of it. He asked me where I came from, asked for more details about my home country (Canada), joked about British language education, and kept on talking and talking—with occasional rejoinders from the rest of his group. As they continued to inquire about me, my sense of sociability and politeness kicked in, and I found myself asking about them, their lives, their hometowns, and so on. Back and forth, we got to know each other. Relentlessly affable in the face of my forceful disinterest, this young man and his friends succeeded in making me warm to them and eventually care about their festive fortunes.

So, when they raised the question of how likely they were to get into the club, I began to feel protective and responsible for them. I told them that I had never had any trouble getting in (which was true but admittedly misleading, considering our differences and the relatively few times I had been to this club); I told them that they should avoid speaking English loudly while waiting in line, present themselves as two smaller groups, and (for the next night, when they planned to try Berghain) look a little less "straight"—in every sense of the term. If I had been in Paris, where I had been living the year before, I could have mustered a vaguely Parisian accent and told the bouncer that they were with me; my German proficiency at that time, however, was too low to provide any help, and I did not have *Stammgast* (regular guest) status at Watergate to use as leverage.

As we neared the front of the line, the bouncer approached to let the next group of people enter the box office. Having read my situation better than I had expected, he sent me in with the people waiting in front of me, while keeping my new acquaintances back for the next group to be admitted. As I went in, I looked over my shoulder and gave them a half-encouraging / half-apologetic wave, hoping that the bouncer would see this signal and read it as an indication that they were also the "right" kind of tourists. After passing through and checking my jacket at the coat check, I hurried back to the entryway to look for them; it had taken several minutes for me to check my coat, so I was unsure if they had already come through and dived into the growing crowd on the dancefloor.

And so it was that this group of British lads on holiday, whom minutes earlier I had been studiously ignoring while enjoying a certain smug schadenfreude at their failure to move smoothly within Berlin's techno *Leit-subkultur*, inspired me to spend the rest of the night/morning scanning the room for evidence of their successful entry. I don't think they ever made it, to be honest. "If I see them tomorrow night at Berghain," I told myself, "I'll have to apologize for not being the intrepid rave-sherpa they took me to be."[43]

At the door of Watergate that evening back in 2008, I was trying to pass as a member of Berlin's electronic music scene or, failing that, as a certain kind of tourist—but not *that* kind of tourist. In retrospect, my concerns about dress, language, and behavior represented a sort of implicit understanding of how door policies worked at Berlin nightlife establishments. The best way to get inside a club, obviously, is to already be an "insider," a familiar face with local connections and scene-specific knowledge. But if you do not (yet) have that status and those resources, then you can at least perform "insiderness" and hope that the door staff will take this as an indication of your likelihood to integrate successfully into the crowd inside. Similarly, my initial reluctance to socialize with that group of young British men behind me in the queue arose from my own understanding of the process of subcultural assessment to which we would all be soon subjected, under the discerning eye of the bouncer. At the time, I was certain that these men failed to perform as either insiders or well-integrated outsiders. Unsure of the legibility of my own status, I felt pressured to make a convincing performance of (sub)cultural integration and to distance myself from those who seemed likely to fail this impending test of "fitting in."

The door of a nightclub is "not merely a site of inclusion or exclusion; it also offers opportunities for assessment and surveillance."[44] The interactions that take place between door staff and partygoers are instances of culturally productive discipline in which the terms of scene-specific belonging are invoked, evaluated, challenged, affirmed, renewed, revised, and otherwise taught by example. The affective contours of these encounters can range from friendly greeting to stern rebuff to earnest (but asymmetrical) negotiation. Temporally, the selection process extends well beyond the bouncer's performative utterance of "come in" or "not tonight": potential guests are already being watched and evaluated as they approach and stand in the queue, and the manner in which they engage with each other and with door staff is subject to careful appraisal—as my own experience at the door of Watergate illustrates. Even after a decision has been made and conveyed, bouncers will often make note of how their interlocutors respond. In fact, one of the first tips I received from a Berghain "regular" when I first moved to Berlin was that one should always politely say good-bye to the bouncers when leaving the club. "They have an incredible memory for faces," he said, as we stumbled out of the club and into daylight, "and they remember people who are nice on the way out as well as on the way in."

In any case, the criteria used in this assessment remain mostly hidden behind a veil of professional discretion. These matters are rarely discussed openly, and in Berlin, door staff do not offer explanations to patrons for their decisions. But this is where the long-term immersion of fieldwork comes in handy: from my position as a participant-observer standing in the queue of several different clubs on numerous occasions, I could glean some patterns of selection by observing the interactions of people approaching the door before me, trying the door myself, and conversing with other partygoers in the queue as well as on the dancefloor. *Partygoers conduct fieldwork in their own way*, often described as "doing your time" in the scene: repeated attendance at parties and interaction with other participants contributes to a fragmentary archive of implicit subcultural knowledge. Although difficult to articulate in a systematic fashion, this knowledge circulates in the form of heuristic maxims, tentative generalizations, and vague instructions. For example, large, boisterous groups are rarely welcome at most nightclubs, and their exclusion is "an unwritten but well-understood part of the night-time code."[45] Gender is also a factor in that men are unlikely to gain entry—especially in groups—unless they are accompanied by women. This gender selection shifts correspondingly at gay, lesbian, and queer clubs, combined with efforts to limit the presence of heterosexual guests.[46] Many Berliner clubs also select for age, preferring to admit partygoers in their midtwenties or older, with the exception of a handful of venues that target students. Appropriate dress clearly plays a role as well, although what counts as "appropriate" is often difficult to define and specific to particular clubs or event promoters. It is somewhat easier to define what is inappropriate dress for Berliner clubs, which includes glamorous, expensive-looking clothing as well as the blandly conservative attire associated with middle-class privilege—or, as is sometimes the case, working-class approximations thereof. While the door staff at these clubs ostensibly seek to weed out the "boring" and "conservative" bourgeoisie, Sarah Thornton's observation of class in the UK club scene also applies to Berlin: middle-class youth gain access to "underground" club scenes through a stylized performance of "classlessness" that is less available to those in the working classes.[47]

Fair-skinned and/or ethnic German partygoers generally have an easier time getting in, whereas the outcomes for people of color seem to intersect with class and cultural code-switching, dependent on their success in articulating a degree of cultural distance from the city's guest workers and refugees. For example, I am a Canadian of mixed Peruvian-Colombian ancestry, with a vaguely "Mediterranean" appearance that often functions as a racial Rorschach test: depending on the length of my curly hair, the grooming of my facial hair, recent exposure to sunlight, and where I am traveling, I can "read" as *criollo* white (in Latin America), Latino, Iberian Spanish or Portuguese, Greek, Turkish, Lebanese, Moroccan, or Sephardic Jewish (of which I do have patrilineal ancestry). Despite my phenotypical similarity to the Levantine and Anatolian majority of Berlin's (post)migrant population, I rarely encountered refusal at the doors of Berliner clubs. I did, however, wear a pair of large-gauge earrings, keep my beard short, keep my hair too short for curls to form, wear jeans and running shoes accompanied by brightly colored graphic T-shirts, approach the door alone or in the company of mostly fairer-skinned companions, initiate conversation in German whenever possible, and move and speak in a manner expressive of queer masculinity. I also learned never to react with anything but docility in the presence of Berliner bouncers, regardless of how much aggression they might show me; I was aware that white-German culture imagined only a limited range of "brown boy" identities, and they were mostly associated with violence. I may have been vaguely brown when I presented myself to the door of these nightclubs, but a complex set of both verbal and nonverbal cues seemed to enable a subtle disambiguation, providing implicit reassurances that my ethnicity was not an indicator of "trouble." Even now, it is not clear to me how much of my performance of "disidentification" was conscious or unconscious.[48]

Perhaps one of the more distinctive patterns of selection for Berlin is the ambivalent welcome that tourists receive, seen as both disruptive and beneficial to the local scene's diversity and (financial) vitality. Door staff appear to discriminate between different kinds of tourists who, as the Watergate anecdote earlier suggests, are expected to perform a degree of fluency with local dance music subculture in order to pass as the "right" kind of tourist. They are assessed for their subcultural fluency and their capacity to adopt localized modes of behavior, dress, and speech. Notably, this does not require one to be German or Berliner or even a Berlin techno-scenester— although it certainly helps—but rather to show that one has adapted in some way to the local subculture of Berliner electronic dance music. One's adaptability is demonstrated partially through language but also through modes of dress and bodily habitus that index the possession of such microcultural knowledge.

Whether seasoned scenesters, local "expats" (read: relatively privileged migrants), or curious tourists, those who stand at the door of Berliner nightclubs are assessed for their knowledge of and adherence to the Leitsubkultur of the city's electronic dance music scenes. The notion of a "leading subculture" may seem contradictory at first, in that the Leitkultur of German immigration policy can be understood as an articulation of hegemonic culture, which was usually positioned in opposition to subculture within the Gramscian framework of "Birmingham School" subcultural studies as it developed throughout the latter half of the twentieth century.[49] This neat binary opposition between the dominant and the dominated, however, fails to account for the messiness of power relations and cultural hierarchies "on the ground" or "in the field." Within the narrower scope of an underground music scene, for example, there exist alternative, smaller-scale hierarchies through which certain microcultural formations enjoy dominance over others.[50] And so, in the context of Berliner nightlife, my use of the term *Leitsubkultur* relies on a more literal translation that emphasizes *leading* a given cultural field rather than total hegemony; it refers to a certain set of microcultural values and practices that function as privileged points of reference for subcultural belonging, while still recognizing a plurality of microcultures within a given scene. *Leitsubkultur* also recognizes that the dominance of a "leading subculture" places differently encultured actors at a disadvantage in accessing subcultural institutions. In any case, the *Leitsubkultur* of Berliner clubbing is a largely implicit, vaguely defined, but concretely implemented microcultural framework that serves as criteria for door selection as well as guidance for participants' self-fashioning and comportment.[51] Crucially, *Leitsubkultur* is the bundle of knowledge and skills that both partygoers and gatekeepers use to manage access to Berlin's nightlife institutions.

When I began my fieldwork in Berlin, the challenges of the Berliner door apparatus were already widely known within the international online networks of electronic dance music. Popular electronic music websites such as *Resident Advisor* featured ongoing discussions about getting into Berlin clubs, including advice and personal accounts of successful and unsuccessful attempts.[52] Aggregated together, these online discussions provided enterprising "techno-tourists" with an archive of collective subcultural knowledge, from which they could gain useful information about local practices and expectations in order to avoid being lumped in with the "bad" casual party tourists whom bouncers systematically excluded. Interestingly, much of the advice found in these forums focused not only on performances of a particular identity, style, or group membership but also on forms of behavior in the queue that were likely to be read by door staff as indicative of one's behavior inside the club. This advice included admonitions to avoid appearing drunk or high, speaking loudly, acting rowdy, and seeming overserious or nervous. Any implication that nightlife establishments may preferentially admit people of a particular ethnicity, social class, or sexuality tended to lead to "flame wars," as supporters of these establishments would often vigorously deny these characterizations. It is also for this reason, I believe, that several of my fieldwork contacts in Paris—who deplored the explicitly classist and often-racist door politics of their home city—were more comfortable expressing support for the modes of selection they witnessed when they traveled to Berlin. Take, for example, these comments by Marie:

> MARIE: I think that it really is about behavior. When you show up in front of the door of someone you don't know, or a place where you haven't been before . . . I think people will adapt to the venue. And that's what I criticize [when] a guy shows up in tourist mode, like, "We're going here because they say it's good or it's fashionable," or something. I think that, if we let in too many people like this or if they become the majority, that can really ruin your night. (Paris, 2009)

What Marie describes in this passage (and Frank in the previous section, too) is a technique of door selection described in an ethnography of British bouncers as the "attitude test," in which a bouncer carefully examines the behavior of guests as they approach the door and interact with staff—which sometimes includes observing their responses to being denied entry or told to wait.[53] Kira Kosnick also describes something similar in her study of the door policy of Gayhane, a queer "Oriental" club night in Berlin's Kreuzberg district, in the middle of one of the city's oldest and densest Turkish-German neighborhoods.[54] The monthly party offered a protected space for queers hailing from local Anatolian and Levantine postmigrant communities, but as the party became more well known, it was soon overwhelmed with successive waves of white-European gay men, straight-identified Turkish-German and Kurdish-German women, and ultimately straight men. The resulting mix provided the setting for a rash of homophobic, genderphobic, and transphobic "incidents," some of them violent. The door staff responded by trying to select more stringently for queer sexualities, but this posed a challenge, since sexuality is more difficult to "read" off a body than ethnicity or gender expression. Nonetheless, as Kosnick writes, the ability "to sense if someone shares queer identifications and/or desires is a crucial (and sometimes life-saving) competence for queers."[55] And so, the (mostly queer) door staff found themselves employing a version of the "attitude test" informed by "gaydar," in which they would closely scrutinize eye contact, brief conversations with door staff, and interactions with other guests in the queue in order to assess queer affinities. Much like gaydar, this process involves the intuitive assessment of queer sensibilities through fleeting interactions and brief appraisals of nonverbal cues. Similarly, my informal conversations with those who worked at the doors of Berlin's electronic dance music clubs revealed that many of them considered those few seconds of interaction with prospective guests to be the core of their decision-making process. Notably, Berghain—a club that struggles to deal with a rise in popularity expanding well beyond its original target audience and far outstripping the venue's attendance capacity—has a bank of closed-circuit television screens just inside the door of the club, connected to cameras trained on various parts of the queue. Since the queue in front of this club can easily extend up to two hundred meters long during the busy hours of the night, this extension of the surveillance capacities of the door apparatus also facilitates assessment, providing the door staff with more time to observe prospective guests who are usually less restrained in their behavior when they are still far from the door.

This attitude test, however, is "soaked in discretionary practice," which risks obfuscating more categorical forms of discrimination.[56] Although selection by behavior may seem less problematic than selection by categories of identity, this becomes less certain when one considers that these observable behaviors are produced by bodies that are nonetheless legible through signifiers of race/ethnicity, class, gender, and sexuality. Bouncers develop "typologies of disrepute" that provide heuristics for risk assessment, categorizing potential guests for their capacity for violence—usually referred to euphemistically as "trouble."[57] Against a discursive background where tropes that associate various forms of "antisocial" behavior with particular identity groups appear in news media, popular discourse, and cultural texts—a situation that is certainly not unique to Germany or France—one might wonder whence nightclub door staff derive some of their assessments of probable behavior and potential "trouble."[58]

How do you know that someone will cause trouble inside the club? What indicators should bouncers read, for example, in order to identify those men who risk being sexually aggressive toward women? For clubs like Berghain or Gayhane that are supposed to offer a safer space for queers, how do you select for sexuality or "gay friendliness"? This sort of selection can arise from legitimate and laudable concerns about creating a safe space for marginalized patrons, especially women and queer people, but the way that this threat is assessed could also rely on racial/ethnic, gendered, and ageist stereotypes. This logic enables bouncers to refuse certain people at the door of their club—young, working-class men of color especially—and then to justify their decision by reframing it as discrimination along lines of antisocial behavior or incorrect moral values rather than identity. One might counter these concerns by pointing to the evident diversity—in both bodily appearance and sartorial style—on the dancefloors of those Berlin nightclubs that practice such stringent forms of selection. This argument, however, fails to account for the possibility that heterogeneity itself may be the product of a selective process that replaces limitless—and therefore uncontrolled—openness with a bounded and filtered diversity.

Embedded Diversity

Like the clubs of the early disco era, many electronic dance music venues in Berlin maintain an "intentionally monitored heterogeneity" that provides the feeling of inclusivity through relative diversity, although it is framed by exclusion.[59] Bar25, for example, was a summertime Berlin bar/nightclub on the banks of the river Spree that was as notorious as Berghain—if not more—for its exclusive door policy. Bar25 began in 2004 as a private party venue for Christoph Klenzendorf and several of his friends, who had been organizing techno parties around Berlin in previous years. This group signed a lease for the property at Holzmarktstraße 24–25 in the Friedrichshain district, a property on the northern bank of the Spree, halfway between the Jannowitzbrücke and Ostbahnhof S-Bahn (light rail) stations and flanking the railway tracks to the east of where they cross over Holzmarktstraße. This was part of a larger stretch of land owned by Berlin's sanitation service, Berlin Stadtreinigungsbetriebe (BSR), extending from Holzmarktstraße 19 to 30. The owners (BSR) had been having difficulties finding tenants for the space, so it agreed to rent a smaller parcel out to Klenzendorf when he approached the company. Klenzendorf's group parked a trailer on the property in August 2004 and proceeded to party "non-stop for six weeks."[60] Over the winter, they initiated plans to create a bar, hostel, and restaurant on the location, which opened in the spring of 2005 as Bar25. Over the years, additional amenities were added (including a circus-themed auditorium, a spa, and a pizza oven), but the core of the location was the bar itself: a Wild West/pioneer–themed log cabin overlooking the Spree. Bar 25's relationship with its landlords was never friendly, but it soon became openly hostile. The bar's premises were located right in the middle of the development area for a major urban renewal project called "Mediaspree," and BSR had plans to capitalize on it. Conflicts between Bar25 and BSR over their property lease and the terms of its renewal became an annual event, eventually leading to the closure of the venue in 2010.

The six-week party that started everything in 2004 also set the tone for Bar25's parties. The venue soon became famous for the "anything goes" hedonism, childlike fantasy, and drug-soaked stamina of its attendees. The club would open on Friday evening and stay open until Monday afternoon, without ever shutting its doors. On Sunday afternoons, it became a favorite spot for partygoers to finish (or extend) a party weekend. Much like Berghain, every eyewitness account of a night out at Bar25—including those I gathered from interviews with Parisian and Chicagoan scene participants who had traveled to Berlin—included certain clichés: excessive drug use, sexual adventure, and/or possessions lost in the fray. An oft-cited and emblematic example would be "the confessional," a seemingly authentic Catholic-church confessional (i.e., a wooden booth with two chambers and a small light) that had been installed near the washrooms in order to ease the demand for toilet stalls; this provided an alternate space for drug consumption, which allowed the toilet stalls to be used for their intended purpose.

Bar25 was also infamous for its severe and often hostile door staff, who frequently refused entry to would-be clubbers and humiliated them while in the queue. In fact, the principal door woman, Steffi, was nicknamed "Door Hitler" by insiders and outsiders alike.[61] If the door policy at Berghain was obscure and unpredictable, the door policy at Bar25 seemed at times entirely incoherent. On the basis of my own experiences as well as on the accounts of fieldwork contacts involved in Berlin's electronic music scenes, the door staff might sometimes select for various forms of insider status—group membership (as a "regular," familiar face), locality (as a Berliner or a German), or style (conforming to a particular "techno hipster" look)—but sometimes the selection appeared to be arbitrary. For example, on a Sunday afternoon in 2009, I was waiting in the queue in front of Bar25, with the intention of joining one of my fieldwork contacts inside. There were approximately one hundred people in the queue, and it was moving very slowly. The woman running the door was turning away nearly half the people who came to the door, usually by pointing at a group of people in line and telling them to leave. Just as I was approaching the front of the line, she turned to a group of six young clubbers, selected three of them, and said in English, "You three can come in. The rest: go somewhere else." I could discern no salient difference in age, gender, ethnicity, or attire between those in this group who had been admitted and those who had been refused. After a brief and awkward exchange among themselves, all six of them left.

FIGURE 6.2 Although Bar25 was a mostly open-air venue, its entrance hid the entire complex from public view with high wooden walls and a tiny entryway. Ullstein bild / ullstein bild via Getty Images.

Although the most visible mechanics of selection at Bar25 often seemed mercurial or aleatoric, those who had long-term experience in the local scene were able to discern a particular Bar25 "type." For example, several of my fieldwork contacts in Berlin used the terms "confetti-heads" or "glitter-heads" (somewhat derisively) in reference both to the venue's tendency to use any excuse to shower patrons with confetti as well as to the frequent—but by no means universal—practice by both employees and regular patrons of applying glitter to the eyes and cheekbones. Beyond the semiotics of confetti and glitter, however, the Bar25 "look" was less a stable set of sartorial signs than an unsystematic agglomeration of intersecting styles. Between my own observations and conversations with local contacts, I began to assemble a list of common-but-not-essential characteristics: a more extreme version of fashion associated with Berlin's alternative/hipster scenes; visible piercings and tattoos; moderately ambiguous gender presentation; hair that is either stylishly disheveled or cropped into something short, angular, and asymmetrical; clothing and accessories that allude to childhood and fairy tales (including costumes); circus-themed outfits; ironic renditions of traditional garb (e.g., lederhosen, journeymen's vests, poet's blouses, peasant dresses); bright colors; and incongruous combinations of "glamour" (e.g., sequins, a feather boa) and "grit" (e.g., torn jeans, a "vintage" T-shirt).[62]

If I and many other partygoers had difficulty "cracking the code" of Bar25's patterns of selection, this was at least in part due to the apparent diversity of the crowd inside.[63] During my first few visits to the venue, I had the impression that the the club's door apparatus had somehow produced a dancefloor that was more heterogeneous in comparison to the queue waiting outside. This perception of diversity, however, was admittedly relative: a variety of languages could be overheard and people of color were visibly present, but the crowd was still predominantly white German; most guests were in their midtwenties, but there was also a "core" crew of regular partygoers well into their thirties and forties; and yet, there was a relatively even mix of genders and a sizeable proportion of queer guests. At the same time, neither the queue nor the dancefloor reflected the diversity of people I would see on the streets of Berlin. According to the local music journalist Tobias Rapp, the apparent diversity of style and self-expression masked class-based homogeneity: "Many of those who end up [at Bar 25] on the weekend are middle-class kids. . . . As diverse as it looks, the social makeup is actually very narrow."[64] He goes on to speculate that the absence of working-class patrons may have had to do with the overtly queer sexuality of the space—which he assumes working-class youth would not tolerate—or perhaps with Bar25's thematic focus on childlike innocence. Notably, Rapp points to a disjuncture between affect and practice, suggesting that "the club isn't actually as diverse and open as it feels. The people here just look that way."[65] As I suggested with regard to liquidarity (in chapter 3), one of the pitfalls of a vague and unarticulated sense of collectivity is that it covers over its fissures and failures. In this sense, it seemed that Bar25's door apparatus selected for an expansive—but not limitless—eclecticism rather than a specific profile, thus producing a filtered and monitored form of heterogeneity that furnished a sense of diversity for the people in attendance.

The Bar25 "type" was thus difficult to delineate in specific terms because its primary characteristic was a kind of studied, neo-bohemian eclecticism. Following Richard Lloyd's modeling of the gentrification process in Chicago's Wicker Park, scholars and journalists have increasingly identified Berlin as a site of "neo-bohemian" urban development and gentrification, especially in the immigrant neighborhoods of former West Berlin (i.e., Kreuzberg, Neukölln, and Wedding) and most of former East Berlin (i.e., Prenzlauer

Berg, Friedrichshain, Pankow).[66] Alan Blum has usefully characterized bohemianism as "not defined by its specific relation to commerce but by the need to dramatize its commitment to a life on its own terms," in a summary of his own work on the role of theatricality in urban scenes.[67] This characterization is particularly apt to Bar25, which is an overtly theatrical space: the architecture and graphic representation of the bar draw from the realm of stage-oriented entertainment (such as circuses, vaudeville, sideshows), and regular patrons frequently dress in clothing that might easily be classified as "costumes" rather than "outfits." In the performative space of this venue, patrons perform their commitment to an individualistic, self-determined, nonconformist, and otherwise "alternative" life, and I would argue that much of the selection at the door has to do with the door staff's impression of how well those individual performances integrate aesthetically into the venue's collective performance of bohemian eccentricity and festive cosmopolitanism.

This argument is supported by Klenzendorf's own words, in an interview in *Ibiza Voice*—an electronic dance music magazine based in Ibiza, Spain, arguably the oldest "techno-tourism" destination:

> One Monday I got up early and looked around the dance floor and we had about 50% foreigners. I thought, "what an amazing crowd." I would say it's the most special crowd you can find. Everyone wants to present themselves in the best, craziest way. We have great friends in Berlin and really nice people from overseas and from Europe. We have a quite strict door. We can only fit 400–500 in the place and we have 2000 people trying to get in. We also do it because *we want people who fit in*. We want people who won't spoil the party. You really feel everybody [here] is in the same boat, nobody is aggressive, everyone is trying to entertain.[68]

Here, Bar25's leading founder describes a scene of exuberant diversity that is produced through deliberate selection—note in particular his emphasis on a substantial proportion of "foreigners," which obliquely addresses complaints from detractors that the door staff's antitourist sentiments bordered on xenophobia. He also enumerates the stakes of this selectivity: avoiding a rupture in the festive atmosphere of the party, maintaining a sense of shared circumstances, downplaying antagonisms, and fostering collective participation in the production of fun. Here, eclecticism's variety is the product not of random and indiscriminate aggregation but rather of careful curatorial intervention. In this respect, Bar25 resembles the "vintage" secondhand clothing stores that are an important element of Berlin's hipster/neo-bohemian scenes and that present a diverse array of "unique" clothing that, in fact, has been carefully curated to capitalize on a relatively narrow range of fashionable eclecticism. What is interesting about the example of Bar25 as well as other clubs such as Berghain and Watergate is how an internal scene of harmonious diversity (on the dancefloor) is embedded in exclusionary technologies that carve this diversity out of a broader, less harmonious world. If everyone in the club seems to fit in, it is because they already got in. In other words, the lack of obvious homogeneity (of class, gender, age, and so on) is not a reliable indicator of inclusivity or equal accessibility.

In the nightclubs of Berlin, diversity is *embedded* in technologies of discipline that are enforced through selection and self-selection. Much like the "embedded capitalism" of Keynesian economics—in which the technologies of (national) control that embed capitalism are meant to minimize the risks of liberal markets and lend them stability while preserving their profit-generating benefits—nightclubs manage the risks of openness to alterity by deploying an enclosing apparatus of controlled entry. This embedded diversity sustains a space of safe and mostly harmonious cosmopolitanism by first passing everyone through a process of selection that filters out differently different people, that is, those whose difference poses a threat to a club's *Leitsubkultur*.[69] The door apparatus in which this diversity is embedded rejects certain "unintegrated" or "unassimilable" bodies, primarily on the basis of a visual and interactive assessment of subcultural integration that disproportionately impacts partygoers who are some combination of straight, nonwhite, male, and young. By clearing the dancefloor of inconvenient differences, this selective process creates a social space of anodyne diversity, within which an ethos of nondiscriminatory inclusivity can be more easily promoted and performed. Crucially, this entire process, of testing for subcultural integration in order to produce a scene of harmonious cosmopolitanism, relies on establishing and policing the boundaries between benign variation and intolerable aberrance.[70]

Reading the scene of the club door as an assessment of subcultural integration also recasts the selection process as a sort of audition for acceptance, placing a focus on the clubber's appeal to join a space of inclusion while also revealing how the bouncer's gesture of admission or refusal is productive of norms and identities. This reading arises from an interview with Fantômette, who framed the approach to the door of Berghain / Panorama Bar in poignant terms:

FANTÔMETTE: They make a selection in order to ensure that the people who get in will also be inside the *ambiance* of the event. And so when you go there, you hope to be a part [*faire partie*] of a tribe. And in fact, if you get in, you're part of the tribe. It's gratifying, you see. And I think that's why we're willing to take the risk of being turned away: because we would really like to get in. (Paris, 2009)

For Fantômette, to get in is to have one's desire to belong confirmed. It constitutes an admission into social space as much as physical space, which produces a social form of pleasure through an ongoing cycle of query and response, risk and reward. This feeling of both validation and belonging also provides another basis for liquidarity, a sense of intimacy with others who have made it past the door.

A similar dynamic was also at play in New York's disco scene in the early 1970s, according to Vince Aletti, a music journalist who was the first to pen an article on the burgeoning disco scene for *Rolling Stone*.[71] In a later interview, Aletti ruminates on the intimate atmosphere of David Mancuso's The Loft: "What was important to me about the Loft was this whole cultural mix that was going on there, and it really felt like this sort of New York melting pot that totally worked. And David made it clear that everybody was there because he wanted them to be there, and so you felt very brotherly toward other people."[72] In this passage, Aletti describes a scene of harmonious diversity, both as a "cultural mix" and as the quintessentially American "melting pot." Notably, it is a diversity that *works*, and he attributes its success to the social curatorship of Mancuso, whose Loft ran on an exclusive membership system. For Aletti, this sense of being personally chosen for inclusion fostered a feeling of "brotherly" intimacy. Although discussing dance scenes more than three decades and nearly 6,400 kilometers apart, both Fantômette and Aletti recount how a system of local, small-scale selection can provide an affective basis for conviviality that combines the *communitas* of liminality with the chosenness of elitism. It stages an improbable scene of distinction without discrimination by displacing the act of exclusion to the dancefloor's spatial and temporal margins. At venues such as these, social misfits and cultural outsiders find a space where they are not only welcome but chosen, special, and desirable. Not every outsider is chosen, however, and this gap between feeling and practice is where the unfinished business of utopian belonging hides.

Embedded diversity and the accompanying sense of loose belonging across heterogeneity (liquidarity) that electronic music scenes foster rely on a process of recognition, selection, and ordering that both places limits on acceptable difference and produces a "safe" space of encounter with alterity. In so doing, they exclude those forms of difference that are judged to be incompatible with the local *Leitsubkultur*, the "leading subculture" that is the dominant microcultural paradigm within the local music scene (or even within a specific club). At the level of both the nation-state and the urban nightclub, processes of belonging produce unassimilated difference as an excess, a kind of difference that is both illegible and all too legible to these institutions. Thus, an institution's attempts to control and harmonize difference—to domesticate it—is constantly haunted by a stubborn remainder, and those forms of vague belonging that arise in these conditions, such as liquidarity, can serve to ideologically minimize the significance of such unassimilated difference while pragmatically managing its continued presence.

I should clarify here that in no way do I wish to claim that the diversities cultivated by Berlin's electronic dance music venues (or multicultural policy for that matter) are invalid or that they are no better than xenophobia and enforced cultural homogeneity. Heterogeneity need not be universal in scope in order to be recognizable as some form of diversity, and these institutions still provide a relatively safe environment for an encounter with difference. What concerns me here, however, is how a presumed opposition between homogeneity and heterogeneity can hide inequities of access by allowing scenes of managed diversity to be misrecognized as discrimination-free zones. The ambivalent dynamics of embedded diversity enable both partygoers and door staff to manage the dissonance between a utopian desire for unproblematically inclusive collectivity and the practices of exclusion that help make the experience of cosmopolitan conviviality possible. If a good club is full of "familiar strangers," as Thornton puts it, we would do well to ask what happened to the unfamiliar ones.[73]

EPILOGUE

A Talkative Stranger

Sometime before noon on a Sunday morning in April 2009, I was in Panorama Bar, the smaller "house music"–oriented room in the Berlin nightclub Berghain.[1] I had been partying—at times alone, at times with friends and strangers—since early the previous evening, and I was beginning to feel tired. I left the dancefloor to get a drink and to splash some water on my face in the restroom. The restrooms in Berghain have no mirrors, an expression of the club's "antiglamour" ethos; but this lack of mirrors also spares partygoers like me that moment of looking at oneself in the mirror and thinking, "Wow, I'm a mess. I should go home." As I was coming out of the restroom, a tall man whom I vaguely recognized from previous nights here stopped me in front of the large, trough-like washbasin.

> **FAMILIAR STRANGER:** Hey, I bet you like house music [*his arm over my shoulders*].
>
> **LUIS:** Yep! I sure do [*my hand on his back*].
>
> **FAMILIAR STRANGER:** In fact, I think you love house music [*reaching under his shirt and moving his hand rhythmically over his chest, simulating a beating heart*].

LUIS: Lemme think about it . . . yes. Yes I do [*feigning uncertainty / humorous understatement*].

FAMILIAR STRANGER: You see, man, I've lived here in Berlin for many years and soon I have to move far away and so I am very high tonight and house music has always been so important for me and when I come to Berghain it is so nice to see people who love the music and don't just do drugs but drugs are sometimes nice and everybody likes to have fun but it makes me happy to see people like you who are here for the music.

LUIS: Yes, totally. [?]

Written the day after this encounter, my rendering of his unpunctuated stream of consciousness is probably less florid and wide ranging than it actually was. Based on his dilated pupils, grinding jaw, and bursts of pressured speech, it is likely that he was as high as he claimed to be. At the time, I was not sure I understood everything that he was saying (despite the conversation being in English), but it seemed that all he needed from me was a sort of approving, reflective presence. I just needed to say yes, smile, put my hand on his back when he draped his arm around my shoulder, look him in the eyes, listen, and nod—in other words, expressive and legible gestures of intimacy. Perhaps I was humoring him, but I would not dismiss this as false intimacy, either; even if I was not in the same "headspace" as he was, the encounter was still close, both spatially and affectively. There is something about the simple fact of being in one another's presence and coming into contact that allows for warmth to pass where understanding and knowledge sometimes cannot.

Moments like this are what this book set out to explain: moments of glancing contact within vaguely defined social worlds that nonetheless unfold with surprising intimacy. And after several chapters that have approached such moments from various angles, much can be said about this vignette. First, our interaction was intensely tactile; in a busy unisex restroom, this stranger initiated contact with me by draping an arm around my shoulders as he addressed me, without even the conventional social preliminaries of an introduction or an exchange of names. I reflexively put a hand on the small of his back, and we conducted the rest of our conversation in a half embrace. Second, we were in a festive setting: the affective tone of the atmosphere was high and both of us had been through intense experiences that had "loosened us up" socially (and perhaps psychically). If this encounter were to have taken place on a daylit street, for example, I doubt he would have disclosed as much or been so emotionally effusive. Third, this effusiveness was nonetheless prompted by events in his "daytime" life, emerging from of a sense of impending loss as commitments from this sphere of life impacted his access to a nocturnal world that was clearly important to him. Fourth, his first words established a sense of intimacy with me by anticipating a shared taste in music: "I bet you like house music." He then intensified this projection by replacing "like" with "love" and mimicking a heartbeat with a hand under his shirt. And the prolix oratory that followed made it clear that his expansive sense of fellow feeling and community was based on an affinity with (and emotional commitment to) house music, which he implicitly projected onto the people around him (including me); this projected affinity, in turn, created a sense of solidarity with fellow partygoers that was vaguely defined but affectively intense. Fifth, for all of the affective intensity and intimacy of the encounter, our exchange was relatively thin in information: we hardly learned anything about each other, aside from the fact that he was leaving Berlin soon and we both loved house music. But despite this apparent shallowness, there was a connection at a tactile level, a point of commonality at a music-aesthetic level, and a moment of attunement at an affective level.

What gives rise to this sense of warm conviviality among strangers? At popular electronic music events in cities such as Berlin, Paris, and Chicago in the years leading up to the "EDM boom" of the 2010s, how did a seemingly random assortment of dancers accrue the characteristics of an intimate gathering? For the partygoers, promoters, performers, and other stakeholders with whom I have spoken, the answer has always been music, first and foremost. In most cases, music provides both the setting and the occasion for first contact with others. Whether it is specific recordings, niche genres, or broader sonic aesthetics, music serves as a collective and public point of affective attachment through which are relayed a range of optimistic projections about shared aesthetics, affinities, values, and practices. These sanguine hunches of common (sub)culture may turn out to be mistaken to some degree, but the lack of interpersonal knowledge characteristic of such gatherings helps keep such disappointment in abeyance while sustaining a sense of vague belonging to a space, a sound, a happening. For many of those whom I interviewed, the relative anonymity of these nightlife settings created openings for surprising intimacy by conveniently (and perhaps strategically) camouflaging markers of social difference that would normally inhibit social engagement, replacing them with a sense of nonidentitarian liminal fellowship or *communitas*.[2] This *liquidarity*—this fluid solidarity—thrives on incoherence about what makes it cohere; it flourishes in situations in which the terms of togetherness remain vague. But this feeling of inchoate sociability is also fragile, easily punctured when irreconcilable differences, antagonisms, and grievances rise to the surface. Indeed, while liquidarity can make conviviality among heterogeneous crowds feel easier and smoother, it also risks smoothing over underlying frictions and fractures. In this way, music plays an ambivalent role in underground music scenes, serving as the primary anchor for their sense of coherence amid the anonymous flux of nightlife while also providing a euphonious alibi to the incoherence that still persists underneath.

Music also plays a significant role in the intensification of corporeal intimacies on the dancefloor of electronic music events, evoking heightened tactility through rich sonic textures. Electronic dance music reads "feeling" as a *triple entendre*, referencing affective experience, tactile perception, and eroticized fleshy contact. The manner in which this music connects these registers of feeling is itself threefold: beats, flesh, and grain. Dance music evokes physical and affective impact through its "beats," the continuous stream of percussive sounds common to this genre that index objects striking, rubbing, and vibrating. These beats impact bodies through energetic fluctuations in air pressure, with the transient spikes of their amplitude envelopes and their bone-rattling, amplified bass frequencies. Many subgenres of electronic dance music—especially the minimal and microhouse styles that were pervasive during my fieldwork for this book—feature sound samples that allude to vibrant flesh through their timbre, often sampling sounds arising from real-world flesh as part of an extended sonic palette. Finally, electronic dance music shows an aesthetic preference for rich, complex sonic grain, which enables a cross-modal mapping of texture between the microstructures of sound and surface—and, thus, between hearing and feeling. In this sense, texture is an "amodal" phenomenon that is not just reserved for tactile perception; instead, it is an aspect of the microstructuring of the lived world that can be simultaneously registered across a range of sensory channels.

And so, electronic dance music's textural mappings between hearing, touch, and affect engage haptically with dancers and imbue dancefloors with a sense of tactile immersion. These find expression in surprisingly intimate instances of bodily proximity and contact, which reflect subcultural touch norms that are fluid, vague, mostly tacit, but nonetheless clearly divergent from everyday "respectable" public comportment. Fueled not only by texture-rich music but also by the physical exertions of dancing, scene-specific histories of sexual subculture, intoxicants, and the hedonism associated with nightlife settings, these dancefloors constitute a "counterpublic" of corporeal conviviality that transgresses dominant notions of bodily decorum. These intimacies, however, also arise from vague desires and pleasures that trouble the boundaries of sexuality and bodily sovereignty. Asymmetries of power and privilege still persist on these dancefloors, and so instances of tactile stranger-intimacy always risk spilling over into sexual harassment and coercion. This risk is all the more difficult to mitigate in nightlife settings, where nonverbal communication prevails, intoxication may be a factor, and bodies are usually pressed together tightly. Nearly all of the women I interviewed, for example, evinced some degree of ambivalence on the topic of tactile stranger-intimacy, articulating a desire both to enjoy dance music events free from unwelcome touch and to be able to enjoy the full range of opportunities for tactile pleasure and connection. And both of these desires point to an implicit utopian wish for a world where these two conditions need not be mutually exclusive.

The term "vibe" came up in many interviews as a means to explain stranger-intimacy at musical events. An abbreviated form of "vibration," it circulates as an affective concept that connects sound, resonance, synchronization, entrainment, and attunement through the common phenomenon of periodic movement. For most, vibe-based stranger-intimacy begins with music and with the belief that music encodes affective content that is available for those who are able to perceive and receive it. It is this underlying logic of the vibe, for example, that undergirds interviewees' explanations that a shared taste in electronic dance music somehow ensures interpersonal compatibility in values, practices, and affective dispositions. Vibration serves as an emic model for the transmission and circulation of affect through a dancefloor, and for some interviewees, the phenomenon of sympathetic resonance provides a more detailed account of how sound brings bodies into affective attunement. Indeed, one can combine academic theories of emotional contagion and rhythmic entrainment to produce a model of affective entrainment through social dancing that can account for the convergence of collective feeling commonly held to be one of the primary pleasures of electronic dance music culture. Many partygoers—especially those with some experience as DJs or producers—attributed to music and musicians a capacity to shape, punctuate, and modulate collective affect, usually in cycles of excitation and release. These moments of musical and affective convergence not only generate intimacy through fellow feeling but also index collectivity through coordinated action and thus engender an emergent sense of sociality among strangers.

A certain esprit de corps also arises out of the intensities of adventure and misadventure. Although electronic dance music scenes are more often associated with smooth sociability and euphoric leisure, many partygoers still confess a taste for rough experience, for escapades that offer wildness, intensity, serendipity, and destabilization. Such rough experiences induce processes of psychic unraveling—*coming undone*—that are often remembered fondly, even if they were overwhelming at the time. These often entail (temporary, reversible) cognitive erasures, altered states, and affective extremes, which stretch and unravel subjectivity in ways that also render interpersonal boundaries and social structures more plastic. When practiced collectively, coming undone unravels the self in ways that can facilitate intimacy through derailment, while the cyclic rhythms of unraveling and rebinding create openings for small-scale, incremental-but-utopian transformations. Rough experience can also go terribly wrong, however, and so partygoers are wary of these risks and take measures to mitigate them—especially women, queers, and people of color.

Additionally, part of what makes a crowd of random strangers on a dancefloor feel intimate is that they are not as random as they seem. At most electronic dance music events, the crowd is a carefully curated subset of the world of strangers outside, chosen for their likelihood of subcultural compatibility. Most electronic dance music venues and promoters use a range of relatively subtle tactics of passive filtration that are common to most "underground" music scenes, such as hidden venues and low-profile operations; targeted, narrow-channel advertising (e.g., word of mouth, posters in record shops, flyers at the exits of similar events, mailing lists, and social media); avoidance of mainstream media exposure; subcultural mentorship (i.e., the induction of new partygoers by older ones); and various inconvenient-but-not-insurmountable obstacles to entry (e.g., cost, distance to venue, cryptic or elliptical information, and seedy venues). All of these tactics are credited with weeding out inappropriate guests, based on the assumption that a properly motivated (and cultivated) partygoer would find their way through effort, research, and social networks. Notably, interviewees saw music as the prime motivator behind these efforts—thus ethically justifying these forms of exclusivity as selection by musical taste—but this overlooks the ways in which these filters could still prove insurmountable for dedicated fans who simply lacked the necessary resources to overcome these obstacles (e.g., money, transportation, free time, and both social and cultural capital).

At many electronic dance music events—especially in Berlin—the spontaneous affinity and easy cosmopolitanism of their crowds emerge out of more active forms of filtration, usually located at the physical threshold of the venue. Its most overt form is the "selection" that takes place at the door of nightclubs, based on intuitive, interactive, but also strategically vague decision-making processes. The responsibility for selection may be spread across the entire *door apparatus*, which can include bouncers, box-office staff, and event-specific "hosts," but most often bouncers take the leading role. Much like passive filters, door selection tends to select for some form of subcultural compatibility, but the details of this process are difficult to discern and substantiate—not least of all due to the guardedness of door staff concerning this topic. Nonetheless, national European debates on multiculturalism, immigration, and cultural integration provide a preliminary vocabulary for describing the underlying logics of the door apparatus, which seem to assess prospective partygoers for some indication of integration into local *Leitsubkultur* (leading subculture), that is, one microcultural formation among many that serves as a privileged paradigm for membership as well as self-fashioning within an "underground" scene. Some techniques of selection involve a subtle reading of bodily habitus, sartorial markers, nonverbal communication, and probing interactions with door staff, but the most conspicuous instances of filtration are those that seek to exclude "trouble" (i.e., violence and disorder), based on "typologies of disrepute" that primarily impact people of color, working-class youth, and heterosexual men.[3] But judging from the apparent heterogeneity of the crowds on the dancefloor of several Berliner venues, it is difficult to pin down a specific "look" or "type" that represents the local *Leitsubkultur*. A closer look at these crowds, however, reveals a carefully curated eclecticism that renders a microcosm of cosmopolitanism composed of a relatively narrow range of difference. The scenes of "happy" cosmopolitanism at many electronic dance music events are thus the result of an *embedded diversity*, in which a heterogeneous crowd is embedded within an apparatus of exclusion set to minimize the risks of uncontrolled diversity. Deployed at the threshold of the venue, the door apparatus serves to exclude troublesome alterity in order to produce an interior crowd of purely benign diversity. And so, the intimacy attendant at these events arises partly from these modes of filtration—both active and passive—which contribute to the production of a crowd of "familiar strangers": excitingly strange, but only so much.

And, finally, intimacy emerges out of a collective sense of utopian possibility, a sense that a world better than this one might soon dawn over the horizon. This utopian feeling arises performatively, through enactments of effortless stranger-sociability, freedom, cosmopolitanism, and aesthetic affinity that are easier to perform convincingly when inconvenient differences are left outside, at the door. These musical and corporeal performances provide a sense of what a utopia of postidentitarian belonging might feel like, rather than a coherent model of how it would function. Liquidarity, for example, entails a performance of utopian ecumenical conviviality experienced more through collective feeling and fleeting interactions than through structured representation. There is also utopian striving in the subcultural practice of coming undone through rough experience, especially the openings it creates for serendipity and transformation through self-imposed nonsovereignty. Utopian aspirations are even intertwined with exclusionary practices of filtration and selection, which aim to curate and monitor an embedded diversity that expresses a yearning for harmonious heterogeneity in contexts of oppression and antagonism.

Intimacy and Utopia in the Shadow of Orlando

I learned of the Orlando massacre right after returning home to Birmingham, following a week spent teaching at a summer school in Prague. After the plane landed and began to slowly approach our arrival gate, I fired up my mobile phone with the intention of scrolling through my social media feeds as a calming distraction before facing yet another tense encounter with the United Kingdom's Border Force. Instead, I found news reports from Orlando in all of my feeds. At the time, the reports mentioned an "active shooter" with potential hostages, but little else was known about the attacker, the circumstances, or the death toll. All I knew was that a bunch of queer Latinxs had been attacked in the place where they went to dance, feel safe, hook up, and celebrate another week of survival.

Unable to do much more than worry helplessly, I went into a sort of self-protective lockdown. I reposted one of the news links with the comment, "Welp, everything is terrible again," and then shut off my internet connectivity for several hours. Mercifully, I had a date with two friends for a "Sunday pub dinner" somewhere in the countryside west of Birmingham;

for a couple of hours, they kept me distracted with talk of vegetarian pub grub, canals, longboats, music festivals, and BBC radio comedy while my mind struggled to right itself.

In the meanwhile, as I was out being distracted with dinner, further details about the shooting were coming to light. The shooting began shortly after 2:00 A.M. on Sunday, June 11, 2016, when a heavily armed man walked in through the front door of Pulse, a gay nightclub that was hosting a "Latin Night" as part of local Pride Weekend celebrations. The first "breaking news" dispatches reported at least twenty dead and many more wounded. Soon afterward, the shooter was holed up in the club's toilets with several hostages. The shooter was Omar Mateen, a twenty-nine-year-old American-born local resident and security guard of Afghan heritage. Rumors were circulating that he had called 911 (emergency dispatch) before the shooting rampage to swear allegiance with ISIL (Islamic State of Iraq and the Levant). About three hours after the shooting began, it was all over: Mateen was dead by police gunfire, and the surviving hostages were released. As police entered the venue to tend to the wounded, the casualties rose to nearly fifty dead and more than fifty injured. As the day wore on, accounts by survivors began to surface that recounted bar staff and guests alike risking their lives to help others escape. Local news outlets began to collect and publish text messages, voice messages, and recorded phone calls from hostages who had been trapped inside—in many cases capturing their last moments. A message on Twitter began to circulate widely, pointing out that many closeted Latinx queers had just been outed by television footage of the shooting or by having to call home from a hospital bed. Later in the same day, Mateen's father denied that his son had any connections to Islamist extremist groups, offering instead homophobia as a potential motive—a motive supported by his former coworkers, who characterized him as not only violently homophobic but also misogynist and racist. Although investigations and trials completed two years later would argue that Mateen's choice of target was last-minute and not necessarily based on the perceived sexuality of the club, the details that were available in the immediate aftermath of the massacre strongly implied that he had targeted the queerness, *latinidad*, and transness of Pulse's partygoers. Despite the shooting taking place at a "Latin Night" in a queer club during Pride Weekend, most national and international news failed to mention the racial and sexual dimensions of the shooting until queer Latinx activists criticized the coverage on social media. That night and in the days that followed, American public culture showed itself reluctant to mourn brown queer lives.

When I got home, I was pulled into a feedback loop of horror, sadness, and anger: force-feeding my outrage with every news update, posting frustrated status updates, commiserating with other queer and brown friends through public comment threads as well as private messengers, and so on. I got into bed late in the morning and had trouble getting to sleep, and for the rest of the week, I struggled to return to any semblance of productive work. I felt more than just absentminded. As the days and weeks went on, however, I found myself more closely connected to a network of queers, people of color, and allies than I had been before. Friends and acquaintances reached out through various channels of communication to "check in," to express support, to spill out their own mess of feelings, to remap past traumas to the present, to share weblinks to commentary that was either uplifting or further infuriating, or just to confirm that they were not the only ones still aching.

A renewed sense of intimacy within queer club culture seems to have emerged under the shadow of the Orlando massacre, one grounded in a similarly renewed sense of shared risk and struggle. In the days immediately following the shooting, the internet was awash with the testimonies of queer clubgoers, attesting to the importance of musical refuges such as

FIGURE E.1 Mourners outside a memorial service at the Cathedral Church of Saint Luke in Orlando, Florida, in support of shooting victims from Pulse nightclub, on Saturday, June 18, 2016. Al Diaz / Miami Herald / Tribune News Service via Getty Images.

Pulse. Marea Stamper (The Blessed Madonna), a queer DJ and producer from the Chicago scene who in the previous three years had become an international touring artist and a vocal proponent of political activism within club culture, described Pulse as "exactly the kind of hometown club that saved my life. It is the kind of place that let me live as a young person."[4] Daniel Leon-Davis, a local resident who grew up in close proximity to Pulse, recounted his first revelatory visit to the club as a high-school senior; for him, the club's significance was not just personal but collective: "Pulse was not just my safe haven, but a safe haven for hundreds of LGBTQ individuals in Orlando."[5] Four days after the shooting, the prominent popular culture magazine *The Fader* published an interview with two queer Latinx party promoters in Washington, DC, Kristy LarAt and Precolumbian (Sofia Chaska), who described events such as theirs ("Maracuyeah") and Pulse's "Latin Night" as "necessary spaces of resistance"; for them, such spaces offered not only escape from oppression but also opportunities to release and channel their frustrations in constructive ways.[6] Although hardly perfect utopias, these dancefloors provided spaces where queers of color could collectively imagine, play out, and *feel* a world less toxic than this one.

Some of the online responses to the Orlando massacre were remarkable in the intimacy of their tone and content, especially those addressed to an imagined intergenerational community of queers and Latinxs. Often writing in the second person or the first-person plural, these commentators posted deeply affective "open letters" to their queer and brown brethren on public blogs and through social media channels. In particular, the post-Orlando discourse reactivated traumatic memories of violence across several generations of queers, prompting them to connect this fresh new trauma to older ones still in living memory, such as the HIV/AIDS crisis and the post-Stonewall backlash. One of the most moving of these was a series of posts by a Twitter user under the pseudonym "Supergrover" (@fuzzlaw), a commentator on issues of criminal justice in the Baltimore area who also identified herself as an "aging dyke":

> I'm an aging dyke, so I'm just going to get this out of my system: kids, y'all 35 and under, this wasn't supposed to happen to you.
>
> The generation ahead of us knocked down the wall: Stonewall. Initial visibility. Standing proud. Being out. They suffered the consequences.
>
> Backlash. Violence. The Upstairs Lounge in New Orleans. Guns fired at the places they dared to gather.

Then AIDS swept in and devastated the community. Reagan and his ilk laughed at our suffering. They closed ranks. Cared for one another. Tended the dying and buried the dead. There's a reason why most 60+ gay leaders are women. See the genocide underneath the demographics.

Then, the mid-90's. Anti-retroviral drugs came along. Our men started surviving. We began to flourish, stand up, stand out more strongly. . . .

With every step of progress came backlash. But we pushed. And we pushed. And there weren't any Upstairs Lounges. No Matthew Shepards. . . .

But we were winning. Then, Pulse. 50 dead. 50 wounded. Babies. Kids. The ones we fought so hard to protect from the backlash. . . .

We never wanted you to know about this. We never wanted you to experience this. It's why we fought, and fight, so hard. . . .

It permeates our society. It is so much better than it was, yet remains so awful. It's why our generation kept fighting, and keeps fighting.

But it's time for our generation to teach the next. Welcome to the fight for your lives, kids. We're with you. We'll guide you.

The world is not a safe space, and it only gets safer when you fight like hell for it. We weren't given the spaces we have.

We'd still take a bullet for you, literally, and figuratively. You were just never supposed to have to take a bullet for us.[7]

In the series of thirty tweets (from which the preceding have been excerpted), she explicitly addresses a younger generation of queers, addressing them frequently as "kids" and alternating between the second-person plural ("y'all") and the first-person plural to narrate a story of care, solidarity, and political pedagogy. To convey her sense of heartbreak, she traces a timeline of antiqueer violence—Stonewall, UpStairs Lounge, responses to AIDS crisis, and Matthew Shepard—describing how the political advances in LGBTQIA+ rights after the Shepard murder raised hopes that the worst of the violence was behind them. The Orlando massacre, however, not only reconnected this tragic timeline to the present but far surpassed previous antiqueer attacks in its scale and brutality. Indeed, some of the more reflective news stories that circulated later that week situated the Orlando attack within this longer history of homophobic mass violence.[8] This historical perspective brought the violent past of queer struggle uncomfortably close, implicitly questioning whether contemporary political advances toward queer visibility and institutional recognition had substantially increased the chances of queer survival. The trans Twitter user Kylie Jack (@ixKylie) captured this disheartening realization with bleak humor, writing, "47 years after Stonewall and we're still like," followed by a screenshot taken from a smartphone "To-Do List" application, titled "Gay Agenda" but having only one entry in the list: "survive."[9] Notably, the check box was left unchecked.

The Orlando massacre was especially shocking for people involved in queer nightlife not only because the attack took place in a queer nightclub but also because it occurred during a period of flourishing for their scenes. In 2014, when I wrote a revisionist history of sexuality in dance music for *Resident Advisor*—an article I wrote in response to the erasures of sexuality and race that seemed to stem from the influx of mainstream attention during the EDM "boom"—I closed the article with a brief survey of some of the queer, sex-positive party crews that were just beginning to gain notoriety beyond their local scenes at the time.[10] Two years later (and three months before Orlando), Andrew Ryce devoted an entire feature article in the same magazine to a growing network of queer party crews that he described as "America's Gay Techno Underground."[11] These two magazine articles bookend a two-year period when various media outlets, bloggers, and artists sought to "reclaim" dance music from a straight, white, middle-class mainstream and recenter it around burgeoning queer scenes by insisting on electronic dance music's queer, Black and brown, working-class, inner-city roots. By 2016, queer nightlife was resurgent and vibrant again, and its increasing visibility seemed to herald growing acceptance by a wider public. All of this may have been indeed the case, but Orlando did much to deflate this sense of political and cultural progress.

It is out of this discursive landscape in the days following Orlando that an "intimate public" took shape, a sphere of affective belonging based on the assumption that personal experiences of (sexual, racial) oppression are sufficiently similar in their affective contour to provide a basis for solidarity across other differences and distances.[12] This public mode of queer intimacy existed well before the Orlando massacre, but this most recent and very public tragedy provided a new instance of common affective experience, that is, the irruption of homophobic violence into a queer dancefloor. Many responses to the attack described queer nightclubs as "sanctuaries," alluding to the desecration of a sacred, sacrosanct space in order to express the gravity of the violation. In *Remezcla*, an online magazine of alternative Latin culture, Veronica Bayetti Flores notes that Pulse was not only a nocturnal sanctuary of dancing, companionship, and self-realization, "where many of us experienced our whole selves for the first time," but also "an important community center," providing support for HIV prevention,

breast-cancer awareness, and immigrant rights.[13] Queer nightclubs like Pulse are spaces of cultural and corporeal survival for queer people of color, and so the resurgence of queer public intimacy in the wake of the Orlando massacre had its affective basis in a renewed awareness that we are not even safe in our own spaces, on the dancefloors of our own making.[14] On the day that the shooting happened, just before I tried (and failed) to finally go to sleep, I posted a tweet that encapsulated this realization neatly: "What us queers are reminded of with #Orlando is: 1) There are no truly safe spaces; 2) Safe spaces are a vital need." Queers, women, people of color, and trans folk repeatedly find themselves caught in between these apparently irreconcilable conditions, and the friction they create permeates our nightlives with a persistent hum of precarity. As much as we might go out to escape our troubles, they have a way of following us into the club.

Trouble in Transition

> *There will come a time in your life*
> *When you will ask yourself a series of questions:*
> *Am I happy with who I am?*

Am I happy with the people around me?
Am I happy with what I am doing?
Am I happy with the way my life is going?
Do I have a life,
Or am I just living?
Do not let these questions restrain or trouble you.
Just point yourself in the direction of your dreams,
Find your strength from the sound,
And make your transition.
Make your transition. (Make your transition) (×4)[15]

Although released in 2002, "Transition" became an "instant classic" of De-troit techno, with its mix of funk and futurism. The track begins with a sparse beat-backbeat combination of kick drum and hi-hats reminiscent of Chicago house, set against a background of chorused strings playing a single high-pitched note. On the last beat of every four bars (i.e., every sixteen beats), two slightly syncopated synthesizer "stabs" mark the end of a metric cycle while briefly destabilizing the sense of metric flow. After this cycle has repeated four times (i.e., sixty-four beats), a masculine voice enters, followed soon after by a female voice that repeats his questions. As the voices reach a sort of spoken-word refrain, repeating "make your transition" eight times, the track's sonic texture fills out with skittering, syncopated synth chords and a bent electric-guitar lick that interlocks with its own echoes in a manner reminiscent of Steve Reich. This track was com-posed and released by Underground Resistance, a Detroit collective of DJs and producers who combine anticapitalist and antiracist politics, Afrofu-turist themes, and military imagery in their artistic output. In a manner similar to "conscious rap," Underground Resistance prioritizes reaching out to Black youth—especially in recession-era Detroit—with messages of political resistance, transformation, and independence encoded into lyrics, track titles, and even vinyl runout groove etchings. Rooted in the racial and class struggles of Detroit, many of their tracks have a utopian outlook that resonates with Ernst Bloch's notion of a "concrete utopia," focusing dreams and desires toward building a better future through transformation—although, notably, the focus of this particular track is on individual self-transformation rather than collective action.[16] "Transition" sets an affective tone of excitement and determination and combines it with a spoken-word text that calls on listener-dancers to assess their situations, ask if things could be better, find "strength from the sound" (of techno), and "make your transition" toward a better life.

As inspiring and positive as the message may be, the track encourages potentially uncomfortable introspection, such as, "Do I have a life, or am I just living?" Considering that nightclubs can serve as sanctuaries for those who find no solace elsewhere in their lives, the answers to such questions may be hard to face. Not all transitions are redemptive narratives of self-realization. Not everyone can enjoy unalloyed access to utopian feeling. Indeed, exclusion from such experiences may have played an important role in the Orlando massacre. I can still remember that queasy sinking feeling I had when I read the first reports from Pulse's surviving clientele, claiming that the shooter, Omar Mateen, maintained a profile on a well-known gay dating app (Grindr) and frequented the club. I was braced for this revelation to fuel smugly pathologizing narratives of queer brokenness that would distract from an overdue discussion of the convergence of racism, homophobia, Islamophobia, transphobia, and gun violence in the United States. While this account was undermined by contradictory statements from his family and police, the accounts of the Pulse clientele furnished one of the most compelling explanations for why he targeted that nightclub: revenge. According to these accounts, Mateen would often visit the club, drink excessively, and complain about his wife; but he would find scarce companionship at the club, ultimately becoming frustrated with the ostracization he experienced as a married, straight-identified (but allegedly flexible) Middle Eastern man in this queer Latinx space. Later FBI investigations would report that no evidence could be found of Mateen living a closeted gay life—no photographs, text messages, pornography, mobile-phone apps, or cellular-tower location data.[17] Although these reports were released within weeks of the shooting, the "embittered closet case" narrative remained a popular one in queer public discourse—especially among queers of color. What shared, intersecting queer and Latinx experience did this narrative tap into?

Although touted as sanctuaries of acceptance and fellowship, queer nightclubs can still be sites of alienation for queers of color, for "fats" and "femmes," for trans and gender-nonbinary people, for the disabled, for the aged, for those who fall outside of prevailing norms of attractiveness. But this alienation does not necessarily sever their attachment to the utopian promises of musical fellowship, smooth intimacy, and erotic conviviality that these venues embody; if anything, it only renders this attachment more complex, dissonant, and difficult to manage. A few days after the Orlando massacre, for example, an acquaintance of mine—gay, male, white, able-bodied, slim, comfortably middle-class and privileged—posted on his Facebook timeline a rebuke of those queers who were writing "utopian" encomiums to queer nightclubs as sanctuaries and safe spaces, arguing that many of these same politically minded queers had previously complained about the social exclusion and body shaming that takes place at these venues. Smug in his certainty that he was calling out hypocrisy among his sexual cohort, he failed to imagine the possibility that, for underprivileged queers, nightclubs could be both uplifting and alienating at the same time. Indeed, this combination of help and hurt makes nightlife all the more toxic for them. There is a certain "cruel optimism" in maintaining an attachment to a nightlife world that hurts you, obstructs you, and diminishes you in certain ways—but still provides essential support for surviving the much more malignant world outside its doors.[18] Our ability to absorb this sort of dissonance seems boundless when it is key to our survival under worse conditions. But the potential for affective backlash is

FIGURE E.3 Mourners signing what appears to be a nightclub couch at a memorial down the road from the Pulse nightclub on June 18, 2016, in Orlando, Florida. Spencer Platt / Getty Images News via Getty Images.

just as vast when the optimism runs out and all that is left is woundedness, despair, and resentment.

And so, these worlds of warm liquidarity are still places of suffering, hidden to varying degrees under the fluid dynamics of vague belonging. As DJ Sprinkles states in her spoken-word introduction to *Midtown 120 Blues*, "The House Nation likes to pretend clubs are an oasis from suffering, but suffering is *in here*, with us."[19] In the network of ballroom/vogue scenes that now encompasses a wide geographic range both online and offline, common terms of appraisal such as "living" and "slaying" are only partly hyperbole; they reference the stakes of everyday survival for many participants. In a way, queer nightlife worlds are quite fragile: they tether precarious lives, dampen intolerable circumstances, and bracket irreconcilable antagonisms; they offer an ambivalent bargain between belonging and identity, solace and struggle. Although these nightlife scenes nourish a sense of collectivity under challenging circumstances and provide access to experiences of kinship and community that are out of reach of many partygoers in their everyday lives, they also lubricate the perpetuation of toxic circumstances. For some partygoers, the fluid stranger-intimacy found on the dancefloors of electronic dance music events helps make the suffering, struggle, and sheer fucked-up-ness of their world survivable—but it also renders these conditions tolerable, okay, livable, and perhaps something to which they can envision resigning themselves. Although these spaces offer valuable opportunities for broad fellowship in an increasingly mobile and mixed world, the vagueness that makes such utopian collectivity possible leaves important questions unanswerable: Are these dancefloors *just utopian enough* to keep on "just living," or do they provide a necessary refuge—a place where precarious partygoers can gather their energies, "find strength in the sound," and make their transition?

Introduction

1. My use of the term "the dancefloor" throughout this book reflects its
    doubled meaning in electronic dance music scenes, where it designates
    the physical space where dancing occurs *and* serves as a metonym for
    "the party" as a whole. In interviews and conversations with partygoers,
    actual dancefloors always remained the central point of reference for
    discussing parties and music scenes. Similarly, most of the ethnographic
    fieldwork I conducted took place on or near dancefloors, while the result-
    ing book shuttles constantly between the narrower and broader mean-
    ings of the term.

2. "Electronic dance music" (EDM) is a broad term originally developed in
    academic and journalistic contexts to refer to any style of post-disco,
    sample-based dance music without reducing it to its venues (e.g., "club
    music," "rave music"), prioritizing one style over others (e.g., "techno
    music"), or conflating it with different musical fields that have already
    laid claim to "electronic music" (e.g., "electroacoustic music"). How-
    ever, a recent popularization of the term—particularly its acronym—in
    mainstream media has accrued a new meaning, such that "EDM" can also
    refer to a narrower range of dance music genres that gained global main-
    stream popularity during the 2010s (e.g., dubstep, trap; for an overview
    of the "EDM boom," see Matos, *Underground Is Massive*). Since this newer
    usage has mostly involved the acronym "EDM," I avoid the acronym in
    this book and instead employ the full phrase "electronic dance music"
    (or "post-disco dance music") to invoke the term's initial meaning as a
    metacategory of popular dance music genres that make prominent use
    of sound samples and share a common origin in disco. When discussing
    concrete cases, I employ specific terms such as "deep house" or "mini-
    mal techno." In any case, the scholarly use of the term continues still
    with *Dancecult: Journal of Electronic Dance Music Culture* (since 2009). For

examples of this scholarly usage, see Fikentscher, *"You Better Work!"*; Hes-
mondhalgh, "International Times"; Loza, "Sampling (Hetero)sexuality";
McLeod, "Genres, Subgenres, Sub-Subgenres, and More"; Fink, *Repeating
Ourselves*; Garcia, "On and On"; M. Butler, *Unlocking the Groove*; Farrugia,
Beyond the Dance Floor; Fraser, "Spaces, Politics, and Cultural Economies";
Matos, *Underground Is Massive*.

3.   For ease of reading, I mostly use the term "partygoers" to refer to the
     people involved in the electronic dance music scenes where I conducted
     fieldwork. Although a more technical term like "scene participants"
     might be more precise, its repeated use soon becomes cumbersome,
     while "partygoers" is more contextually valid and intuitive for a
     broader readership—including readers who are themselves partygo-
     ers. For similar reasons, the terms "party" and "dance party" often stand
     in for "electronic dance music event."

4.   See also Ana Hofman's critical review of the affective turn in ethnomu-
     sicology as well as special issues on this topic in *Ethnomusicology Forum*
     and *Culture, Theory and Critique*: Desai-Stephens and Reisnour, "Musical
     Feelings and Affective Politics"; Graber and Sumera, "Interpretation,
     Resonance, Embodiment"; Hofman, "Affective Turn in Ethnomusicology."

5.   See the introduction to Lauren Berlant's *Female Complaint* for a definition
     of "intimate publics" as porous structures of belonging, where member-
     ship is based on feeling and shared affective experience. Also of relevance
     here is Michael Warner's account of "counterpublics," alternative public
     spheres that are characterized by embodied copresence flouting hege-
     monic norms of decorum. On a related point, Keira Kosnick notes how
     face-to-face encounters with strangers at a queer "Oriental" (Anatolian,
     Levantine) dance party in Berlin helped to mitigate concerns about self-
     imposed ghettoization. Berlant, *Female Complaint*; Kosnick, "Out on the
     Scene"; Warner, *Publics and Counterpublics*.

6.   Georg Simmel makes a similar reflection in his essay on "the stranger,"
     noting how the stranger's position outside of local social webs sometimes
     prompts their interlocutors to divulge information they would normally
     withhold from their social peers. Simmel, "Stranger."

7.   In addition to Dyer's original article, see also several articles reflect-
     ing on its historical circumstances and impact, in volume 58 of *New
     Formations*: Dyer, "In Defense of Disco"; Lawrence, "In Defence of Disco
     (Again)." In addition to *Saturday Night Fever*, see also *Thank God It's Friday*,
     a disco-themed comedy film that featured a soundtrack by the famed
     disco producer Giorgio Moroder as well as the legendary vocalist Donna
     Summer appearing in a supporting (and singing) role. Badham, *Saturday
     Night Fever*; Klane, *Thank God It's Friday*.

8.   The first decade of the twenty-first century saw several significant
     publications on the utopian promise of dancefloors (especially queer

ones), such as Amico, "I Want Muscles"; Amico, "Su casa es mi casa"; Bollen, "Queer Kinesthesia"; Buckland, *Impossible Dance*; Echols, *Hot Stuff*; Hutton, *Risky Pleasures?*; Muñoz, *Cruising Utopia*; Race, "Death of the Dance Party"; Rivera-Servera, "Choreographies of Resistance."

9. Scholarship and journalism on disco have gone through cycles of "revival" over the past two decades, generating a growing archive of histories and memoirs. Haden-Guest, *Last Party*; Reynolds, *Energy Flash*; Brewster and Broughton, *Last Night a DJ Saved My Life*; Lawrence, *Love Saves the Day*; Shapiro, *Turn the Beat Around*; Echols, *Hot Stuff*.

10. Aletti, "Vince Aletti Interviewed," 455. See also Aletti's landmark report on New York's nascent disco scene, "Discotheque Rock '72."

11. "The disco and its lifestyle has helped to contribute to a more harmonious fellowship towards all creeds and races." New York mayor Edward Koch, quoted in Lawrence, *Love Saves the Day*, 308.

12. The O'Jays, "Love Train," Philadelphia International Records ZS8-3754, vinyl, 7″, 1972; Sister Sledge, "We Are Family," Cotillion 44251, vinyl, 7″, 1979.

13. Oddly enough, a complete history of Chicago's post-disco dance music scenes has yet to be written, although Salkind's recent monograph provides substantial coverage for the city's queer-of-color scenes: Salkind, *Do You Remember House?* Nonetheless, the city appears prominently in nearly every historical account of house music, such as Brewster and Broughton, *Last Night a DJ Saved My Life*; Collin and Godfrey, *Altered State*; Feige and Müller, *Deep in Techno*; Gilbert and Pearson, *Discographies*; Kyrou, *Techno rebelle*; Reynolds, *Energy Flash*; Silcott, *Rave America*; Thornton, *Club Cultures*.

14. Joe Smooth Inc. featuring Anthony Thomas, "Promised Land," D.J. International Records DJ-905, vinyl EP, 12″, 1987. Notably, much of house music's utopianism draws on Christian tropes of salvation and paradise, particularly from Black gospel traditions; in fact, one would be hardpressed to find house vocalists active in the 1980s who did not begin their singing career in church. Many thanks to Michael Castelle for pointing this out to me during a conversation on this topic.

15. Fingers Inc., "Can You Feel It?," Jack Trax JTX-20, vinyl EP, 12″, 1988.

16. Robert Owens in Fingers Inc., "Can You Feel It?"

17. Not coincidentally, this track also exists in a reedited "Spoken Word MLK" version, where Owens's sermon is replaced with a recording of Dr. Martin Luther King Jr.'s "I Have a Dream" speech.

18. For accounts of the early acid house scene in the United Kingdom and its connections to the club cultures of the Balearic, see Collin and Godfrey, *Altered State*; Halfacree and Kitchin, "Madchester Rave On"; Reynolds, *Energy Flash*; Thornton, *Club Cultures*.

19. This comparison between the acid house boom of 1989 and the Summer of Love was first made in the pages of the subcultural magazine *i-D*: Heley and Collin, "Summer of Love 1989."

20. Langlois, "Can You Feel It?"

21. For a detailed account of rave's arrival to North America, see Silcott, *Rave America*.

22. "Generation X" refers to the generation born between the early 1960s and the late 1970s, following the postwar "baby boom." Members of this cohort were in their teens and twenties during the 1990s, grappling with a job market already saturated with baby boomers and the global economy sliding into recession. Henseler, *Generation X Goes Global*.

23. For an account of New York's dance music scenes in the 1980s and early 1990s, see Fikentscher, "Popular Music and Age Stratification"; Fikentscher, *"You Better Work!"*; Lawrence, *Love Saves the Day*. Although the musical curatorship of Larry Levan has been largely credited with shaping the New York house music sound during the 1980s, Tim Lawrence has argued for the importance of The Saint's roster of DJs for developing a "gay white aesthetic" that tended more toward Eurodisco, New Wave, and Hi-NRG dance music. He also argues that The Saint's DJs developed a smooth and seamless mixing technique that supplanted Levan's rough-cut style by the end of the decade. Lawrence, "Forging of a White Gay Aesthetic."

24. Serious Intention, "You Don't Know (Special Remix)," Easy Street Records EZS-7512, vinyl EP, 12", 1984.

25. Around 1990, New York's ballroom culture gained rapid visibility due to the release of the documentary film *Paris Is Burning*, Judith Butler's landmark book on gender performativity, and Madonna's hit music video "Vogue" (1990). Livingston, *Paris Is Burning*; J. Butler, *Gender Trouble*. For more recent critical work on ballroom culture, see Bailey, *Butch Queens Up in Pumps*; Jackson, "Improvisation in African-American Vernacular Dancing"; Jackson, "Social World of Voguing"; moore, *Fabulous*; Muñoz, *Cruising Utopia*.

26. For some preliminary reading on the intersection of techno and Afrofuturism, see Eshun, *More Brilliant than the Sun*; McCutcheon, "Techno, Frankenstein, and Copyright"; Schaub, "Beyond the Hood?"

27. For a detailed account of the first years of the "EDM boom" in North America, see Matos, *Underground Is Massive*.

28. Dyer, "In Defense of Disco."

29. For an analysis of Marx and Engels's critique of utopian socialism (including a bibliography of relevant texts from both revolutionary and utopian socialists), see Paden, "Marx's Critique of the Utopian Socialists."

30. Bloch, *Principle of Hope*.

31. On concrete utopias, see Bloch, *Principle of Hope*, 1:146.

32. Bloch, *Principle of Hope*, 1:75, 94 (emphasis added).

33. For repetition as structures of expectation in electronic dance music, see M. Butler, *Unlocking the Groove*; Garcia, "On and On."

34. In a similar vein of limited-scope utopianism, Hutton argues that "clubbing is not about apathy, it is a rejection of a world that has failed clubbers and a move towards creating a new worldview—if only for the weekend." Hutton, *Risky Pleasures?*, 12.

35. Muñoz, *Cruising Utopia*; Dolan, "Performance, Utopia."

36. Two key texts on queer antirelationality and the danger of heteroreproductive futurity are Bersani, *Homos*; Edelman, *No Future*.

37. Many thanks, again, to Michael Castelle for this turn of phrase.

38. Dyer, "Entertainment and Utopia."

39. "The use of massed violins takes us straight back, via Hollywood, to Tchaikovsky, to surging, outpouring emotions. . . . [Diana Ross's "Ain't No Mountain High Enough"] with its lyrics of total surrender to love, its heavenly choir and sweeping violins, is perhaps one of the most extravagant reaches of disco's romanticism. . . . [Ross's records] express the intensity of fleeting emotional contacts." Dyer, "In Defense of Disco," 22.

40. Dyer, "In Defense of Disco," 23.

41. George E. Marcus has been the most prominent advocate of this methodological approach, while a more recent multiauthor volume, *Mobile Methods*, provides an update through the framework of mobility studies. Marcus, "Ethnography in/of the World System"; Marcus, "What Is at Stake"; Marcus, "Beyond Malinowski"; Büscher, Urry, and Witchger, *Mobile Methods*.

42. Will Straw's foundational essay on music scenes defines them as "systems of articulation" that link the local to the global (or at least the extralocal). Andy Bennett and Richard A. Peterson's edited volume on music scenes extends this definition to include translocal scenes, which span multiple locales, and virtual scenes, which exist primarily online. Bennett and Peterson, *Music Scenes*; Straw, "Systems of Articulation."

43. The impact of increasing mobility on Berlin's electronic music scenes is the focus of a still-ongoing research project of mine, which has thus far resulted in a few publications: Garcia, "At Home, I'm a Tourist"; Garcia, "Techno-tourism"; Garcia, "With Every Inconceivable Finesse."

44. At the beginning of fieldwork (2006), I would orient myself in any city by visiting specialist vinyl record shops and perusing the flyers left by the door. By 2008, party promoters in all three cities were using social media platforms (primarily Facebook), and by 2011, the online media platform *Resident Advisor* had effectively monopolized event listings and ticketing globally.

45. Since all three fieldwork sites are large cities, this book focuses mainly on minimal electronic dance music events at nightclubs as well as in the ephemeral, clandestine spaces of raves. For the study of electronic dance music in festival settings, see the edited volume *Weekend Societies*, among others: F. Holt, "Music Festival Video"; Motl, "Dashiki Chic";

O'Grady, "Interrupting Flow"; Park, "Searching for a Cultural Home"; Partridge, "Spiritual and the Revolutionary"; Ruane, "Harm Reduction or Psychedelic Support?"; St. John, *Technomad*; St. John, "Neotrance and the Psychedelic Festival"; St. John, *Local Scenes*; St. John, *Weekend Societies*; Wergin, "Destination 'Three Days Awake.'"

46. "Club cultures contain hierarchies within themselves, which result not in a unified culture but fragmented clusters which share the term 'club culture,' that maintain their own dance styles, music genres and behaviours." Hutton, *Risky Pleasures*, 11.

47. Nye, "Love Parade, Please Not Again."

48. Despite the lack of print historiography, two documentary films on Chicago's early house scene have been released, both of which feature interviews and oral histories: Eberhart, *UnUsual Suspects*; Ramos, *Maestro*. In addition to these films, Salkind's recent monograph combines archival research, oral histories, and performance ethnography to narrate the first decade of house music in Chicago: Salkind, *Do You Remember House?*

49. Silcott, *Rave America*, 103.

50. Lloyd, "Neo-Bohemia"; Wilson and Taub, *There Goes the Neighborhood*.

51. Although Doreen Massey was the first to identify "hypersegregation," many other scholars have since continued this line of investigation: Massey and Denton, "Hypersegregation"; Massey and Denton, *American Apartheid*; Wilkes and Iceland, "Hypersegregation in the Twenty-First Century"; Wacquant, *Urban Outcasts*.

52. Although there is yet no monograph that focuses on Paris's post-disco scenes exclusively, nearly every French-language work on *la techno* provides a historical sketch of electronic dance music in France that centers primarily on Paris. Gaillot, *Multiple Meaning*; Kyrou, *Techno rebelle*; Racine, *Le phénomène techno*; Hampartzoumian, *Effervescence techno*; Mabilon-Bonfils, *La fête techno*; Vaudrin, *La musique techno*.

53. The term "techno" is already confusing enough in English, since it can be used to refer to all of electronic dance music as a metastyle or to a particular style associated with Detroit and Berlin. In France, *la techno* can be used even more broadly to speak of virtually any kind of electronic music, including music that is not dancefloor oriented. Throughout this book, the term *la techno* will appear in italics when referring to this broader French genre category. In all other cases, the term refers to the musical style.

54. See Entertainments (Increased Penalties) Act, 1990, c. 20 (England, Wales, Scotland); and Criminal Justice and Public Order Act, 1994, c. 33 (England, Wales, Scotland, N. Ireland).

55. Birgy, "French Electronic Music," 226.

56. For several extensive quotations of especially vitriolic condemnation of *la techno* in French public discourse, see Racine, *Le phénomène techno*, 112–14.

57. Looseley, *Popular Music in Contemporary France*.
58. Looseley, *Popular Music in Contemporary France*, 187.
59. Racine, *Le phénomène techno*, 135.
60. For a historical sketch of Le Pulp and its legacy, including some interviews with participants, see Garcia, "Alternate History of Sexuality."
61. See Uwe Schütte's introduction to *German Pop Music*, which provides a broader timeline of popular music in Germany, from the postwar era to the early twenty-first century.
62. Rapp, *Lost and Sound*, 30–34.
63. For the debate around "creative clusters" and their impact on cities, see Florida, *Rise of the Creative Class*; Florida, *Flight of the Creative Class*; Cooke and Lazzeretti, *Creative Cities, Cultural Clusters*; Heebels and van Aalst, "Creative Clusters in Berlin." The initially celebratory account of the "creative classes" has come under criticism for the accuracy of its analysis of statistical data sets, for failing to account for its negative impact on the freelancing creative classes themselves (i.e., the "flexibilization" of labor markets that create job volatility), and for the gentrification of urban space that their "clusters" tend to exacerbate. Sassen, "Global Cities and Survival Circuits"; Hoyman and Faricy, "It Takes a Village"; Shatkin, "Geography of Insecurity." This latter issue has been a point of great tension since the beginning of Berlin's push for postreunification urban redevelopment, which has only been intensified by the recent influx of "new tourism" that fixates on these gentrifying, "neo-bohemian" neighborhoods. Bernt and Holm, "Exploring the Substance and Style of Gentrification"; Bader and Bialluch, "Gentrification and the Creative Class"; Novy and Huning, "New Tourism (Areas) in the 'New Berlin.'"
64. Rapp, *Lost and Sound*, 105.
65. For a more detailed reflection on the methods used for this project, see Garcia, "Editor's Introduction"; Garcia, "Feeling the Vibe."
66. O'Grady, "Interrupting Flow."
67. This method is modeled after Fiona Buckland's pioneering work in the queer nightclub scenes of Manhattan, where she had to adapt her fieldwork methods to similar circumstances. Buckland, *Impossible Dance*.
68. Here and throughout the book, I use the term "fieldwork contact" instead of the more conventional "informant" or "consultant," as I believe that "contact" better conveys the social realities of my relationship with these people, many of whom were (or came to be) acquaintances and friends.
69. Other scholars of popular music have also used snowball sampling to study music scenes where participants are wary of outside scrutiny, such as Death Metal (Purcell), hip-hop (Jeffries), and popular musicians (primarily rock and pop) who license their work for television advertising (Klein): Jeffries, *Thug Life*; Klein, *As Heard on TV*; Purcell, *Death Metal Music*.

70. In other publications, I have reflected more extensively on invisibility as survival in queer-of-color nightlife, although this theme returns in the epilogue of this book, where I discuss the aftermath of the Orlando massacre of 2016: Garcia, "Whose Refuge, This House?"; Garcia, "Editor's Introduction"; Garcia, "Feeling the Vibe."

71. This shift can be tracked across two feature articles for *Resident Advisor*, published two years apart: Garcia, "Alternate History of Sexuality"; Ryce, "America's Gay Techno Underground."

72. An example of historiographic work would be Tim Lawrence's histories of dance music in New York in the 1970s and 1980s, while Mark Butler's books on composition and performance in techno provide an emblematic example of research based in musical analysis. Lawrence, *Love Saves the Day*; Lawrence, *Life and Death on the New York Dance Floor*; M. Butler, *Unlocking the Groove*; M. Butler, *Playing with Something That Runs*. There are nonetheless some notable exceptions to this pattern, including Jeremy Gilbert and Ewan Pearson's cultural-critical *Discographies* as well as a body of ethnographic research embedded in the substyles of psychedelic trance (especially "Goa trance" and "psytrance"): Gilbert and Pearson, *Discographies*; D'Andrea, *Global Nomads*; Saldanha, *Psychedelic White*; St. John, *Technomad*; St. John, *Global Tribe*.

73. Particularly influential for my approach to affect is the work of Lauren Berlant, Sianne Ngai, Eve K. Sedgwick, Kathleen Stewart, and Nigel Thrift, all of whose work spans several disciplines and areas of study: Berlant, *Female Complaint*; Berlant, *Cruel Optimism*; Ngai, *Ugly Feelings*; Sedgwick, *Touching Feeling*; Stewart, *Ordinary Affects*; Thrift, *Non-Representational Theory*. For an overview of affect theory and the "affective turn," see Clough and Halley, *Affective Turn*; Gregg and Seigworth, *Affect Theory Reader*.

74. Fiona Buckland's study of queer nightlife in New York is based in dance ethnography and performance studies, while Alejandro Madrid writes about "nor-tec" (electronic *norteño* music from Tijuana) through the lens of ethnomusicology and Latin American studies, and Ben Malbon engages in a critical geography of British urban clubbing. Buckland, *Impossible Dance*; Madrid, *Nor-Tec Rifa*; Malbon, *Clubbing*. Although not as tightly focused on dancefloor encounters, both Rebekah Farrugia and Fiona Hutton provide important accounts of how women experience and navigate club spaces: Farrugia, *Beyond the Dance Floor*; Hutton, *Risky Pleasures?*

75. This book's focus on slippery and vague belonging resonates with Kiri Miller's *Traveling Home*, which examines how a radically diverse group of singers can share a sense of belonging through collective music making; although we examine contrasting sites and scenes, we find similar forms of strategic avoidance being used to lubricate encounters with difference.

76. Ngai, *Ugly Feelings*, 7–8.

77. See the introductory chapter of Muñoz's *Cruising Utopia* for an elucidation of how Bloch's utopianism can inform queer politics.

78. For Bloch's concrete utopias, see Bloch, *Principle of Hope*, 1:146.

79. For an introduction to thick description as ethnographic method, see Geertz, "Thick Description."

1. Touch and Intimacy on the Dancefloor

1. For a more detailed recounting of this event, see the corresponding field note posted to my fieldwork blog: Garcia, "Souvenir 03."

2. For this conceptualization of cultural intimacy through shared embarrassment, see Herzfeld, *Cultural Intimacy*, 1–6; and for an ethnomusicological application of this idea to the role of sentimentality in Turkish popular musics, see Stokes, *Republic of Love*, 32–34.

3. "Vibe" as a vernacular Anglophone term for diffuse and contagious affect has an especially long history of use in electronic dance music scenes. See chapter 4 for more discussion of this term in relation to affect theory, and for a review of scholarly literature on the topic, see Garcia, "Feeling the Vibe."

4. Unwelcome touch also impacts people of color as well as trans and queer folks differently and disproportionately. Since my interviewees were mostly white and cisgendered, the ethnographic data I collected on this issue focused mainly on (mostly white) cis women's experiences.

5. Some scholars of Japanese corporeal culture have also worked to counter stereotypes of Japanese intimate relations (as nonverbal, nontactile, indirect, and unemotional) by focusing on practices of cosleeping (Tahhan, "Depth and Space in Sleep"), bathing rituals (Clark, *Japan, a View from the Bath*), and parent-child or teacher-child tactility (Ben-Ari, *Body Projects in Japanese Childcare*; Tahhan, "Blurring the Boundaries between Bodies").

6. Although a more recent review article on empirical studies of interpersonal touch research does not seem to have been published yet, see nonetheless Gallace and Spence, "Science of Interpersonal Touch."

7. Henley, "Status and Sex"; Henley, *Body Politics*. For an example of the warmth/nurturing approach to touch research, see Mehrabian, *Nonverbal Communication*. For an approach centered on sexual interest, see Jourard and Rubin, "Self-Disclosure and Touching."

8. Henley, "Status and Sex," 91. Following this hypothesis, see also Goffman, "Nature of Deference and Demeanor"; Major, Schmidlin, and Williams, "Gender Patterns in Social Touch," 634.

9. Major, Schmidlin, and Williams, "Gender Patterns in Social Touch," 640.

10. See Major, "Gender Patterns in Touching Behavior"; Stier and Hall, "Gender Differences in Touch." At the time of this writing, most quantitative research conducted on interpersonal touch assumes heterosexuality on the part of the test subjects and their social settings. This raises questions about how well such research will predict or describe the touch behaviors that I have observed during my fieldwork, where a spectrum of queer sexualities are often well represented (at least in the minimal techno and house scenes studied here).

11. These studies are reviewed in Gallace and Spence, "Science of Interpersonal Touch."

12. In the absence of more recent examples of cross-cultural studies of tactility, some pioneering studies can be found among Jourard, "Exploratory Study of Body-Accessibility"; Remland and Jones, "Cultural and Sex Differences"; Remland, Jones, and Brinkman, "Proxemic and Haptic Behavior"; Remland, Jones, and Brinkman, "Interpersonal Distance, Body Orientation, and Touch." For the (not uncontroversial) categorizations of "contact culture" and "noncontact culture," see Hall, *Hidden Dimension*; Montagu, *Touching*.

13. The use of the term "proxemics" in this research literature differs from Michel Maffesoli's theorization of the same term, in that these studies mainly seek to provide a category for norms and behaviors that manage bodily proximity (rather than physical contact). There is nonetheless some relevance to this project in Maffesoli's formulation, in that the spatial clustering of human activity over time creates a sense of community that transcends those who invoke it. Maffesoli's theorization of proxemics can be found in *Time of the Tribes*, chap. 6.

14. Henley, *Body Politics*; Major, Schmidlin, and Williams, "Gender Patterns in Social Touch."

15. Guerrero and Andersen, "Waxing and Waning of Relational Intimacy."

16. For discussions of the underground/mainstream binary in club culture, as well as its limits, see Redhead, *Rave Off*; Thornton, *Club Cultures*.

17. Two books were central in establishing this conceptualization of subculture through the subversion of dominant culture, both of which came out of the "Birmingham School" of cultural studies, that is, the Centre for Contemporary Cultural Studies at the University of Birmingham (now defunct): Hall and Jefferson, *Resistance through Rituals*; Hebdige, *Subculture*.

18. Warner, *Publics and Counterpublics*, 112.

19. Warner, *Publics and Counterpublics*, 119. See also an analysis and extension of Warner's counterpublics concept in Deem, "Stranger Sociability," 446–51.

20. Humphreys, *Tearoom Trade*. See also Hollister's critique and revision of the concept of "interaction membranes," which Humphreys adapted

from Erving Goffman's sociology of games to describe a delimited space designated for play: Hollister, "Beyond the Interaction Membrane."

21. "Habitus" can be understood here to refer to behaviors that are deeply embodied, mostly unconscious, and tied to class and upbringing—although Bourdieu's conceptualization of this term is more complex. For a more in-depth discussion, see Bourdieu, *Outline of a Theory of Practice*; Bourdieu, *Distinction*.

22. Due to the agendas of many funding bodies that support research on recreational drugs, it is difficult to find scholarly writing that describes the recreational/subjective effects of drugs, rather than adverse effects and long-term health risks. Nonetheless, a few review articles are available: Britt and McCance-Katz, "Brief Overview"; Hart et al., "Acute Physiological and Behavioral Effects"; Kavanaugh and Anderson, "Solidarity and Drug Use"; Liechti and Vollenweider, "Acute Psychological and Physiological Effects"; Nestler, "Is There a Common Molecular Pathway for Addiction?"

23. Lee and Guerrero, "Types of Touch."

24. Jones and Yarbrough, "Naturalistic Study."

25. Although this "narcissistic apolitical escapism" critique of rave culture was commonplace in both popular and scholarly discourse at the time, notable examples can be found in the "Birmingham School" of subculture studies, such as Melechi, "Ecstasy of Disappearance."

26. Spinoza, *Ethics*. For a more in-depth discussion of affect and affect theory, see chapter 4.

27. Hutton, *Risky Pleasures?*, 14–15.

28. The earliest example I could find of a prominent publication addressing unwelcome touch on the dancefloor of electronic dance music events was Fiddy and Mixmag Staff, "We Need to Talk about Sexual Harassment." Although I have yet to find a definitive historical account of how the notion of "safe(r) spaces" entered electronic dance music scenes, it most likely came through the queer and feminist subscenes, drawing on the practices of riot grrrl and lesbian scenes going back to at least the early 1990s.

29. Hutton, *Risky Pleasures?*, 95.

30. Hutton, *Risky Pleasures?*, 95.

31. For detailed descriptions and analyses of situations in which the conversion of intimacy and flirtation into saleable labor produces pragmatic strategies aimed at bridging the gap between desire and necessity, see Anne Allison's ethnographic work on/in the Tokyo hostess-club scene: *Nightwork*.

32. Hutton, *Risky Pleasures?*, 25.

33. Hutton, *Risky Pleasures?*, 25.

34. For further discussion of "counterpublics," see especially Warner, *Publics and Counterpublics*, chap. 1.

35. As Lauren Berlant puts it, "therapy saturates the scene of intimacy, from psychoanalysis and twelve-step groups to girl talk, talk shows, and other witnessing genres." Berlant, "Intimacy," 4. For examples of explicitly normative and therapeutic definitions of intimacy, see Jamieson, *Intimacy*; Kasulis, *Intimacy or Integrity*.

36. Prager, *Psychology of Intimacy*, 18–32.

37. Some examples of critical, nonnormative approaches to intimacy would include Berlant, *Intimacy*; Berlant and Warner, "Sex in Public"; Bromley, "Failures of Intimacy"; Plummer, *Intimate Citizenship*; Povinelli, *Empire of Love*; Probyn, *Outside Belongings*; Warner, *Publics and Counterpublics*.

38. Sedgwick, *Touching Feeling*, 17.

39. Berlant, "Intimacy," 1.

40. "Iconic" here makes reference to the icon in Peircean semiotics: a sign whose referentiality is based on resemblance to its object. Peirce, *Essential Peirce*, 2:460–61.

2. Sonic Tactility

1. This chapter expands on an earlier article published in the inaugural issue of *Sound Studies*: Garcia, "Beats, Flesh, and Grain: Sonic Tactility and Affect in Electronic Dance Music," *Sound Studies* 1, no. 1 (2015): 59–76.

2. Many of these titles correspond to multiple recordings, but an example for each phrase mentioned here would include the following: Omar featuring Stevie Wonder, "Feeling You (Henrik Schwarz Remix)," *The Remixes*, Peppermint Jam PJMS0140, vinyl, 12″, 2010; Sylvester, "You Make Me Feel (Mighty Real)," Fantasy 12FTC 160, vinyl, 12″, 1978; Donna Summer, "I Feel Love," Casablanca Records NBD 20104, vinyl, 12″, 1977; Nightcrawlers, "Push the Feeling On," Great Jones 162-530 620-1, vinyl, 12″, 1992; K. Hand, "Feel," *On a Journey*, !K7 Records !K7R001cd, compact disc, 1995.

3. Fingers Inc., "Can You Feel It?," Jack Trax JTX-20, vinyl, 12″, 1988; Chez Damier, "Can You Feel It," KMS KMS035, vinyl, 12″, 1992; NY Stomp, "Can You Feel It? E.P.," Illusion Recordings ILL003, vinyl, 12″, 2012. While there are innumerable tracks with "feel it" in the title, two examples that were prominent during fieldwork are John Tejada, "Feel It," *Where*, Palette Recordings PAL-050 LP, 2 vinyl, 12″, 2008; Scuba, "Feel It," *Back and 4th* (compilation), Hotflush Recordings HFLP005, 3 vinyl, 12″, 2011.

4. For a relevant example of comparative genre analysis, see Charles Kronengold's analysis of disco tracks as a nexus of exchange of genre

conventions with "new wave" pop and album-oriented rock, "Exchange Theories in Disco."

5. This is primarily the case in styles such as techno, house, trance, and its various substyles. The "breakbeat"-based styles of "hardcore" breaks, jungle, drum'n'bass, and dubstep use asymmetrical pulse cycles that more closely resemble hip-hop's "beats" and "breaks."

6. The Gathering is a recording project/moniker initially started by the Chicago house producer Chez Damier in 2004; it was revived in 2010 with the addition of the Parisian producers Jef K (also the manager of Silver Network records) and Chris Carrier. The Gathering, "In My System (Jef K SystemMix)," Silver Network SILVER 027, vinyl, 12", 2010.

7. Davide Squillace, "The Other Side of Bed," *What about the Vice*, Desolat X008, vinyl, 12", 2010.

8. Excerpt begins at 46:34 of Classen, *Feiern*.

9. Pinch and Trocco, *Analog Days*, 59–60.

10. Goodman, *Sonic Warfare*, 18.

11. Goodman, *Sonic Warfare*, 196.

12. Matthew Herbert, *Bodily Functions*, Studio!K7!K7097CD, compact disc, 2001.

13. Matthew Herbert, *Bodily Functions (Special 10th Anniversary Edition)*, Accidental AC66CD, 2 compact discs, 2012.

14. Herbert, "Personal Contract for the Composition of Music."

15. Smalley, "Defining Timbre," 35.

16. Smalley, "Defining Timbre," 36.

17. For an overview of Peircean semiotics, as well as its applications to music and sound, see Peirce, *Essential Peirce*; Tomlinson, "Sign, Affect, and Musicking"; Turino, *Moving Away from Silence*.

18. Early on in the era of "glitch music" and "post-digital aesthetics," Kim Cascone proposed definitions of both terms that emphasized the sounds of failing recording technology as an elegiac trope for the unfulfilled promises of the "digital revolution" of the 1980s and '90s: Cascone, "Aesthetics of Failure."

19. Remix: M.A.N.D.Y. and Booka Shade, "O Superman feat. Laurie Anderson (Reboot's 20 Cubans Rework)," Get Physical Music GPM098.1, vinyl, 12", 2008. Original source material: Laurie Anderson, "O Superman," Warner Bros. Records DWBS 49888, vinyl, 12", 1981.

20. Kerri Chandler, "Pong (Bones and Strings Rework)," *Pong (Ben Klock Unreleased Mixes)*, Deeply Rooted House DRH018R, limited pressing, gray translucent vinyl, 12", 2009.

21. Pierre Schaeffer's writings are best approached through Chion's "study guide" to Schaeffer's landmark treatise, both of which have only been translated relatively recently: Chion, *Guide des objets sonores*; Chion, *Guide to Sound Objects*; Schaeffer, *Traité des objets musicaux*; Schaeffer, *Treatise on Musical Objects*.

22. In contrast to Schaeffer, Barthes's definition of "grain" was limited to the human voice; his conceptualization focused on finding the traces of the singer's flesh and bones in the sound of their voice. Barthes, "Grain of the Voice." The original French term that Schaeffer uses, *entretien*, is difficult to translate precisely, although in everyday usage it is closest to "maintenance" in English. This has been translated variously as "sustainment" (see Dack and North's translation of both Schaeffer and Chion) and "continuant phase" (Smalley). I have chosen to use "sustain" instead, in order to emphasize its conceptual and formal similarities with "sustain" as an element of the ADSR amplitude envelope described earlier in this chapter. Chion, *Guide to Sound Objects*; Schaeffer, *Treatise on Musical Objects*; Smalley, "Spectromorphology: Explaining Sound-Shapes." Schaeffer, quoted in Chion, *Guide to Sound Objects*, 171.

23. In addition to the original French edition and the English translation, this massive classificatory table of musical objects can be found in Chion's guide to Schaeffer's treatise, which presents slight differences in translation into English: Schaeffer, *Traité des objets musicaux*, 584–87; Schaeffer, *Treatise on Musical Objects*, 464–69; Chion, *Guide to Sound Objects*, 197–200.

24. All translations by the author, although corresponding page numbers in Dack and North's translation are provided for comparison. Schaeffer, *Traité des objets musicaux*, 551–52; Schaeffer, *Treatise on Musical Objects*, 439–41.

25. Schaeffer, *Traité des objets musicaux*, 554–55; Schaeffer, *Treatise on Musical Objects*, 441–42.

26. Schaeffer, *Traité des objets musicaux*, 551; Schaeffer, *Treatise on Musical Objects*, 439.

27. Schaeffer, *Traité des objets musicaux*, 551; Schaeffer, *Treatise on Musical Objects*, 439.

28. Smalley, "Spectromorphology and Structuring Processes," 72.

29. Smalley, "Spectromorphology and Structuring Processes," 72.

30. Various artists, *Clicks & Cuts 3*, Mille Plateaux MP116, 2 compact discs, 2002; Philip Sherburne quoted in Goodman, *Sonic Warfare*, 121.

31. Roads, *Microsound*, 86.

32. For an introduction to the "forward masking effect" in hearing, see Buser and Imbert, *Audition*.

33. Roads, *Microsound*, 105.

34. Oliver Hacke, "Millepieds (SLG Remix)," Level Records LVL-06, vinyl, 12″, 2006.

35. Lee Jones, "Safari (Stimming Remix)," Aus Music AUS0813, vinyl, 12″, 2008.

36. Niederflur, "z.B.," *Min2MAX*, M_nus MINUS40CD, compact disc, 2006; Martin Dawson and Glimpse, "No One Belongs Here More than You," Crosstown Rebels CRM070, vinyl, 12″, 2011.

37. For further reading on Marks's notion of "haptic visuality," see Marks, *Skin of the Film*; Marks, *Touch*.

38. Marks, *Skin of the Film*, 162.

39. For the anatomy and physiology of the ear, see Møller, *Hearing*, and Beament, *How We Hear Music*. See also Veit Erlmann's *Reason and Resonance*, a historical study of the development of otology (that is, the science of hearing) in relation to modern theories of the thinking and feeling subject, particularly as he traces the ways that the mechanics of hearing troubled the ideal of "rational" subjectivity.

40. For historical accounts of tactile hearing aids before the invention of cochlear implants, see Mills, "On Disability and Cybernetics"; Schürmann et al., "Hands Help Hearing"; Summers, *Tactile Aids*.

41. Sedgwick, *Touching Feeling*, 13. See also Bora, "Outing Texture."

42. For Gibson's definition and elaboration of "affordance," see Gibson, *Ecological Approach to Visual Perception*, 127.

43. Spinoza, *Ethics*. For theoretical accounts of Spinozan *affectus* that resonate with affordance theory's foregrounding of potential action, see Bergson, *Matter and Memory*; Deleuze and Guattari, *What Is Philosophy?*; Massumi, *Parables for the Virtual*.

44. Sedgwick, *Touching Feeling*, 15. See also Bora, "Outing Texture."

45. Goodman, *Sonic Warfare*, 47.

46. Sedgwick, *Touching Feeling*, 16.

47. For Deleuze's conceptualization of "molar" versus "molecular," particularly in analogy to social relations, see Deleuze and Guattari, *Thousand Plateaus*, 283–96.

3. Liquidarity

1. Since this book focuses primarily on the period from 2006 to 2010, it does not cover the rise of politically oriented rave collectives in the mid-2010s—especially those formed around feminist, queer, nonwhite, and/or postmigrant identities. These collectives define belonging more explicitly through identity-based communities, and they set expectations for ethical behavior through antiharassment / safer space policies as well as accountability procedures that have been adapted from feminist and antiracist activist cultures.

2. For relevant scholarship on taste, see Bourdieu, *Distinction*, and Thornton, *Club Cultures*. For ritual, see Turner, *Ritual Process*, and van Gennep, *Rites of Passage*. And for reading/viewing publics, see Berlant, *Female Complaint*, and Warner, *Publics and Counterpublics*.

3. *Éléctro* is an abbreviation of "electroclash," a style emergent in the early 2000s that fused contemporary house with 1980s electro-pop, New Wave,

and synth rock. It is characterized by a preponderance of arpeggiated synthesizer chords, heavy use of EQ filters, distortion, and deadpan vocals, all of which signal a certain nostalgia for the sounds of 1980s music.

4. Ostgut was also the subject of a feature article for the Red Bull Music Academy, which features interviews with DJs, clubgoers, and promoters. Waltz, "Nightclubbing."

5. Up to the time of this writing, Berghain holds a special "Snax" fetish night every year on the weekend of Holy Week, in Easter. Since 2011, the club has also been holding a sports-themed fetish night in late autumn, called "FC Snax." For more history and ethnography about this event, see Garcia, "With Every Inconceivable Finesse."

6. When newly renovated unisex bathrooms were opened in Panorama Bar in the winter of 2009, the statements made by Berghain management in electronic newsletters and flyers highlighted the fact that the new bathroom stalls were on average two square meters (21.5 square feet) larger than the previous ones—an improvement that required no explanation for Berghain's regular clientele.

7. Sherburne, "Techno."

8. "Top 100 Clubs"; Resident Advisor Staff, "RA Club Awards."

9. For further reading, see also Imre van der Gaag's architectural and cultural history of Snax, Ostgut, and Berghain, "Function Follows Form," which provides a more detailed historical narrative of the pre-Berghain years as well as precise descriptions of the built environments that they occupied.

10. See the website of Karhard Architektur (http://www.karhard.de), the firm that directed the renovations to Berghain, for numerous images of the exterior and interior of Berghain.

11. Also, see "Im Reich des Wahnsinns" for a hand-drawn floor plan of each floor, accompanied by tongue-in-cheek descriptions of each space. The floor plan was created by the artist Chrisse Kunst (http://www.chrisse kunst.de/), whose drawings also include a postapocalyptic landscape surrounding a still-standing Berghain.

12. During renovations to Panorama Bar in the winter of 2010, this image was replaced by another Tillmans photo of a man's exposed anus; this ignited a backlash among club regulars, who started a Facebook page demanding, "We want our vagina back!" Tillmans's black-and-white "Freischwimmer" prints were replaced by two other, multicolored ones in the same style (and equally massive dimensions). Berghain continues to rotate its considerable art collection every few years, much like art galleries with large archives, like the Sammlung Boros. Notably, while Berlin nightlife was effectively shut down during the COVID-19 pandemic, Berghain reopened temporarily as a socially distanced art gallery/ museum.

13. I have developed a more detailed account of this this tension between inclusive ethos and exclusive practices in earlier work: Garcia, "Pathological Crowds"; Garcia, "Crowd Solidarity"; Garcia, "Alternate History of Sexuality."

14. A few historical accounts of the disco era consider its ethos in some detail, such as Echols, *Hot Stuff*; Fikentscher, *"You Better Work!"*; Lawrence, *Love Saves the Day*; and Lawrence, "I Want to See All My Friends."

15. An account of rave's countercultural and hippie inheritance can be found especially in accounts of the UK "acid-house" scene and global psytrance scenes, such as Collin and Godfrey, *Altered State*; D'Andrea, *Global Nomads*; Reynolds, *Energy Flash*; Rietveld, *This Is Our House*; Silcott, *Rave America*; St. John, *Rave Culture and Religion*; Sylvan, *Trance Formation*; and Thornton, *Club Cultures*.

16. For a contemporary journalistic account of the "Second Summer of Love," see Heley and Collin, "Summer of Love 1989."

17. I draw my approach to "reparative reading" from Eve Kosofsky Sedgwick's essay contrasting reparative/depressive and paranoid reading, relating them, respectively, to "weak" and "strong" theory. For more detail on this epistemological framework, see Sedgwick, *Touching Feeling*, chap. 4.

18. For examples of additive theories of collectivity centered around taste communities, totems, and group leaders, see, respectively, Southerton, "Consuming Kitchens"; Durkheim, *Elementary Forms of Religious Life*; Freud, *Group Psychology*.

19. For examples of subtractive theories of collectivity focused on ritual *communitas*, see Turner, *Ritual Process*, and van Gennep, *Rites of Passage*. For crowd anonymity, see Tarde, *Laws of Imitation*, and Le Bon, *Crowd*.

20. Thornton, *Club Cultures*, 111.

21. For an introduction to "techno-tourism" in Berlin, see Rapp, *Lost and Sound*; Garcia, "At Home, I'm a Tourist"; Garcia, "Techno-tourism."

22. For "cultural capital," see Bourdieu, *Distinction*; and for "subcultural capital," see Thornton, *Club Cultures*.

23. For a selection of scholarship that employs high/low cultural distinctions to examine the intersection of taste and social class, see Simmel, "Philosophy of Fashion"; Gans, *Popular Culture and High Culture*; Bourdieu, *Distinction*; Gronow, *Sociology of Taste*; and D. Holt, "Distinction in America?" Scholarship tracking the emergence of omnivore/eclectic/cosmopolitan tastes as a new articulation of social class flourished in the 1990s and early 2000s: Peterson, "Understanding Audience Segmentation"; Peterson and Kern, "Changing Highbrow Taste"; Bryson, "Anything but Heavy Metal"; T. Bennett, Emmison, and Frow, *Accounting for Tastes*; López Sintas and García Álverez, "Omnivores Show Up Again"; and Swirski, *From Lowbrow to Nobrow*.

24. For two influential studies of how taste-based consumption can generate new identities that do not align neatly with social class, see Southerton, "Consuming Kitchens," and Savage, "Musical Field."

25. In Lynn Jamieson's clinical-psychological definition of intimacy, she identifies "detailed interpersonal knowledge" as a crucial element of an intimate relationship. I use the term here to highlight the ways in which dancefloor intimacy diverges from normative forms of intimacy. Jamieson, *Intimacy*.

26. Miller, *Traveling Home*, 36.

27. Miller, *Traveling Home*, 37.

28. Miller, *Traveling Home*, 116.

29. Victor Turner's writing on liminality and *communitas* remains essential reading for ritual studies, although this theorization is deeply indebted to the early twentieth-century scholarship of Arnold van Gennep and Émile Durkheim: Durkheim, *Elementary Forms of Religious Life*; van Gennep, *Rites of Passage*; Turner, *Ritual Process*.

30. For early studies of rave in subculture studies, see, e.g., McRobbie, "Shut Up and Dance"; Redhead, *Rave Off*; Redhead, *Subculture to Clubcultures*; and Thornton, *Club Cultures*. A broader introduction to the field of subculture studies in general can be found in Hall and Jefferson, *Resistance through Rituals*. Ritual theory is especially present in ethnographic work dedicated to "festival" events, especially those featuring psychedelic trance / "psytrance," in which aesthetics, bodily practices, and partygoers' discourse often invite comparisons to Turner's account of ritual. For an introduction to the subfield of "psytrance" studies, see St. John, "Rave Culture and Religion"; St. John, "Neotrance and the Psychedelic Festival."

31. See also Graham St. John's critique of the concept of the *limen*, which raises similar issues and provides a review of previous anthropological scholarship that questions the Turnerian account of liminality. St John, "Alternative Cultural Heterotopia."

32. Berlant, *Female Complaint*, viii.

33. Notably, affect is central to how intimate publics are formed, in a manner similar to Fiona Hutton's term "emotional communities," which she coins to describe club scenes as communities built around shared feeling. Hutton, *Risky Pleasures*?

34. Berlant, *Female Complaint*, 4.

35. Berlant, "Intimacy," 1.

36. A similarly fluid additive mode of crowd cohesion can be found in the work of the geographer Arun Saldanha. He develops a contrasting but complementary account of cohesion in his study of race and tourism in the "Goa trance" scene in Goa, India. Through participant-observation as a legibly Indian cis man, he develops an affect-informed theory of white

racial "viscosity" as a way of explaining how certain spaces and times in the Goa scene would attract white hippies and ravers while remaining impenetrable to Indian revelers. In addition to the fluid analogies of the two approaches, both share a focus on how problematic exclusions are obfuscated. Saldanha, *Psychedelic White*, 49–52.

37. Dueck, *Musical Intimacies and Indigenous Imaginaries*, 6.
38. Dueck, *Musical Intimacies and Indigenous Imaginaries*, 5.
39. Dueck, *Musical Intimacies and Indigenous Imaginaries*, 7.
40. A selection of influential cultural theories that emphasized movement and fluidity as a means of accounting for globalization and neoliberal capitalism would include Appadurai, *Modernity at Large*; Beck, *Cosmopolitan Vision*; Castells, *Rise of the Network Society*; Giddens, *Consequences of Modernity*; Sassen, *Globalization and Its Discontents*; Sassen, "Global Cities and Survival Circuits"; Urry, *Mobilities*.
41. Zygmunt Bauman wrote a series of books that explored the theoretical possibilities of liquid metaphors to interpret contemporary societal changes. Here, I am especially influenced by the first in this series, *Liquid Modernity*, as well as *Liquid Love*.
42. Bauman, *Liquid Modernity*, 13.
43. See Bauman's discussion in *Liquid Love* of "top pocket relationships" and "semi-detached couples" as evidence of a rising tendency to view stable relationships as burdens rather than support (x–xi).
44. A paradigmatic (and landmark) example of this line of queer critique would be Warner, *Trouble with Normal*.
45. Landmark publications that theorize "agonistic" politics include Laclau and Mouffe, *Hegemony and Socialist Strategy*; Mouffe, *Agonistics*; Rancière, *Disagreement*. In my own writing on agonism in nightlife economies of London and Berlin, I have drawn most directly from Mouffe's work. Garcia, "Agonistic Festivities."
46. Warner, *Publics and Counterpublics*.

4. Thickening Something

1. This is the same party and afterparty, in fact, that featured in the opening to chapter 1, where Lola and I later embraced, kissed, and called ourselves best friends after having met for the first time merely twelve hours earlier.
2. Later, a remix/edit of "Bakerman" by the New York–based duo Soul Clap (Aux Music, 2010) became ubiquitous, on the crest of a wave of popularity for downtempo disco edits during 2010. Old deep house tracks also enjoyed a renaissance at this time, such as Blaze's "Lovelee Dae (20:20 Vision Remix)" (Playhouse, 1998).

3. For a more extensive review of "vibe" as a vernacular metaphor for affect within electronic dance music, see Garcia, "Feeling the Vibe"; Witek, "Feeling at One."

4. Cusick, "Musicology, Torture, Repair"; Cusick, "You Are in a Place Out of the World."

5. Goodman, "Speed Tribes"; Goodman, *Sonic Warfare*.

6. On the notion of nonalive matter being nonetheless vibrant and active as a nonhuman force, see J. Bennett, *Vibrant Matter*.

7. See Graham St. John's reflections on the centrality of "vibe" to electronic dance music experience ("Writing the Vibe") as well as his article "Neotrance and the Psychedelic Festival," the latter of which provides an overview of electronic dance music scholarship with respect to the concept of "vibe," particularly in relation to *communitas*. A reading list on this topic could include Sommer, "C'mon to My House"; Taylor, *Strange Sounds*; Siokou, "Seeking the Vibe"; Takahashi and Olaveson, "Music, Dance, and Raving Bodies"; Gerard, "Selecting Ritual"; Olaveson, "'Connectedness' and the Rave Experience"; Rill, "Rave, Communitas, and Embodied Idealism"; and St. John, "Trance Tribes and Dance Vibes." See also my article on "vibe" in electronic dance music scenes, which provides a more detailed review of this literature from the perspective of affect theory: Garcia, "Feeling the Vibe." Paul Berliner's ethnographic monograph *Thinking in Jazz* provides an illuminating example of "vibe" in nightlife culture outside of electronic dance music. Of particular interest is the chapter titled "Vibes and Venues," in which Berliner uses the term "vibes" to reference both the acoustical properties of a space and the general (affective) atmosphere of the performance environment, thus implying a connection between sound and mood/atmosphere.

8. Other writers have similarly employed "attunement," "tuning in," or similar terms to describe a process of coming into a relation of shared experiential flux (Schutz, "Making Music Together"; Schutz, "Fragments on the Phenomenology of Music"), of mutual attention (Schutz, *Phenomenology of the Social World*), of intensified awareness of and sympathy with one's surrounding sonic environment (Schafer, *Soundscape*), and of affective alignment with an atmosphere or "affective tone" (Goodman, *Sonic Warfare*). Notably, all of these writers use music and sound to account for the development and intensification of relationships to others and to one's environment.

9. Spinoza, *Ethics*. For an indispensable review of the broader range of theories of affect, of which the Spinoza-Deleuze genealogy is but one, see Thrift, "Intensities of Feeling."

10. Although many of Deleuze's writings touch on affect as a concept, a selection of readings and commentary would include Deleuze, *Cinema 1*; Deleuze, *Spinoza*; Deleuze, *Expressionism in Philosophy*; Seigworth, "From

Affection to Soul." It is impossible to provide a representative overview of this broad stream of "affect theory," but my own pathway through this theory (by year of publication) includes Grosz, *Space, Time, and Perversion*; Probyn, *Outside Belongings*; Sedgwick, *Touching Feeling*; Grosz, *Time Travels*; Shouse, "Feeling, Emotion, Affect"; Povinelli, *Empire of Love*; Clough and Halley, *Affective Turn*; Saldanha, *Psychedelic White*; Stewart, *Ordinary Affects*; Berlant, *Female Complaint*; Thrift, *Non-representational Theory*; Race, *Pleasure Consuming Medicine*; Mazzarella, "Affect"; Mazzarella, "Myth of the Multitude"; Eng, *Feeling of Kinship*; Pope, "Hooked on an Affect."; and Berlant, *Cruel Optimism*. See especially Gregg and Seigworth's *Affect Theory Reader*, which offers not only a varied sampling of landmark readings on affect but also an editors' introduction that serves as an accessible overview of affect theory as a whole.

11. Massumi, *Parables for the Virtual*, 14.

12. Goodman, *Sonic Warfare*, xv.

13. Goodman, *Sonic Warfare*, 47.

14. Goodman, *Sonic Warfare*, 172.

15. For scholarly efforts at describing DJ techniques that articulate affect, some early examples would include Hadley, "'Ride the Rhythm'"; Fikentscher, *"You Better Work!"*; M. Butler, *Unlocking the Groove*; Montano, "DJ Culture."

16. Roland Clark, "I Get Deep," Shelter Records SHL-1032, vinyl, 12″, 2000; Late Nite Tuff Guy, "I Get Deeper," TBot's All Nite House Party (no catalog number), limited edition vinyl, 12″, 2007, later released as part of a compilation of remixes: DJ Le Roi feat. Roland Clark, "I Get Deep (Late Night Tuff Guy Remix)," *I Get Deep*, Get Physical Music GPM160, MP3 file (320 kbps), 2012.

17. Rework, "Anyway I Know You," Playhouse 43, vinyl, 12″, 2000.

18. Clark, "I Get Deep," 2:38–3:10; emphasis indicates falsetto.

19. M. Butler, *Unlocking the Groove*.

20. M. Butler, *Unlocking the Groove*, 91.

21. M. Butler, *Unlocking the Groove*, 92.

22. For an overview of the "emotional scaffolding" model and other neuro-cognitive theories of how music impacts emotional cognition, see Krueger, "Affordances and the Musically Extended Mind"; Witek, "Feeling at One."

23. Equalizers (or an equalization filter) can be understood as a set of band-pass filters—that is, filters that amplify or attenuate a signal across a specified range of frequencies. The most rudimentary equalizers in a DJ's mixer will usually provide control over the bass and treble frequency ranges, while more sophisticated equipment will provide a filter for the "mid" (middle) range and/or subdivide these ranges into narrower frequency bands. Most contemporary DJ mixers include one or two side

channels with high-pass, band-pass, and low-pass filters that can be extended across the whole frequency spectrum, enabling "filter sweep" effects. An echo or delay effect is a device that takes an incoming audio signal and repeats it one or multiple times, at specified time intervals and with specified levels of attenuation, thus creating an "echo" effect. A "reverb" (reverberation) effect is one that emulates the complex accumulation of echoes and dissipation that would occur in a particular enclosed space, thus creating ringing and dampening effects that create a sense of space; although mechanical devices have been used for this effect (e.g., chamber reverberators and plate reverberators), electronic dance music performance technologies are usually digital, using algorithms to reproduce these processes of echo and absorption. The flanging effect entails combining an incoming signal with itself, with this second identical signal delayed by a microtemporal interval, which is usually measured in the milliseconds. This phase-shifted combination creates amplifications and cancellations in the waveforms across particular frequencies that are related to each other by the harmonic series. Gradual changes in the delay interval between the two signals will cause these "peaks and notches" to sweep up and down the frequency spectrum.

24. London, *Hearing in Time*, 12.
25. For conceptualizations and studies of "flow" experience, see Csikszentmihalyi, *Flow*; Krueger, "Affordances and the Musically Extended Mind"; Trost, "Time Flow and Musical Emotions"; and Witek, "Feeling at One."
26. Trost, "Time Flow and Musical Emotions," 210. See also Krueger, "Affordances and the Musically Extended Mind"; Witek, "Feeling at One."
27. The explicit processes of social entrainment, especially impression management, have been extensively described and discussed by Erving Goffman in his interactionist and theatrical approach to social self-presentation. See Goffman, *Presentation of Self in Everyday Life*; Kelly and Barsade, "Mood and Emotions."
28. For a substantial literature review (up to 2014) of affective synchronization in psychology and sociology as well as philosophy, see Bösel, "Affective Synchronization."
29. Hatfield, Cacioppo, and Rapson, *Emotional Contagion*, 151.
30. For a sample of studies of afferent feedback in face-to-face interactions, see: Bavelas et al., "Motor Mimicry as Primitive Empathy"; Bernieri, Reznick, and Rosenthal, "Synchrony, Pseudosynchrony, and Dissynchrony"; Capella, "Mutual Influence in Expressive Behavior"; Hatfield, Cacioppo, and Rapson, *Emotional Contagion*; and Kelly and Barsade, "Mood and Emotions."
31. Barsade, "Ripple Effect."
32. Bösel, "Affective Synchronization," 91.

33. Bösel, "Affective Synchronization," 90–93; Trost, "Time Flow and Musical Emotions."
34. Kelly and Barsade, "Mood and Emotions."
35. Chapple, *Culture and Biological Man*; Warner et al., "Rhythmic Organization of Social Interaction."
36. Bartel and Saavedra, "Collective Construction."
37. Gabriel Tarde developed a model of facial mirroring similar to "afferent feedback" in his account of affective contagion in crowds (*Laws of Imitation*), while Gustave Le Bon imagined a "collective mind" emerging out of the accumulation of individual psyches (*Crowd*). Although both nineteenth-century French crowd theorists shared a tendency to depict crowds as volatile and irrational, Le Bon was more alarmist. Le Bon was an elitist openly opposed to universal suffrage, and his writings frequently demonized working-class voters as "electoral mobs," ascribing to them the same risks and dangers. Other relevant studies that critique and update the field of crowd psychology include Borch and Knudsen, "Postmodern Crowds"; Canetti, *Crowds and Power*; Hemment, "Affect and Individuation"; and Jaguaribe, "Carnival Crowds."
38. Durkheim, *Rules of Sociological Method*; Durkheim, *Elementary Forms of Religious Life*.
39. Ahmed, "Collective Feelings," 28.
40. The relationship between collective music making and social relations is a foundational research aim of ethnomusicology. Although most ethnomusicologists engage with this topic in some form, a selection of ethnographies that engage with affect and collective musicking would include Benamou, *Rasa*; Desai-Stephens and Reisnour, "Musical Feelings and Affective Politics"; Dueck, *Musical Intimacies and Indigenous Imaginaries*; Feld, "Sound Structure as Social Structure"; MacMillen, "Affective Block"; Miller, *Playing Along*; and Turino, *Moving Away from Silence*.
41. Hall, *The Dance of Life*; Turino, *Moving Away from Silence*.
42. Turino, *Moving Away from Silence*, 111.
43. Turino, *Moving Away from Silence*, 111.
44. Margulis, "Repetition and Emotive Communication."
45. On the predominance of repetition in electronic dance music, see Fink, *Repeating Ourselves*; Garcia, "On and On."
46. "Musicking" derives from "music" but inflected as a verb, rather than a noun. Christopher Small proposed this term to focus on music as a process and to include all forms of musical involvement: "To music is to take part, in any capacity, in a musical performance, whether by performing, by listening, by rehearsing or practicing, by providing material for performance (what is called composing), or by dancing." Small, *Musicking*, 9.
47. Turino, *Moving Away from Silence*, 111; emphasis in original.

48. Austin, *How to Do Things with Words*; Tambiah, *Performative Approach to Ritual*.
49. Tambiah, "Form and Meaning of Magical Acts," 221.
50. Friedson, *Remains of Ritual*.
51. Friedson, *Remains of Ritual*, 115.
52. Friedson, *Remains of Ritual*, 115.
53. Ngai, *Ugly Feelings*.
54. Tompkins's notion of affect is substantially different from the Spinoza-Deleuze-Massumi genealogy discussed earlier in the chapter, in that it is based on empirical studies and directed toward clinical practitioners of psychology. Tompkins developed his notion of affect in response to Freud's system of drives (and in contradistinction from other cognitive, motor, perceptual, and homeostatic systems), with the particularity of affects being that they amplify and combine other systems without the object specificity of those systems (such as breathing being specific to a particular mix of gases). Tomkins defines affects as having three characteristics: (1) urgency, in the sense of drawing attention and eliciting action; (2) abstractness, in the sense that its urgency is not object specific but rather only vaguely indexes more complex underlying processes; and (3) generality, in that it can be coassembled with other systems and mediate between them. A more detailed definition of Tomkinsonian affect is not possible here, but see Sianne Ngai's *Ugly Feelings* for further elaborations (especially the chapter on "tone") as well as several edited collections and readers of his work: Sedgwick, Frank, and Alexander, *Shame and Its Sisters*; Tomkins and Demos, *Exploring Affect*; and Tomkins and Karon, *Affect, Imagery, Consciousness*.
55. For an analysis of improvised music (mostly free jazz) using systems theory, emergence, and "swarm intelligence" as a form of emergent intelligence, see Borgo, *Sync or Swarm*.

5. The Sweetness of Coming Undone

1. Dominica, "Gotta Let You Go," Micmac Records, Inc. MIC-304, vinyl 12", 1994.
2. Although the page is now dormant, earlier activity on the Panorama Bar Music page on Facebook can be found here: http://www.facebook.com /panoramabarmusic/.
3. Berlant, *Cruel Optimism*, 1.
4. Race, *Pleasure Consuming Medicine*.
5. See Masomenos's website, https://masomenos.fr (accessed December 18, 2022).

6. Examples of these can be found at Masomenos's website: https://maso menos.fr/JUKEBOX-MUSIC-SHOP (accessed December 18, 2022).

7. Michael Herzfeld defines "cultural intimacy" as "the recognition of those aspects of a cultural identity that are considered a source of external embarrassment but that nevertheless provide insiders with their assurance of common sociality." Herzfeld, *Cultural Intimacy*, 3.

8. This anecdote involves several other characters—some of whom are not official participants in this research project—and explicit accounts of drug use, so I have obfuscated some identifying details and given single-use pseudonyms to everyone else involved in this narrative.

9. Most ethnographic anecdotes included here are edited versions of posts made to a blog where I recorded shorthand field notes during the research phase of this project. The post for this anecdote can be found in Garcia, "Kompakt Label Night @ Le Rex."

10. See, for example, the online magazine / community website *Resident Advisor* (http://www.residentadvisor.net; https://ra.co/), which conducted yearly polls of its members. Since polling began in 2006, Villalobos has been listed either at or very near the top of "Best DJ" listings. The polls were discontinued in 2017, with a brief explanation published as a staff editorial: "Opinion: Why We're Stopping the RA Polls."

11. Most media devoted to electronic music, whether online or in print, feature "DJ charts" prominently. These are lists submitted by well-known DJs, listing recently released tracks that they frequently play in their sets. This "charting" of a track is taken to be an endorsement by that particular DJ, which in turn is used to drive sales. This system functions much like a peer-review system (in contrast to the music-review system, where ratings are assigned by professional music critics, who are rarely high-profile DJs). The DJ charts are often aggregated statistically by media platforms to create metacharts, with formulaic titles such as "100 Most Charted Tracks of November."

12. See, for example, reviews of Villalobos's music on *Resident Advisor* (Staff of Resident Advisor, "Ricardo Villalobos"), *Little White Earbuds* ("Tag Archive: Ricardo Villalobos"), or *Pitchfork* ("Ricardo Villalobos: Reviews"), the latter of which primarily focuses on "indie" rock but has heaped critical praise on Villalobos for several years.

13. Ricardo Villalobos, "Que Belle Epoque 2006," Frisbee Tracks FT067, vinyl 12″, 2006.

14. This expressive break in vocal register can be compared to the "cry break" in country music, Mexican *rancheros*, folk-pop, and numerous traditions of ritual wailing. Sonically similar to how the voice breaks when sobbing, the cry break, as Greg Urban claims, is "arguably the most transparent index of crying" ("Ritual Wailing in Amerindian Brazil," 390). As Aaron

Fox helpfully describes it, cry breaks "vividly express the upwelling of bodily processes in the sound-stream of texted song" (*Real Country*, 281). Although the lyrics of Villalobos's vocal sample have been reduced to unintelligible vocables, the indexing of overwhelming affect remains. In addition to Urban and Fox, a sample of early research on cry breaks and ritualized weeping would include Feld, *Sound and Sentiment*; Feld, "Wept Thoughts"; and Tolbert, "Women Cry with Words."

15. Ricardo Villalobos, "Easy Lee" and "What You Say Is More Than I Can Say," *Alcachofa*, Playhouse CD08, CD, 2003.

16. M. Butler, *Unlocking the Groove*, 141–46.

17. This opening phrase repeats later on in the track and nearly reaches the end of the statement: "And it's time to lose my mind" (02:31).

18. See Mark Spicer's account of "accumulative form" in popular music, in "(Ac)cumulative Form in Pop-Rock Music," especially his analysis of Radiohead's "Packt like Sardines in a Crushd Tin Box." See also the penultimate chapter in Mark Butler's *Unlocking the Groove*, "Form from the Record to the Set," which draws on both formalist musical analyses and ethnographic interviews with techno producers.

19. Roland Clark, "I Get Deep," Shelter Records SHL-1032, vinyl 12″, 2000, 2:38–3:10; emphasis indicates falsetto.

20. For an analysis of drug use as a form of "non-sovereignty" that provides release from normativity, see especially the chapter "Exceptional Sex," in Race, *Pleasure Consuming Medicine*. See also Race, "Recreational States."

21. For discussion of "disappearance" through raving and its political ramifications (from a subculture studies perspective), see Melechi, "Ecstasy of Disappearance"; St. John, "Rave Culture and Religion."

22. Blanchot, *Infinite Conversation*, 203.

23. Blanchot, *Infinite Conversation*, 207.

24. Pini, *Club Cultures and Female Subjectivity*.

25. Hutton, *Risky Pleasures?*, 18.

26. Hutton, *Risky Pleasures?*, 25.

27. Race, *Pleasure Consuming Medicine*, 115.

28. Race, *Pleasure Consuming Medicine*, 166.

29. Race, *Pleasure Consuming Medicine*, 166.

30. Lacan, *Ethics of Psychoanalysis*; Lacan, "Subversion of the Subject."

31. For accounts of self-deterritorialization (adapted from Deleuze and Guattari) in electronic dance music, see especially the scholarship on psychedelic trance, including D'Andrea, *Global Nomads*; Deleuze and Guattari, *Mille plateaux*; and St. John, *Technomad*.

32. D'Andrea, *Global Nomads*.

33. As discussed in the introduction, Muñoz's *Cruising Utopia* provides a crucial and critical queer perspective on utopianism that draws from Ernst Bloch's account of hope in relation to utopian politics in *Principle of Hope*.

34. In "Entertainment and Utopia," a study of mid-twentieth-century American musical films, Richard Dyer proposes that utopianism in popular entertainment is more often expressed through feeling than representation.

6. Bouncers, Door Policies, and Embedded Diversity

1. Fikentscher, "It's Not the Mix," 136.
2. Fikentscher, "It's Not the Mix," 127.
3. Thornton, *Club Cultures*, 56.
4. Søgaard, "Bouncers, Policing," 43.
5. Chicago, as a fieldwork site, is largely absent from this chapter for a number of reasons. First, this chapter focuses on Berlin as the club scene with the richest and most internationally (in)famous discourse around "door policy" work. Second, while France shares a supranational European context with Germany that facilitates concise comparison, including Chicago would require a historical survey and academic literature review of immigration/cultural policy in North America. As a result, integrating Chicago in a nonsuperficial way would balloon this chapter to an unwieldy length. Nonetheless, some Chicagoan interviewees are quoted here regarding their experiences in Berlin, and a few comparisons to "door work" in the Chicago scene can be found in the notes.
6. Hobbs et al., *Bouncers*, 119–20.
7. On risk management among bouncers, through participant ethnography, see Monaghan, "Doorwork and Legal Risk."
8. As discussed previously in relation to liquidarity, Sarah Thornton developed the concept of "subcultural capital" as an extension and adaptation of Bourdieu's "cultural capital," oriented toward the internal hierarchies of subcultures rather than those of dominant culture(s): Thornton, *Club Cultures*.
9. Although difficult to conduct in an embedded manner (especially for nonwhite ethnographers), there is a growing archive of ethnographic studies of nightclub door staff: Hobbs et al., *Bouncers*; Kosnick, "Out on the Scene"; Monaghan, "Doorwork and Legal Risk"; and Søgaard, "Bouncers, Policing."
10. Deborah Talbot's *Regulating the Night* is a notable example of an ethnographic project that consults a range of nightlife workers, rather than only bouncers.
11. Hobbs et al., *Bouncers*.
12. Comment threads across *Resident Advisor* were all deleted in 2019, in an effort to curb harassment and hate speech on the platform. Nonetheless, the event listing for "Promote Diversity" (September 12–13, 2013) is still

available; see Resident Advisor Staff, "Berlin: Events: Promote Diversity." The editorial staff at *Resident Advisor* explained the rationale behind the deletion of comment threads; see "Opinion: Why We're Closing Comments."

13. Helm, "How the Bouncer of Berghain Chooses."
14. "Integration."
15. See also *Der Spiegel*'s thorough English-language synopsis of the Sarrazin controversy. Bode et al., "Man Who Divided Germany."
16. Prochasson, "Expulsions de Roms."
17. Nowicki, "Présentation générale," paras. 1–4.
18. Freeman, "Immigrant Incorporation in Western Democracies," 946.
19. Vertovec and Wessendorf, "Introduction," 4.
20. Vertovec and Wessendorf, "Introduction," 6–12.
21. For the German notion of "parallel societies" (*Parallelgesellschaften*), see Heitmeyer, "Für türkische Jugendliche in Deutschland."
22. For one of the more forceful criticisms of multiculturalism on French republican grounds, see Amselle, *Affirmative Exclusion*.
23. Multiculturalism as a cultural policy has been the subject of considerable scholarly debate; a selection that bears on European contexts would include Brubaker, *Citizenship and Nationhood*; Favell, *Philosophies of Integration*; Klopp, *German Multiculturalism*; Freeman, "Immigrant Incorporation in Western Democracies"; Geschiere, *Perils of Belonging*; Koopmans, "Trade-Offs between Equality and Difference"; Schönwälder, "Germany"; and Simon and Sala Pala, "'We're Not All Multiculturalists Yet.'"
24. Schönwälder, "Germany."
25. For a historical survey of the guest-worker system in West Germany, see Korte, "Labor Migration and the Employment of Foreigners"; Bade, *Population, Labour, and Migration*; Bade, "From Emigration to Immigration"; and Klopp, *German Multiculturalism*.
26. Schönwälder, "Germany."
27. Liebig, "Labour Market Integration."
28. Schmalz-Jacobsen, Hinte, and Tsapanos, *Einwanderung, und Dann?*; Klopp, *German Multiculturalism*.
29. Hoffmann, *Die unvollendete Republik*; Hoffmann, "Das 'Volk'"; Brubaker, *Citizenship and Nationhood*; Kanstroom, "Wer sind wir wieder?"; Klopp, *German Multiculturalism*.
30. Klopp, *German Multiculturalism*.
31. Zimmermann et al., *Immigration Policy and the Labor Market*; Schönwälder, "Germany."
32. Klopp, *German Multiculturalism*.
33. Schönwälder, "Germany."
34. Adrian Favell provides a thorough account of France as an "assimilationist" nation-state, in *Philosophies of Integration*.

35. Amselle, *Affirmative Exclusion*, xiii.

36. Brubaker, *Citizenship and Nationhood*; Silverman, *Deconstructing the Nation*; Geschiere, *Perils of Belonging*.

37. Simon and Sala Pala, "'We're Not All Multiculturalists Yet.'"

38. Brubaker, *Citizenship and Nationhood*; Silverman, *Deconstructing the Nation*.

39. Wieviorka, *Une société fragmentée?*; Simon, "Le modèle français de discrimination." Simon, "Les jeunes de l'immigration"; Simon, "France and the Unknown Second Generation"; Simon, "Choice of Ignorance"; Bleich, *Race Politics in Britain and France*.

40. Simon and Sala Pala, "'We're Not All Multiculturalists Yet.'"

41. Ignatieff, *Blood and Belonging*.

42. Ignatieff, *Blood and Belonging*, 3–4.

43. Most ethnographic anecdotes included here are edited versions of posts made to a blog where I recorded shorthand field notes during the research phase of this project. The direct link to this anecdote can be found at Garcia, "Watergate."

44. Hobbs et al., *Bouncers*, 121.

45. Hobbs et al., *Bouncers*, 122.

46. For a study of the complexities of door selection for a queer "oriental" (read: Middle Eastern) night in Berlin, see Kosnick, "Out on the Scene."

47. Thornton, *Club Cultures*, 90–91, 101–2.

48. For "disidentification," see Muñoz, *Disidentifications*.

49. For an overview of the "Birmingham School" and some of its applications to popular music scenes, see Clarke et al., "Subcultures, Cultures and Class"; Hall and Jefferson, *Resistance through Rituals*; Hebdige, *Subculture*; and Redhead, *Subculture to Clubcultures*.

50. Muggleton and Weinzierl, *Post-subcultures Reader*; Thornton, *Club Cultures*.

51. This chapter focuses exclusively on Berlin as an ethnographic site to develop this notion of *Leitsubkultur*—that is, the prioritization of one subcultural "way of life" over others, as a hegemonic "guiding example" that disadvantages those who approached Berlin's electronic music scenes through different subcultural frameworks. Although the performance and appraisal of subcultural knowledge is most visible at the doors of Berlin clubs, where such selection is usually overt, similar dynamics are at play in Paris and Chicago, albeit in subtler ways. At Le Rex in Paris, for example, it was common for door staff to quiz clubbers on the names of artists playing that night. And in Chicago, as recounted briefly in chapter 3, most loft parties and illicit "underground" events managed access through extended social networks that could be seen as an ecosystem of microcultural "crews" with varying proximity to the music scene's "leading" subculture.

52. All of these discussions on *Resident Advisor* have been lost since the website deleted all of the user comments on its articles in 2019. For an

example from a different website, see the extensive "Berghain" thread on the mnml.nl discussion board.

53. Hobbs et al., *Bouncers*, 122.
54. Kosnick, "Out on the Scene."
55. Kosnick, "Out on the Scene," 21.
56. Hobbs et al., *Bouncers*, 122.
57. Hobbs et al., *Bouncers*, 122–23.
58. In a study of Danish "color-blind policing," the ideology of color blindness combined with violent stereotypes of ethnically marked men to enable covert discriminatory practices at the doors of clubs: Søgaard, "Bouncers, Policing."
59. Fikentscher, "It's Not the Mix," 136.
60. Rapp, *Lost and Sound*, 174.
61. Rapp, *Lost and Sound*, 46.
62. In addition to amateur video clips easily searchable through video-sharing sites such as YouTube (especially with the search term "Bar25"), the promotional reel for a proposed documentary on Bar 25 includes a compressed sequence of crowd footage that can serve as a preliminary example of the bar's sartorial and architectural style: 25FilmsBerlin, "Bar25—Days Out of Time Trailer."
63. May and Chaplin, "Cracking the Code."
64. Rapp, *Lost and Sound*, 179.
65. Rapp, *Lost and Sound*, 179.
66. Lloyd, "Neo-Bohemia"; Lloyd, *Neo-Bohemia*. The scholarly literature on gentrification in Berlin is vast, but a sampling of publications relevant to this project would include Reimann, "Transition from People's Property to Private Property"; Häussermann, Holm, and Zunzer, *Stadterneuerung in der Berliner Republik*; Bernt and Holm, "Exploring the Substance and Style of Gentrification"; Färber, "Flourishing Cultural Production"; Bader and Bialluch, "Gentrification and the Creative Class"; and Novy and Huning, "New Tourism (Areas) in the 'New Berlin.'"
67. This definition of bohemianism appeared on a website for a research project led by Alan Blum and hosted by the Culture of Cities Centre at York University (Canada), which was published in 2004 but has since been deleted. For an archived version, see Blum, "New Directions for Research." This research project expands on ideas first published in Blum, "Scenes"; Blum, *Imaginative Structure of the City*.
68. Klenzendorf, "Bar 25" (emphasis added). The odd, intransitive use of "entertain" here may have to do with the lexical proximity between "to entertain" (*unterhalten*) and "to converse, to chat" (*sich unterhalten*) in German. Klenzendorf may have been describing the crowd as eager to *engage with* rather than amuse each other.

69. This notion of embedded diversity is comparable to Reuben A. Buford May's theorization of "integrated segregation," in which "individuals in public space, rather than experiencing unfettered interaction with others, . . . are socially bound to interaction with those social types like themselves" (*Urban Nightlife*, 8). He developed this concept to account for a nightlife district in a southern US university town, which was perceived locally as a racially "integrated" zone, even though bars and clubs were effectively segregated and partygoers tended to avoid contact with racial others on the street. Although May's analytic focus is broader, including public urban space and seeing little evidence of integration *within* clubs, his notion of integrated segregation helps to understand how embedded diversity can provide a seemingly harmonious cosmopolitanism on the dancefloor: door staff may curate an idealized form of heterogeneity at the door, but partygoers can nonetheless self-segregate within the club space, as a means of avoiding conflict and protecting themselves from aggression.
70. It should be noted that these practices of embedded diversity primarily serve the emotional comfort of white partygoers, who are less likely to experience the failures and inequities of this system firsthand. In an article written for the Black-centered media platform *The Root*, Michael Harriot writes about the protective nature of whiteness: "Whiteness offers respite. The greatest privilege that whiteness affords is the ability to overlook racism, hate, and inequality. Whiteness is a fireproof suit in a world that is on fire and no one—not even me—is even asking you to help us extinguish the blaze. But please stop acting like the heat is all in our head or that you figured out how to make yourself inflammable." Harriot, "How to Be."
71. Aletti, "Discotheque Rock '72."
72. Aletti, *Disco Files 1973–78*, 456.
73. Thornton, *Club Cultures*, 111.

Epilogue

1. See chapter 3 for a more detailed description of the club.
2. For *communitas* as an anthropological concept related to the experience of ritual, see chapters 3 and 4 in this book as well as Turner, *Ritual Process*, and Turner, "Liminal to Liminoid."
3. For "typologies of disrepute" in the context of nightclub bouncers, see chapter 6 and also Hobbs et al., *Bouncers*, 122.
4. The Blessed Madonna (Marea Stamper) / @Blessed_Madonna, Twitter post, June 12, 2016. This post was deleted in 2020, when she changed her

Twitter user handle to reflect a change in her artist moniker. The entirety of the post is nonetheless preserved in several contemporary journalistic sources, including Julius, "Nightlife Community Condemns Mass Shooting."

5. Leon-Davis, "Site of the Orlando Shooting."
6. Saxelby, "Why Queer Latinx Parties Are Necessary."
7. Supergrover, "I'm an aging dyke."
8. Barbaro, "It's Sacred."
9. Kylie Jack (@ixKylie), Twitter post, June 12, 2016. This post was deleted sometime after I took the screenshot included here (August 25, 2016).
10. Garcia, "Alternate History of Sexuality in Club Culture."
11. Ryce, "America's Gay Techno Underground."
12. For "intimate publics," see chapter 3 and also the introduction to Berlant, *Female Complaint.*
13. Bayetti Flores, "Pulse Nightclub Shooting."
14. For a sampling of scholarship on brown and Black queer dancefloors, see Amico, "Su casa es mi casa"; Bailey, *Butch Queens Up in Pumps*; Buckland, *Impossible Dance*; Muñoz, *Cruising Utopia*; and Rivera-Servera, "Choreographies of Resistance."
15. Underground Resistance (producer: Mad Mike), "Transition," *Inspiration/ Transition* (EP), Underground Resistance UR-3000, vinyl 12″, 2002.
16. For "concrete utopias," see the introduction to this book as well as Bloch, *Principle of Hope.*
17. Hennessy-Fiske, "FBI Investigators Say."
18. Berlant, *Cruel Optimism.*
19. DJ Sprinkles, aka Terre Thaemlitz, "Introduction," *Midtown 120 Blues,* Mule Musiq, mule musiq cd 9, CD, 2009.

Ahmed, Sara. "Collective Feelings: Or, the Impressions Left by Others." *Theory, Culture & Society* 21, no. 2 (2004): 25–42. https://doi.org/10.1177/0263276404042133.

Aletti, Vince. *The Disco Files 1973–78: New York's Underground, Week by Week*. Edited by Frank Broughton and Bill Brewster. London: DJhistory.com, 2009.

Aletti, Vince. "Discotheque Rock '72: Paaaaarty!" *Rolling Stone*, September 13, 1973.

Aletti, Vince. "Vince Aletti Interviewed." In *The Disco Files 1973–78: New York's Underground, Week by Week*, edited by Frank Broughton and Bill Brewster, 453–67. London: DJhistory.com, 2009.

Allison, Anne. *Nightwork: Sexuality, Pleasure, and Corporate Masculinity in a Tokyo Hostess Club*. Chicago: University of Chicago Press, 1994.

Amico, Stephen. "'I Want Muscles': House Music, Homosexuality and Masculine Signification." *Popular Music* 20, no. 3 (2001): 359–78.

Amico, Stephen. "Su casa es mi casa: Latin House, Sexuality, Place." In *Queering the Popular Pitch*, edited by Sheila Whiteley and Jennifer Rycenga, 131–51. New York: Routledge, 2006.

Amselle, Jean-Loup. *Affirmative Exclusion: Cultural Pluralism and the Rule of Custom in France*. Translated by Jane Marie Todd. 2nd ed. Ithaca, NY: Cornell University Press, 2003.

Appadurai, Arjun. *Modernity at Large: Cultural Dimensions of Globalization*. Minneapolis: University of Minnesota Press, 1996.

Austin, J. L. *How to Do Things with Words*. The William James Lectures, 1955. Oxford: Oxford University Press, 1962.

Bade, Klaus J. "From Emigration to Immigration: The German Experience in the Nineteenth and Twentieth Centuries." In *Migration Past, Migration Future: Germany and the United States*, edited by Klaus J. Bade and Myron Weiner, 1–38. Providence, RI: Berghahn Books, 1997.

Bade, Klaus J. *Population, Labour, and Migration in 19th- and 20th-Century Germany*. New York: Berg, 1987.

Bader, Ingo, and Martin Bialluch. "Gentrification and the Creative Class in Berlin-Kreuzberg." In *Whose Urban Renaissance? An International Comparison of Urban Regeneration Strategies*, edited by Libby Porter and Kate Shaw, 93–102. New York: Routledge, 2009.

Badham, John, dir. *Saturday Night Fever*. Los Angeles: Paramount Pictures, 1977. Film.

Bailey, Marlon M. *Butch Queens Up in Pumps: Gender, Performance, and Ballroom Culture in Detroit*. Ann Arbor: University of Michigan Press, 2013.

Barbaro, Michael. "'It's Sacred': A Gay Refuge, Turned into a War Zone." *New York Times*, June 13, 2016. https://www.nytimes.com/2016/06/14/us/gay-bars-his tory.html.

Barsade, Sigal G. "The Ripple Effect: Emotional Contagion and Its Influence on Group Behavior." *Administrative Science Quarterly* 47, no. 4 (2002): 644–75. https://doi.org/10.2307/3094912.

Bartel, Caroline A., and Richard Saavedra. "The Collective Construction of Work Group Moods." *Administrative Science Quarterly* 45, no. 2 (2000): 197–231. https://doi.org/10.2307/2667070.

Barthes, Roland. "The Grain of the Voice." In *Image, Music, Text*, translated by Stephen Heath, 179–89. New York: Hill and Wang, 1977.

Bauman, Zygmunt. *Liquid Love: On the Frailty of Human Bonds*. Cambridge: Polity Press, 2003.

Bauman, Zygmunt. *Liquid Modernity*. Cambridge: Polity Press, 2000.

Bavelas, Janet Beavin, Alex Black, Charles R. Lemery, and Jennifer Mullett. "Motor Mimicry as Primitive Empathy." In *Empathy and Its Development*, edited by Nancy Eisenberg and Janet Strayer, 317–38. Cambridge: Cambridge University Press, 1987.

Bayetti Flores, Veronica. "The Pulse Nightclub Shooting Robbed the Queer Latinx Community of a Sanctuary." *Remezcla*, June 13, 2016. https://remezcla.com /features/music/pulse-nightclub-sanctuary/.

Beament, James. *How We Hear Music: The Relationship between Music and the Hearing Mechanism*. Rochester, NY: Boydell Press, 2001.

Beck, Ulrich. *The Cosmopolitan Vision*. Translated by Ciaran Cronin. Cambridge: Polity Press, 2006.

Benamou, Marc. *Rasa: Affect and Intuition in Javanese Musical Aesthetics*. New York: Oxford University Press, 2010.

Ben-Ari, Eyal. *Body Projects in Japanese Childcare: Culture, Organization and Emotions in a Preschool*. Surrey, UK: Curzon, 1997.

Bennett, Andy, and Richard A. Peterson, eds. *Music Scenes: Local, Translocal and Virtual*. Nashville, TN: Vanderbilt University Press, 2004.

Bennett, Jane. *Vibrant Matter: A Political Ecology of Things*. Durham, NC: Duke University Press, 2010.

Bennett, Tony, Michael Emmison, and John Frow. *Accounting for Tastes: Australian Everyday Cultures*. Cambridge: Cambridge University Press, 1999.

"Berghain." mnml.nl discussion board. Accessed July 21, 2021. https://www.mnml
.nl/phpBB3/viewtopic.php?t=64444.

Bergson, Henri. *Matter and Memory*. New York: Zone Books, 1991. Orig. 1896.

Berlant, Lauren. *Cruel Optimism*. Durham, NC: Duke University Press, 2011.

Berlant, Lauren. *The Female Complaint: The Unfinished Business of Sentimentality in
American Culture*. Durham, NC: Duke University Press, 2008.

Berlant, Lauren, ed. *Intimacy*. Chicago: University of Chicago Press, 2000.

Berlant, Lauren. "Intimacy: A Special Issue." In *Intimacy*, edited by Lauren Berlant,
1–8. Chicago: University of Chicago Press, 2000.

Berlant, Lauren, and Michael Warner. "Sex in Public." *Critical Inquiry* 24, no. 2
(1998): 547–66. https://doi.org/10.1086/448884.

Berliner, Paul. *Thinking in Jazz: The Infinite Art of Improvisation*. Chicago: University
of Chicago Press, 1994.

Bernieri, Franck J., J. Steven Reznick, and Robert Rosenthal. "Synchrony, Pseudosynchrony, and Dissynchrony: Measuring the Entrainment Process in
Mother-Infant Interactions." *Journal of Personality and Social Psychology* 54,
no. 2 (1988): 243–53. https://doi.org/10.1037/0022-3514.54.2.243.

Bernt, Matthias, and Andrej Holm. "Exploring the Substance and Style of Gentrifi-
cation: Berlin's 'Prenzlberg.'" In *Gentrification in a Global Context: The New Urban
Colonialism*, edited by Rowland Atkinson and Gary Bridge, 106–20. New York:
Routledge, 2005.

Bersani, Leo. *Homos*. Cambridge, MA: Harvard University Press, 1995.

Birgy, Philippe. "French Electronic Music: The Invention of a Tradition." In
Popular Music in France from Chanson to Techno: Culture, Identity, and Society,
edited by Hugh Dauncey and Steve Cannon, 225–42. Aldershot, UK:
Ashgate, 2003.

Blanchot, Maurice. *The Infinite Conversation*. Minneapolis: University of Minnesota
Press, 1993.

Bleich, Erik. *Race Politics in Britain and France: Ideas and Policymaking since the 1960s*.
Cambridge: Cambridge University Press, 2003.

Bloch, Ernst. *The Principle of Hope*. 3 vols. Cambridge, MA: MIT Press, 1986. Orig.
1938–1947.

Blum, Alan. *The Imaginative Structure of the City*. Montreal: McGill–Queen's University Press, 2003.

Blum, Alan. "New Directions for Research: Bohemianism." Culture of Cities
Centre (York University, Canada), 2004. https://web.archive.org/web
/20041225210223/http://www.yorku.ca/cities/city/projects/z7dir-dex.html.

Blum, Alan. "Scenes." *Public* 22/23, Cities/Scenes (2001): 7–35. https://public
.journals.yorku.ca/index.php/public/article/view/30324.

Bode, Kim, Jörg Blech, Katrin Elger, Markus Feldenkirchen, Jan Fleischhauer,
Christoph Hickmann, Guido Kleinhubbert, et al. "The Man Who Divided
Germany." *Der Spiegel*, September 9, 2010. http://www.spiegel.de/interna
tional/germany/0,1518,715876,00.html.

Bollen, Jonathan. "Queer Kinesthesia: Performativity on the Dance Floor." In *Dancing Desires: Choreographing Sexualities On and Off the Stage*, edited by Jane Desmond, 285–314. Madison: University of Wisconsin Press, 2001.

Bora, Renu. "Outing Texture." In *Novel Gazing: Queer Readings in Fiction*, edited by Eve Kosofsky Sedgwick, 94–127. Durham, NC: Duke University Press, 1997.

Borch, Christian, and Britta Timm Knudsen. "Postmodern Crowds: Re-inventing Crowd Thinking." *Distinktion: Scandinavian Journal of Social Theory* 14, no. 2 (2013): 109–13. https://doi.org/10.1080/1600910x.2013.821012.

Borgo, David. *Sync or Swarm: Improvising Music in a Complex Age*. New York: Continuum, 2005.

Bösel, Bernd. "Affective Synchronization, Rhythmanalysis and the Polyphonic Qualities of the Present Moment." In *Timing of Affect: Epistemologies, Aesthetics, Politics*, edited by Marie-Luise Angerer, Bernd Bösel, and Michaela Ott, 87–102. Zurich: Diaphanes Verlag, 2014.

Bourdieu, Pierre. *Distinction: A Social Critique of the Judgement of Taste*. Cambridge, MA: Harvard University Press, 1984.

Bourdieu, Pierre. *Outline of a Theory of Practice*. Cambridge: Cambridge University Press, 1977.

Brennan, Teresa. *The Transmission of Affect*. Ithaca, NY: Cornell University Press, 2004.

Brewster, Bill, and Frank Broughton. *Last Night a DJ Saved My Life: The History of the Disc Jockey*. New York: Grove Press, 2000.

Britt, Gena Covell, and Elinore F. McCance-Katz. "A Brief Overview of the Clinical Pharmacology of 'Club Drugs.'" *Substance Use & Misuse* 40, nos. 9–10 (2005): 1189–201. https://doi.org/10.1081/ja-20006630.

Bromley, James M. "Failures of Intimacy in English Renaissance Literature." PhD diss., Loyola University, 2007.

Brubaker, Rogers. *Citizenship and Nationhood in France and Germany*. Cambridge, MA: Harvard University Press, 1992.

Bryson, Bethany. "'Anything but Heavy Metal': Symbolic Exclusion and Musical Dislikes." *American Sociological Review* 61, no. 5 (1996): 884–99. http://www.jstor.org/stable/2096459.

Buckland, Fiona. *Impossible Dance: Club Culture and Queer World-Making*. Middletown, CT: Wesleyan University Press, 2002.

Büscher, Monika, John Urry, and Katian Witchger. *Mobile Methods*. Abingdon, UK: Routledge, 2011.

Buser, Pierre A., and Michel Imbert. *Audition*. Cambridge, MA: MIT Press, 1992.

Butler, Judith. *Gender Trouble: Feminism and the Subversion of Identity*. New York: Routledge, 1990.

Butler, Mark J. *Playing with Something That Runs: Technology, Improvisation, and Composition in DJ and Laptop Performance*. Oxford: Oxford University Press, 2014.

Butler, Mark J. *Unlocking the Groove: Rhythm, Meter, and Musical Design in Electronic Dance Music*. Bloomington: Indiana University Press, 2006.

Canetti, Elias. *Crowds and Power*. London: Gollancz, 1962.

Capella, Joseph N. "Mutual Influence in Expressive Behavior: Adult–Adult and Infant–Adult Dyadic Interaction." *Psychological Bulletin* 89, no. 1 (1982): 101–32. https://doi.org/10.1037/0033-2909.89.1.101.

Cascone, Kim. "The Aesthetics of Failure: 'Post-digital' Tendencies in Contemporary Computer Music." *Computer Music Journal* 24, no. 4 (2000): 12–18.

Castells, Manuel. *The Rise of the Network Society*. Cambridge, MA: Blackwell, 1996.

Chapple, Eliot Dismore. *Culture and Biological Man: Explorations in Behavioral Anthropology*. New York: Holt, Rinehart and Winston, 1970.

Chion, Michel. *Guide des objets sonores: Pierre Schaeffer et la recherche musicale*. Paris: Institut national de la communication audiovisuelle, 1983.

Chion, Michel. *Guide to Sound Objects: Pierre Schaeffer and Musical Research*. Translated by John Dack and Christine North. Leicester, UK: Electro Acoustic Research Site (EARS) Project, De Montfort University, 2009.

Clark, Scott. *Japan, a View from the Bath*. Honolulu: University of Hawai'i Press, 1994.

Clarke, John, Stuart Hall, Tony Jefferson, and Brian Roberts. "Subcultures, Cultures and Class." In *Resistance through Rituals: Youth Subcultures in Post-war Britain*, edited by Stuart Hall and Tony Jefferson, 35–74. London: Hutchinson, 1976.

Classen, Maja, dir. *Feiern*. True People; Intergroove, 2006. Film.

Clough, Patricia T., and Jean Halley. *The Affective Turn: Theorizing the Social*. Durham, NC: Duke University Press, 2007.

Collin, Matthew, and John Godfrey. *Altered State: The Story of Ecstasy Culture and Acid House*. London: Serpent's Tail, 1997.

Cooke, Philip, and Luciana Lazzeretti. *Creative Cities, Cultural Clusters and Local Economic Development*. Cheltenham, UK: Edward Elgar, 2008.

Csikszentmihalyi, Mihaly. *Flow: The Psychology of Optimal Experience*. New York: Harper and Row, 1990.

Cusick, Suzanne G. "Musicology, Torture, Repair." *Radical Musicology* 3 (2008). http://www.radical-musicology.org.uk.

Cusick, Suzanne G. "'You Are in a Place Out of the World': Music in the Detention Camps of the 'Global War on Terror.'" *Journal of the Society for American Music* 2 (2008): 1–27. https://doi.org/10.1017/S1752196308080012.

D'Andrea, Anthony. *Global Nomads: Techno and New Age as Transnational Countercultures in Ibiza and Goa*. London: Routledge, 2007.

Deem, Melissa. "Stranger Sociability, Public Hope, and the Limits of Political Transformation." *Quarterly Journal of Speech* 88, no. 4 (2002): 444–54. https://doi.org/10.1080/00335630209384391.

Deleuze, Gilles. *Cinema 1: The Movement-Image*. Translated by Hugh Tomlinson and Barbara Habberjam. Vol. 1. Minneapolis: University of Minnesota, 1986.

Deleuze, Gilles. *Expressionism in Philosophy: Spinoza*. New York: Zone Books, 1990. Orig. 1968.

Deleuze, Gilles. *Spinoza: Practical Philosophy*. San Francisco: City Lights Books, 1988. Orig. 1970.

Deleuze, Gilles, and Félix Guattari. *Mille plateaux: Capitalisme et schizophrénie*. Paris: Éditions de Minuit, 1980.

Deleuze, Gilles, and Félix Guattari. *A Thousand Plateaus: Capitalism and Schizophrenia*. Translated by Brian Massumi. Vol. 2. Minneapolis: University of Minnesota Press, 1987. Orig. 1980.

Deleuze, Gilles, and Félix Guattari. *What Is Philosophy?* New York: Columbia University Press, 1994.

Desai-Stephens, Anaar, and Nicole Reisnour. "Musical Feelings and Affective Politics." *Culture, Theory and Critique* 61, nos. 2–3 (2020): 99–111. https://doi.org/10.1080/14735784.2021.1878468.

Diebold, David. *Tribal Rites: San Francisco's Dance Music Phenomenon, 1978–1988*. Northridge, CA: Time Warp, 1986.

Dolan, Jill. "Performance, Utopia, and the 'Utopian Performative.'" *Theatre Journal* 53, no. 3 (2001): 455–79. https://doi.org/10.1353/tj.2001.0068.

Dueck, Byron. *Musical Intimacies and Indigenous Imaginaries: Aboriginal Music and Dance in Public Performance*. New York: Oxford University Press, 2013.

Durkheim, Émile. *The Elementary Forms of Religious Life: A Study in Religious Sociology*. Translated by Joseph Ward Swain. London: G. Allen and Unwin, 1915.

Durkheim, Émile. *The Rules of Sociological Method*. Translated by W. D. Halls. Edited by Steven Lukes. New York: Free Press, 1901.

Dyer, Richard. "Entertainment and Utopia." *Movie* 24 (Spring 1977): 2–13. Reprinted in *Only Entertainment*, 19–35. London: Routledge, 2002.

Dyer, Richard. "In Defense of Disco." *Gay Left*, no. 8 (Summer 1979).

Eberhart, Chip, dir. *The Unusual Suspects: Once upon a Time in House Music*. Chicken Lunch Films, 2005. Film.

Echols, Alice. *Hot Stuff: Disco and the Remaking of American Culture*. New York: Norton, 2010.

Edelman, Lee. *No Future: Queer Theory and the Death Drive*. Durham, NC: Duke University Press, 2004.

Eng, David L. *The Feeling of Kinship: Queer Liberalism and the Racialization of Intimacy*. Durham, NC: Duke University Press, 2010.

Erlmann, Veit. *Reason and Resonance: A History of Modern Aurality*. New York: Zone Books, 2010.

Eshun, Kodwo. *More Brilliant than the Sun: Adventures in Sonic Fiction*. London: Quartet Books, 1998.

Färber, Alexa. "Flourishing Cultural Production in Economic Wasteland: Three Ways of Making Sense of a Cultural Economy in Berlin at the Beginning of the Twenty-First Century." In *Creative Urban Milieus: Historical Perspectives on Culture, Economy, and the City*, edited by Martina Hessler and Clemens Zimmermann, 409–28. Frankfurt: Campus Verlag, 2008.

Farrugia, Rebekah. *Beyond the Dance Floor: Female DJs, Technology and Electronic Dance Music Culture*. Bristol, UK: Intellect, 2012.

Favell, Adrian. *Philosophies of Integration: Immigration and the Idea of Citizenship in France and Britain*. New York: St. Martin's Press, 1998.

Feige, Marcel, and Kai-Uwe Müller. *Deep in Techno: Die ganze Geschichte des Movements* [Deep in techno: A history of the movement in its entirety]. Berlin: Schwarzkopf and Schwarzkopf, 2000.

Feld, Steven. *Sound and Sentiment: Birds, Weeping, Poetics, and Song in Kaluli Expression*. Philadelphia: University of Pennsylvania Press, 1982.

Feld, Steven. "Sound Structure as Social Structure." *Ethnomusicology* 28, no. 3 (1984): 383–407.

Feld, Steven. "Wept Thoughts: The Voicing of Kaluli Memories." In *South Pacific Oral Traditions*, edited by Ruth H. Finnegan and Margaret Rose Orbell, 85–108. Bloomington: Indiana University Press, 1995.

Fiddy, Chantelle, and Mixmag Staff. "We Need to Talk about Sexual Harassment in Nightclubs." *Mixmag*, April 13, 2015. https://mixmag.net/read/we-need-to -talk-about-sexual-harassment-in-nightclubs-blog.

Fikentscher, Kai. "'It's Not the Mix, It's the Selection': Music Programming in Contemporary DJ Culture." In *DJ Culture in the Mix: Power, Technology, and Social Change in Electronic Dance Music*, edited by Bernardo Attias, Anna Gavanas, and Hillegonda Rietveld, 123–49. New York: Bloomsbury, 2013.

Fikentscher, Kai. "Popular Music and Age Stratification: The Case of Underground Dance Music in the Post-disco Period." In *Popular Music: Style and Identity*, edited by Will Straw, 89–94. Montreal: Centre for Research on Canadian Cultural Industries and Institutions, 1995.

Fikentscher, Kai. *"You Better Work!" Underground Dance Music in New York City*. Hanover, NH: Wesleyan University Press, 2000.

Fink, Robert. *Repeating Ourselves: American Minimal Music as Cultural Practice*. Berkeley: University of California Press, 2005.

Florida, Richard. *The Flight of the Creative Class: The New Global Competition for Talent*. New York: HarperBusiness, 2005.

Florida, Richard. *The Rise of the Creative Class: And How It's Transforming Work, Leisure, Community and Everyday Life*. New York: Basic Books, 2002.

Fox, Aaron A. *Real Country: Music and Language in Working-Class Culture*. Durham, NC: Duke University Press, 2004.

Fraser, Alistair. "The Spaces, Politics, and Cultural Economies of Electronic Dance Music." *Geography Compass* 6, no. 8 (2012): 500–511. https://doi.org/10.1111/j .1749-8198.2012.00505.x.

Freeman, Gary P. "Immigrant Incorporation in Western Democracies." *International Migration Review* 38, no. 3 (2004): 945–69.

Freud, Sigmund. *Group Psychology and the Analysis of the Ego*. New York: Boni and Liveright, 1922.

Friedson, Steven M. *Remains of Ritual: Northern Gods in a Southern Land*. Chicago: University of Chicago Press, 2009.

Gaillot, Michel. *Multiple Meaning: Techno, an Artistic and Political Laboratory of the Present*. Translated by Warren Niesluchowski. Paris: Editions Dis Voir, 1998.

Gallace, Alberto, and Charles Spence. "The Science of Interpersonal Touch: An Overview." *Neuroscience & Biobehavioral Reviews* 34, no. 2 (2010): 246–59. https://doi.org/10.1016/j.neubiorev.2008.10.004.

Gans, Herbert J. *Popular Culture and High Culture: An Analysis and Evaluation of Taste*. New York: Basic Books, 1974.

Garcia, Luis-Manuel. "Agonistic Festivities: Urban Nightlife Scenes and the Sociability of 'Anti-social' Fun." *Annals of Leisure Research* 21, no. 4 (2018): 462–79. https://doi.org/10.1080/11745398.2017.1398097.

Garcia, Luis-Manuel. "An Alternate History of Sexuality in Club Culture." *Resident Advisor*, 2014. https://ra.co/features/1927.

Garcia, Luis-Manuel. "At Home, I'm a Tourist: Musical Migration and Affective Citizenship in Berlin." *Journal of Urban Cultural Studies* 2, nos. 1–2 (2015): 121–34. https://doi.org/10.1386/jucs.2.1-2.121_1.

Garcia, Luis-Manuel. "Beats, Flesh, and Grain: Sonic Tactility and Affect in Electronic Dance Music." *Sound Studies* 1, no. 1 (2015): 59–76. https://doi.org/10.1080/20551940.2015.1079072.

Garcia, Luis-Manuel. "Crowd Solidarity on the Dance Floor in Paris and Berlin." In *Musical Performance and the Changing City: Post-industrial Contexts in Europe and the United States*, edited by Fabian Holt and Carsten Wergin, 227–55. New York: Routledge, 2013.

Garcia, Luis-Manuel. "Editor's Introduction: Doing Nightlife and EDMC Fieldwork." *Dancecult: Journal of Electronic Dance Music Culture* 5, no. 1 (2013): 3–17. https://doi.org/10.12801/1947-5403.2013.05.01.01.

Garcia, Luis-Manuel. "Feeling the Vibe: Sound, Vibration, and Affective Attunement in Electronic Dance Music Scenes." *Ethnomusicology Forum* 29, no. 1 (2020): 21–39. https://doi.org/10.1080/17411912.2020.1733434.

Garcia, Luis-Manuel. "Kompakt Label Night @ Le Rex." *Luis in Paris* (blog), November 1, 2008. http://luisinparis.blogspot.com/2008/11/affect-and-unintimacy-at-lerex.html.

Garcia, Luis-Manuel. "On and On: Repetition as Process and Pleasure in Electronic Dance Music." *Music Theory Online* 11, no. 4 (2005). https://mtosmt.org/issues/mto.05.11.4/mto.05.11.4.garcia.html.

Garcia, Luis-Manuel. "Pathological Crowds: Affect and Danger in Responses to the Love Parade Disaster at Duisburg." *Dancecult: Journal of Electronic Dance Music Culture* 2, no. 1 (2011). https://doi.org/10.12801/1947-5403.2011.02.01.15.

Garcia, Luis-Manuel. "Souvenir 03: The Welcome Home (with Seuil)." *Luis in Paris* (blog), September 5, 2009. http://luisinparis.blogspot.com/2009/09/souvenir-03-welcome-home-with-seuil.html.

Garcia, Luis-Manuel. "Techno-tourism and Postindustrial Neo-romanticism in Berlin's Electronic Dance Music Scenes." *Tourist Studies* 16, no. 3 (2016): 276–95. https://doi.org/10.1177/1468797615618037.

Garcia, Luis-Manuel. "Watergate: Kiki's Birthday." *Luis in Paris* (blog), July 11, 2008. http://luisinparis.blogspot.com/2008/07/awkwardness-intimacy-and-charm.html.

Garcia, Luis-Manuel. "Whose Refuge, This House? The Estrangement of Queers of Color in Electronic Dance Music." In *The Oxford Handbook of Music and Queerness*, edited by Fred Everett Maus and Sheila Whiteley. Oxford: Oxford University Press, 2018.

Garcia, Luis-Manuel. "'With Every Inconceivable Finesse, Excess, and Good Music': Sex, Affect, and Techno at Snax Club in Berlin." In *Dreams of Germany: Musical Imaginaries from the Concert Hall to the Dance Floor*, edited by Neil Gregor and Thomas Irvine, 73–96. New York: Berghahn Books, 2019.

Geertz, Clifford. "Thick Description: Toward an Interpretive Theory of Culture." In *The Interpretation of Cultures*, 3–30. New York: Basic Books, 1973.

Gerard, Morgan. "Selecting Ritual: DJs, Dancers and Liminality in Underground Dance Music." In *Rave Culture and Religion*, edited by Graham St. John, 167–84. London: Routledge, 2004.

Geschiere, Peter. *The Perils of Belonging: Autochthony, Citizenship, and Exclusion in Africa and Europe*. Chicago: University of Chicago Press, 2009.

Gibson, James Jerome. *The Ecological Approach to Visual Perception*. Boston: Houghton Mifflin, 1979.

Giddens, Anthony. *The Consequences of Modernity*. Stanford, CA: Stanford University Press, 1990.

Gilbert, Jeremy, and Ewan Pearson. *Discographies: Dance Music, Culture, and the Politics of Sound*. New York: Routledge, 1999.

Goffman, Erving. "The Nature of Deference and Demeanor." *American Anthropologist* 58, no. 3 (1956): 473–502. https://doi.org/10.1525/aa.1956.58.3.02a00070.

Goffman, Erving. *The Presentation of Self in Everyday Life*. Garden City, NY: Doubleday, 1959.

Goodman, Steve. *Sonic Warfare: Sound, Affect, and the Ecology of Fear*. Cambridge, MA: MIT Press, 2010.

Goodman, Steve. "Speed Tribes: Netwar, Affective Hacking and the Audio-Social." In *Cultural Hacking: Kunst des Strategischen Handelns*, edited by Franz Liebl and Thomas Düllo, 139–55. Vienna: Springer, 2004.

Graber, Katie J., and Matthew Sumera. "Interpretation, Resonance, Embodiment: Affect Theory and Ethnomusicology." *Ethnomusicology Forum* 29, no. 1 (2020): 3–20. https://doi.org/10.1080/17411912.2020.1808501.

Gregg, Melissa, and Gregory J. Seigworth, eds. *The Affect Theory Reader*. Durham, NC: Duke University Press, 2010.

Gronow, Jukka. *The Sociology of Taste*. London: Routledge, 1997.

Grosz, Elizabeth A. *Space, Time, and Perversion: Essays on the Politics of Bodies*. New York: Routledge, 1995.

Grosz, Elizabeth A. *Time Travels: Feminism, Nature, Power*. Durham, NC: Duke University Press, 2005.

Guerrero, Laura K., and Peter A. Andersen. "The Waxing and Waning of Relational Intimacy: Touch as a Function of Relational Stage, Gender and Touch Avoidance." *Journal of Social and Personal Relationships* 8, no. 2 (1991): 147–65. https://doi.org/10.1177/0265407591082001.

Haden-Guest, Anthony. *The Last Party: Studio 54, Disco, and the Culture of the Night*. New York: William Morrow, 1997.

Hadley, Daniel. "'Ride the Rhythm': Two Approaches to DJ Practice." *Journal of Popular Music Studies* 5 (1993): 58–67.

Halfacree, Keith H., and Robert M. Kitchin. "'Madchester Rave On': Placing the Fragments of Popular Music." *Area* 28, no. 1 (1996): 47–55.

Hall, Edward T. *The Dance of Life: The Other Dimension of Time*. Garden City, NY: Anchor Press/Doubleday, 1983.

Hall, Edward T. *The Hidden Dimension*. Garden City, NY: Doubleday, 1966.

Hall, Stuart, and Tony Jefferson. *Resistance through Rituals: Youth Subcultures in Postwar Britain*. London: Hutchinson, 1976.

Hampartzoumian, Stéphane. *Effervescence techno ou la communauté trans(e)cendantale*. Paris: L'Harmattan, 2004.

Harriot, Michael. "How to Be a Better White Person in 2020." *The Root*, January 9, 2020. https://www.theroot.com/how-to-be-a-better-white-person-in-2020-1840868641.

Hart, Carl L., Erik W. Gunderson, Audrey Perez, Matthew G. Kirkpatrick, Andrew Thurmond, Sandra D. Comer, and Richard W. Foltin. "Acute Physiological and Behavioral Effects of Intranasal Methamphetamine in Humans." *Neuropsychopharmacology* 33, no. 8 (2007): 1847–55. https://doi.org/10.1038/sj.npp.1301578.

Hatfield, Elaine, John T. Cacioppo, and Richard L. Rapson. *Emotional Contagion*. Cambridge: Cambridge University Press, 1994.

Häussermann, Hartmut, Andrej Holm, and Daniela Zunzer. *Stadterneuerung in der Berliner Republik: Modernisierung in Berlin-Prenzlauer Berg*. Opladen, Germany: Leske + Budrich, 2002.

Hebdige, Dick. *Subculture: The Meaning of Style*. London: Methuen, 1979.

Heebels, Barbara, and Irina van Aalst. "Creative Clusters in Berlin: Entrepreneurship and the Quality of Place in Prenzlauer Berg and Kreuzberg." *Geografiska Annaler Series B: Human Geography* 92, no. 4 (2010): 347–63. https://doi.org/10.1111/j.1468-0467.2010.00357.x.

Heitmeyer, Wilhelm. "Für türkische Jugendliche in Deutschland spielt der Islam eine wichtige Rolle." *Die Zeit* (Hamburg), August 23, 1996.

Heley, Mark, and Matthew Collin. "Summer of Love 1989." *i-D*, September 1989. http://www.djhistory.com/features/summer-of-love-1989.

Helm, Burt. "How the Bouncer of Berghain Chooses Who Gets into the Most Depraved Party on the Planet," *GQ*, July 25, 2015. http://www.gq.com/story/berghain-bouncer-sven-marquardt-interview.

Hemment, Drew. "Affect and Individuation in Popular Electronic Music." In *Deleuze and Music*, edited by Ian Buchanan and Marcel Swiboda, 76–94. Edinburgh: Edinburgh University Press, 2004.

Henley, Nancy M. *Body Politics: Power, Sex, and Nonverbal Communication*. Englewood Cliffs, NJ: Prentice-Hall, 1977.

Henley, Nancy M. "Status and Sex: Some Touching Observations." *Bulletin of the Psychonomic Society* 2, no. 2 (1973): 91–93.

Hennessy-Fiske, Molly. "FBI Investigators Say They Have Found No Evidence That Orlando Shooter Had Gay Lovers." *Los Angeles Times*, June 23, 2016. https://www.latimes.com/nation/la-na-orlando-gay-fbi-20160623-snap-story.html.

Henseler, Christine, ed. *Generation X Goes Global: Mapping a Youth Culture in Motion*. New York: Routledge, 2013.

Herbert, Matthew. "Personal Contract for the Composition of Music [Incorporating the Manifesto of Mistakes]." Matthewherbert.com, 2005, rev. 2011. http://dev.matthewherbert.com/about-contact/manifesto/.

Herzfeld, Michael. *Cultural Intimacy: Social Poetics in the Nation-State*. 2nd ed. New York: Routledge, 2005.

Hesmondhalgh, David. "International Times: Fusions, Exoticisms, and Antiracism in Electronic Dance Music." In *Western Music and Its Others: Difference, Representation, and Appropriation in Music*, edited by Georgina Born and David Hesmondhalgh, 280–304. Berkeley: University of California Press, 2000.

Hobbs, Dick, Philip Hadfield, Stuart Lister, and Simon Winlow. *Bouncers: Violence and Governance in the Night-Time Economy*. Oxford: Oxford University Press, 2003.

Hoffmann, Lutz. "Das 'Volk'—Zur ideologischen Struktur eines unvermeidbaren Begriffs." *Zeitschrift für Soziologie* 20, no. 3 (1991): 191–208.

Hoffmann, Lutz. *Die unvollendete Republik: Einwanderungsland oder deutscher Nationalstaat*. Köln: PapyRossa Verlag, 1990.

Hofman, Ana. "The Affective Turn in Ethnomusicology." *Muzikologija* 18 (2015): 35–55. https://doi.org/10.2298/MUZ1518035H.

Hollister, John. "Beyond the Interaction Membrane: Laud Humphreys' Tearoom Tradeoff." *International Journal of Sociology and Social Policy* 24, nos. 3–5 (2004): 73–94. https://doi.org/10.1108/01443330410790885.

Holt, Douglas B. "Distinction in America? Recovering Bourdieu's Theory of Tastes from Its Critics." *Poetics* 25, nos. 2–3 (1997): 93–120. https://doi.org/10.1016/s0304-422x(97)00010-7.

Holt, Fabian. "Music Festival Video: A 'Media Events' Perspective on Music in Mediated Life" [In French]. *Volume!* 14, no. 2 (2018): 202. https://www.cairn.info/revue-volume-2018-1-page-202.htm.

Hoyman, Michele, and Christopher Faricy. "It Takes a Village: A Test of the Creative Class, Social Capital and Human Capital Theories." *Urban Affairs Review* 44, no. 3 (January 2009): 311–33. https://doi.org/10.1177/1078087408321496.

Humphreys, Laud. *Tearoom Trade: Impersonal Sex in Public Places*. New York: Aldine, 1975.

Hutton, Fiona. *Risky Pleasures? Club Cultures and Feminine Identities*. Aldershot, UK: Ashgate, 2006.

Ignatieff, Michael. *Blood and Belonging: Journeys into the New Nationalism*. New York: Farrar, Straus and Giroux, 1994.

"Im Reich des Wahnsinns." *Süddeutsche Zeitung Magazin*, April 8, 2009. http://sz -magazin.sueddeutsche.de/texte/anzeigen/28877.

"Integration: Merkel Erklärt Multikulti Für Gescheitert." *Der Spiegel*, October 16 2010. http://www.spiegel.de/politik/deutschland/integration-merkel -erklaert-multikulti-fuer-gescheitert-a-723532.html.

Jackson, Jonathan David. "Improvisation in African-American Vernacular Dancing." *Dance Research Journal* 33, no. 2 (2001): 40–53.

Jackson, Jonathan David. "The Social World of Voguing." *Journal of the Anthropological Study of Human Movement* 12, no. 2 (2002): 26–42.

Jaguaribe, Beatriz. "Carnival Crowds." *The Sociological Review* 61, no. S1 (2013): 69–88. https://doi.org/10.1111/1467-954X.12054.

Jamieson, Lynn. *Intimacy: Personal Relationships in Modern Societies*. Cambridge: Polity Press, 1998.

Jeffries, Michael P. *Thug Life: Race, Gender, and the Meaning of Hip-Hop*. Chicago: University of Chicago Press, 2011.

Jones, Stanley E., and Elaine Yarbrough. "A Naturalistic Study of the Meanings of Touch." *Communication Monographs* 52, no. 1 (1985): 19–56. http://search .ebscohost.com/login.aspx?direct=true&db=ufh&AN=10005796&site=ehost -live.

Jourard, Sidney M. "An Exploratory Study of Body-Accessibility." *British Journal of Social and Clinical Psychology* 5, no. 3 (1966): 221–31. https://doi.org/10.1111/j .2044-8260.1966.tb00978.x.

Jourard, Sidney M., and Jane E. Rubin. "Self-Disclosure and Touching: A Study of Two Modes of Interpersonal Encounter and Their Inter-relation." *Journal of Humanistic Psychology* 8, no. 1 (Spring 1968): 39–48. https://doi.org/10.1177 /002216786800800104.

Julius, Britt. "Nightlife Community Condemns Mass Shooting at Pulse Nightclub." *Vice*, June 12, 2016. https://www.vice.com/en/article/z45zwx/pulse-shooting -reactions.

Kanstroom, Daniel. "Wer sind wir wieder? Laws of Asylum, Immigration, and Citizenship in the Struggle for the Soul of the New Germany." *Yale Journal of International Law* 18, no. 1 (1993): 155–211.

Kasulis, Thomas P. *Intimacy or Integrity: Philosophy and Cultural Difference*. Honolulu: University of Hawai'i Press, 2002.

Kavanaugh, Philip R., and Tammy L. Anderson. "Solidarity and Drug Use in the Electronic Dance Music Scene." *Sociological Quarterly* 49 (2008): 181–208.

Kelly, Janice R., and Sigal G. Barsade. "Mood and Emotions in Small Groups and Work Teams." *Organizational Behavior and Human Decision Processes* 86, no. 1 (2001): 99–130. https://doi.org/10.1006/obhd.2001.2974.

Klane, Robert, dir. *Thank God It's Friday*. Columbia Pictures, 1978. Film.

Klein, Bethany. *As Heard on TV: Popular Music in Advertising*. Farnham, UK: Ashgate, 2009.

Klenzendorf, Christoph. "Bar 25: Partying in the Sun, Berlin Style." *Ibiza Voice*, February 1, 2008. http://www.ibiza-voice.com/story/news/1364.

Klopp, Brett. *German Multiculturalism: Immigrant Integration and the Transformation of Citizenship*. Westport, CT: Praeger, 2002.

Koopmans, Ruud. "Trade-Offs between Equality and Difference: Immigrant Integration, Multiculturalism and the Welfare State in Cross-National Perspective." *Journal of Ethnic and Migration Studies* 36 (2010): 1–26.

Korte, Hermann. "Labor Migration and the Employment of Foreigners in the Federal Republic of Germany since 1950." In *Guests Come to Stay: The Effects of European Labor Migration on Sending and Receiving Countries*, edited by Rosemarie Rogers, 29–49. Boulder, CO: Westview Press, 1985.

Kosnick, Kira. "Out on the Scene: Queer Migrant Clubbing and Urban Diversity." *Ethnologia Europaea* 38, no. 2 (2008): 19–30.

Kronengold, Charles. "Exchange Theories in Disco, New Wave, and Album-Oriented Rock." *Criticism* 50, no. 1 (2008): 43–82. https://doi.org/10.1353/crt.0.0050.

Krueger, Joel. "Affordances and the Musically Extended Mind." *Frontiers in Psychology* 4, article no. 1003 (2013). https://doi.org/10.3389/fpsyg.2013.01003.

Kyrou, Ariel. *Techno rebelle: Un siècle de musiques électroniques*. Paris: Denoël, 2002.

Lacan, Jacques. *The Ethics of Psychoanalysis, 1959–1960*. New York: Norton, 1997.

Lacan, Jacques. "The Subversion of the Subject and the Dialectic of Desire in the Freudian Unconscious." In *Écrits*, edited by Bruce Fink, 355–415. New York: Norton, 2006.

Laclau, Ernesto, and Chantal Mouffe. *Hegemony and Socialist Strategy: Towards a Radical Democratic Politics*. London: Verso, 1985.

Langlois, Tony. "Can You Feel It? DJs and House Music Culture in the UK." *Popular Music* 11, no. 2 (1992): 229–38.

Lawrence, Tim. "The Forging of a White Gay Aesthetic at The Saint, 1980–84." *Dancecult: Journal of Electronic Dance Music Culture* 3, no. 1 (2011): 4–27.

Lawrence, Tim. "In Defence of Disco (Again)." *New Formations* 58 (2006): 128–46.

Lawrence, Tim. "'I Want to See All My Friends at Once': Arthur Russell and the Queering of Gay Disco." *Journal of Popular Music Studies* 18, no. 2 (2006): 144–66. https://doi.org/10.1111/j.1533-1598.2006.00086.x.

Lawrence, Tim. *Life and Death on the New York Dance Floor, 1980–1983*. Durham, NC: Duke University Press, 2016.

Lawrence, Tim. *Love Saves the Day: A History of American Dance Music Culture, 1970–1979*. Durham, NC: Duke University Press, 2003.

Le Bon, Gustave. *The Crowd: A Study of the Popular Mind*. 2nd ed. London: T. F. Unwin, 1897.

Lee, Josephine W., and Laura K. Guerrero. "Types of Touch in Cross-Sex Relationships between Coworkers: Perceptions of Relational and Emotional Messages, Inappropriateness, and Sexual Harassment." *Journal of Applied Communication Research* 29, no. 3 (2001): 197–220. https://doi.org/10.1080/00909880128110.

Leon-Davis, Daniel. "The Site of the Orlando Shooting Wasn't Just a Gay Nightclub. It Was My Safe Haven." Fusion.net, June 12, 2016. https://fusion.tv/story/312960/pulse-orlando-safe-haven/.

Liebig, Thomas. "The Labour Market Integration of Immigrants in Germany." OECD *Social, Employment and Migration Working Papers*, no. 47. Paris: OECD Publishing, 2007. https://doi.org/10.1787/238411133860.

Liechti, Matthias E., and Franz X. Vollenweider. "Acute Psychological and Physiological Effects of MDMA ('Ecstasy') after Haloperidol Pretreatment in Healthy Humans." *European Neuropsychopharmacology* 10, no. 4 (2000): 289–95. https://doi.org/10.1016/S0924-977X(00)00086-9.

Livingston, Jennie, dir. *Paris Is Burning*. Miramax, 1990. Film.

Lloyd, Richard D. *Neo-Bohemia: Art and Commerce in the Postindustrial City*. 2nd ed. New York: Routledge, 2010.

Lloyd, Richard D. "Neo-Bohemia: Art and Neighborhood Redevelopment in Chicago." *Journal of Urban Affairs* 24, no. 5 (2002): 517–32.

London, Justin. *Hearing in Time: Psychological Aspects of Musical Meter*. New York: Oxford University Press, 2004.

Looseley, David. *Popular Music in Contemporary France: Authenticity, Politics, Debate*. Oxford: Berg, 2003.

López Sintas, Jordi, and Ercilia García Álverez. "Omnivores Show Up Again: The Segmentation of Cultural Consumers in Spanish Social Space." *European Sociological Review* 18, no. 3 (2002): 353–68. https://doi.org/10.1093/esr/18.3.353.

Loza, Susana. "Sampling (Hetero)sexuality: Diva-ness and Discipline in Electronic Dance Music." *Popular Music* 20, no. 3 (2001): 349–57.

Mabilon-Bonfils, Béatrice, ed. *La fête techno: Tout seul et tous ensemble*. Paris: Autrement, 2004.

MacMillen, Ian. "Affective Block and the Musical Racialisation of Romani Sincerity." *Ethnomusicology Forum* 29, no. 1 (2020): 81–106. https://doi.org/10.1080/17411912.2020.1815551.

Madrid, Alejandro L. *Nor-Tec Rifa! Electronic Dance Music from Tijuana to the World*. Oxford: Oxford University Press, 2008.

Maffesoli, Michel. *The Time of the Tribes: The Decline of Individualism in Mass Society*. London: Sage, 1996.

Major, Brenda. "Gender Patterns in Touching Behavior." In *Gender and Nonverbal Behavior*, edited by Clara Alexandra Weiss Mayo and Nancy M. Henley, 15–37. New York: Springer, 1981.

Major, Brenda, Anne Marie Schmidlin, and Lynne Williams. "Gender Patterns in Social Touch: The Impact of Setting and Age." *Journal of Personality and Social Psychology* 58, no. 4 (1990): 634–43. https://doi.org/10.1037/0022-3514.58.4.634.

Malbon, Ben. *Clubbing: Dancing, Ecstasy and Vitality*. New York: Routledge, 1999.

Marcus, George E. "Beyond Malinowski and after Writing Culture: On the Future of Cultural Anthropology and the Predicament of Ethnography." *Australian Journal of Anthropology* 13, no. 2 (2002): 191–99.

Marcus, George E. "Ethnography in/of the World System: The Emergence of Multi-sited Ethnography." *Annual Review of Anthropology* 24 (1995): 95–117.

Marcus, George E. "What Is at Stake—and Is Not—in the Idea and Practice of Multi-sited Ethnography." *Canberra Anthropology* 22, no. 2 (1999): 6–14.

Margulis, Elizabeth Hellmuth. "Repetition and Emotive Communication in Music versus Speech." *Frontiers in Psychology* 4, no. 167 (2013): 1–4. https://doi.org/10.3389/fpsyg.2013.00167.

Marks, Laura U. *The Skin of the Film: Intercultural Cinema, Embodiment, and the Senses*. Durham, NC: Duke University Press, 2000.

Marks, Laura U. *Touch: Sensuous Theory and Multisensory Media*. Minneapolis: University of Minnesota Press, 2002.

Massey, Douglas S., and Nancy A. Denton. *American Apartheid: Segregation and the Making of the Underclass*. Cambridge, MA: Harvard University Press, 1993.

Massey, Douglas S., and Nancy A. Denton. "Hypersegregation in U.S. Metropolitan Areas: Black and Hispanic Segregation along Five Dimensions." *Demography* 26, no. 3 (1989): 373–91. https://doi.org/10.2307/2061599.

Massumi, Brian. *Parables for the Virtual: Movement, Affect, Sensation*. Durham, NC: Duke University Press, 2002.

Matos, Michaelangelo. *The Underground Is Massive: How Electronic Dance Music Conquered America*. New York: Dey Street Books, 2015.

May, Reuben A. Buford. *Urban Nightlife: Entertaining Race, Class, and Culture in Public Space*. New Brunswick, NJ: Rutgers University Press, 2014.

May, Reuben A. Buford, and Kenneth Sean Chaplin. "Cracking the Code: Race, Class, and Access to Nightclubs in Urban America." *Qualitative Sociology* 31, no. 1 (2008): 57–72. https://doi.org/10.1007/s11133-007-9084-7.

Mazzarella, William. "Affect: What Is It Good For?" In *Enchantments of Modernity: Empire, Nation, Globalization*, edited by Saurabh Dube, 291–309. New York: Routledge, 2009.

Mazzarella, William. "The Myth of the Multitude, or, Who's Afraid of the Crowd?" *Critical Inquiry* 36, no. 4 (2010). https://doi.org/10.1086/655209.

McCutcheon, Mark A. "Techno, Frankenstein, and Copyright." *Popular Music* 26, no. 2 (2007): 259. https://doi.org/10.1017/S0261143007001225.

McLeod, Kembrew. "Genres, Subgenres, Sub-subgenres, and More: Musical and Social Differentiation with Electronic/Dance Music Communities." *Journal of Popular Music Studies* 13, no. 1 (2001): 59–76. https://doi.org/10.1080/152422201317071651.

McRobbie, Angela. "Shut Up and Dance: Youth Culture and Changing Modes of Femininity." *Young* 1, no. 2 (1993): 13–31. https://doi.org/10.1177/110330889300100202.

Mehrabian, Albert. *Nonverbal Communication*. Chicago: Aldine, 1972.

Melechi, Antonio. "The Ecstasy of Disappearance." In *Rave Off: Politics and Deviance in Contemporary Youth Culture*, edited by Steve Redhead, 29–40. Aldershot, UK: Avebury, 1993.

Miller, Kiri. *Playing Along: Digital Games, YouTube, and Virtual Performance*. Oxford: Oxford University Press, 2012.

Miller, Kiri. *Traveling Home: Sacred Harp Singing and American Pluralism*. Urbana: University of Illinois Press, 2008.

Mills, Mara. "On Disability and Cybernetics: Helen Keller, Norbert Wiener, and the Hearing Glove." *differences* 22, nos. 2–3 (2011): 74–111. https://doi.org/10.1215/10407391-1428852.

Møller, Aage R. *Hearing: Anatomy, Physiology, and Disorders of the Auditory System*. 2nd ed. Amsterdam: Academic Press, 2006.

Monaghan, Lee F. "Doorwork and Legal Risk: Observations from an Embodied Ethnography." *Social & Legal Studies* 13, no. 4 (2004): 453–80. https://doi.org/10.1177/0964663904047329.

Montagu, Ashley. *Touching: The Human Significance of the Skin*. New York: Columbia University Press, 1971.

Montano, Ed. "DJ Culture in the Commercial Sydney Dance Music Scene." *Dancecult: Journal of Electronic Dance Music Culture* 1, no. 1 (2009): 81–93. https://doi.org/10.12801/1947-5403.2009.01.01.05.

moore, madison. *Fabulous: The Rise of the Beautiful Eccentric*. New Haven, CT: Yale University Press, 2018.

Motl, Kaitlyne A. "Dashiki Chic: Color-Blind Racial Ideology in EDM Festivalgoers' 'Dress Talk.'" *Popular Music and Society* 41, no. 3 (2018): 250–69. https://doi.org/10.1080/03007766.2018.1519094.

Mouffe, Chantal. *Agonistics: Thinking the World Politically*. London: Verso, 2013.

Muggleton, David, and Rupert Weinzierl. *The Post-subcultures Reader*. Oxford: Berg, 2003.

Muñoz, José Esteban. *Cruising Utopia: The Then and There of Queer Futurity*. New York: New York University Press, 2009.

Muñoz, José Esteban. *Disidentifications: Queers of Color and the Performance of Politics*. Minneapolis: University of Minnesota Press, 1999.

Nestler, Eric J. "Is There a Common Molecular Pathway for Addiction?" *Nature Neuroscience* 8, no. 11 (2005): 1445–49. https://doi.org/10.1038/nn1578.

Ngai, Sianne. *Ugly Feelings*. Cambridge, MA: Harvard University Press, 2005.

Novy, Johannes, and Sandra Huning. "New Tourism (Areas) in the 'New Berlin.'" In *World Tourism Cities: Developing Tourism off the Beaten Track*, edited by Robert Maitland and Peter Newman, 87–108. New York: Routledge, 2009.

Nowicki, Joanna. "Présentation générale: La cohabitation culturelle ; Un enjeu politique." In *La cohabitation culturelle*, 9–24. Paris: CNRS Editions, 2010.

Nye, Sean. "Love Parade, Please Not Again: A Berlin Cultural History." *ECHO* 9, no. 1 (2009): 1–50. http://www.echo.ucla.edu/Volume9-Issue1/nye/nye1.html.

O'Grady, Alice. "Interrupting Flow: Researching Play, Performance and Immersion in Festival Scenes." *Dancecult: Journal of Electronic Dance Music Culture* 5, no. 1 (2013): 18–38. https://doi.org/10.12801/1947-5403.2013.05.01.02.

Olaveson, Tim. "'Connectedness' and the Rave Experience: Rave as New Religious Movement?" In *Rave Culture and Religion*, edited by Graham St. John, 85–106. London: Routledge, 2004.

Paden, Roger. "Marx's Critique of the Utopian Socialists." *Utopian Studies* 13, no. 2 (2002): 67–91. http://www.jstor.org/stable/20718467.

Park, Judy Soojin. "Searching for a Cultural Home: Asian American Youth in the EDM Festival Scene." *Dancecult: Journal of Electronic Dance Music Culture* 7, no. 1 (2015): 15–34. https://doi.org/10.12801/1947-5403.2015.07.01.01.

Partridge, Christopher. "The Spiritual and the Revolutionary: Alternative Spirituality, British Free Festivals and the Emergence of Rave Culture." *Culture and Religion: An Interdisciplinary Journal* 7, no. 1 (2006): 41–60. https://doi.org/10.1080/01438300600625408.

Peirce, Charles S. *The Essential Peirce: Selected Philosophical Writings*. Edited by Nathan Houser and Christian J. W. Kloesel. 2 vols. Bloomington: Indiana University Press, 1992.

Peterson, Richard A. "Understanding Audience Segmentation: From Elite and Mass to Omnivore and Univore." *Poetics* 21, no. 4 (1992): 243–58. https://doi.org/10.1016/0304-422x(92)90008-q.

Peterson, Richard A., and Roger M. Kern. "Changing Highbrow Taste: From Snob to Omnivore." *American Sociological Review* 61, no. 5 (1996): 900–907.

Pinch, T. J., and Frank Trocco. *Analog Days: The Invention and Impact of the Moog Synthesizer*. Cambridge, MA: Harvard University Press, 2002.

Pini, Maria. *Club Cultures and Female Subjectivity: The Move from Home to House*. Basingstoke, UK: Palgrave, 2001.

Plummer, Kenneth. *Intimate Citizenship: Private Decisions and Public Dialogues*. Seattle: University of Washington Press, 2003.

Pope, Richard. "Hooked on an Affect: Detroit Techno and Dystopian Digital Culture." *Dancecult: Journal of Electronic Dance Music Culture* 2, no. 1 (2011): 24–44. https://doi.org/10.12801/1947-5403.2011.02.01.02.

Povinelli, Elizabeth A. *The Empire of Love: Toward a Theory of Intimacy, Genealogy, and Carnality*. Durham, NC: Duke University Press, 2006.

Prager, Karen Jean. *The Psychology of Intimacy*. New York: Guilford, 1995.

Probyn, Elspeth. *Outside Belongings*. New York: Routledge, 1996.

Prochasson, David. "Expulsions de Roms, un 'mode d'emploi' explicite." *Le Canard Social*, September 9, 2010. http://www.lecanardsocial.com/Article.aspx?i=193.

Purcell, Natalie J. *Death Metal Music: The Passion and Politics of a Subculture*. Jefferson, NC: McFarland, 2003.

Race, Kane. "The Death of the Dance Party." *Australian Humanities Review*, no. 30 (2003). http://australianhumanitiesreview.org/2003/10/01/the-death-of-the-dance-party/.

Race, Kane. *Pleasure Consuming Medicine: The Queer Politics of Drugs*. Durham, NC: Duke University Press, 2009.

Race, Kane. "Recreational States: Drugs and the Sovereignty of Consumption." *Culture Machine* 7 (2005). http://svr91.edns1.com/~culturem/index.php/cm/article/view/28/35.

Racine, Etienne. *Le phénomène techno: Clubs, Raves, Free-Parties*. Paris: Imago, 2002.

Ramos, Josell, dir. *Maestro*. Artrution Productions; Sony, 2004. Film.

Rancière, Jacques. *Disagreement: Politics and Philosophy*. Minneapolis: University of Minnesota Press, 1999.

Rapp, Tobias. *Lost and Sound: Berlin, Techno and the Easyjet Set*. Translated by Paul Sabin. Berlin: Innervisions, 2010.

Redhead, Steve. *Rave Off: Politics and Deviance in Contemporary Youth Culture*. Aldershot, UK: Avebury, 1993.

Redhead, Steve. *Subculture to Clubcultures: An Introduction to Popular Cultural Studies*. Oxford: Blackwell, 1997.

Reimann, B. "The Transition from People's Property to Private Property: Consequences of the Restitution Principle for Urban Development and Urban Renewal in East Berlin's Inner-City Residential Areas." *Applied Geography* 17, no. 4 (October 1997): 301–13. https://doi.org/10.1016/s0143-6228(97)00023-4.

Remland, Martin S., and Tricia S. Jones. "Cultural and Sex Differences in Touch Avoidance." *Perceptual and Motor Skills* 67, no. 2 (1988): 544–46. https://doi.org/10.2466/pms.1988.67.2.544.

Remland, Martin S., Tricia S. Jones, and Heidi Brinkman. "Interpersonal Distance, Body Orientation, and Touch: Effects of Culture, Gender, and Age." *Journal of Social Psychology* 135, no. 3 (1995): 281–97. https://doi.org/10.1080/00224545.1995.9713958.

Remland, Martin S., Tricia S. Jones, and Heidi Brinkman. "Proxemic and Haptic Behavior in Three European Countries." *Journal of Nonverbal Behavior* 15, no. 4 (1991): 215–32. https://doi.org/10.1007/bf00986923.

Resident Advisor Staff. "Berlin: Events: Promote Diversity." *Resident Advisor*, September 12, 2013. https://www.residentadvisor.net/event.aspx?509118.

Resident Advisor Staff. "Opinion: Why We're Closing Comments." *Resident Advisor*, January 3, 2019. https://ra.co/features/3386.

Resident Advisor Staff. "Opinion: Why We're Stopping the RA Polls." *Resident Advisor*, November 22, 2017. https://ra.co/features/3105.

Resident Advisor Staff. "RA Club Awards: Best Club." *Resident Advisor*, July 24, 2008. https://ra.co/features/932.

Resident Advisor Staff. "Ricardo Villalobos: Music Reviews." *Resident Advisor*. Accessed December 20, 2022. https://ra.co/dj/ricardovillalobos/editorial.

Reynolds, Simon. *Energy Flash: A Journey through Rave Music and Dance Culture*. London: Picador, 1998.

"Ricardo Villalobos: Reviews." *Pitchfork*. Accessed December 20, 2022. http://pitchfork.com/artists/4505-ricardo-villalobos/.

Rietveld, Hillegonda. *This Is Our House: House Music, Cultural Spaces, and Technologies*. Brookfield, VT: Ashgate, 1998.

Rill, Bryan. "Rave, Communitas, and Embodied Idealism." *Music Therapy Today: A Quarterly Journal of Studies in Music and Music Therapy* 7, no. 3 (2006): 648.

Rivera-Servera, Ramón H. "Choreographies of Resistance: Latina/o Queer Dance and the Utopian Performative." *Modern Drama* 47, no. 2 (Summer 2004): 269–89. https://doi.org/10.1515/9780822393856-019.

Roads, Curtis. *Microsound*. Cambridge, MA: MIT Press, 2001.

Ruane, Deirdre. "Harm Reduction or Psychedelic Support? Caring for Drug-Related Crises at Transformational Festivals." *Dancecult: Journal of Electronic Dance Music Culture* 7, no. 1 (2015): 55–75. https://doi.org/10.12801/1947-5403.2015.07.01.03.

Ryce, Andrew, "America's Gay Techno Underground." *Resident Advisor*, March 7, 2016. https://ra.co/features/2642.

Saldanha, Arun. *Psychedelic White: Goa Trance and the Viscosity of Race*. Minneapolis: University of Minnesota Press, 2007.

Salkind, Micah E. *Do You Remember House? Chicago's Queer of Color Undergrounds*. New York: Oxford University Press, 2019.

Sarrazin, Thilo. *Deutschland schafft sich ab: Wie wir unser Land aufs Spiel setzen*. 10th ed. Munich: Deutsche Verlags-Anstalt, 2010.

Sassen, Saskia. "Global Cities and Survival Circuits." In *American Studies: An Anthology*, edited by Janice A. Radway, 185–93. Malden, MA: Wiley-Blackwell, 2009.

Sassen, Saskia. *Globalization and Its Discontents: Essays on the New Mobility of People and Money*. New York: New Press, 1998.

Savage, Mike. "The Musical Field." *Cultural Trends* 15, nos. 2–3 (2006): 159–74. https://doi.org/10.1080/09548960600712975.

Saxelby, Ruth. "Why Queer Latinx Parties Are Necessary Spaces of Resistance." Interview with Kristy LarAt and Precolumbian. *Fader*, June 16, 2016. https://www.thefader.com/2016/06/16/kristy-la-rat-precolumbian-latinx-spaces-interview.

Schaeffer, Pierre. *Traité des objets musicaux, essai interdisciplines*. Paris: Éditions du Seuil, 1966.

Schaeffer, Pierre. *Treatise on Musical Objects: An Essay across Disciplines*. Translated by Christine North and John Dack. Oakland: University of California Press, 2017.

Schafer, R. Murray. *The Soundscape: Our Sonic Environment and the Tuning of the World*. Rochester, VT: Destiny Books, 1993.

Schaub, Christoph. "Beyond the Hood? Detroit Techno, Underground Resistance, and African American Metropolitan Identity Politics." *Forum for Inter-American Research* 2, no. 2. (2009). http://interamerica.de/current-issue/schaub/.

Schmalz-Jacobsen, Cornelia, Holger Hinte, and Georgios Tsapanos. *Einwanderung, und Dann? Perspektiven einer neuen Ausländerpolitik*. Munich: Knaur, 1993.

Schönwälder, Karen. "Germany: Integration Policy and Pluralism in a Self-Conscious Country of Immigration." In *The Multiculturalism Backlash: European Discourses, Policies and Practices*, edited by Steven Vertovec and Susanne Wessendorf, 152–69. Abingdon, UK: Routledge, 2010.

Schürmann, Martin, Gina Caetano, Veikko Jousmäki, and Riita Hari. "Hands Help Hearing: Facilitatory Audiotactile Interaction at Low Sound-Intensity Levels." *Journal of the Acoustical Society of America* 115, no. 2 (February 2004): 830–32.

Schütte, Uwe, ed. *German Pop Music*. Berlin: De Gruyter, 2017.

Schutz, Alfred. "Fragments on the Phenomenology of Music." In *In Search of Musical Method*, edited by F. Joseph Smith, 23–71. London: Gordon and Breach, 1976.

Schutz, Alfred. "Making Music Together: A Study in Social Relationship." *Social Research* 18, no. 1 (1951): 76–97.

Schutz, Alfred. *The Phenomenology of the Social World*. Translated by George Walsh and Frederick Lehnert. Evanston, IL: Northwestern University Press, 1967.

Sedgwick, Eve Kosofsky. *Touching Feeling: Affect, Pedagogy, Performativity*. Durham, NC: Duke University Press, 2003.

Sedgwick, Eve Kosofsky, Adam Frank, and Irving E. Alexander. *Shame and Its Sisters: A Silvan Tomkins Reader*. Durham, NC: Duke University Press, 1995.

Seigworth, Gregory J. "From Affection to Soul." In *Gilles Deleuze: Key Concepts*, edited by Charles J. Stivale, 159–69. Montreal: McGill–Queen's University Press, 2005.

Shapiro, Peter. *Turn the Beat Around: The Secret History of Disco*. New York: Faber and Faber, 2005.

Shatkin, Gavin. "The Geography of Insecurity: Spatial Change and the Flexibilization of Labor in Metro Manila." *Journal of Urban Affairs* 31, no. 4 (2009): 381–408.

Sherburne, Philip. "Techno." *Pitchfork*, May 9, 2007. https://pitchfork.com/features/techno/6604-techno/.

Shouse, Eric. "Feeling, Emotion, Affect." *M/C Journal* 8, no. 6 (2005). https://doi.org/10.5204/mcj.2443.

Silcott, Mireille. *Rave America: New School Dancescapes*. Toronto: ECW Press, 1999.

Silverman, Maxim. *Deconstructing the Nation: Immigration, Racism, and Citizenship in Modern France*. London: Routledge, 1992.

Simmel, Georg. "The Philosophy of Fashion." In *The Consumption Reader*, edited by David B. Clarke, Marcus A. Doel, and Kate M. L. Housiaux, 238–245. London: Routledge, 2003.

Simmel, Georg. "The Stranger." In *The Sociology of Georg Simmel*, edited and translated by Kurt Wolff, 402–8. New York: Free Press, 1950.

Simon, Patrick. "The Choice of Ignorance: The Debate on Ethnic and Racial Statistics in France." *French Politics, Culture & Society* 26, no. 1 (2008): 7–31.

Simon, Patrick. "France and the Unknown Second Generation." *International Migration Review* 37, no. 4 (2003): 1091–119.

Simon, Patrick, ed. "Le modèle français de discrimination: Un nouveau défi pour l'antiracisme." *Mouvements*, no. 4 (1999): 1–176.

Simon, Patrick. "Les jeunes de l'immigration se cachent pour vieillir : Représentations sociales et catégories de l'action publique." *VEI Enjeux* 121 (2000): 23–38.

Simon, Patrick, and Valérie Sala Pala. "'We're Not All Multiculturalists Yet': France Swings between Hard Integration and Soft Anti-discrimination." In *The Multiculturalism Backlash: European Discourses, Policies and Practices*, edited by Steven Vertovec and Susanne Wessendorf, 92–110. Abingdon, UK: Routledge, 2010.

Siokou, Christine. "Seeking the Vibe." *Youth Studies Australia* 21, no. 1 (2002): 11–18.

Small, Christopher. *Musicking: The Meanings of Performing and Listening*. Hanover, NH: University Press of New England / Wesleyan University Press, 1998.

Smalley, Denis. "Defining Timbre—Refining Timbre." *Contemporary Music Review* 10, no. 2 (1994): 35–48. https://doi.org/10.1080/07494469400640281.

Smalley, Denis. "Spectromorphology: Explaining Sound-Shapes." *Organised Sound* 2, no. 2 (1997): 107–26. https://doi.org/10.1017/S1355771897009059.

Smalley, Denis. "Spectromorphology and Structuring Processes." In *The Language of Electroacoustic Music*, edited by Simon Emmerson, 61–93. Basingstoke, UK: Macmillan, 1986.

Søgaard, Thomas Friis. "Bouncers, Policing and the (in)Visibility of Ethnicity in Nightlife Security Governance." *Social Inclusion* 2, no. 3 (2014): 40–51. https://doi.org/10.17645/si.v2i3.34.

Sommer, Sally. "C'mon to My House: Underground-House Dancing." *Dance Research Journal* 33, no. 2 (2001): 72–86. https://doi.org/10.2307/1477805.

Southerton, Dale. "Consuming Kitchens: Taste, Context and Identity Formation." *Journal of Consumer Culture* 1, no. 2 (2001): 179–203.

Spicer, Mark. "(Ac)cumulative Form in Pop-Rock Music." *twentieth-century music* 1, no. 1 (2004): 29–64.

Spinoza, Benedictus de. *Ethics*. Translated by G. H. R. Parkinson. New York: Oxford University Press. 2000.

Stewart, Kathleen. *Ordinary Affects*. Durham, NC: Duke University Press, 2007.

Stier, Deborah S., and Judith A. Hall. "Gender Differences in Touch: An Empirical and Theoretical Review." *Journal of Personality and Social Psychology* 47, no. 2 (August 1984): 440–59. https://doi.org/10.1037/0022-3514.47.2.440.

St. John, Graham. "Alternative Cultural Heterotopia and the Liminoid Body: Beyond Turner at Confest." *Australian Journal of Anthropology* 12, no. 1 (2001): 47–66. https://doi.org/10.1111/j.1835-9310.2001.tb00062.x.

St. John, Graham. *Global Tribe: Technology, Spirituality and Psytrance*. Sheffield, UK: Equinox, 2012.

St. John, Graham, ed. *The Local Scenes and Global Culture of Psytrance*. New York: Routledge, 2010.

St. John, Graham. "Neotrance and the Psychedelic Festival." *Dancecult: Journal of Electronic Dance Music Culture* 1, no. 1 (2009): 35–64. https://doi.org/10.12801/1947-5403.2009.01.01.03.

St. John, Graham, ed. *Rave Culture and Religion*. London: Routledge, 2004.

St. John, Graham. "Rave Culture and Religion: An Overview." In *Rave Culture and Religion*, edited by Graham St. John, 1–25. London: Routledge, 2004.

St. John, Graham. *Technomad: Global Raving Countercultures*. London: Equinox, 2009.

St. John, Graham. "Trance Tribes and Dance Vibes: Victor Turner and Trance Dance Culture." In *Victor Turner and Contemporary Cultural Performance*, 149–73. New York: Berghahn Books, 2008.

St. John, Graham, ed. *Weekend Societies: Electronic Dance Music Festivals and Event-Cultures*. New York: Bloomsbury Academic, 2017.

St. John, Graham. "Writing the Vibe: Arts of Representation in Electronic Dance Music Culture." *Dancecult: Journal of Electronic Dance Music Culture* 5, no. 1 (2013). https://doi.org/10.12801/1947-5403.2013.05.01.11.

Stokes, Martin. *The Republic of Love: Cultural Intimacy in Turkish Popular Music*. Chicago: University of Chicago Press, 2010.

Straw, Will. "Systems of Articulation, Logics of Change: Communities and Scenes in Popular Music." *Cultural Studies* 5, no. 3 (1991): 368–88.

Summers, Ian R. *Tactile Aids for the Hearing Impaired*. Hoboken, NJ: Wiley, 1992.

SuperGrover (@fuzzlaw). "I'm an aging dyke, so I'm just going to get this out of my system: kids, ya'll 35 and under, this wasn't supposed to happen to you." Twitter, June 13, 2016. https://twitter.com/fuzzlaw/status/742364635777667072.

Swirski, Peter. *From Lowbrow to Nobrow*. Montreal: McGill–Queen's University Press, 2005.

Sylvan, Robin. *Trance Formation: The Spiritual and Religious Dimensions of Global Rave Culture*. New York: Routledge, 2005.

"Tag Archive: Ricardo Villalobos." *Little White Earbuds*. Accessed December 18, 2022. http://www.littlewhiteearbuds.com/tag/ricardo-villalobos/.

Tahhan, Diana Adis. "Blurring the Boundaries between Bodies: *Skinship* and Bodily Intimacy in Japan." *Japanese Studies* 30, no. 2 (2010): 215–30. https://doi.org/10.1080/10371397.2010.485552.

Tahhan, Diana Adis. "Depth and Space in Sleep: Intimacy, Touch and the Body in Japanese Co-sleeping Rituals." *Body and Society* 14, no. 4 (2008): 37–56. https://doi.org/10.1177/1357034X08096894.

Takahashi, Melanie, and Tim Olaveson. "Music, Dance, and Raving Bodies: Raving as Spirituality in the Central Canadian Rave Scene." *Journal of Ritual Studies* 17, no. 2 (2003): 72–96. https://www.jstor.org/stable/44368995.

Talbot, Deborah. *Regulating the Night: Race, Culture and Exclusion in the Making of the Night-time Economy*. Aldershot, UK: Ashgate, 2007.

Tambiah, Stanley J. "The Form and Meaning of Magical Acts." In *Modes of Thought: Essays on Thinking in Western and Non-Western Societies*, edited by Robin Horton and Ruth H. Finnegan, 199–229. London: Faber and Faber, 1973.

Tambiah, Stanley J. *A Performative Approach to Ritual*. London: British Academy, 1981.

Tarde, Gabriel de. *The Laws of Imitation*. Translated by Elsie Worthington Clews Parsons. Gloucester, MA: P. Smith, 1962. Orig. 1890.

Taylor, Timothy. *Strange Sounds: Music, Technology, and Culture*. New York: Routledge, 2001.

Thornton, Sarah. *Club Cultures: Music, Media and Subcultural Capital*. Hanover, NH: Wesleyan University Press, 1996.

Thrift, Nigel. "Intensities of Feeling: Towards a Spatial Politics of Affect." *Geografiska Annaler. Series B, Human Geography* 86, no. 1 (2004): 57–78. http://www.jstor.org/stable/3554460.

Thrift, Nigel. *Non-representational Theory: Space, Politics, Affect*. New York: Routledge, 2008.

Tolbert, Elizabeth. "Women Cry with Words: Symbolization of Affect in the Karelian Lament." *Yearbook for Traditional Music* 22 (1990): 80–105.

Tomkins, Silvan S., and E. Virginia Demos. *Exploring Affect: The Selected Writings of Silvan Tomkins*. Cambridge: Cambridge University Press, 1995.

Tomkins, Silvan S., and Bertram P. Karon. *Affect, Imagery, Consciousness*. 4 vols. New York: Springer, 1962.

Tomlinson, Gary. "Sign, Affect, and Musicking before the Human." *boundary 2* 43, no. 1 (2016): 143–72. https://doi.org/10.1215/01903659-3340673.

"Top 100 Clubs / 1. Berghain." *DJ Mag*, 2009. https://djmag.com/top100clubs/2009.

Trost, Wiebke. "Time Flow and Musical Emotions: The Role of Rhythmic Entrainment." In *Timing of Affect: Epistemologies, Aesthetics, Politics*, edited by Marie-Luise Angerer, Bernd Bösel, and Michaela Ott, 207–24. Zurich: Diaphanes Verlag, 2014.

Turino, Thomas. *Moving Away from Silence: Music of the Peruvian Altiplano and the Experience of Urban Migration*. Chicago: University of Chicago Press, 1993.

Turner, Victor Witter. "Liminal to Liminoid in Play, Flow and Ritual." *Rice University Studies* 60, no. 3 (1974): 53–92.

Turner, Victor Witter. *The Ritual Process: Structure and Anti-structure*. Chicago: Aldine, 1969.

25FilmsBerlin. "Bar25—Days Out of Time Trailer—English Subtitles." YouTube. Accessed August 17, 2021. https://youtu.be/HQpZQj3TY80.

Urban, Greg. "Ritual Wailing in Amerindian Brazil." *American Anthropologist* 90, no. 2 (1988): 385–400.

Urry, John. *Mobilities*. Cambridge: Polity Press, 2007.

van der Gaag, Imre. "Function Follows Form: How Berlin Turns Horror into Beauty." *Failed Architecture*, January 28, 2014. http://failedarchitecture.com/berlin-horror-beauty/.

van Gennep, Arnold. *The Rites of Passage*. Translated by Monika B. Vizedom and
    Gabrielle L. Caffee. Chicago: University of Chicago Press, 1960. Orig. 1927.

Vaudrin, Marie-Claude. *La musique techno, ou, Le retour de Dionysos: Je rave, tu raves,
    nous rêvons*. Paris: Harmattan, 2004.

Vertovec, Steven, and Susanne Wessendorf. "Introduction: Assessing the Backlash
    against Multiculturalism in Europe." In *The Multiculturalism Backlash: European
    Discourses, Policies and Practices*, edited by Steven Vertovec and Susanne Wes-
    sendorf, 1–31. Abingdon, UK: Routledge, 2010.

Wacquant, Loïc J. D. *Urban Outcasts: A Comparative Sociology of Advanced Marginality*.
    Cambridge: Polity Press, 2008.

Waltz, Alexis. "Nightclubbing: Berlin's Ostgut." Red Bull Music Academy, Septem-
    ber 24, 2013. http://daily.redbullmusicacademy.com/2013/09/nightclubbing
    -ostgut.

Warner, Michael. *Publics and Counterpublics*. New York: Zone Books, 2002.

Warner, Michael. *The Trouble with Normal: Sex, Politics, and the Ethics of Queer Life*.
    New York: Free Press, 1999.

Warner, Rebecca M., Daniel Malloy, Kathy Schneider, Russell Knoth, and Bruce
    Wilder. "Rhythmic Organization of Social Interaction and Observer Ratings
    of Positive Affect and Involvement." *Journal of Nonverbal Behavior* 11, no. 2
    (1987): 57–74. https://doi.org/10.1007/BF00990958.

Wergin, Carsten. "Destination 'Three Days Awake': Cultural Urbanism at a Popular
    Music Festival Outside the City." In *Musical Performance and the Changing City:
    Post-industrial Contexts in Europe and the United States*, edited by Fabian Holt and
    Carsten Wergin, 102–26. New York: Routledge, 2013.

Wieviorka, Michel, ed. *Une société fragmentée? Le multiculturalisme en débat*. Paris: La
    Découverte, 1996.

Wilkes, Rima, and John Iceland. "Hypersegregation in the Twenty-First Century."
    Demography 41, no. 1 (2004): 23–36. https://doi.org/10.1353/dem.2004.0009.

Wilson, William J., and Richard P. Taub. *There Goes the Neighborhood: Racial, Ethnic,
    and Class Tensions in Four Chicago Neighborhoods and Their Meaning for America*.
    New York: Knopf, 2006.

Witek, Maria A. G. "Feeling at One: Socio-affective Distribution, Vibe and Dance
    Music Consciousness." In *Music and Consciousness II*, edited by Eric Clarke,
    David Clarke, and Ruth Herbert, 93–112. Oxford: Oxford University Press, 2019.

Zimmermann, Klaus F., Holger Bonin, Holger Hinte, and René Fahr. *Immigration
    Policy and the Labor Market: The German Experience and Lessons for Europe*. Berlin:
    Springer, 2007. https://doi.org/10.1007/978-3-540-68382-7.

Note: Page numbers in *italics* indicate figures and tables.

attack (sound synthesis), 69; attack-effluvium continuum, 83; microstructures, 80

"attitude test," 206–7; as indicator of risk, 57–58; and intuition, 119–20. *See also* door selection

audience demographics: Berlin, 25–26; Chicago, 18; Paris, 23

audio engineering, 68, 77. *See also* sound synthesis

auditory space, 81–82

Austin, J. L., 146

authenticity, 8, 41, 136; and altered states, 50–51; of dancefloor intimacy, 62, 128

avoidance of personal discourse, 116–17

Aymara rituals, 145, 146

"Bakerman" (Laid Back), 127, 253n2

ballroom culture, 11, 233, 238n25

Bar25 (Berlin), 210; door policies, 208–9; layout and décor, 212; theatricality, 212

Barthes, Roland, 79, 248n22

bass. *See* low-frequency sounds; subbass

bass kicks, 67–68; breakdowns, 137

"bass materialism," 72, 133

Bataille, George, 177

Batofar (Paris), 21, 106

Bauman, Zygmunt, 92, 122, 123, 253n41

beats, 66, 67–72, 129; "withholding the beat," 137–38, 140. *See also* sonic tactility

becoming/unbecoming (Deleuze), 90, 181

belonging, 40, 91, 97, 116; categories of, 98, 113; and identity, 120, 184; members-only policies, 8; narratives of, 108; politics of, 186; shared affect, 144, 145. *See also* door selection; solidarity; subcultural knowledge

Benard, Alexis (Seuil), 39, 158

Berghain (Berlin), 92, 94, 213; door policy, 95, 160; entrance, 199; Lab.Oratory, 100; layout and décor, 99–100; "Promote Diversity" events, 189

Berghain / Panorama Bar (Berlin), 2–3, 24, 69, 92–93, 94, 151–52, 216–17

Berlant, Lauren, 63, 92, 119–23, 152, 236n5

Berlin: as fieldwork site, 23, 25; Friedrichshain district, 93, 208, 212; gentrification, 23, 211–12, 241n63; Kreuzberg district, 93, 197, 206, 211; post-disco scene, 23–26

Berlin clubs: Club der Visionäre, 68; discretionary door policies, 185; Mediaspree, 208; Ostgut, 93; terminology, 17; tourists, 199–201. *See also* Bar25 (Berlin); Berghain (Berlin); Berghain / Panorama Bar (Berlin); Watergate (Berlin)

Berlin Stadtreinigungsbetriebe (BSR), 208

Berliner, Paul, 254n7

Birmingham School, 204, 244n17

Black community, 8, 11, 18, 28–29, 54, 228, 230

Black vernacular speech, 65

Blanchot, Maurice, 177, 178

Bloch, Ernst, 12

Blum, Alan, 212

bodily decorum, 3–4, 40, 48, 115; violations of, 37, 53. *See also* stranger-intimacy; stranger-sociability

Bodily Functions (Matthew Herbert), 73–75

bodily habitus, 44, 48–50, 55–56; transformation of, 49–50

bodily proximity, 42, 47, 89, 219, 244n13

bodily timbre, 73–79

body noises (sampled), 73–75

bohemianism, 211–12

Booka Shade, 78

booking agents, 110, 152

Bora, Renu, 67, 88, 89–90

bouncers, 94–96, 110–11, 189–90, 201, 202–3; door apparatus, 186–88. *See also* door selection

Bouncers: Violence and Governance in the Night-time Economy (Hobbs et al.), 188

Bourdieu, Pierre, 112, 261n8

box office. *See* door selection

bpitchcontrol (label), 198

"breakdowns," 137

Brekete ritual, 146–47

Brennan, Teresa, 53

Butler, Mark J., 137, 171

"Can You Feel It?" (Larry Heard), 9–10
capitalism, 122, 213
Chandler, Kerri, 78
Chicago: East Garfield Park, 39, 157; as fieldwork site, 16, 18–19, *19*, 261n5; gentrification, 18; South Loop, 38, 158
Chicago clubs: club culture, 48; door policies, 186; harassment in, 56–57; post-disco, 8–10; terminology, 17; touch norms, 43. *See also* Souvenir parties (Chicago)
Chion, Michel, 79
Christopher Street Day (Berlin), 152
citizenship, 192–97. *See also* belonging; immigration policy
citoyenneté, 192, 194–95
Classen, Maja, 125
classism, 205–6, 211
Clicks & Cuts 3, 83
clouds (sounds), 84, 85, 86
Club Cultures (Thornton), 183–84
Club der Visionäre (Berlin), 68
Club Regret (Chicago), 112, 157–58
clubs: distinguished by attitudes, 57–58; gay, 8, 10–11; mainstream, 23, 56–57; as sites of resistance, 225–26; target audiences, 206–7; techno, 47, 50–51. *See also* soundworlds; venues
code-switching, 203–4
collective cohesion: definition, 104–5; through music and dancing, 128. *See also* additive cohesion; subtractive cohesion
"collective effervescence," 144–45, 146. *See also* ritual
collectivity, 92, 104–5, 211; burgeoning, 145, 148–50; musicking, 4, 145–46, 257n46; nighttime, 114–15
color blindness, 196, 264n58. *See also* racism
Columbia-Princeton Electronic Music Center, 69
coming undone, 151–82; musical analogues, 168–74; nonheroic aspirations of, 181–82; as self-fashioning, 175–79; sweetness of, 174–82

communitas, 105, 117–18, 214, 219; and "vibe," 254n7
community. *See* collective cohesion; solidarity
compression, 68
computer-assisted analysis, 76
confetti-heads, 210
conflict avoidance, 58
connoisseurship, 107, 167–68
consent, 46
consumerist self-fashioning, 113
corporeal copresence, 3, 46, 117, 126, 236n5
cosmopolitanism, 107, 184, 185, 212–13, 222–23, 265n69. *See also* embedded diversity
Costes, Joan, 156–57
cottaging, 46
counterpublics, 6, 45–48, 61, 92, 123, 220, 236n5; touch norms, 46–47. *See also* intimate publics
crowds: vs. groups, 143; musical affect, 134–35, 138; psychology of, 4, 143, 257n37; tactile experience of, 50, 51. *See also* anonymity
cruel optimism, 152, 232
cruising counterpublic, 46
Cruising Utopia (Muñoz), 13–14
cry breaks, 169, 259n14
Cubase, 70
cuica (friction drum), 75
cultural capital, 112, 128, 187, 222, 261n8
cultural intimacy and shared embarrassment, 40, 158, 259n7
cultural theory, 31
curation of diversity, 184–85, 209–14. *See also* door selection; exclusionary practices
Cusick, Suzanne, 129
cuts, 137–38, 140

dancefloor, *135*; bodily contact, 4, 38–39, 49–50, 98; as complex system, 150; as counterpublic, 6–7, 61; hierarchies, 8, 114–17, 204–5; as refuge, 7–8, 35, 225–26; safety and risk, 54–55, 57–58; site

Engels, Friedrich, 12

entrainment, 141–45, 147, 220

envelopment aesthetic, 87–88, 219

equality ethos, 102

equalizers (EQs), 140, 255n23

Ethics (Spinoza), 52

ethics of proximity, 58

ethnic minorities, 122; political recognition of, 192–93

ethnicity: and citizenship, 194–95; and door selection, 203–4

ethnographers, 15–16

ethnographic approach, 15–31, 187–88; dialogic interviewing, 154–55; site selection, 15–17; snowball sampling, 28, 109, 241n69

ethnography, 31

ethnomusicology, 4, 145–46; methodology, 26–27

ethnonationalism, 122, 197. *See also* multiculturalism

everyday life, 115; affect in, 149–50; avoided as topic, 116; decorum, 3, 4; identity, 115; stranger-intimacy, 114–15; touch in, 51, 58; utopian reprieve from, 153–54, 176–77. *See also* capitalism; patriarchy

E-Werk (Berlin), 23, 94

exclusionary practices, 102; and curated diversity, 209–14; at the door, 185, 195–96; hard obstacles, 110–11; multiculturalism as, 195; soft obstacles, 110–12. *See also* door selection

experimental music, 48. *See also* sound synthesis

fashion, 199–200, 203; Bar25, 210–11

Fast Fourier Analysis, 76

"Feel It" (John Tejada), 65–66

feeling: double meaning, 65, 89; study of, 4. *See also* sensory modes

feelings, 14, 31, 51–52, 89, 147; expressed through dance, 126–29, 133–34; and sense of belonging, 120, 143–44; and Spinozan affect, 132; and tactility, 63. *See also* affect; emotions

Feiern (documentary film), 68, 125–26, 127

Female Complaint, The (Berlant), 119–21, 236n5

femininity: acceptable forms of, 42, 60–61; policing of, 38, 178; womanhood as genre, 119

Fête de la Musique, 21

fieldwork: Berlin, 23–26; Chicago, 18–19; methods and demographics, 26–31; Paris, 19–23; site selection, 15–17

Fikentscher, Kai, 184–85

Fingers Inc., 9

"flow," 141

"Foreign Bodies" (Matthew Herbert), 74–75; sound sources, 77

forward masking effect, 84

found sounds, 77

Fourier, Charles, 12

France: anti-immigrant sentiment, 191; civic belonging, 188; homophobia, 189; multiculturalism, 192; political use of techno, 21; touch norms, 49. *See also* Paris

frequencies, inaudible, 72

frequency bandwidth, 85; layering, 86

Friedson, Steven M., 146

Fruity Loops, 70

Fulbright fellowships, 16

Funkpark Rechenzentrum (Rummelsburg), 109

Funktion One sound system, 94, 99

Garnier, Laurent, 20

Gastarbeiter (guest workers), 193, 203. *See also* immigration policy

gated sounds, 68, 86, 169

gay fetish events, 93, 99

Gay Left, 7

gaydar, 206

Gayhane (Berlin), 206

gender and touch, 43–44. *See also* touch

gender minorities and kinship ties, 122–23

gender studies, 31

gender-based violence, 57–59; threat of, 46

genderphobia, 206

Generation X, 10, 30, 236n22

gentrification: Berlin, 23, 211–12, 241n63; Chicago, 18

Germany: anti-immigrant sentiment, 190; citizenship, 193; civic belonging, 188; German Democratic Republic (East Germany), 2; immigration policy, 204; multiculturalism, 192; reunification, 193. *See also* Berlin

Get Physical Music (record label), 136

Gibson, James J., 89

glitch, 77, 83, 85, 247n18

glitter-heads, 210

global nomads. *See* techno-tourists

globalization, 121–22

Goffman, Erving, 43

"good night out," a, 154, 156–62, 163–65, 169, 182. *See also* "peak moments"

Goodman, Steve (aka Kode9), 72, 89; on "sonic warfare," 130

"Gotta Let You Go" (Dominica), 151, 152

grain, 66, 78, 79–88; continuous grains, 86; density and texture, 85; grains of sound, 84; iteration grains, 86; iterative/discontinuous, 82–83; material grain, 83; pitch and granularity, 79, 85; resonance grains, 86; Schaeffer's taxonomy, 80–82, 81; as threshhold phenomenon, 90

Grands Boulevards clubs, 23

guest list. *See* door selection

guest workers (*Gastarbeiter*), 193, 203. *See also* immigration policy

guiro, 82–83

Haçienda (Manchester), 20

Hall, Edward T., 145

haptic perception, 51, 52–53, 67–72; hearing and, 87; vision and, 67, 87. *See also* sensory modes

Hardy, Ron, 18

harm-reduction measures, 55

Harriot, Michael, 265n70

Hawtin, Richie, 110

hearing, 72, 76, 83, 84, 87, 219. *See also* grain; sonic tactility

Heartthrob (Jesse Siminski), 2

hegemony and subalterity, 46–47

Henley, Nadine, 43–44

Herbert, Matthew, 73; *Bodily Functions*, 73–75

Herzfeld, Michael, 259n7

heterosexual audiences, 10, 18, 203

heterosexuality, 60, 244n10

high volumes, 34, 69, 70, 72, 87. *See also* sonic tactility

homophobia, 231; antiqueer violence, 206, 224–29; global rise in anti-gay legislation, 188–89

hope, 12, 13

Höppner, Nick, 68–69

hostile environments, 109

house, 8–10, 94, 102; Paris, 93

house, acid, 10, 102

house, deep, 67–68, 107

house, garage, 11, 102

house, "ketamine," 168, 172

house, minimal, 49; Berlin, 23–26; connoisseurship, 167–68; music, 73, 77, 85, 86; respect for personal boundaries, 57; touch norms, 53

house, progressive, 56

hugging, 63

human voice: grain, 80; unraveling in Villalobos, 169; vocal samples and meter in Villalobos, 169–74, 170

Humphrey, Laud, 46

Hurley, Steve "Silk," 18

Hutton, Fiona, 54, 57, 60, 178

"I Get Deep" (Roland Clark), 135–36, 174–75

Ibiza (Spain), 181, 212

Ibiza Voice, 212

identity: and belonging, 120; formation, 112; loss as release, 176–77, 178; as selection criterion, 207; unrelated to attunement, 131–32

Ignatieff, Michael, 197

imaginaries (Dueck), 121

immigrant communities, 190–95; anti-immigrant sentiment, 190–91; Berlin, 211–12; Chicago, 18, 28–29

musical techniques, 77, 135–37, 140–41, 255n23

musique concrète, 73

MUTEK festival (Montréal), 161

Nathan, Piotr, 99

nationalism, 191–92, 197. *See also* multiculturalism

neo-bohemianism, 211–12

New York City, 8, 10, 11–12, 184

Ngai, Sianne, 31, 147

nightclubs. *See* clubs; venues

nighttime, 92, 114–18

"No One Belongs Here More than You" (Martin Dawson and Glimpse), 86

noise gate, 68

noise music, 43, 48

No-Longer-Conscious, the (Bloch), 13

noncontact culture, 44

nonknowledge, 177, 178

nonverbal communication: and cruising, 46; studies of, 44

Not-Yet-Conscious, the (Bloch), 13

nu-disco, 106

Nye, Sean, 17

"O Superman feat. Laurie Anderson (Reboot's 20 Cubans Rework)" (Booka Shade), 78

O$_2$ World (arena), 93

olfactory transfer of affect, 53

Ordinary Affects (Stewart), 148, 149

organizational behavior studies, 141–42, 143

Ostgut (Berlin), 93

OstGut Ton, 69, 152

"Other Side of Bed, The" (Davide Squillace), 68

Owens, Robert, 9

Panorama Bar. *See* Berghain / Panorama Bar (Berlin)

Parables for the Virtual (Massumi), 132

Paradise Garage (New York), 10

Paris: audience demographics, 23; as fieldwork site, 16, 19–23, 22; post-disco scene, 20–21

Paris clubs: club culture, 48; door policies, 205–6; minimal scene, 21, 23; right to entry, 186; terminology, 17; touch norms, 43, 56

Paris Is Burning (documentary film), 11

Paris Paris (Paris), 106

partygoers: adaptation to local norms, 49, 201–4; avoiding talk of norms, 102–4; ecstatic experiences and subjectivity, 177–78; ethical responsibilities among, 96, 119–20; as ethnographic informants, 154–55; negative stereotypes, 37; performing "insiderness," 201–2; self-fashioning for door selection, 205; social class, 211; techno-tourists, 17; undesirable, 111; use of this term, 236n3; views of stranger-intimacy, 41–42. *See also* dancers; techno-tourists

patriarchy, 15, 43, 54; norms of, 59–60

"PCCOM" ("Personal Contract for the Composition of Music"; Matthew Herbert), 73

"peak moments," 13, 126–28, 135–37. *See also* coming undone; thickening of the social

perception: as topic of research, 43. *See also* sensory modes; tactility

perceptual threshholds, 34, 89; and sonic grain, 83, 84

percussion loops, 169, 170, 171–72

percussive amplitude envelope, 69, 70

performance practice, 135–37, 140–41. *See also* musical articulation of affect

personal space, 49–50. *See also* bodily habitus

Petite Maison Éléctronique, 93

physical excitation and affect, 52, 132–33

Pini, Maria, 177–78

Pitchfork, 94

"planet of drums," 72

police, 157, 161–62

techno, minimal, 85, 106; connoisseurship, 167–68; fans, 107; "Feel It" (John Tejada), 65–66; Heartthrob (Jesse Siminski), 3

techno music, 94; experience of, 69

Techno Parade, The, 21

techno parties, 103; Chicago, 52

techno scenes: Chicago, 43, 47–48, 56–57; respect for personal boundaries, 57; touch norms, 47–48, 53

techno/neo-hippie, 181

techno-tourists, 17, 110, 185; Berlin, 24–25, 198–201, 204–5, 212; Ibiza-Goa-Pune circuit, 181

Telefónica O$_2$ Germany, 93

temporality: dislocation, 115; and queer theory, 14

texture, social. *See* rough experiences; smooth experiences; thickening of the social

texture, sonic, 66, 72, 86, 137, 230; perception of, 82–83, 88; and rhythm, 83; smooth and rough, 156, 168–69. *See also* grain

Thatcher, Margaret, 10, 12

theatricality, 211–13

thickening of the social, 124–50; affective intensity, 125–28; entrainment, 141–44; musical articulation of affect, 128–41

Thinking in Jazz (Berliner), 254n7

Thomas, Anthony, 9

Thornton, Sarah, 105, 183, 185, 215, 261n8

threshhold phenomena, 90

Thrift, Nigel, 92

Tillmans, Wolfgang, 99

timbre, 66; definition, 75–76; psycho-acoustic approach to, 82; as semiotic trace (index), 76–77. *See also* grain

togetherness, 5, 147, 219; on the dance-floor, 92–98. See also *communitas*; liquidarity

Tomkins, Silvan, 147, 258n54

Toronto, 10

touch, 4, 32, 37–38; and affect, 51–53, 88; avoidance of, 44, 49, 60; bodily contact, 38–39; bodily habitus, 44,

48–50, 55–56; expressive modes, 51–52; friendly vs. sexual, 57; gender asymmetry hypothesis, 43–44; and intimacy, 62–64; perceptions of, 42–43; as term, 51; theories of, 43–44; "touching," dual meaning of, 62–63; unwelcome, 38, 42, 45, 53–55, 57–58, 220, 243n4. *See also* haptic perception; sensory modes; sexual harassment; tactility

touch norms: cultural differences, 42–45, 55–56; differences between scenes, 48; touch privilege, 44, 53–54

Touching Feeling (Sedgwick), 63, 88

track titles, 9, 65, 78, 167, 230

tracks: "Foreign Bodies," 74–75, 77; "Mil-lepieds (SLG Remix)," 85–86, 87; "In My System (Jef K System Mix)," 67–68; "No One Belongs Here More than You," 86; "O Superman feat. Laurie Anderson (Reboot's 20 Cubans Rework)," 78; "The Other Side of Bed," 68; "Pong (Bones and Strings Rework)," 78, 87; "Safari (Stimming Remix)," 86; "You're Un-known to Me," 74; "z. B.," 86, 87

Traité des objets musicaux (Schaeffer), 79–83

trance, 56; Goa, 11; psychedelic, 11, 181; and ritual theory, 117, 252n30

transient (sound synthesis), 69–70

Transmission of Affect, The (Brennan), 53

transphobia, 112, 206, 231

Tresor (Berlin), 23, 24, 94

"tribes," 105–7, 213–14. *See also* belonging; door selection

trigger events (sound synthesis), 69

Turino, Thomas, 145, 146

Turner, Victor, 117, 252n29

"turning the beat around," 171

Twilo (New York), 11

Ugly Feelings (Ngai), 31, 147

underground parties, 11–12, 19, 47; collective selection, 111–12; Paris, 23; as safer spaces, 57–58. *See also* raves; Souvenir parties (Chicago)

Underground Resistance (UR), 11, 230